Cases in Congressional Campaigns
Riding the Wave
Second Edition

Edited by
Randall E. Adkins
David A. Dulio

Routledge
Taylor & Francis Group

NEW YORK AND LONDON

First published 2012
by Routledge
711 Third Avenue, New York, NY 10017

Simultaneously published in the UK
by Routledge
2 Park Square, Milton Park, Abingdon, Oxon OX14 4RN

Routledge is an imprint of the Taylor & Francis Group, an informa business

Library of Congress Cataloging in Publication Data
Cases in Congressional campaigns : incumbents playing defense / [edited by] Randall E. Adkins, David A. Dulio.
   p. cm.
   [etc.]
   1. United States. Congress—Elections, 2008. 2. Elections—United States—History—21st century. 3. Political campaigns—United States—History—21st century. 4. United States—Politics and government—2001–2009. I. Adkins, Randall E. II. Dulio, David A.
   JK19682008 .C37 2010
   324.973'0931—dc22
   2009027648

ISBN: 978-0-415-89516-3 (hbk)
ISBN: 978-0-415-89517-0 (pbk)
ISBN: 978-0-203-80306-6 (ebk)

Typeset in Goudy
by EvS Communication Networx, Inc.

Printed and bound in the United States of America on acid-free paper
by Walsworth Publishing Company, Marceline, MO

Cases in Congressional Campaigns

After Barack Obama's historic 2008 victory, Democrats were riding high. But a number of tough fights on policy initiatives put Democrats in a difficult position leading up to the 2010 congressional elections. With nearly all the electoral gains Democrats made during 2006 and 2008 now lost, this race became one of the most dramatic shifts in congressional power in history.

Adkins and Dulio provide a clear explanation of the macro-political trends in this election cycle, followed by twelve in depth and fascinating case studies of House and Senate toss up races. Framed by a common set of questions and topics, each chapter focuses on the micro-political effects active in the individual campaigns. Furthermore, the editors discuss how the 2010 cycle fits into the existing literature on campaigns and elections, conclusions about what we learned in 2010, and speculation on what might be ahead in 2012.

In addition, the companion website provides instructors with useful teaching tools, including sample assignments and PowerPoint slides with graphs and videos.

Randall E. Adkins is the Ralph Wardle Diamond Professor of Arts and Sciences and Chair of the Department of Political Science at the University of Nebraska at Omaha.

David A. Dulio is Associate Professor and Chair of Political Science at Oakland University in Rochester, MI.

For our children

Ross and Ryan

Abby and Sophia

Contents

List of Tables   ix
List of Figures   xi
Acknowledgments   xiii

1 Riding the Wave   1
   DAVID A. DULIO AND RANDALL E. ADKINS

2 Reid vs. Angle in Nevada's Senate Race: Harry Houdini Escapes the
   Wave   32
   DAVID F. DAMORE

3 Edwards vs. Flores in Texas' Seventeenth Congressional District:
   The Perfect Storm   55
   VICTORIA A. FARRAR-MYERS AND DANIEL DAVIS SLEDGE

4 Boxer vs. Fiorina in California's Senate Race: The Wave Stopped at
   the Sierra Nevada   78
   CASEY B. K. DOMINGUEZ

5 Mitchell vs. Schweikert in Arizona's Fifth Congressional District: A
   Rematch in the Desert   97
   JENNIFER A. STEEN

6 Kirk vs. Giannoulias in Illinois' Senate Race: Scandal and
   Competition to Replace a President   117
   WAYNE STEGER

7   Bass vs. Kuster in New Hampshire's Second Congressional District:
    Riding the Wave to a Comeback   139
    DANTE J. SCALA AND ANDREW E. SMITH

8   Rubio vs. Crist vs. Meek in Florida's Senate Race: Coming Out of
    Nowhere   160
    SETH C. MCKEE AND STEPHEN C. CRAIG

9   Marshall vs. Scott in Georgia's Eighth Congressional District: The
    Power of Incumbency Fails   181
    CHARLES S. BULLOCK, III AND KAREN P. OWEN

10 Feingold vs. Johnson in Wisconsin's Senate Race: The Maverick
    Icon Meets His Match   201
    DAVID T. CANON

11 Chabot vs. Driehaus in Ohio's First Congressional District: The
    Rematch in the City of Seven Hills   219
    RANDALL E. ADKINS AND GREGORY A. PETROW

12 Toomey vs. Sestak in Pennsylvania's Senate Race: Moderation
    Doesn't Pay   239
    ROBIN KOLODNY

13 Schauer vs. Walberg in Michigan's Seventh Congressional District:
    Money Helps Create the Wave   259
    DAVID A. DULIO AND JOHN S. KLEMANSKI

14 The Wave Recedes, but Which Way Will the Tide Turn?   280
    RANDALL E. ADKINS AND DAVID A. DULIO

    About the Contributors   290
    About the Editors   295

List of Tables

1.1 Congressional Candidate Fundraising and Spending, 2010   20

1.2 Party Campaign Committee Fundraising and Spending, 2010   21

2.1 Congressional Vote Scores for Harry Reid, 1987–2010   37

2.2 Reid and Angle Campaign Receipts and Disbursements by Reporting Period, 2009–2010   41

2.3 General Election Spending by Outside Groups in Nevada's Senate Race, 2010   43

3.1 Congressional Vote Scores for Chet Edwards, 1991–2010   60

3.2 Campaign Finance Data for Texas' 17th Congressional District Campaigns, 2004–2010   62

3.3 Vote Totals in Texas' 17th Congressional District by County, 2004–2010   69

3.4 Predicted and Actual Vote Percentages in Texas' 17th Congressional District Based on PVI Rating, 2004–2010   71

4.1 Congressional Vote Scores for Barbara Boxer, 1993–2010   83

4.2 Campaign Finance Data for California's Senate Campaigns, 2004 & 2010   84

4.3 Boxer and Fiorina Campaign Receipts and Disbursements by Reporting Period, 2009–2010   91

5.1 Congressional Vote Scores for Harry Mitchell, 2007–2010   99

5.2 Campaign Finance Data for Arizona's 5th Congressional District Campaigns, 2006–2010   110

5.3 Summary of Campaign Spending in Arizona's 5th Congressional District, 2010   110

6.1 Congressional Vote Scores for Mark Kirk, 2001–2010   123

6.2 Campaign Finance Data for Illinois' Senate Campaigns, 2004–2010   126

6.3 Kirk and Giannoulias Campaign Receipts and Disbursements by Reporting Period, 2009–2010   127

6.4 State and National Political Party Spending in Illinois' Senate Race, 2010   129

6.5 Spending by Outside Groups in Illinois' Senate Race, 2010   131

7.1 Congressional Vote Scores for Charlie Bass, 1995–2006   145
7.2 Campaign Finance Data for New Hampshire's 2nd Congressional
     District Campaigns, 2002– 010   152
7.3 Bass and Kuster Receipts and Disbursements by Reporting Period,
     2009–2010   153
8.1 Party Affiliation of Florida Voters, 1986–2010   163
8.2 Campaign Finance Data for Florida's Senate Campaigns, 2004–2010 170
8.3 Voter Characteristics and Senate Preferences in Florida, 2010   173
8.4 Opinion of Political Conditions and Senate Preferences in
     Florida, 2010   174
9.1 Congressional Vote Scores for Jim Marshall, 2003–2010   185
9.2 Campaign Finance Data for Georgia's 8th Congressional District
     Campaigns, 2006–2010   191
9.3 Marshall and Scott Receipts and Disbursements by Reporting
     Period, 2009–2010   192
10.1 Congressional Vote Scores for Russ Feingold, 1993–2010   204
10.2 Campaign Finance Data for Wisconsin's Senate Campaigns, 2004
      & 2010   210
10.3 Feingold and Johnson Campaign Receipts and Disbursements by
      Reporting Period, 2009–2010   211
10.4 Number of Ads Run by Russ Feingold, Ron Johnson, and their
      Supporters, 2010   214
11.1 Congressional Vote Scores for Steve Dreihaus and Steve Chabot,
      1995–2010   223
11.2 Campaign Finance Data for Ohio's 1st Congressional District
      Campaigns, 2002–2010   231
11.3 Driehaus and Chabot Receipts and Disbursements by Reporting
      Period, 2009–2010   232
11.4 Comparison of Election Results for Ohio's 1st District, 2008
      and 2010   235
12.1 Congressional Vote Scores for Arlen Specter, 1981–2010   242
12.2 Congressional Vote Scores for Pat Toomey, 1999–2004   245
12.3 Congressional Vote Scores for Joe Sestak, 2007–2010   246
12.4 Pennsylvania Statewide Election Results, 2010   249
12.5 Campaign Finance Data for Pennsylvania's Senate Campaigns,
      2004–2010   251
12.6 Campaign Activity by Outside Group in the Pennsylvania
      Senate Race, 2010   252
13.1 Campaign Finance Data for Michigan's 7th Congressional
      District Campaigns, 2006–2010   269
13.2 Schauer and Walberg Receipts and Disbursements by Reporting
      Period, 2009–2010   271
13.3 Mark Schauer Vote Percentages by County, 2008 & 2010   275

List of Figures

1.1 Support for Health Care Reform, August 2009–October 2010. 6

1.2 Congressional Job Approval, January 2001–November 2010. 7

1.3 Midterm Gains or Losses by the President's Party, 1934–2010. 8

1.4 Barack Obama Job Approval, January 2009–November 2010. 9

1.5 Barack Obama Job Approval, by Party Identification, January 2009–November 2010. 10

1.6 Direction of the Nation, September 2008–November 2010. 11

1.7 Support for Reelecting Members of Congress in Midterm Elections, 1994–2010. 12

1.8 Party Identification, 1990–2010. 15

1.9 Generic Congressional Ballot, March 2010–October 2010. 16

1.10 Enthusiasm for Voting in 2010 Midterm Election, March 2010–October 2010. 17

2.1 Nevada Voter Registration, 2000–2010. 33

4.1 Boxer vs. Fiorina Polling Results, 2009–2010. 89

5.1 Cumulative Spending for Candidates in Early Voting States, Non-early Voting States, and in Arizona's 5th Congressional District, Labor Day through Election Day, 2010. 103

6.1 Senate Candidate Support in Illinois' Senate Campaign, 2010. 133

7.1 Party Identification in New Hampshire's 2nd Congressional District, May 1999–September 2010. 142

7.2 Charlie Bass Favorability Ratings, October 2001–September 2010. 144

7.3 Bass vs. Kuster Polling Results, 2010. 154

7.4 Voter Turnout of Core Partisans in New Hampshire's 2nd Congressional District, 2000–2010. 156

8.1 Rubio vs. Crist vs. Meek Polling Averages, 2010. 169

Acknowledgments

Riding the Wave is the second edition of *Cases in Congressional Campaigns* and we are very excited that we have the opportunity to put forth another set of case studies that investigate some of the most important congressional elections from the most recent election cycle. As with the first edition of *Cases*, this book was not possible had it not been for the hard work and dedication of a number of individuals. First, we wish to thank the contributors to the first edition. They produced quality work and working with them provided us with a great deal of satisfaction in putting together that volume. That experience made us want to do it all over again.

Of course, a great deal of thanks goes to the contributors to this volume. None of the individuals who wrote chapters for this book needed to take on this project. It was a lot of work for each of them and they are all very busy with their own research agendas. Each of the authors also endured our editorial queries and comments that asked them to think about and revise their chapters even more than they already did. Having these great scholars take time to contribute to our book is very much appreciated.

We also deeply appreciate the dedication of the staff at Routledge Press. Specifically, we would like to thank Michael Kerns, the Acquisitions Editor, for his encouragement and assistance in every stage of the publication process. Our work with Michael goes back to the first edition. We hope the experience of that first volume made him want to work with us again as much as we wanted to work with him. Also at Routledge, Mary Altman has been a tremendous asset from day one as she helped us navigate the various processes and tasks needed to complete this edition. Production Editor Alf Symons and Lynn Goeller and the team at EvS have proved to be very devoted professionals. We also wish to thank those who anonymously reviewed the book. Their comments proved very constructive and encouraged us to make a number of revisions that improved the book considerably.

At the University of Nebraska at Omaha, Adkins would foremost like to express his appreciation to the students in his campaigns and elections class who followed each of the congressional races in this volume with great passion and in great detail. Adkins would also like to thank David Boocker, Dean of the College of Arts and Sciences, for his commitment to the research and creative activity of the faculty of the College. Thanks are also due to Elizabeth O'Connor for her research assistance.

At Oakland University, Dulio would like to thank his Elections and Voting Behavior and Political Campaigns students; they have made him a better teacher and scholar through their questions and insights, and by challenging him to think about various questions related to American campaigns, many of which are at the center of this book. Dulio would also like to thank Provost Virinder Moudgil and Dean of the College of Arts and Sciences Ron Sudol for their support of faculty research and for providing an environment in which scholars can thrive.

Our families deserve special thanks. Our homes are built through the love and commitment our families provide, and our wives and children are the rare and beautiful treasures that fill the rooms.

Finally, we hope that you, the reader, will get as much pleasure from reading this book as much as we did putting it together.

1 Riding the Wave[1]

David A. Dulio and Randall E. Adkins

On the evening of November 2, 2010, Republicans across the nation celebrated major gains in the midterm elections, but as the votes were counted all eyes focused on one person—Ohio Representative John Boehner. Congressman Boehner became Speaker of the House, when he took the gavel from former Speaker Nancy Pelosi (D-CA) on January 5, 2011. In his Election Night victory speech, Boehner clearly described the message Republicans saw in the election results when he said, "Across the country right now, we're witnessing a repudiation of Washington. A repudiation of big government and a repudiation of politicians who refuse to listen to the American people."[2] In the same speech, Boehner also sent the message to President Obama that it was his policies that were being rejected, saying, "While our new majority will serve as your voice in the people's house, we must remember, it's the president who sets the agenda for our government. The American people have sent an unmistakable message to him tonight, and that message is, change course."[3] In the election cycle following arguably one of the more change-oriented elections in recent history, the public seemed to be clamoring for change once again.

The 2010 midterm elections marked the second consecutive historic election for the United States. Of course, the 2008 presidential election was historic for many reasons; indeed the nation chose its first African-American president, Barack Obama, who was elected on the promise of "Change we can believe in." The campaign of 2010 and the election results, however, also offer important historical markers. First, at the end of the day on November 2, President Obama's party lost a total of 63 House seats and control of the House of Representatives. This number represents more seats lost in that chamber than in any election since 1938, including the historic 1994 midterm election when the Democrats lost 58 seats. Second, while Republicans also gained seats in the United States Senate—a total of six—they failed to win the ten seats they needed to take control of that chamber. This too is historic, not because of the gains Republicans made, but because of the gains they did not. Since World War II, party control of the U.S. House has changed seven times in midterm election cycles (1946, 1948, 1952, 1954, 1994, 2006, and 2010). In each instance, control of the Senate changed hands as well, that is until 2010. This midterm marked the first time where control of the Senate did not switch when control of the

House changed.[4] In addition to the federal elections, the 2010 state legislative elections were historic. Republicans gained nearly 700 seats in state legislative chambers across the nation, and starting in 2011 have control of more state legislatures than any time since 1928.

Midterm elections are often described as a referendum on the president, who was of course elected only two years earlier. The idea is simple. The president was elected based on promises he made during the campaign, but he does not appear on the ballot during midterms. Should the public be pleased with the president's performance, his party benefits in the next election cycle and will likely gain seats; should the public be displeased with the president's performance, his party pays the price and loses seats in the midterm elections. On Election Night, Speaker-to-be Boehner's comments noted above clearly fit the mold of the latter.

Analysis of such critical midterm elections is important for many reasons. Without question the 2010 elections fundamentally changed government, politics, and policy choice for the foreseeable future, at least for the second half of President Obama's first term in office.[5] For our purposes here, however, this election cycle offers an important opportunity to examine congressional campaigns and elections broadly. The 2010 elections allow us to examine how and why Americans sometimes use midterm elections as a referendum on the president. The lessons from 2010 will be informative for future midterms in 2014, 2018, and beyond. Candidates running for office in those years will face some of the same obstacles as candidates running in 2010. By examining the election context and campaign strategies and tactics of candidates in 2010, we will be better prepared to understand the dynamics of future campaigns as they unfold during the election cycle. Examining competitive congressional campaigns in the 2010 cycle will also provide an opportunity to explore the effects of the specific factors at work that produced such historic results.

The subtitle of this book is *Riding the Wave*. The term "wave" or "wave election" refers to reinforcing economic, political, and social forces that produce an electoral environment that substantially favors one political party over the other (typically the party out of power) and result in significantly higher electoral turnover. In 2010 these forces included a weak economy, an increasingly unpopular president, and an energized Republican electorate. Most notably the results of this particular wave election included large gains made by Republicans that put them back in charge of the House and altered the balance of power in the Senate (and Washington more generally). These results, to a great degree, were only possible because of the underlying dynamics.

While larger factors fueled the Republican wave in 2010, the individual campaigns of those running for seats in the U.S. House of Representatives and U.S. Senate are the focus of this book. We will examine the factors that buoyed Republicans on their way to their large gains but we will also examine specific campaigns and how these dynamics influenced individual outcomes. Republicans were helped to their large electoral gains by a number of "macro-political" factors. These were a big part of the political environment in 2010 and helped create a wave that crashed into the political landscape on Election Day. How did these factors develop and how did Republicans take advantage of them? Did Republicans win simply because of these macro-political dynamics, or were there factors relevant to individual races ("micro-political" elements) at play? Were there common strategies and tactics that Republican candidates employed that produced results? If so, what were they and how did Republicans take advantage of them? Where Republicans won, was the contest simply about national issues, or were there also local concerns debated?

In spite of the Republican wave, Republicans did not win all the seats that were contested in 2010. While Republicans had no chance to win many seats (for reasons we explore later), Democrats managed to come out victorious in some of the races that were most promising for Republicans to win. One could argue that Republicans actually underperformed. There are several races, especially Senate contests, where the Republican candidate probably should have won, but did not. How did Democrats manage to hang on to these seats? Were there some areas of the nation that were not impacted by the wave, where the factors that allowed Republicans to win so many seats were not as important? If so, did this mean local issues were more important than national issues? Alternatively, were there particular strategies and tactics employed by Democrats that helped them win these races? Or, was there something about the candidates who were running that created a favorable environment for Democrats? In short, how did Democrats defeat Republicans during this wave? These are important questions for students of campaigns and elections to understand not just for 2010, but in future election cycles that may include a similar electoral landscape.

The Shifting Tides

Any number of factors impact election outcomes. Some of these are micro-political dynamics that are active in individual campaigns and unique to each race. These might be the fundraising prowess of the candidates in the race, strategic and tactical decisions made by the campaigns, or certain issues that are specific to a race because they are important to voters in that district or state (the auto industry in Michigan, or dairy farming in Wisconsin, for example). The chapters that follow explore the way these kinds of factors and dynamics impacted congressional campaigns across the nation.

In this chapter, however, we will focus on the macro-political factors that affected all 435 House races and more than 30 Senate races in the 2010 election cycle. Macro-political factors are national-level forces over which candidates have no real control, but to which their campaigns must respond. Unlike the micro-political factors over which candidates can exert influence through the actions inside their own campaign, such as raising more campaign funds than the opponent in order to purchase additional time to air television advertisements, macro-political factors such as the state of the economy or the public approval of the president are out of a candidate's control. Rather, candidates must navigate their campaigns through a myriad of very dynamic and sometimes highly salient macro-political factors in order to win. In other words, macro-political factors set the stage for the campaign by determining the political battleground on which candidates must compete. In the months leading up to the 2010 election cycle, macro-political factors exposed an electoral environment that would be difficult for most, if not all, Democrats. Indeed, a number of predictions using macro-political factors by political scientists showed Democrats losing dozens of seats in the House and a number of Senate seats.[6] Should we have seen the big gains by Republicans coming?

While a variety of factors set the stage for the 2010 congressional races, most pundits and scholars focused their attention on the economy. In short, when the economy does well, the political party in power is rewarded at the ballot box. Likewise, when the economy does poorly, voters punish the political party in power. Heading into the 2010 election cycle, there were no economic indicators that looked positive. The recession that started in 2008 was the main culprit and unemployment or underemployment were the issues about which most Americans were concerned. By February 2009, the unemployment rate had risen above 8 percent. Coming into office with a recession in full swing, President Obama, along with the Democratic Congress, acted quickly to stave off even higher unemployment and even bleaker economic conditions. The White House worked with Congress to design and pass a legislative agenda intended to encourage job growth by spending government dollars on infrastructure, social welfare, and education projects, as well as provide extended unemployment benefits, targeted tax cuts, and other incentives. At the time, a report from the chair of the President's Council of Economic Advisors, Christina Roemer, projected that if the American Recovery and Reinvestment Act (or what came to be known as the "stimulus bill") was enacted the unemployment rate would not rise above 8 percent.[7] In spite of the passage of the stimulus bill, the unemployment rate grew. It passed 9 percent by May of 2009, 10 percent by October of 2009, and hovered there through Election Day.

Unemployment along with other bad economic news haunted the Administration and Democrats running for reelection throughout the 2010 election cycle. Sluggish growth in the Gross Domestic Product, rising home foreclosures, and signals of worldwide economic problems complicated matters and put Democrats in a precarious position. In 2008, voters entrusted them to get the nation back on sound economic footing, but economic indicators in 2009 and 2010 clearly showed they had not been as successful as they, or the nation, had hoped.

The weak economy was not the only factor that created the wave everyone witnessed on Election Day in 2010. Democrats enjoyed unified control of government throughout 2009 and 2010, led by President Obama, House Speaker Nancy Pelosi, and Senate Majority Leader Harry Reid (D-NV).[8] This period of unified government allowed the Democrats to pass a number of legislative initiatives they had longed to address since they last enjoyed unified government—the 103rd Congress from 1993 to 1994.

One issue in particular stands out from the rest. During his campaign for the White House, Senator Obama pledged to reform the health care system. In coordination with the Democratic leaders in Congress, President Obama pressed forward with his health care initiative in spite of the grave economic problems that the country faced. The battle over health care reform took many twists and turns. Originally, the idea of health care reform was quite popular with the American public. Survey research conducted in mid-2009 found large majorities of the public supported the idea of a "major overhaul" of the U.S. health care system (62 percent), and an even larger number thought that it was "very important" that Congress pass a reform bill that year (68 percent).[9] Moreover, another survey found that 75 percent of Americans favored changing the health care system so that all Americans have insurance that covers necessary medical care.[10]

As the debate turned to specific aspects of the plan before Congress, however, support for the idea eroded for a number of reasons. For instance, pluralities of the public feared that the reform ideas would worsen their own medical care and increase their own costs for health care (34 percent each).[11] Other provisions, such as how the new law would be paid for and the idea of a "public option," were also met with negative public reaction. By the end of July 2009, more Americans opposed the plan before Congress than supported it—47 percent to 42 percent.[12] In spite of this, both the House and Senate each passed their own versions of a health care reform bill in July 2009.

It is typical for the Congress to recess for the month of August. During this time members of Congress return to their districts or states for work periods dedicated to meeting with and helping constituents. The recess in August of 2009, however, was unlike any ever seen before. As they typically do, many members of Congress held town hall-style meetings with constituents. Attendance was unusually high for this type of event; constituents who attended the meetings were not happy about either version of health care reform passed by the House or Senate. Many who attended the meetings were very passionate, if not confrontational, in letting their legislator know how they felt. It was common to see the news, national or local, cable or network, show video of a legislator questioned, challenged, and even berated at a town hall meeting over the health care bills that had just passed.[13]

There were a number of actions on health care reform between August 2009 and November 2010, including more debate in Congress over different ideas and possible compromises, and a nationally televised health care summit at Blair House with the President and prominent members of Congress from both parties. There was even an attempt to pass the bill through the House with a little-used parliamentary procedure and a last-minute deal to secure the votes needed to pass the bill. In the end, the Patient Protection and Affordable Care Act of 2010 was signed by President Obama March 23, 2010.

Public support for health care reform never reached the levels of early 2009. In fact, after August 2009, opposition to the reform bill continued to outpace support (see Figure 1.1). What is more striking, however, was the intensity of the opposition. At no point were those who strongly supported the health care reform within five percentage points of those who were strongly opposed to the idea, and most of the time the difference was more than 10 percentage points.

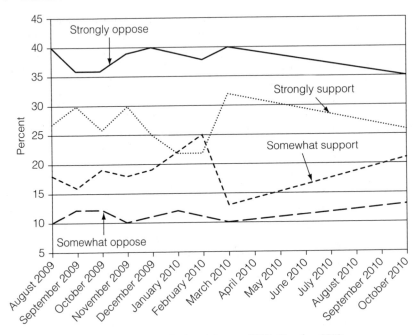

Figure 1.1 Support for Health Care Reform, August 2009–October 2010.
Source: ABC News / Washington Post Poll, various dates. Complete question wording: "Overall, given what you know about them, would you say you support or oppose the changes to the health care system that have been enacted by (Congress) and (the Obama Administration)? Do you feel that way strongly or somewhat?" Prior to February 10, 2010, the wording included: "proposed changes ... that are being developed by ...", http://www.washingtonpost.com/wp-srv/politics/polls/postpoll_10052010. html?sid=ST2010100500023 (accessed November 23, 2010).

Moreover, throughout the debate and after, opposition to the bill was at or above 50 percent.

Given the economic difficulties facing the nation and the opposition to the health care reform bill that was passed by the House and Senate, it should be no surprise that the American public had a dim view of the Congress. Starting in the summer of 2003, more Americans disapproved of the job Congress was doing than approved (see Figure 1.2). Congressional disapproval reached a new height during the 2006 midterm elections and the Democrats won enough seats to take control of both the House and Senate from Republicans for the first time since 1994. Unfortunately for Democrats, congressional approval remained low even after they took over the leadership of the Congress.

Indeed, the American public has almost always held the Congress in relatively low esteem. As John Hibbing and Elizabeth Theiss-Morse argue, Congress is the most disliked branch of government; the presidency and the Supreme Court enjoy much higher approval ratings.[14] Part of the reason for the low congressional approval is that today Congress is on public display thanks to 24-hour

cable news coverage as well as C-SPAN broadcast of many congressional proceedings. With Congress on display in the media fishbowl, the public gets to see
the legislative process at work. As the Framers intended, congressional deliberation includes policy disagreement and partisan bickering, both of which the
public dislikes. As Otto Von Bismark famously noted, "Laws are like sausages.
It's better not to see them being made."

With highly intense partisan debate over the economy, health care and other
contentious issues, the public's dislike for Congress reached a modern zenith during the 111th Congress. While congressional approval rating improved in early
2009, likely due to the good will afforded President Obama and his Democratic
counterparts on the Hill immediately following his inauguration, the improvement did not last long. Congressional approval reached nearly 40 percent in
March of 2009 after passage of the stimulus bill and during deliberation of legislation that intended to help struggling homeowners (see Figure 1.2). This approval
was short-lived, however. Soon thereafter, Congress extended loans to two automakers (General Motors and Chrysler) to fend off bankruptcy and passed the
original versions of health care reform. In tandem, these led to another spike
in congressional disapproval. Obviously, low congressional approval negatively
impacted the campaigns of many incumbents that decided to seek reelection,
especially Democrats, and even discouraged some incumbents from running.

As noted above, midterm congressional elections are often viewed as a referendum on the performance of the president. While voters have an opportunity

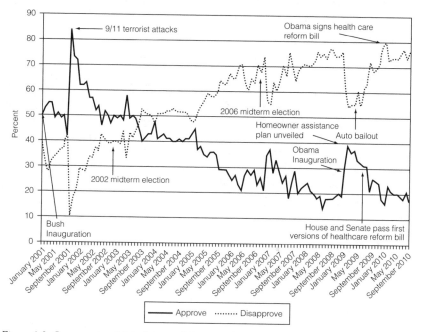

Figure 1.2 Congressional Job Approval, January 2001–November 2010.
Source: Gallup Poll, various dates, http://www.gallup.com (accessed November 13, 2010).

to vote retrospectively when an incumbent president runs for reelection, the president is not on the ballot in midterm elections. Evidence suggests that as a result, voters in midterm elections use the president's party in Congress as a proxy or an opportunity to send a message to the president. In other words, when the public approves of the president's job performance, voters reward his party in Congress. When the public disapproves of the president's job performance, voters punish his party in Congress. History is rarely on the side of the president's party and, unfortunately for Democrats, this trend continued in 2010. The president's party has lost seats in the House of Representatives in every midterm election since the Great Depression except 1934, 1998, and 2002 (see Figure 1.3). In the Senate, the president's party has lost seats in every midterm since the Great Depression except 1934, 1962, 1970, and 2002. Most often, the losses for the president's party were minor, but at times they have been substantial. Notably, just four years after winning a sufficient number of seats to wrestle control from the Republicans in the House, the Democrats under President Franklin Roosevelt lost 71 seats in 1938. In 1942, his party lost another 55 seats. On other occasions, the Democrats under President Johnson lost 47 House seats in 1966, and in the 1994 elections the Democrats under President Clinton lost 52 House seats. On the other side of the aisle, Presidents Eisenhower and Ford each saw

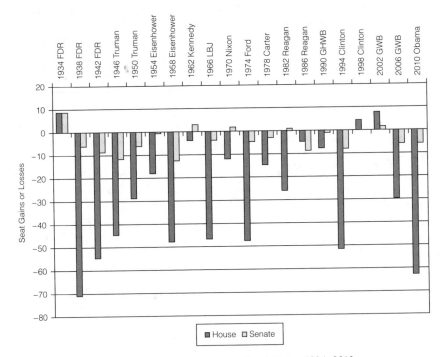

Figure 1.3 Midterm Gains or Losses by the President's Party, 1934–2010.
Source: University of California, Santa Barbara, The American Presidency Project, "Seats in Congress Gained/Lost by the President's Party in Mid-Term Elections," http://www.presidency.ucsb.edu/data/mid-term_elections.php (accessed December 16, 2010).

their party lose 48 House seats in the midterm congressional election. In other words, we should have seen Democratic losses coming. The loss of 63 seats by the Democrats under President Obama is second only to FDR's 71 seats in 1938 (see Figure 1.3). Of course, Senate gains or losses are much smaller because only a fraction of the party's seats are up for reelection,[15] but the net loss of six seats in 2010 is still higher than average.

Most analysis, journalists, and prognosticators were predicting Democratic losses because of these historical trends. The question was how many seats the Democrats would lose. The nation's economic difficulties and the displeasure with Congress as an institution suggested the losses would be large. Another consideration that factored into the equation was the president's own approval rating. If midterm elections are, in fact, referenda on the president's job performance, then the president's approval rating should be a good indicator of how his party would fare at the ballot box.

Barack Obama entered the Oval Office in January of 2009 amidst a backdrop of hope and optimism created by his successful presidential campaign. Presidents often enjoy a "honeymoon" period early in their presidency where they enjoy good relations with the Congress and the news media, and high public approval ratings. President Obama entered office with nearly 70 percent approval, the highest starting approval rating since President Jimmy Carter in 1977 (see Figure 1.4). President Obama's high public approval ratings, however, did not last

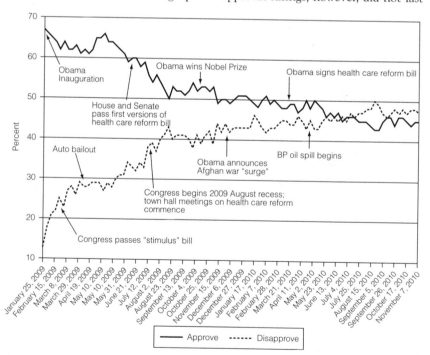

Figure 1.4 Barack Obama Job Approval, January 2009–November 2010.
Source: Gallup Poll, various dates, http://www.gallup.com (accessed November 13, 2010).

long. With the exception of a spike in his public approval during early May of 2009, President Obama's approval among the public steadily declined, hitting 50 percent in August of 2009 then rebounded somewhat before going below the 50 percent mark in November of 2009. Overall, the president's job approval fell below 50 percent faster than any post-World War II president except Gerald Ford and Bill Clinton. Where it took approximately ten months for Obama to drop to the 50 percent mark, Ford did so in three and Clinton in four.[16] More importantly, more Americans disapproved of his job performance than approved by July of 2010, which lasted until Election Day. The 50 percent threshold is critical for a president and his party in midterm elections. In midterms since 1946, the president's party lost an average of 36 seats in the House and more than five in the Senate when his approval rating was below 50 percent.

Especially important in 2010 was the president's job approval among self-identified independent voters. In 2008, Obama received 52 percent of the independent vote, which proved to be an important element in his electoral coalition. The president's public support among independent voters mirrored his support with the nation as a whole; it started relatively high and fell after a few months of steady ratings (see Figure 1.5). His approval among independents, however, started lower (about 60 percent) and fell below 50 percent faster (after only about 6 months in office); Obama saw his approval among this vital

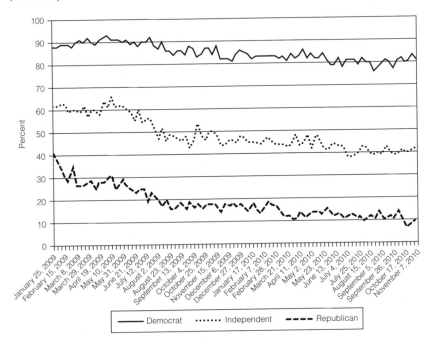

Figure 1.5 Barack Obama Job Approval, by Party Identification, January 2009–November 2010.
Source: Gallup Poll, various dates, http://www.gallup.com (accessed November 13, 2010).

group even fall below 40 percent for several periods before Election Day. The job approval ratings of both Democratic and Republican partisans followed expected patterns. Democrats were more likely to stand by the president and he suffered only a minor dip in public approval. Republicans, on the other hand, abandoned the president rather quickly and his approval among Republicans by Election Day was less than 10 percent.

The American public was not only disappointed in the job performance of the president and the Congress, but they were dissatisfied with the general direction the country was heading well before Election Day. One of the most accessible measures utilized by public opinion pollsters is a question that asks whether the country is heading in the "right direction" or is "off on the wrong track." Dating back as far as 2004, more voters viewed the country as off on the wrong track than headed in the right direction. President George W. Bush fought this problem throughout his second term, and it clearly hurt him in the 2006 midterm elections. This sentiment reached an all-time high in October 2008 when 73 percent of all Americans said the nation was headed in the wrong direction (see Figure 1.6). After President Obama was elected, however, the trend shifted. More and more Americans reported that things were headed in the right direction between November of 2008 and May of 2009. Between May and June of

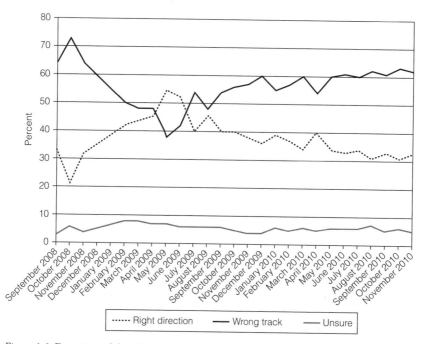

Figure 1.6 Direction of the Nation, September 2008–November 2010.
Source: Ipsos/Reuters Poll. Complete question wording: "Generally speaking, would you say things in this country are heading in the right direction, or are they off on the wrong track?" Data from http://www.pollingreport.com/right.htm (accessed November 26, 2010).

2009, for the first time in more than five years, more Americans said things were going in the right direction than reported things off on the wrong track.[17] Beginning in July 2009, however, Americans had started to sour on the direction of the nation again, and the gap between those who saw things headed in the right direction and those who viewed the country off on the wrong track grew steadily. By Election Day, the difference between the two figures was more than 30 percent. Although the new administration started 2009 with the hope ignited during the campaign, the trend clearly signaled bad signs for Democrats in the upcoming midterm elections.

Heading into the 2010 midterm elections, the American public was not happy with either the leadership in Washington or the direction the country was headed. Major pieces of legislation passed in Congress and signed into law by the president, at least in part, contributed to this feeling among the public. As we noted above, however, Barack Obama was not on the ballot and voters could not take out there frustration on him. On the other hand, they could voice their dissatisfaction with their votes for the House and Senate. Typically, however, most members of Congress are reelected. In fact, since 1994, the reelection rate for members of the House seeking reelection never fell below 90 percent; even in Senate contests, which are often much more competitive, incumbents seeking reelection never had a reelection rate below 79 percent since 1988.[18]

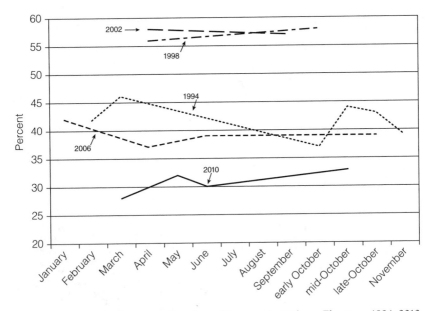

Figure 1.7 Support for Reelecting Members of Congress in Midterm Elections, 1994–2010.
Source: Gallup Poll, various dates, http://www.gallup.com (accessed November 13, 2010).
Note: Lines represent percent saying most members of Congress deserve reelection. Complete question wording: "Please tell me whether you think each of the following political office-holders deserves to be re-elected, or not.... most members of Congress."

The 2010 election cycle appeared to be something clearly different. Overall, voters were not in the mood to send most members of Congress back to Washington for another term. Gallup Polls that surveyed voters throughout the election season showed only about 30 percent of Americans reported that most members should be reelected (see Figure 1.7). In five midterm elections dating back to 1994, this was the lowest percentage of support for reelection to Congress that Gallup found, yet another signal pointing to big gains by the Republicans. Even as Election Day drew near, only 30 to 35 percent of respondents said most members should be reelected. During the midterm elections of 2006—another wave election that swept enough Democrats into office for them to take control of Congress—the figures were similar, but not as Gallup found in 2010. Comparing these election cycles to the more incumbent-friendly elections of 1998 and 2002, an entirely different picture emerges. In these years, between 55 and 60 percent of those surveyed responded that most members of Congress deserved to be reelected.

The implication for the results of the 2010 midterm elections was clear. While some might characterize the electoral context facing Democrats in 2010 as not friendly, others might characterize it as downright hostile. The tide that brought the Democrats into Congress in 2006 and Barack Obama into the White House in 2008 had shifted.

The Wave Crests

In the 2010 election cycle these macro-political factors reinforced each other helping to produce a third consecutive wave election. Alone, however, they were likely not enough to produce the outcome that we saw on Election Day. Republicans needed this kind of political environment to be able to retake the House and make gains in the Senate, but other factors and dynamics were also at work that produced the results of this election cycle. These were also macro-political factors, but were not focused on elected officials or the policies they were pursuing during the 111th Congress. These factors were related to partisanship, excitement about voting on Election Day, and campaign finance.

On Election Night, victorious Kentucky GOP Senate candidate Rand Paul (son of former GOP presidential primary candidate Ron Paul) said in his victory speech, "… tonight, there's a tea-party tidal wave …"[19] Senator-elect Paul was not referencing the effects of American colonists dumping British tea into Boston Harbor in 1773 that were part of the events leading to the Revolutionary War. Rather, Paul was referencing the modern Tea Party, a grassroots[20] movement made up of individuals who are displeased with the direction of the nation, and specific policies of the Obama Administration and the Democratic Congress. The Tea Party was a major development that had a particular impact on the 2010 election cycle and it deserves special attention.

Commentator Rick Santelli of CNBC is often credited with starting the movement. In February of 2009 he went into a tirade on the floor of the New York Stock Exchange where he "called for a modern-day Boston Tea Party protest of President Obama's proposal to help Americans [who were facing foreclosure] with their mortgages."²¹ Three days earlier, however, Seattle resident Keli Carender held the first Tea Party rally (although it was not billed as such at the time). She organized a rally to protest the stimulus bill making its way thought Congress; calling the bill the "porkulus" because she believed it contained wasteful spending that would not help the economy.²²

Although the Tea Party movement started small, it grew quickly. After only about 100 people showed up at Carender's first rally in February 2009, a Tax Day Tea Party six weeks later on April 15 drew over 1,000 people.²³ Small gatherings like those that Carender organized started popping up all across the country and before long there were dozens, if not hundreds, of local Tea Party organizations holding rallies that drew thousands and in some cases tens-of-thousands of supporters. The attitudes expressed by Santelli and Carender each reflect why most Tea Party activists got involved—they were calling for limits to what they felt was out of control government spending and greater intrusion into the lives of average Americans. The debate over issues like health care reform only further fanned the flames of Tea Party activists.

Before long more established politicians became involved in the Tea Party movement. Republicans like former Texas House member and Majority Leader Dick Armey and Sarah Palin, the GOP vice presidential candidate in 2008, were identified as leaders within the Tea Party movement. Armey led an organization called FreedomWorks and Palin offered her counsel to the Tea Party Express. In addition, a large number of Republican candidates in House and Senate across the country (including some whose races are covered in this book) took up the banner of the Tea Party in an effort to win over its burgeoning number of supporters and growing political clout. By the middle of 2009, the Tea Party was on every candidate's radar screen, Democrat and Republican, with each trying either to take advantage of it or mitigate its impact in the upcoming election. The Tea Party movement generated an enthusiasm among Republican voters about public affairs, specifically the 2010 election, not seen in recent years.

In spite of the zeal of Republican voters in 2010, Democrats still had a foundational advantage in the electorate. Simply stated, more Americans call themselves Democrats than call themselves Republicans. Democrats have held an advantage in party identification for decades. In fact, the only time more Americans reported identifying with the GOP was in 1995, just prior to the Republican takeover of the House and Senate in the 104th Congress (see Figure 1.8). This meant that if Democrats could get their voters to the polls, they might be able to hold off many of the Republican challengers.

Unfortunately for Democrats, political ideology is not perfectly correlated with party identification. In other words, the percentages of Americans who view themselves as conservative, liberal, and moderate do not closely match the percentages who say they are Republican, Democrat, and independent, respectively. Between the early 1990s and the mid-2000s, more Americans called themselves moderates (about 40 percent) than labeled themselves conservative (roughly 38 percent) or liberal (about 20 percent).²⁴ After a period in

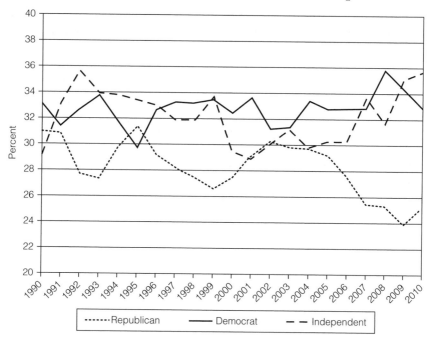

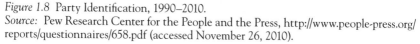

Figure 1.8 Party Identification, 1990–2010.
Source: Pew Research Center for the People and the Press, http://www.people-press.org/reports/questionnaires/658.pdf (accessed November 26, 2010).

the mid-2000s when self-identified conservatives reached parity with moderates, trends in political ideology (and to some extent in party identification) began to shift in 2009 and continued to shift in 2010. During this time, more Americans began to call themselves conservative than moderate or liberal. In fact, this marked only the second time since 1990 that more Americans called themselves conservative than moderate; and the gap between the two was the highest it has ever been with roughly 40 percent saying they were conservative and 35 percent moderate.

Over time, Democrats have enjoyed other foundational advantages as well. One indicator referred to as the "generic ballot" is useful in forecasting how candidates of the two parties will fare in the upcoming election. When the Gallup organization measures this they asks survey respondents, "If the elections for Congress were being held today, which party's candidate would you vote for in your congressional district—the Democratic Party's candidate or the Republican Party's candidate?" Since Gallup started asking this question in 1950, Democrats have routinely led Republicans. The only time the GOP led the generic ballot was in 1994. In 2010, the generic ballot measure looked eerily similar to 1994. Republicans reached parity with Democrats and at some points held historic leads (see Figure 1.9). Given that Democrats had regularly enjoyed an advantage on this indicator, Republicans pulling even and then later leading the Democrats on the generic ballot signaled a wave of substantial proportion.

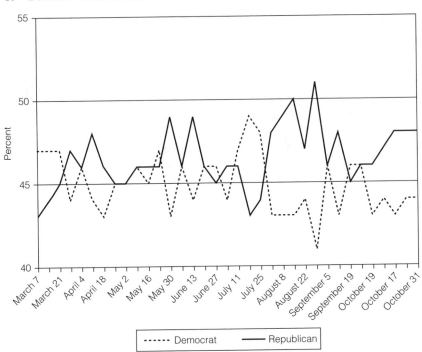

Figure 1.9 Generic Congressional Ballot, March 2010–October 2010.
Source: Gallup Poll, various dates, http://www.gallup.com (accessed November 13, 2010).

Measures of party identification, ideology, or even a generic ballot choice can sometimes be misleading because the collective views of the American public are not what matters on Election Day. Campaigns are won by candidates who get their voters to turn out and cast ballots. While it is difficult to forecast exactly who will turn out to vote, pollsters can predict with a good degree of accuracy who will show up at the polls. A good indicator is how excited someone is about voting. For example, the Gallup organization asks survey respondents, "Would you say you are enthusiastic or not enthusiastic about voting in this year's congressional elections?" One of the major storylines of the 2010 election cycle was the "enthusiasm gap" between Republicans and Democrats. In short, Republicans, particularly conservative Republicans and Tea Party activists, were much more excited about voting than were Democrats (see Figure 1.10). One might even say that Democrats were dreading going to the polls in November, while Republicans were champing at the bit. Although there was a late spike in enthusiasm among Democrats, they failed to close the gap because enthusiasm among Republicans increased too.

In spite of the macro-political factors that obviously reinforced each other, the dynamics present on Election Day were still probably insufficient to produce the outcome with which Democrats were eventually confronted. Republicans still needed to tap potential campaign contributors for funding. Both the Tea

Party movement and the enthusiasm gap were clear signs that the GOP would raise the funds necessary to pick up seats in Congress. In addition to this, there were structural changes at work in the campaign finance system that buoyed the strength of the Republican wave.

Although 2010 brought a number of changes, seismic structural changes occurred in the way that campaigns were financed, producing the most expensive midterm election in history. Reform of the federal campaign finance system has been debated among scholars, pundits, and analysts for more than a century. Indeed, federal campaign finance laws date back almost as far as the Civil War. The first noticeable effort by Congress to level the campaign finance playing field included the Tillman Act (1907), followed by the Federal Corrupt Practices Act (1910). The Tillman Act made it illegal for banks and corporations to make direct contributions to a candidate for federal office. The Federal Corrupt Practices Act established requirements for multi-state parties "to report any contribution or expenditure made in connection with campaigns for the House of Representatives," but only after the election was over.[25] The 1910 law was amended in 1911 to include spending limits and other disclosure requirements, but much of this new law was struck down by the Supreme Court in *Newberry v. United States*. The law was amended again in 1925 to meet Constitutional scrutiny in terms of disclosure of campaign money. The Taft-Hartley Act (1947)

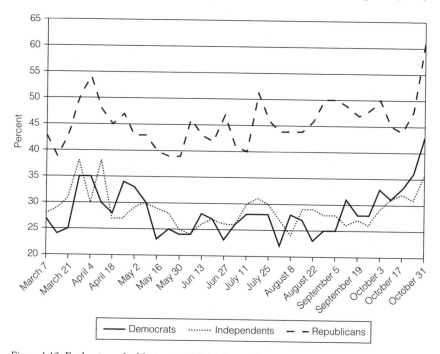

Figure 1.10 Enthusiasm for Voting in 2010 Midterm Election, March 2010–October 2010.
Source: Gallup Poll, various dates, http://www.gallup.com (accessed November 13, 2010).
Note: Lines represent percentage saying they were "very enthusiastic" about voting.

made permanent the provisions of the Smith-Connelly Act (1943), which prohibited unions from contributing directly to candidates campaigns (matching the ban on corporate contributions in 1907).

The seismic change impacting this election was announced on January 21, 2010, by the Supreme Court in the decision *Citizens United v. Federal Election Commission*. This decision fundamentally reshaped American elections, especially as it relates to the early campaign finance laws. While corporations were banned from contributing directly to candidates for political office in the early 20th century and unions were banned from contributing in the mid-20th century, more recent law had restricted their efforts to become involved in elections independently of candidates' campaigns. In particular, the Federal Election Campaign Act (FECA) "prohibited corporations and unions from using their treasury funds for making expenditures influencing federal elections—including political advertising known as express advocacy, which explicitly calls for election or defeat of federal candidates."[26] To circumvent this, corporations and unions could create political action committees (PACs) to fund this type of activity, but they were still bound by other aspects of the FECA. In addition, the Bipartisan Campaign Reform Act of 2002 "prohibited corporate and union treasuries from funding broadcast advertisements … that mention clearly identified federal candidates … within 60 days of a general election or 30 days of a primary election."[27] Clearly, this statute significantly limited the role of corporations and unions in American elections. In effect, "corporations that wanted to air at least some messages referring to federal candidates during periods preceding elections either had to establish a PAC to receive voluntary contributions in order to fund the ads or forgo the advertising altogether."[28]

After the *Citizens United* decision, while corporations and unions were still prohibited from making direct contributions to candidates' campaigns, the restrictions on expenditures from their general treasuries that called for the election or defeat of a candidate for federal office no longer existed. This created the potential for corporations and unions to spend hundreds of millions to influence the 2010 elections. It also created the possibility for new organizations to be created simply in order to raise and spend money to influence elections. Familiar organizations such as the U.S. Chamber of Commerce—a group friendly to Republican candidates—and the Service Employees International Union (SEIU)—a group friendly to Democratic candidates—as well as new organizations such as American Crossroads and 60 Plus Association—both groups friendly to Republicans—were very active in 2010.

In the 2010 midterm election cycle, over $294 million was spent by groups other than candidates' campaigns and the two major political parties, compared to the 2006 midterm election cycle when less than $69 million was spent by outside groups.[29] This money is important because of the sum total, the increase over the previous midterm election cycle, and the likely connection to the *Citizens United* decision. Most of all, however, it is important because of the collective impact that it had on individual campaigns in 2010.

On average, individual candidate campaigns in House races were fairly even in 2010, in terms of raising and spending campaign cash. The average GOP candidate spent about $1 million and the average Democrat spent nearly $1.3 million (see Table 1.1).[30] In many races, however, especially the most competitive of the cycle, Democratic candidates had a large fundraising advantage over the Republican opponents. In 109 of the most competitive races tracked by the *New York Times*, "Democratic candidates ... outraised their opponents overall by more than 30 percent ... And Democratic candidates ... significantly outspent their Republican counterparts over the last few months [of the election cycle] in those contests, $119 million to $79 million."[31] For example, in Florida's 8th Congressional District race, Representative Alan Grayson raised over $5.1 million while his challenger, Daniel Webster, raised only $1.3 million; Representative Walter Minnick, in Idaho's 1st District race, raised $2.4 million compared to challenger Paul Labrador's $603,000; and in New York's 25th District, Representative Dan Maffei raised over $2.7 million while his challenger, Ann Marie Buerkle, raised only about $550,000.[32] The margin of victory in each of these races was two percentage points or less.

After all the funds were tallied, the GOP held the advantage in Senate races as their candidates raised and spent more than Democrats overall. In addition, the average GOP candidate raised roughly $2.5 million more and spent about $1.7 million more than the average Democratic Senate candidate. Similar to the closest House races, however, Democrats in the most competitive Senate contests enjoyed a fundraising advantage over Republicans throughout most of the election cycle. For example, in her losing bid to keep her seat in Arkansas, Blanche Lambert Lincoln raised $10.5 million while her challenger, John Boozman, raised only $3.2 million; Senator Michael Bennett in Colorado raised nearly $11.5 million compared to his opponent Ken Buck's $3.8 million; and in Washington's race, Senator Patty Murray raised nearly $11 million to challenger Dino Rossi's $7.3 million.[33] In an interesting twist, some other GOP Senate candidates made a late fundraising surge to get even with their Democratic rivals. This surge came late—near the end of September—and marked "the first time in the two-year election cycle that Republican candidates for the Senate raised more than Democrats in the closest races."[34] For example, challenger and Tea Party activist Sharron Angle raised over $21 million in her unsuccessful effort to defeat Senate Majority Leader Harry Reid, who raised $17 million. In Pennsylvania, Republican Pat Toomey was able to out raise his opponent, Democrat Joe Sestak, $14.8 million to $11.8 million.[35]

The Democratic Party's campaign committees in the House and Senate also held a large advantage in fundraising over their GOP counterparts (see Table 1.2). These funds were largely spent to supplement candidate campaign spending.[36] Some money was spent to help candidates who were being outraised by their opponents. For example, in Michigan's 9th District, the National Republican Congressional Committee (NRCC) spent over $2 million to help Andrew "Rocky" Raczkowski who trailed Representative Gary Peters in fundraising.

Table 1.1 Congressional Candidate Fundraising and Spending, 2010.

	Number of candidates	Total raised	Total from PACs	Total from individuals	Total spent	Average raised	Average spent
			House				
Democrats	391	$474,163,797	$190,329,760	$262,986,591	$496,221,682	$1,212,695	$1,269,109
Republicans	412	$460,816,468	$128,297,256	$289,339,041	$429,450,338	$1,118,487	$1,042,355
			Senate				
Democrats	34	$227,866,222	$36,917,637	$168,644,997	$237,865,361	$6,701,948	$6,996,040
Republicans	38	$348,528,913	$40,289,533	$210,707,629	$330,161,933	$9,171,813	$8,688,472

Source: Center for Responsive Politics, "2010 Overview; Stats at a Glance," http://www.opensecrets.org/overview/index.php?cycle=2010&Type=G&Display=T (accessed June 20, 2011).

The NRCC also spent more than $840,000 to help Cory Gardner in Colorado's 4th Congressional District who was running against Representative Betsy Markey.[37] Democrats also spent heavily to help their candidates. The Democratic Congressional Campaign Committee (DCCC) spent over $1.4 million to help Representative Bobby Bright fend off a challenge from Martha Roby in Alabama's 2nd District, and they spent $1.2 million to assist John Salazar from Colorado's 3rd District in his race against challenger Scott Tipton (even though Salazar had more money than Tipton).[38] In total, the NRCC and DCCC spent $1 million or more on 41 candidates (14 Republicans, 27 Democrats).[39] Not all candidates, however, received help from their party. Both parties made difficult decisions in the closing days of the campaign. While their total figures represent large fundraising hauls, both parties were still dealing with limited resources in numerous competitive races and they could not spend money on a race if it was not going to be effective.[40]

Strong fundraising by both Democratic candidates and the party's congressional campaign committees gave Democrats the resources they needed to compete in a year when all the other macro-political factors were clearly working against them. This advantage, however, was neutralized by spending from outside organizations that raised and spent money to help Republicans. According to the non-partisan Center for Responsive Politics, which tracks money in political campaigns, of the top 10 groups who spent money during 2010, eight tilted to the conservative side of the political spectrum and helped Republican candidates. The aforementioned U.S. Chamber of Commerce spent nearly $33 million on ads that helped get Republicans elected. Two groups new to the electoral landscape, and formed after the *Citizens United* decision—American Crossroads and Crossroads Grassroots Policy Strategies—spent $21.5 million and $17 million, respectively, on campaign communications to help GOP candidates.[41] Of course, Democratic groups were active too. Two major public

Table 1.2 Party Campaign Committee Fundraising and Spending, 2010.

Committee	Total raised	Total spent
Democratic National Committee	$224,457,439	$223,910,984
Republican National Committee	$196,336,723	$210,769,855
Democratic Senatorial Campaign Committee	$129,543,443	$129,086,445
National Republican Senatorial Committee	$84,513,719	$68,099,551
Democratic Congressional Campaign Committee	$163,896,053	$163,582,280
National Republican Congressional Committee	$133,779,119	$132,098,633
All Democratic Party committees[a]	*$814,974,337*	*$759,042,694*
All Republican Party committees[a]	*$586,594,377*	*$589,574,971*

[a] These include state party committees as well.

Source: Center for Responsive Politics, "Political Parties Overview," http://www.opensecrets.org/parties/index.php (accessed June 20, 2011).

employee unions—Service Employees International (SEIU) and the American Federation of State, County and Municipal Employees (AFSCME)—spent $15.7 million and $12.6 million, respectively.[42] When all was said and done, the two parties and their candidates were on roughly equal financial footing in the 2010 cycle. In the most competitive races, candidates of both parties had enough money in their coffers to campaign effectively, and when they did not a party committee or outside group spent money to help level the playing field.

Caught in the Undertow

The macro-political factors surrounding 2010 strongly suggested a significant defeat for the party in power, but who, specifically, was in trouble? Which candidates were most in danger of defeat? While that answer can be provided in one word—Democrats—there were clearly some Democrats who were in more trouble than others. Even though the GOP picked off 63 seats in the House and 6 in the Senate, there were many other Democrats who won and some won by safe a margin. For instance, in Florida's 23rd Congressional District Alcee Hastings won by a margin of 79 percent to 21 percent over his GOP opponent; in Alabama's 7th District Terry Sewell won 73 percent to 28 percent; John Lewis won by nearly 50 points in Georgia's 5th District; and in California a number of Democrats won by large margins including Barbara Lee (9th) and Xavier Becerra (31st) who each received 84 percent of the vote, and Karen Bass (33rd) who received 86 percent of the vote.

The fact that so many Democrats were able to win convincingly points to a well established fact of congressional elections. Some seats in the House and Senate are almost guaranteed victories for the Democratic Party while others are sure wins for the GOP, even in a tumultuous year like 2010. This allows Democrats like those noted above to win easily in a bad year for their party. These seats are commonly referred to as "safe" seats. In these races, the candidate of the party with the advantage typically faces little, if any, opposition and the outcome is rarely in doubt. In most election cycles, the vast majority of seats in the House are considered safe, while Senate contests are generally more competitive. In a typical year between 370 and 380 of the 435 House seats are considered safe. This leaves only a relative handful of seats that are competitive.

One factor that made 2010 different was the large number of seats that were competitive. In comparison to the typical election, about twice as many seats were competitive. The *Cook Political Report*, a very well-regarded political newsletter in Washington, D.C. headed by Charlie Cook, a long-time election analyst, handicaps each of the 435 House districts into seven categories each election year. Those that are competitive are either "likely Democratic," "lean Democratic," "Democratic toss up," "Republican toss up," "lean Republican," and "likely Republican." All other seats are considered safe. In the final assessment by the *Cook Report* in 2010, 135 seats were in one of the six competitive categories. This is compared to 2006, another "wave" election, in which 88 seats were competitive, and 2002 when only 67 were competitive.[43] In 2010, the vast majority of the competitive seats were, as one would expect, Democratic seats. Democratic candidates were the ones most likely to lose, but as the number of Democrats who won easily demonstrates, a blanket statement that Democrats were in trouble does not tell the whole story.

Democratic incumbents were certainly wary of reelection in 2010. Those Democrats holding office during the 111th Congress—the two-year period after President Obama's inauguration—were being held accountable for the nation's complex economic problems. Of course, there were Democrats also running against Republican incumbents and Democrats running for open seats. Some of these Democrats even managed to win, such as Cedric Richmond who knocked off GOP incumbent Joseph Cao in Louisiana's heavily Democratic 2nd Congressional District.

Most Democrats running as either challengers or for open seats in 2010 had slim chances of winning. While giving due credit to the campaigns that these individuals ran, there were likely other Democrats that might have made better candidates who simply chose not to run in 2010. In other words, some of the Republican wins may have effectively been determined months or even years before Election Day when individuals made decisions about whether or not to run for office. As Gary Jacobson and Samuel Kernell demonstrate, some would-be candidates act very strategically when deciding whether or not to run for office.[44] The best potential candidates examine the macro-political factors noted earlier, using them to determine whether or not to run and in which election cycle to run. Strategic politicians run for office when the climate is good for their party and sit out elections when the climate is bad for their party (see Chapter 10 by David Canon, however, for an alternative hypothesis). Thus, it is likely that the Democrats with the best chances to defeat Republicans in 2010 were sitting on the sidelines.

Incumbents use a similar decision calculus in when making choices about whether to run for reelection. Rather than go through a difficult election cycle when the prospects of losing are higher than normal, many members of Congress will retire. Seventeen House Democrats decided to retire rather than run for reelection in 2010. Some retirements surprised even the most seasoned election analysts. Many of these representatives, in any other election cycle, would likely have had an easy time getting reelected. Appropriations Committee Chairman, David Obey, from Wisconsin's 7th Congressional District, Patrick Kenney (RI 1st), Vic Snyder (AR 2nd), and Brian Baird (WA 3rd) all decided to throw in the towel. There were also a number of surprising Democratic retirements in the Senate, such as Senators Chris Dodd (CT), Byron Dorgan (SD), and rising star Evan Bayh (IN). Interestingly, 20 Republicans in the House also decided not to run for their seat again, but 12 of these individuals chose to run instead for either a Senate seat or the governorship in their home state (half as many Democrats from the House ran for higher office).

Drilling down a little deeper, we find that a number of Democratic incumbents were in more trouble compared to others in their party. As noted above, some Democratic incumbents won rather handily in 2010. Those who lost, however, can be classified in three groups: those Democrats who were elected in the wave elections of 2006 or 2008; those Democrats who won in 2008 in districts or states that were carried by John McCain in the presidential race; and those Democrats who voted for the signature pieces of President Obama's agenda (health care reform, the stimulus bill, and the American Clean Energy and Security Act of 2009, which was a piece of environmental legislation that came to be known as "cap-and-trade").[45]

In 2006 Democrats won enough seats to take over the majority in the House and Senate and added to those majorities in 2008. In total, Democrats took 52 House seats and 14 Senate seats from Republicans in these two elections. The trouble with this is that many of these victories were in districts or states that typically elect Republicans. Of the 52 House seats—dubbed "majority makers"[46] because they provided Democrats the seats necessary to gain a majority[46]—50 were on the list of competitive races as defined by the *Cook Report*.[47] Of these 50 seats, 34 were in districts that favored the Republican candidate. Thus, these incumbents were at the top of the Republican list of seats to take over in 2010 for good reason. Still, some of these first- or second-term Democrats were in districts that offered them a fighting chance in 2010. For instance, while Iowa's 1st Congressional District was considered a competitive race, according to the *Cook Report* it had a Partisan Voter Index (PVI)[48] of D+2; Democratic incumbent Bruce Braley went on to successfully defend this seat. Others, however, were not so lucky. Moderate Democrat Bobby Bright ran in his first reelection campaign in Alabama's 2nd District, which had a PVI of R+16, and lost to Martha Roby 51 percent to 49 percent. Fellow first-term member Betsy Markey lost in Colorado's 4th District, which had a rating of R+6. In these contests, only one Democrat was able to win a House race in a district with a PVI of R+6, or higher—Jason Altmire beat Keith Rothfus 51 percent to 49 percent in Pennsylvania's 4th District. In total, during 2010, Republicans were able to win 35 of the 52 seats they had lost in the previous two election cycles.

These 35 Democratic defeats, however, make up only about 55 percent of the seats won by Republicans. There were other places where the GOP was able to make gains. Another type of district Republicans focused on was where their presidential candidate, John McCain, did well in 2008. Barack Obama won that election pretty handily, but he did not win in every congressional district in the country. In fact, there were 48 House districts that voted for John McCain but still elected a Democrat to the House. Some of these districts were very competitive at both the House and presidential levels in 2008. For instance, Obama narrowly lost Colorado's 4th, New Mexico's 5th, Florida's 24th, New York's 13th, and Pennsylvania's 3rd and 12th Districts with 49 percent of the vote, but these districts all elected Democrats to the House fairly comfortably. In a year like 2010, however, these districts were seen as potential GOP pick-ups given the political context in which candidates were operating. Other important districts for Republicans were those that elected Democrats in 2008, but were won easily by John McCain. A total of 12 districts elected Democrats to the House where Obama got less than 40 percent of the presidential vote. Even long-time members such as Chet Edwards (TX 17th), Gene Taylor (MS 4th), Ike Skelton (MO 4th), and Marion Berry (AR 1st) needed to worry. In the end, of these 48 Democrats, only 12 managed to win reelection.

Finally, Democrats who voted for President Obama's legislative agenda were also more likely to be vulnerable. As we have noted, several pieces of the president's agenda were controversial and unpopular. Democrats who voted for the stimulus, health care reform, and the cap-and-trade bill were clearly a focus for the GOP. Analyses by scholars after the election have demonstrated that these votes hurt Democrats.[49] This is consistent with other work that shows the public holds members of Congress accountable for votes that they take.[50] Taking just a sample of the most competitive races from 2010—50 competitive districts where Democrats won in 2006 and 2008—we see clear evidence of the impact of these votes. On health care, of the 37 who voted for the reform, 25 lost. On cap-and-trade, of the 34 who voted "aye," 22 lost. On the stimulus bill, of the 47 who voted for it, 33 lost.[51] Those who voted for more than one of these bills were in even more trouble with the voters.

Plan of the Book

The comparative case studies that follow are designed to help us understand congressional elections on multiple levels. We have chosen cases that allow us to study campaigns not only from the perspective of the historic 2010 election cycle but from a broader view as well. Our focus on macro-political factors in this chapter sets up the discussion of mostly micro-political factors in each of the case chapters. These cases will not only enhance our understanding of what happened in 2010 and why it occurred during this particular election cycle, but will also encourage us to think about what the trends, dynamics that were at work, and the outcomes mean for campaigns during future midterm elections.

We chose the cases carefully to allow us to meet the goals of not only understanding congressional elections in the short term but also the long term. As we noted, there are typically two types of congressional elections: those that are waged for "safe" seats where the outcome is, for all intents and purposes, known before Election Day, and competitive races where the campaign goes right down to the wire. All of the races selected for this book were competitive races. Not only are these some of the most important and interesting races of 2010, but a focus on competitive races will allow us to think about what these races can tell us in future years. Competitive races are the ones that are focused on most heavily by many actors during an election cycle including political parties, interest groups, and the press. In addition, the races included here were some of the most expensive in the country. For instance, in the Nevada Senate race, the two candidates combined to spend nearly $38.7 million. In Pennsylvania, political parties and outside groups spent $25.6 million. In Texas' 17th District the candidates spent a combined $6.1 million. In Michigan's 7th District, non-candidate entities spent an unbelievable $8.5 million. Competitive and expensive races are where the action is in every election cycle, and understanding what happens in these races during 2010 can help us understand future cycles as well.

The chapters that follows was written by first-rate scholars who were "on the ground" in the district or state in which the campaign was waged.[52] These individuals followed the actions of the candidates, saw the television ads that were aired, received the direct mail pieces that were sent, and in many cases had access to one or both campaigns. In other words, these scholars are *the* experts on the campaign they followed. The book, however, is more than a collection of essays about twelve separate campaigns. Rather, the case studies were designed to be an interconnected group. To this end, each chapter has two important similarities. First, each has a common focus—addressing the issue of "the wave" that occurred in 2010 and what that meant for this particular campaign. For instance, while all the races were competitive, some had fairly large margins of victory. This is not an indictment of those who categorized the races as such. Indeed, they were competitive at one point, but the GOP wave was so high that in some instances it carried a Republican to a big win for a normally highly competitive seat. Second, each chapter is unified by common threads running through the case. We believe this creates a more cohesive collection that analyzes the main research question, but also creates a volume where each case study is singing the same tune even though each chapter has a different voice. Each race does stand out in its own right, however, as the idiosyncrasies and unique aspects of the individual campaigns are brought out by the authors.

It was former Speaker of the House Tip O'Neill (D-MA) who famously uttered the axiom, "All politics is local." To help reflect this, each case includes an examination of important micro-political factors at work in the campaign that took place in that particular district or state. These common micro-political elements include, a short description of the district or state where the campaign was waged; the demographics and electoral trends of the district or state; and whether one party typically enjoys an advantage over the other on different measures of partisan strength (election results, party identification, and the like). In addition the mood of the electorate leading up to the campaign and subsequent election is discussed.

Each case also includes a discussion of the electoral and political context leading up to the 2010 election cycle that helps to understand why the race was competitive in the first place. This was a bad year for Democrats generally, but why was this particular race competitive? Was the Democrat tied to President Obama and other Democratic leaders? Was the incumbent a bad "fit" for the district or state where voters felt that he or she did not represent them in Congress?

Congressional elections begin and end with the candidates vying for elected office. While this book is about more than just Democratic officeholders seeking reelection, the fact is that many of the most important races in 2010 were where a sitting Democrat was defeated. In these instances the cases pay close attention to the incumbent. In particular, it is important to know his or her political record. This also speaks to the question of why this officeholder landed on the endangered incumbents list. What was the incumbent's record of performance and what were his or her vulnerabilities? Did the incumbent support President Obama on the important policies noted above as well as other legislation? Did the incumbent take unpopular positions on either national or local issues? David Mayhew noted many years ago that members of Congress would likely not get in trouble with their constituents by being on the losing side of an issue, but they very well could get into hot water by being on the wrong side of an issue important to voters.[53] In addition, were Democratic incumbents trying to fend off challenges by touting the vitality of the constituency service they had performed, or bragging about federal dollars (i.e., earmarks) that had come back to the district under their watch? Moreover, as we noted above, Republicans fielded strong candidates in most of these races. Therefore, each case pays special attention to what got these individuals into the race this time. Were the challengers acting strategically, as Jacobson and Kernell would tell us?

The most important part of each chapter focuses on how the campaign was waged. Here the focus is on the issues driving the campaign as well as the strategies and tactics employed by each candidate and his or her campaign. Were national issues front and center, as Republicans would have liked, or were local concerns the focus, as Democrats hoped? Without question the economy was the number one issue nationally. How did the candidates address this issue? How about other items on President Obama's agenda including health care reform, cap-and-trade, and the stimulus? In terms of strategy and tactics, the cases focus on the money that was raised and spent as well as what it was spent on. How did the candidates communicate with voters? What was the role of television advertising and what issues were discussed? How much money did the candidates raise and how did they spend it? In short, how did the Republican use the favorable electoral climate to his or her advantage, and how did the Democrat try to stop the wave from crashing down on them?

The 2010 election cycle also included important new wrinkles to congressional elections. Chief among these was the *Citizens United* decision. In the wake of this, special attention is paid to the importance of non-candidate activity, specifically spending by political party committees and outside interest groups. In addition, any role that the Tea Party had in the race is an area of primary focus.

Finally, each chapter includes an analysis of the factors that determined why the winning candidate came out on top. For those races that ended up not being as close as they originally were predicted, this involves a discussion of what turned the tide and led to the larger margin of victory than was expected. In those that were close right until Election Day, the factors that put one candidate over the top are detailed. At the end of the book, we return to a more general discussion in the conclusion. Here we revisit both the macro-political factors outlined above as well as the micro-political analyses from each case chapter to make some generalizations about what we learned in 2010 by addressing these competitive races. While the case studies in this book focus on campaigns in one election cycle, this book is about more than just 2010. The lessons uncovered by the authors of these comparative case studies will be important for scholars and students in coming congressional elections; they do not apply only to Democrats running in a tough year for their party or to Republicans trying to take advantage of the wave that hit on November 2, 2010. Rather, they apply to all candidates running in competitive races. For instance, while the 2012 elections will be impacted by a much different context—congressional reapportionment and redistricting will have taken place, President Obama will have finished his first term and be on the ballot again in 2012, Republicans will have been looked to for solutions to major public policy questions, and many others we cannot yet point to—many of the same lessons will still apply. These are important to consider as we look ahead; after all, the next wave might crash down on the GOP.

Notes

1 Many different metaphors are used in describing campaigns and elections. Some of the metaphors used can be very graphic and sometimes even violent. Indeed, the very word campaign comes from its usage as a military term. The events chronicled in this book occurred on or prior to Election Day, which was on November 2, 2010. Since then, however, two very tragic events occurred. Both are frequently used as metaphors to describe certain aspects of campaigns and elections. First, on January 8, 2011, an assassination attempt was made on the life of Representative Gabriel Giffords of Arizona's 8th Congressional District. Fortunately, she survived. Unfortunately, many others did not. Arizona's 8th District is a marginal congressional district, and while Representative Giffords won a close reelection battle in 2010, her district was on the list of congressional races that Republicans publicly "targeted" for takeover. In the aftermath of the shootings in Tucson, a dialog began about the appropriateness of using the word "target" to refer to an electoral contest or an individual candidate. The idea that a district or state is "targeted" by some entity interested in the outcome of a campaign, however, has been around for decades. The second tragic event occurred on March 11, 2011, when a 9.0 magnitude earthquake occurred off the coast of Japan. This earthquake caused an extremely destructive tsunami to hit the coast of Japan, resulting in a tremendous loss of both life and property. The effects of this event will be felt for a very long time. Given these events, we have avoided the terms "target," "tsunami," and "tidal wave" in the text of the book, except where they were used in direct quotation of a politician, pundit, journalist, or campaign professional. We offer our sympathies to the victims of both events and pray for a speedy recovery.
2. CNN, November 3, 2010, http://157.166.255.31/TRANSCRIPTS/1011/02/se.05. html (accessed November 26, 2010).
3. Ibid.
4. On the other hand, there have been instances where control of the Senate has changed but control of the House did not with 1986 being the most recent example.
5. We will leave the discussion of how to pundits and commentators.
6. A number of press articles note these predictions. See, for example, Mike Dorning, "Democrats' Midterm Election Fortunes May Be Measured in Disposable Incomes," Bloomberg, June 1, 2010 (http://www.bloomberg.com/news/2010-06-01/ roman-dmytriv-needs-more-money-in-his-pocket-to-make-ends-meet-with-obama. html); and Seth Masket and John Sides, "Dems Will Lose Seats—But Not Why You Think," *New York Daily News*, May 28, 2010 (http://www.nydailynews.com/ opinions/2010/05/28/2010-05-28_dems_will_lose_seats__but_not_why_you_ think.html) (both accessed December 15, 2010).

7. See "The Job Impact of the American Recovery and Reinvestment Act," Politico. com, http://www.politico.com/static/PPM116_obamadoc.html (accessed December 15, 2010).

8. The other scenario is divided government which is when the two parties split control of the elected offices at the federal level (the U.S. House, U.S. Senate, and the presidency). Divided government has been the norm in American politics since World War II.

9. Diageo/Hotline Poll, June 4–7, 2009, http://www.pollingreport.com/health7.htm (accessed December 15, 2010).

10. Pew Research Center poll, June 10–14, 2009, http://www.pollingreport.com/ health7.htm (accessed December 15, 2010).

11. Gallup Poll, July 24–25, 2009, http://www.pollingreport.com/health7.htm (accessed December 15, 2010).

12. National Public Radio Poll, July 22–26, 2009, http://www.pollingreport.com/ health7.htm (accessed December 15, 2010).

13. Many of these videos can still be found on YouTube.

14. John R. Hibbing and Elizabeth Theiss-Morse, *Congress as Public Enemy: Public Attitudes Towards American Political Institutions* (New York: Cambridge University Press, 1995).

15. Only one-third of all Senate seats are up every two years. See the different Senate classes at http://senate.gov/general/contact_information/senators_cfm.cfm (accessed December 16, 2010). It is noteworthy, however, that there were 37 Senate contests in 2010 due to retirements or other circumstances that led to the need to hold special elections in several states.

16. Jeffrey M. Jones, "Obama Job Approval Down to 49 percent," Gallup.com, November 20, 2009, http://www.gallup.com/poll/122627/Obama-Job-Approval-Down-49. aspx (accessed December 16, 2010).

17. We should note that in some other polls the right direction figure did not pass the wrong track number; they were close to parity but they did not pass each other. See, for example, data at PollingReport.com, http://www.pollingreport.com/right. htm (accessed December 16, 2010).

18. Note that these percentages are for members who seek reelection. They do not reflect the members who retire or do not run for reelection in order to seek another office. We discuss this as it relates to 2010 below.

19. Quoted in Campbell Robertson, "A Victorious Paul Vows to Stick to Message," *New York Times*, November 2, 2010, http://www.nytimes.com/2010/11/03/us/ politics/03kentucky.html (accessed December 22, 2010).

20. This has been disputed by many on the left.

21. Caitlin Huey-Burns, "Inside the Tea Party Revolution," *U.S. News & World Report*, December 17, 2010, http://politics.usnews.com/opinion/articles/2010/12/17/inside-the-tea-party-revolution.html (accessed December 22, 2010).

22. Kate Zernike, "Unlikely Activist Who Got to the Tea Party Early," *New York Times*, February 27, 2010, http://www.nytimes.com/2010/02/28/us/politics/28keli. html (accessed December 22, 2010).

23. Ibid.

24. Lydia Saad, "Conservatives Continue to Outnumber Moderates in 2010," Gallup Poll, http://www.gallup.com/poll/145271/Conservatives-Continue-Outnumber-Moderates-2010.aspx (accessed December 21, 2010).

25. Anthony Corrado, "Money and Politics: A History of Federal Campaign Finance Law," in *Campaign Finance Reform: A Sourcebook*, eds. Anthony Corrado, Thomas E. Mann, Daniel R. Ortiz, Trevor Potter, and Frank J. Sorauf, pp. 25–60 (Washington, D.C.: Brookings Institution Press).

26. R. Sam Garrett, "Campaign Finance Policy After Citizens United v. Federal Election Commission: Issues and Options for Congress," Congressional

Research Service Report R41054, February 1, 2010, http://assets.opencrs.com/rpts/
R41054_20100201.pdf (accessed December 20, 2010).

27. Ibid.

28. Ibid.

29. Center for Responsive Politics, "Outside Spending," http://www.opensecrets.org/
outsidespending/index.php (accessed December 21, 2010). It is important to note
that any discussion of outside money in 2010 is filled with uncertainty. First, there
can be different definitions of what is truly "outside" money. Some will include
money from both political parties and non-party groups. We choose to consider
these two types of organizations separately so our definition of outside money only
includes non-party organizations. The second area of uncertainty stems from the
fact that different types of organizations have different requirements for what they
must report to the Federal Election Commission. Specifically, groups must report
spending for independent expenditures, electioneering communications, and
communications costs. Other spending does not need to be reported. Therefore,
the $294 million figure we have cited likely understates how much was actually
spent by groups during the election cycle.

30. "2010 Overview; Stats at a Glance," Center for Responsive Politics, http://www.
opensecrets.org/overview/index.php?cycle=2010&Type=G&Display=A   (accessed
December 21, 2010).

31. Michael Luo and Griff Palmer, "Democrats Retain Edge in Campaign Spending," *New York Times*, October 26, 2010, http://www.nytimes.com/2010/10/27/us/
politics/27money.html (accessed December 21, 2010).

32. "Candidate Fundraising and Non-Candidate Spending in House Races – 2010,"
Campaign Finance Institute, http://www.cfinst.org/data/2010Election_NonCandi-
date_House.aspx (accessed December 21, 2010).

33. "Candidate Fundraising and Non-Candidate Spending in Senate Races – 2010,"
Campaign Finance Institute, http://www.cfinst.org/data/2010Election_NonCandi-
date_Senate.aspx (accessed December 21, 2010).

34. Brody Mullins and Danny Yadron, "GOP Senate Hopefuls in Tight Races Get
Money Boost," *Wall Street Journal*, October 18, 2010, http://online.wsj.com/article/
SB10001424052702304898004575556562419110060.html (accessed December 21,
2010).

35. Ibid.

36. There are several ways party money can be spent; they include: a direct contribution, coordinated expenditures, or independent expenditures. See Paul S. Herrnson, *Congressional Elections: Campaigning at Home and in Washington*, 5th ed.
(Washington, D.C.: Brookings Institution Press, 2007), for a description of these
spending strategies.

37. "Candidate Fundraising and Non-Candidate Spending in House Races – 2010,"
Campaign Finance Institute.

38. Ibid.

39. Ibid.

40. See, for example, Jeff Zeleny and Carl Hulse, " Democrats Plan Political Triage to Retain House," *New York Times*, http://www.nytimes.com/2010/09/05/us/
politics/05dems.html (accessed December 21, 2010); and Reid Wilson, "DCCC Ad
Plans Show Internal Disagreement," *National Journal Hotline*, http://hotlineoncall.
nationaljournal.com/archives/2010/09/dccc_ad_plans_s.php (accessed December
21, 2010).

41. "2010 Outside Spending by Groups," Center for Responsive Politics, http://www.
opensecrets.org/outsidespending/summ.php?disp=O   (accessed   December   22,
2010).

42. Ibid. We noted above that figures on outside money are likely understated. It appears that these figures are also understated. In press reports, the SEIU has claimed that it spent nearly $88 million dollars during the 2010 cycle (see, for example, Brody Mullins and John D. Mckinnon, "Campaign's Big Spender Public-Employees Union Now Leads All Groups in Independent Election Outlays," *Wall Street Journal*, October 22, 2010, http://online.wsj.com/article/SB10001424052702 303339504575566481761790288.html (accessed December 21, 2010). We are not comfortable using this figure because we do not know with any certainty what is being included in the total. It may be that SEIU is counting PAC contributions to candidates as well as other unreported figures such as grassroots efforts. Instead, we rely on the Center for Responsive Politics and the expenditures that are required to be reported by groups like these (see note 28 above).

43. Cook Political Report, various issues, http://www.cookpolitical.com/ (accessed December 21, 2010).

44. Gary C. Jacobson and Samuel Kernell, *Strategy and Choice in Congressional Elections* (New Haven, CT: Yale University Press, 1983).

45. We should note that these three categories are neither exhaustive nor mutually exclusive.

46. Sean J. Miller, "Speaker Pelosi's 'Majority Makers' Are Facing Possible Electoral Doom," *The Hill*, October 19, 2010, http://thehill.com/house-polls/thehill-poll-week-3/124937-pelosi-majority-makers-are-facing-electoral-peril (accessed December 20, 2010).

47. We cannot make the same comparisons with Senate contests because, unlike the in the House, the candidates elected in 2006 and 2008 were not on the ballot in 2010. However, of the 14 Senate seats Democrats won over this time frame, 5 seats were in states that typically vote Republican—Alaska, Montana, North Carolina, and Virginia's 2 seats—and in three other states that have voted for recent Republican presidential candidates—Colorado, Ohio, and Missouri.

48. Charlie Cook created a measure called the Partisan Voter Index (PVI) which provides a comparison of how a particular congressional district votes compared to the nation as a whole. A PVI is computed for each district which shows whether it leans to the Republicans or the Democrats. For instance, a district with a PVI of R+4 would mean that the district voted an average of 4 points more Republican than the nation did in the last two presidential elections; a PVI of D+8 would mean the district votes 8 points more Democratic than the nation as a whole.

49. These analyses are found mostly on blogs, but are done by first-rate academics and, we believe, can be trusted in their conclusions. See the work of Eric McGhee (http://www.themonkeycage.org/2010/11/did_controversial_roll_call_vo.html), Seth Masket (http://www.huffingtonpost.com/seth-masket/the-price-of-reform_b_755785.html), and Brendan Nyhan (http://www.brendan-nyhan.com/blog/2010/11/a-first-take-on-election-2010.html) for examples.

50. Stephen Ansolabehere and Philip Edward Jones, "Constituents' Responses to Congressional Roll-Call Voting," *American Journal of Political Science*, vol. 54, no. 3, pp. 583–597.

51. *Washington Post*, "The Pendulum Swings Back," http://www.washingtonpost.com/wp-srv/special/politics/election-2010/incumbent-democrat-analysis/ (accessed December 21, 2010).

52. One exception is the chapter on Ohio's 1st Congressional District. The authors were not in that district during the campaign but they had written a previous case about the campaign from 2008.

53. David R. Mayhew, *Congress: The Electoral Connection* (New Haven, CT: Yale University Press, 1974).

2 Reid vs. Angle in Nevada's Senate Race

Harry Houdini Escapes the Wave*

David F. Damore

From the outside, the Nevada Senate race encapsulated many of the plotlines shaping the 2010 election narrative. First, there were the candidates: Harry Reid, an entrenched, but unpopular Democratic incumbent who not only supported the Obama administration's major policy initiatives, but was the main force pushing the president's agenda through Congress, and Sharron Angle, a Tea Party darling and long-time thorn in the side of the Republican establishment. Then there was the context: a swing state with the highest unemployment, foreclosure, and bankruptcy rates and the sharpest decline in median income in the nation—bad omens for any Democratic incumbent. There was also the money—lots and lots of money. The candidates spent record sums for a Nevada election; national and state party organizations made huge investments; and third-party groups made unprecedented expenditures to either help oust the Senate Majority Leader or push him over the finish line for another term.

Along the way, there was the handful of only-in-Nevada-politics moments highlighted by surreptitious tape recordings, claims of voter suppression and counter-charges of vote fraud, speculation about who might benefit from the state's quirky "none of the above" ballot option, and the fracturing of the state's Republican Party that left in its wake a coup against the party's long-time state legislative leader and the demotion of the rabid anti-Reid editor and publisher from the state's largest newspaper.

These considerations, however, served as backdrop to what appeared to be the final act of a politician practicing his craft with uncanny determination and skill. A politician who over a series of election cycles developed assets and incrementally moved them into place; who, by deftly reading the political terrain, knew when and where to apply pressure to tilt the field to his advantage; and who executed a political strategy meticulously constructed to overcome the most unfavorable political environment in a generation. Indeed, as is detailed below, the seeds of Harry Reid's reelection to the U.S. Senate were sown in 2004, germinated in 2008, and harvested in 2010. So, like a modern day Houdini, Harry Reid escaped the 2010 wave.

Party Building and the Specter of Tom Daschle

On Election Night 2004, Harry Reid enjoyed a rarity in a political career that begun four decades prior as he easily won reelection for his fourth term in the U.S. Senate with 61 percent of the vote (a far cry from his 428 vote victory in 1998). Moreover, the defeat of South Dakota Senator and Minority Leader Tom Daschle positioned Reid to move from Minority Whip to Minority Leader. Yet, while the 2004 election allowed Reid to accrue more power than any Nevada politician in history, it was another in a string of dismal elections for Nevada Democrats. Despite near even registration numbers (see Figure 2.1), Republicans won the state's biggest races. Moreover, because of Reid's clout and the Republican-leaning nature of Nevada, if Reid wanted to avoid being "Daschled" in 2010, then he had his work cut out for him.

The ability of Reid and the Democrats to transform the Nevada political landscape over the next three election cycles was aided by a number of factors. The state has a small (2.6 million) population that is concentrated in Clark and Washoe counties (home of Las Vegas and Reno, respectively) and it is within these counties that constituencies friendliest to the Democratic Party reside. Thus, party building activities in these areas benefit from economy of scale and have significant consequences statewide.

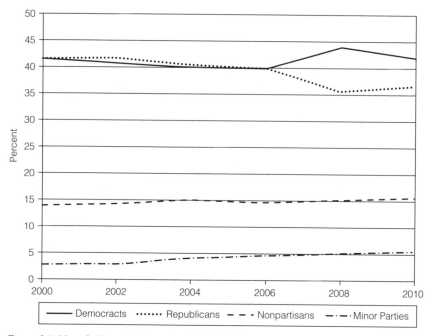

Figure 2.1 Nevada Voter Registration, 2000–2010.
Source: Nevada Secretary of State's Web page, http://nvsos.gov.

Nevada's growth during the prior two decades resulted in a population suggestive of a Democratic demographic advantage as the state is now more urban and ethnically diverse. Specifically, between 2000 and 2010 Nevada's population grew by 35 percent and the share of the state's population concentrated in the urban counties (Clark and Washoe) increased to 88 percent. Much of the growth occurred in the state's Hispanic community (Hispanics, as a share of the population, increased from 20 percent to 27 percent and the non-Hispanic white population decreased from 65 to 54 percent), which increasingly became a top priority of Democratic outreach and mobilization efforts.[1]

Because of the development of a seemingly endless number of gaming properties along the Las Vegas Strip, Nevada is also more union oriented as roughly 16 percent of the state's workforce is union affiliated.[2] The Nevada economy is largely service oriented with 24 percent of the state's workforce employed in the accommodation and food services sector (in comparison less than four percent in manufacturing).[3] Owing to its blue-collar workforce, the state's average annual income of $42,270 is below the national average and only one in five Nevadans have as much as a bachelor's degree (which ranks Nevada 45th out of the 50 states).[4]

The rising Democratic tide over the past decade was also aided by the implosion of the once dominant Republican political operation. Infighting among the party's factions led to power struggles and constant leadership turn-over. This dysfunction was exacerbated by the unwillingness of the state's top Republican office holders to risk their own ambitions and wade into these internecine battles. As a consequence, the Nevada Republican Party stopped doing what it did so well for so long: recruiting electable candidates, raising money, and getting out the vote. Ensign would eventually resign his seat in May of 2011 and Heller was chosen to fill out the remainder of the term.

By far the most pivotal event in the resurgence of the Nevada Democratic Party was the decision of the Democratic National Committee (DNC) to reshape the party's presidential nomination process by including a western state in the early phase of the competition. Nevada was attractive because of the state's concentration of Hispanics, strong union presence, and swing state status. Reid used his clout to successfully lobby the DNC to pick Nevada.[5] Once Nevada was selected, Reid and his newly imported Democratic operatives designed the Democratic caucuses to maximize organization and mobilization.

Yet, despite months of preparation, doubts lingered that the party would be able to execute its ambitious game plan. Indeed, many of the state's political analysts thought that Reid lost his mind as he predicted that caucus turnout would exceed 100,000 given that only 10,000 Democrats participated in 2004. Reid, however, was prophetic as over 117,000 Democrats came out to caucus. While Barack Obama and Hillary Clinton split the state's delegates, the real victor was Reid as by Election Day 2008 Nevada Democrats enjoyed a voter registration advantage of over 100,000 (see Figure 2.1). This advantage certainly impacted the 2008 election as in the end John McCain all but abandoned Nevada and Barack Obama won the state's five Electoral College votes with over 55 percent of the vote—the largest vote share a Democratic presidential candidate received in the state since 1964—and Dina Titus became the first Democratic candidate to win in the 3rd Congressional District. Reid's work earlier in the decade would pay dividends in 2010.

"You Can't Beat Somebody with Nobody" or How to Pick the Least Attractive Opponent

Leading up to 2010, Reid made no secret that he and his staff studied the 2004 South Dakota race and they were determined to avoid the miscalculations that sealed Tom Daschle's fate. First, whereas Daschle ran in a state that was trending Republican, Reid led the transformation of Nevada from a Republican-leaning to a Democratic-leaning state. Second, Daschle's vulnerability caused him to draw a top-tier opponent in John Thune. Ever mindful of the adage that "you can't beat somebody with nobody," the next order of business for Reid was to insure that his opponent was nothing of the caliber that Daschle faced.

In 2005, Reid dispatched with what would have been his toughest opponent, Brian Sandoval, by arranging a federal judicial appointment for the former Nevada Assemblymen, Attorney General, and chair of the state's powerful Gaming Commission.[6] Reid then used his Democratic operation in 2008 to defeat three other potential candidates: state senators Bob Beers and Joe Heck and U.S. Representative Jon Porter (3rd District). Next, Reid's operatives made it known that the Senate Majority Leader planned to raise more than $20 million for his reelection bid and that he would "vaporize" whoever his opponent was. Such a battle, coupled with the prospect that scandal-plagued Republican U.S. Senator John Ensign would be vulnerable to a primary challenge in 2012, caused the last remaining top-tier Republican, Congressman Dean Heller (2nd District), to forgo the race.

Thus, as the 2010 candidate filing deadline approached, the Republicans had no candidate capable of clearing the field, but instead were faced with the prospect of an intra-party fight between the 12 second- and third-tier candidates who entered the primary for the right to challenge Reid. The situation was particularly vexing because the GOP's fortunes were rising nationally due to the deteriorating economy and uncertainty about the Obama administration's health care and stimulus initiatives (the Patient Protection and Affordable Care Act of 2010 and American Reinvestment and Recovery Act, respectively).

The choice of the GOP establishment was Sue Lowden. Lowden, a former beauty queen and television reporter, had a light political resume having served one term in the Nevada Senate and briefly chaired the Nevada Republican Party (see note 5). Lowden's biggest asset, thanks to her marriage to a casino owner, was that she was willing to self-finance her campaign. Lowden, however, was less than agile on the stump and her campaign wallowed for weeks in minor controversies. Lowden's frontrunner status also brought her attention from the Reid campaign, which deployed a video tracker to gather material for television ads run by Reid to undercut Lowden's claims that she was ready for the U.S. Senate. Ultimately, her undoing was comments that she made in discussing her opposition to the health care reform bill where she suggested that patients should be encouraged to barter chickens for medical services.

Once Lowden began to self-destruct, a second front opened against her from the right as the conservative political groups, particularly the Tea Party Express and the Club for Growth, weighed into the primary with over $1 million in television advertising questioning Lowden's conservative bona fides. This move supported Sharron Angle, who was languishing behind Lowden and Danny Tarkanaian. She served in the Nevada Assembly from 1999 to 2005 representing northern Nevada. Since leaving the legislature she had become a perennial candidate who enjoyed mounting primary challenges against establishment politicians as she did in 2006 against Dean Heller for the open 2nd District House seat and in 2008 against Bill Raggio who had served in the Nevada Senate since 1972.

While no one could dispute Angle's conservative credentials—her nickname while in the Nevada Legislature was "41 to Angle" given her propensity to be the only opposition vote in a chamber of 42 members. Angle's primary campaign consisted of a Web page, a few paid staffers working out of her living room, and volunteers energized by the Tea Party movement. After receiving the endorsement of national Tea Party organizations, however, Angle began to gain ground.[7] On primary night, she bested the other eleven candidates with over 40 percent of the vote. Tellingly, a year prior, Harry Reid predicted to U.S. Representative Shelley Berkley (NV-1) that his opponent would be Sharron Angle.[8]

The Devil You Know …

Given that the majority of GOP primary voters did not support Angle, immediate speculation arose about her electability and ability to unify the GOP behind her candidacy. Moreover, pre-primary polls of general election match-ups indicated that while Angle was favored over Reid, her margin was the smallest of the three top Republican candidates. Nevada voters consistently viewed Reid more negatively than positively, as the Senate Majority Leader's favorability ratings continued to linger below 40 percent throughout 2009 and 2010.[9] This trend persisted despite Reid's campaign spending roughly $10 million throughout 2009 and into the first half of 2010 to burnish his image by rolling out a series of television advertisements and mailings centered on the theme "no one can do more."

The problem for Reid was that voters were not interested in rewarding a career politician running on the time tested platform of credit claiming and the delivery of particularistic benefits.[10] Reid was also unable to finesse his way around the Obama administration's policies given that he played prominent roles in passage of health care reform, the stimulus, and the bailout programs begun under George W. Bush and continued by Obama (the Troubled Assets Relief Program (TARP) and the loans to automakers General Motors and Chrysler). Indeed, none of these initiatives resonated in Nevada. For instance, a May 2009 poll found that 37 percent of respondents thought that the stimulus plan was working,[11] while a December 2009 poll indicated support for President Obama's health care plan was at 39 percent in the state.[12] Moreover, because of his long tenure in the Senate, Reid could be portrayed as culpable for the economic downturn and the housing meltdown that hit Nevada particularly hard.

The Majority Leader also operated with a charisma deficit and had a history of malapropisms that reinforced the caricature of Reid as a creature of the Senate unable to viscerally connect with voters.

More generally, as Reid ascended the leadership ladder in the Senate, his congressional voting record became more liberal and more partisan (see Table 2.1). As a consequence, Reid was unable to run under the "Independent like

Table 2.1 Congressional Vote Scores for Harry Reid, 1987–2010

Year	American Conservative Union	Americans for Democratic Action	Party Unity	Presidential Support
2010	0%	75%	95%	97%
2009	8%	95%	96%	99%
2008	16%	70%	84%	43%
2007	0%	85%	95%	39%
2006	12%	90%	93%	57%
2005	4%	100%	92%	38%
2004	21%	90%	83%	61%
2003	21%	70%	95%	53%
2002	10%	85%	94%	71%
2001	20%	100%	96%	65%
2000	12%	90%	94%	92%
1999	12%	90%	92%	82%
1998	20%	90%	78%	76%
1997	8%	85%	83%	84%
1996	15%	85%	79%	78%
1995	9%	80%	74%	75%
1994	4%	85%	85%	90%
1993	24%	60%	86%	88%
1992	23%	80%	75%	37%
1991	33%	65%	75%	51%
1990	30%	61%	79%	44%
1989	21%	65%	71%	63%
1988	28%	55%	76%	56%
1987	19%	80%	88%	40%

Source: CQ's *Politics in America* (Washington, DC: Congressional Quarterly, Inc., 2010 and 2000); The American Conservative Union (http://www.conservative.org); Americans for Democratic Action (http://www.adaction.org); and Congressional Quarterly's vote studies (2009: http://innovation.cqpolitics.com/media/vote_study_2009; and 2010: http://innovation.cq.com/media/vote_study_2010).

Nevada" banner as he did in 1986 and 2004 given that he was now the Senate Majority Leader and an integral part of the Washington establishment. Thus, unable to move his positives or pivot away from his role as a congressional leader, Reid's campaign sought to make the race a choice between the U.S. Senate Majority Leader and Sharron Angle instead of a referendum on Harry Reid.[13]

The strategy employed by the Reid campaign had numerous advantages. Because Angle spent her political career in northern Nevada, she was largely unknown in southern Nevada where the vast majority of the state's electorate resides. Thus, before Angle could put together her general election campaign team, Reid was defining her as "extreme" and "dangerous" in a series of television spots that began hitting the airwaves days after the primary. Reid's early advertising blitz allowed the Majority Leader to frame the campaign's narrative for the media and the electorate, and erase any momentum that Angle may have had coming out of the primary.

Indicative of the Reid campaign's preparation, Reid's spots used Angle's own words culled from interviews and footage provided by the campaign's video trackers to provide veracity to their depiction of Angle. Reid brought attention to a number of Angle's statements including: entitlements have "spoiled our citizenry" with regard to extending unemployment benefits, supporting the nuclear storage facility at Yucca Mountain that Reid worked to kill, making "a lemon situation into lemonade" with regard to her opposition to abortion under any condition including incest, elimination of all insurance mandates with regard to health care, phasing out Social Security and Medicare, privatizing veterans' health care, supporting "second amendment remedies" to facilitate government responsiveness, and general hypocrisy. For example, although she campaigned to eliminate the safety net, she and her husband live on a government pension. By doing this, Reid hoped to draw a sharp contrast and deflect attention from his liabilities.

While Reid prepared for the 2010 election for years, the same could not be said for Angle. Indeed, during the crucial post-primary period, the Angle campaign was essentially non-existent other than to replace her primary Web page with an online contribution appeal.[14] Because her primary campaign was a barebones operation, she had no plan in place for the general election. As a consequence, Angle was forced to play catch-up throughout the campaign to simply react to Reid.

As if her slow start was not problematic enough, Angle's campaign team was divided. On one side sat her trusted advisors who enjoyed the loyalty of the volunteers whose interest in the race was piqued by the Tea Party movement. On the other side were national operatives and associates of the National Republican Senatorial Committee (NRSC) that were brought in to oversee fundraising, communications, and messaging. While the volunteers viewed the professionals as untrustworthy and arrogant, the national operatives responded in kind, and, borrowing from the children's Christmas cartoon, nicknamed the group "The Island of Misfit Toys." The end result was a campaign that spent as much time putting out internal fires as competing against Reid.[15] Unwilling to referee or establish a chain of command, Angle often made matters worse by going off message (e.g., Sharia law has "taken hold" in the United States or questioning the separation of church and state) or scheduling events without informing staff.[16]

Particularly exasperating was Angle's decision to meet privately with Tea Party of Nevada U.S. Senate candidate Scott Ashjian, who, despite having no ties to the movement had qualified himself for the ballot under his newly created party. Although Ashjian's campaign had little traction, Angle feared that he would siphon votes away from her and wanted him out of the race.[17] Ashjian secretly recorded the meeting with Angle and then released it to Jon Ralston, the state's preeminent political commentator. Her campaign staff found out with everyone else via Ralston's blog that Angle promised to use her "juice" to open doors for Ashjian with Republican heavyweights if he would withdraw. Elsewhere, Angle bashed the same Republican establishment by suggesting that the party "lost their standards, they've lost their principles."[18]

Because Angle was sensitive about appearing to sell-out to the GOP establishment, she seemed to run more of a primary as opposed to a general election campaign. She did not move her headquarters to Las Vegas despite the logistical advantages the locale would offer, she preferred to campaign in rural Nevada instead of in the state's vote-rich urban centers, and she gravitated towards media that would allow her to make fundraising appeals. In a Fox News interview, for example, she explained her media strategy as follows: "We needed to have the press be our friend ... We wanted them to ask the questions we want to answer so that they report the news the way we want it to be reported. And when I get on a show and I say send me money to SharronAngle.com, so that your listeners will know that if they want to support me they need to go to SharronAngle.com."[19] As a consequence, most media outlets got little to no attention from the Angle campaign beyond spokesperson boilerplate talking points. Reid, too, was seldom seen as his staff sought to keep the focus on Angle and avoid any new Reidisms.[20]

After spending much of the summer building her war-chest (see below), Angle rolled out her advertising strategy in a series of large ad buys in late summer. The spots were universally negative in tone and focused on two themes. The first laid the blame for Nevada's, and the nation's, economic ills at Reid's feet and featured laundry lists of dismal economic statistics that coincided with Reid's tenure as Senate Majority Leader. The second theme made use of polling data suggesting that Democrats were vulnerable on the immigration issue among nonpartisans (roughly 16 percent of the electorate, see Figure 2.1). In response, the campaign flooded the airwaves with advertisements that linked immigration to the state's economic turmoil.[21]

Although the veracity of the immigration spots were questioned by various fact check organizations, the advertisements tarred Reid as "the best friend an illegal alien ever had" because of his opposition to the Arizona enforcement law and support for tax breaks for illegal immigrants and policies that put "Americans' safety and jobs at risk."[22] The spots received additional criticism owing to their visual images of menacing youths with dark complexions behaving threateningly. At no point did the Angle team use its extensive advertising budget to present Sharron Angle in a positive light and counter the Reid campaign's harsh characterization of her, as Angle was largely absent from her ads. Thus, unable to articulate a counter-narrative through paid or earned media, the Reid campaign's labels of "extreme" and "dangerous" took hold resulting in sharp increases in Angle's negatives.[23]

Money, Money, Money

The non-stop attack ads were fueled by unrelenting fundraising by both Reid and Angle, as well as by significant spending by outside groups. Given his vulnerabilities, Reid raised and spent money aggressively. He geared up his fundraising early in the cycle as he raised about 40 percent of his total before September of 2009 (see Table 2.2). Thereafter, the Senate Majority Leader consistently raised around $2 million each quarter and maintained substantial cash reserves even as he made significant investments in his campaign at the end of 2009 and into 2010. Not surprisingly, given his status as a party leader, about a fifth of Reid's total fundraising came from political action committees (PACs).[24] In particular, trial lawyers, a long-time Democratic ally, were the biggest PAC donors to Reid. In addition, and consistent with Reid's role in shaping the health care and financial regulation legislation during the 111th Congress, PACs associated with health professionals and the pharmaceutical, hospital, insurance, and finance industries invested heavily in the his reelection effort.

Angle's Tea Party credibility and her strategy of using friendly media as a fundraising tool proved to be a boon as she pulled in $14 million in the third quarter alone; unprecedented money for an unknown candidate from a small state. To do this, Angle developed a national fundraising network of nearly 200,000 donors. Reliance on a large pool of small donors was a necessity given Angle's outsider status, which limited her ability to raise money from political action committees (roughly 1 percent of her total contributions came from PACs according to the Center for Responsive Politics). As noted above, until Angle gained the support of various national Tea Party groups in the spring of 2010, she struggled to raise money and she burned through her cash on hand (see Table 2.2). After the primary, Angle raised money at an astonishing pace. At the same time and as is noted in the conclusion, to accrue these funds, her campaign spent a good deal of time and resources on its fundraising operation. Nonetheless, given that fundraising is an indicator of competitiveness and viability, Angle's haul allowed her to project strength and maintain a continuous television presence.

The campaign also featured extensive efforts by outside groups seeking to influence the race. Indeed, while the efficacy of the *Citizens United* decision (see Chapter 1) remains an open question, clear beneficiaries of the Supreme Court decision were Nevada's television station owners. The state's concentrated media markets, inexpensive advertising rates, and highly competitive House and Senate races made Nevada an appealing choice for outside groups hoping to affect the 2010 midterm elections. The race for Nevada's 3rd District

Table 2.2 Reid and Angle Campaign Receipts and Disbursements by Reporting Period, 2009–2010

Reporting Period	Harry Reid			Sharron Angle		
	Receipts	Disbursements	Cash on Hand	Receipts	Disbursements	Cash on Hand
Beginning Cash as of September 30, 2009			$8,732,847.85			$73,377.88
2009 Year End						
(1 October–31 December)	$2,019,548.14	$2,061,208.10	$8,691,187.89	$371,541,30	$344,410.29	$100,508.89
2010 April Quarterly						
(1 January–31 March)	$1,775,009.38	$1,044,719.99	$9,421,477.28	$363,421.42	$348,948.06	$114,982.25
2010 Pre-primary						
(1 April–19 May)	$1,109,450.44	$1,396,251.24	$9,134,676.48	$300,954.51	$288,920.27	$127,016.49
2010 July Quarterly						
(20 May–30 June)	$1,135,189.15	$1,529,563.27	$8,940,302.36	$2,299,428.57	$663,773.25	$1,762,671.81
2010 October Quarterly						
(1 July–30 September)	$2,833,484.08	$7,765,835.50	$4,007,950.94	$14,392,908.99	$12,074,953.32	$4,080,627.48
2010 Pre-general						
(1 October–13 October)	$603,703.55	$3,459,899.15	$1,151,755.34	$3,528,954.46	$4,916,426.69	$2,693,165.25
2010 Post-general						
(14 October –22 November)	$1,972,303.83	$2,947,748.95	$176,310.13	$6,327,399.80	$8,728,565.10	$291,999.95
Total	$11,648,688.57	$20,205,226.19		$27,584,619.05	$27,365,996.98	

Source: Compiled from candidate reports to the Federal Election Commission, Form 3, Lines 23, 24, 26, and 27, various dates.

between Democratic incumbent Dina Titus and Republican Joe Heck garnered more than $7 million in outside spending—the second highest total for any House campaign in 2010.[25] This sum, however, was dwarfed by the $16.8 million in outside spending that the Reid-Angle general election campaign attracted.

In total, 60 organizations spent resources in the Nevada Senate race.[26] Of these groups, 39 worked on Angle's behalf and spent just under $10.5 million, while 21 groups supported Reid and spent a combined $6.3 million. On average, the outside groups spent just over $288,000, with groups backing Reid averaging somewhat more spending than those supporting Angle. There was significant variation among groups as some made token investments, while others were substantially involved in the campaign (see Table 2.3). Parsing the data further, better than three out of four dollars spent by these groups was done to oppose either Reid or Angle, rather than in support of one of the candidates, further adding to the campaign's negative tone.

For Angle, the major players were Crossroads GPS and American Crossroads, conservative 527 political groups organized under the provision in the tax code for which they are named and led by former Bush political advisors Ed Gillespie and Karl Rove. While denying that personal animus was driving the groups' efforts, Rove, who was raised in Sparks, Nevada, has a long and combative relationship with Reid.[27] In total, Crossroads GPS and American Crossroads spent more than $4 million on the race, running negative television spots that sought to blame Reid for the economic downturn. The groups spent heavily during the post-primary period when Angle's had no television presence and thus, provided some push-back against Reid's early spots. Angle was also helped by investments by the National Republican Senatorial Committee (NRSC) and various socially conservative groups (e.g., National Right to Life, the Susan B. Anthony List, and the Faith and Freedom Coalition). Additionally, Angle benefitted, as was the case during the primary, from ad buys by the conservative Tea Party Express and Club for Growth that also attempted to make Reid culpable for economic conditions. She also benefitted from other small government groups (e.g., Citizens United and the 1st Amendment Alliance).

Reid drew outside support from traditional Democratic allies. Various unions (Service Employees International Union (SEIU), American Federation of State, County, and Municipal Employees (AFSCME), and the Nevada State Education Association) spent heavily, as did pro-choice groups (Planned Parenthood and NARAL Pro-Choice America) despite Reid's inconsistent record on abortion. The Democratic Senatorial Campaign Committee (DSCC) also made significant investments on Reid's behalf (see Table 2.3).

Far and away, the group backing Reid that had the most sustained presence was the Patriot Majority. The group was essentially an arm of the Reid campaign and spent nearly $2.5 million during the general election campaign. The group even spent over $300,000 focusing on Sue Lowden during the Republican primary. Patriot Majority received large contributions from many of the groups that were also making independent ad buys in the race (see Table 2.3).[28] Votevets.org, AFSMCE and SEIU contributed $250,000, $300,000, and $445,000,

Table 2.3 General Election Spending by Outside Groups in Nevada's Senate Race, 2010

	Amount	Groups	Mean	Standard Deviation	Minimum	Maximum
Total	$16,810,937	60	$280,182	$568,530	$20	$2,711,745
Angle Backers	$10,435,694	39	$267,582	$511,448	$1,950	$2,711,745
Reid Backers	$6,375,243	21	$303,583	$675,006	$20	$2,489,268
Support Angle	$1,779,440	20	$88,972	$108,393	$350	$387,276
Oppose Reid	$7,488,658	24	$312,027	$520,559	$2,372	$2,253,258
Support Reid	$1,317,096	14	$94,078	$164,530	$20	$595,680
Oppose Angle	$4,458,437	10	$445,844	$795,755	$9	$1,992,222
Top Angle Groups						
1. Crossroads GPS	$2,711,745					
2. American Crossroads	$1,595,234					
3. Ending Spend Fund	$862,432					
4. National Republican Senatorial Committee	$812,041					
5. Our Country Deserves Better PAC (Tea Party Express)	$616,767					
Top Reid Groups						
1. Patriot Majority PAC						$2,489,268
2. Democratic Senatorial Campaign Committee						$2,063,955
3. VoteVets.org Action Fund						$595,680
4. American Federation of State, County, and Municipal Employees						$310,352
5. Service Employees International Union						$225,000

Source: Center for Responsive Politics, http://www.opensecrets.org (accessed March 10, 2011).
Note: Column totals may deviate due to rounding. Some groups that spent in the race were not coded as either spending for or against a specific candidate. These data are included in the totals reported at the top of the table, but are excluded from the figures summarized in the table's middle panel.

respectively to Patriot Majority and the American Federation of Teachers gave $500,000. The group also reaped substantial contributions from Nevada gaming corporations MGM Resorts International ($300,000) and Harrah's (now, Caesars Entertainment; $75,000) and $400,000 from retired insurance executive and Las Vegas real estate entrepreneur Guy David Gundlach.

While not an outside group per se, the Reid campaign's coalition of "Republicans for Reid" was another interest active in the campaign. Led by long-time Nevada operator Sig Rogich, who spent decades in Republican politics including prominent roles in the presidential campaigns of Ronald Reagan and George H. W. Bush, the purpose of "Republicans for Reid" was twofold. First, it accentuated the point that given Nevada's small size, it was not in the state's interest to throw out the Senate Majority Leader regardless of his party affiliation. Second, the group solidified the notion that Angle was outside the mainstream by signaling to moderate Republicans if the Republicans who you have supported are now standing with Reid, then reelecting the Majority Leader may not be so bad given the alternative.

The group, whose membership included much of the state's Republican political, entertainment, legal, and business establishment, played varying roles. For most, involvement was limited to their names being listed on the "Republicans for Reid" page on the Reid campaign's Web site. Others, however, appeared prominently in advertisements. MGM boss Jim Murren (see note 16), Reno mayor Bob Cashell, former Clark County Sheriff Bill Young, and Dema Guinn, the recently widowed wife of former Republican Governor Kenny Guinn, were used with great effect on television and radio. The late endorsement of Reid by Bill Raggio, perhaps the most distinguished northern Nevada Republican of all, was the coup de grâce that likely doomed Angle's prospects in her home county of Washoe.

The Stretch Run

Despite the efforts of so many spending so much to affect the campaign, public polls showed the race within the margin of error (see note 9) heading into the second half of October. The presumed closeness fueled the anticipation surrounding Reid and Angle's lone debate on October 14th, two days before the start of early voting (detailed below). For Angle, the debate was a rare moment when she took the advice of her handlers and spent days sequestered in debate preparation. As a consequence, Angle looked nothing like the "extreme" and "dangerous" caricature put forth by the Reid campaign. Instead, she stuck to her talking points, put Reid on the defensive, and managed, with her "man up Harry Reid" line, to score the debate's only sound bite. Reid, acting on internal polling data indicating that Angle was bleeding moderate Republicans, [29] used the debate to appeal to these voters by suggesting that he admired Supreme Court Justice Antonin Scalia and referring to his friendships with Senate Minority Leader Mitch McConnell and George W. Bush (see note 20).

Any momentum that Angle hoped to gain from the debate, however, was lost when comments that she made during a meeting with the Hispanic Student Union at a Las Vegas area high school were revealed four days later. When confronted about the racial undertones in her immigration spots, Angle responded by saying "I don't know that all of you are Latino. Some of you look a little more Asian to me. I don't know that," and then added that "I've been called the first Asian legislator in our Nevada State Assembly."[30] The videotaped comments quickly circulated in the media. As if Angle's remarks were not problematic enough, they piggybacked on an advertisement produced by a Republican front group called "Latinos for Reform" that ran on a Las Vegas Spanish language radio station that concluded with the plea "Don't vote this November. This is the only way to send them a clear message."[31] The Reid campaign immediately accused Angle and her backers of suppressing the Hispanic vote, which forced the Angle campaign to walk back her comments and denounce the "Latinos for Reform" spot just as voters were heading to the polls.

More generally, these episodes further cemented an already strong relationship between Reid and the Hispanic community.[32] As noted above, after the 2004 election, Nevada Democrats made out-reach to the state's growing Hispanic community a top priority with the result being gradual upticks in Hispanic registration and turnout during the 2006 and 2008 elections with Democrats winning roughly two-thirds of the Hispanic vote. Reid also maintained a constant Spanish language advertising presence throughout the campaign.[33]

In the waning days of the campaign, Angle attempted to shift the focus away from the controversy by putting forth two new lines of attack. The first raised unsubstantiated speculation about Reid's wealth and used his purchase of a condominium in a Washington-area Ritz-Carlton as evidence that Reid was living lavishly while Nevadans were suffering. The second was that Reid "intends to steal this election if he can't win it outright" or so declared Angle campaign attorney Cleta Mitchell in a last-minute fundraising appeal.[34] The campaign's complaints of malfunctioning voting machines and fraud prompted an investigation by the Secretary of State that found no evidence to support the allegations. While the episode did provoke a media storm and was part of a broader Angle strategy to lay the ground work for a potential recount, the move, along with the personal attacks on Reid's finances, smacked of desperation.

Not to be outdone, Reid made a few late tactical changes of his own. After the debate, Reid, who was kept under wraps throughout the campaign, suddenly appeared everywhere accompanied by high profile surrogates designed to appeal to every demographic. For the state's African-American population, there was Reid campaigning with civil-rights giant Representative John Lewis (Georgia 5th); for the Indian-American community there was the actor and Obama political appointee Kal Penn; Commerce Secretary Gary Locke was brought in to solidify Reid's support with the Asian-American community; Ultimate Fighting Championship (UFC) President Dana White and top UFC fighter Chuck Liddell accompanied Reid as he cast his early vote at UNLV; boxing legend Manny

Pacquiao was the main draw at a Reid rally targeting the state's Filipino community; Dolores Huerta, co-Founder of the United Farm Workers, was the speaker at a pre-election event in the Hispanic community; and for the Democratic base there were appearances by Bill Clinton, Joe Biden, and Barack and Michelle Obama on multiple occasions. Angle, too, made appearances with GOP luminaries including former House Speaker Newt Gingrich, John McCain, and Maricopa County Arizona's self-proclaimed "America's Toughest Sherriff" Joe Arpaio.[35] Noticeably absent from any Angle events, however, were the Republican candidates for Nevada's other two high profile races: gubernatorial hopeful Brian Sandoval and 3rd District candidate Joe Heck.

The Reid team also used the closing days of the campaign to goad the media to find Sharron Angle. As noted above, with the exception of friendly outlets, Angle avoided virtually all media contact, did not release her appearance schedule, rarely held public events, and took to employing subterfuge to avoid waiting reporters. The result of the Reid campaign's prodding was news stories featuring footage of Angle running away from reporters that found its way into last-minute Reid ads.[36] The Angle campaign's decision to make her unavailable to the press and the public throughout the campaign was problematic on a number of fronts. Most notably, it played into the Reid campaign's claim that Angle had something to hide—a point that she helped to foster by, for instance, responding to a reporter who ambushed her at McCarran Airport that "I will answer those questions when I'm the senator."[37] Without access to Angle, the media went ahead and reported anyway; often, in a manner that embraced the Reid narrative and contained the very same Angle quotes that appeared in Reid's campaign spots.

While making for good political theater, the late maneuvers were largely beside the point as the campaign was no longer about messaging but about getting out the vote (GOTV). Efforts at GOTV in Nevada are complicated by the popularity of the state's early voting program. Early voting lasts for two weeks prior to Election Day and is used by one-half to two-thirds of voters (votes cast early are not counted until after all polls close on Election Night). In 2010, 60 percent of the vote was cast either early or by mail. The program does offer strategic advantages, however. Because Clark and Washoe counties release early turnout numbers daily, campaigns can gauge how well their voters are turning out and adjust their strategies.

While campaigns universally boast of their turnout operations, rarely do they live up to expectations the way that Reid's did. Despite the nationalization of the race and spending that would exceed $90 a vote—the most for any congressional race during the 2010 cycle—only the opinions of registered Nevada voters mattered. It was here that the Reid held the advantage. His campaign developed a database of one million voters that allowed the campaign to determine who their likely voters were and then follow-up with targeted messaging and canvassers who would electronically communicate information back to headquarters. The campaign's technical savvy coupled with its relentless door-knocking was crucial given internal polling data suggesting that the most frequent midterm voters were less likely to support Reid.[38]

A Reid victory thus required targeting and mobilizing those who were less inclined to vote; a task made even more difficult given the challenging political climate for Democrats, Reid's high unfavorable ratings, and the fact that Reid was running in the decline segment of the surge and decline dynamic.[39] Indeed, the Democratic voter registration advantage from 2008 was reduced by 40,000 (see Figure 2.1) and many of the first time and young voters who came out to support Obama in 2008 were unlikely to vote in 2010. Concerns about the ability of Reid to win the nonpartisan vote led the campaign to gear its late GOTV efforts towards its base. Thus, for the Reid campaign, the endgame involved prodding union leaders to get recalcitrant members to the polls and blanketing Latino neighborhoods with canvassers.[40]

The Angle campaign's ground game, by comparison, was a work in progress. The establishment of the campaign's southern Nevada field offices was entrusted to former volunteers who became paid staffers after the primary.[41] Despite campaign experience that consisted of volunteering for the Angle primary effort, the "Misfit Toys" were expected to hold their own against Reid's team of seasoned veterans. At the same time, because so much of the Angle campaign's resources were allocated to ad buys, little funding was devoted to ground operations. The pressure on the small field staff and the volunteers who flooded the campaign's field offices intensified in the final days of the campaign when an expected Republican surge during early voting failed to materialize. While Republicans did turn out at a higher clip relative to registration figures during early voting, the Democrats held a turnout advantage of roughly 9,000 at the end of the period (60,000 nonpartisans also voted early).

An Angle victory, then, necessitated that the traditional GOP Election Day turnout advantage materialize again, that Angle would be able to minimize Republican defections, and that she could win the nonpartisan vote decisively. The release of early voting results gave Reid a comfortable but surmountable 10-point lead statewide and 12-point advantage in populous Clark County. As results came in from around the state, it quickly became clear that Angle would fall short, as with each update as Reid extended his lead, largely due to an eventual 60,000-plus vote advantage in Clark County. Reid also carried Washoe County, Angle's home turf, despite a Republican registration and turnout advantage and heavy Angle ad buys in the Reno market. The race was called by national media outlets before 9:00 p.m. local time.

In the end, Reid's victory was more decisive than expected as he won over 50 percent of the vote and beat Angle by more than 5 percent. Sixty-five percent of registered voters turned out with near equal numbers of Republicans and Democrats casting votes, along with roughly 120,000 nonpartisan and minor party registrants. The two ballot options that were the source of much speculation, however, turned out to be non-factors. Angle's ham-handed attempt to bully Scott Ashjian out of the race proved to be misguided as Ashjian won less than

6,000 votes. The circulation of last-minute mailers of unknown origin imploring voters to choose the "none of these candidates" option that is available for statewide races in Nevada had little effect as just over 2 percent of voters chose none of the candidates on offer.[42]

A glimmer of good news for Angle was that exit polls indicated that she won the nonpartisan vote. Still, even here the Reid campaign was prescient as its shift to turning out its base may have been the difference maker. At the same time, because turnout among nonpartisans lagged, Angle may have missed her chance for victory. As noted above, while the Angle campaign geared its advertising strategy to appeal to nonpartisans, the campaign failed to coordinate its messaging and field operations to insure that nonpartisans turned out in significant numbers.

Curtain Call

In the aftermath, there was much discussion that Reid was lucky to hold off Angle and that he would have lost to a more moderate and better disciplined candidate. Certainly, there is evidence to suggest this given exit polling data indicating that Angle was unable to unify her party (15 percent of GOP voters defected to Harry Reid). Moreover, as compared to the other Republicans in the primary field, Angle offered a treasure-trove of sound bites that the Reid campaign adroitly mined to define her. Angle's unwillingness to be handled and the decision to ignore the media also brought her unwanted attention at inopportune moments.

While it is unlikely that any other candidate in the primary field would have raised the amount of money that Angle did given her Tea Party appeal, the total dollar amounts obscure as much as they reveal. Given whom her opponent was, Angle likely would have had sufficient resources to compete against Reid without having to spend as much time out of state that she did chasing contributions. Moreover, given that her campaign allocated substantial time and resources to fundraising, but very little to ground operations, it is unclear what her extensive fundraising's real value added was (other than for the direct mail and fundraising firms contracted by her campaign that reaped huge paydays).

More to the point, Angle became the rare exception to Gary Jacobson's law of money in congressional elections.[43] While Reid raised and spent in response to his vulnerability, Angle became the rare challenger to out-raise and out-spend an incumbent and still lose largely because of how her campaign allocated its resources. Angle's national advisors felt that her best chance to win was to match Reid spot for spot on television. Yet, her campaign's cookie-cutter advertisements could have been inserted into any race in the country, provided no counter-narrative to Reid's, and failed to explain what Angle would do if she was in the U.S. Senate. Similarly, the Angle campaign's borderline racist immigration ads likely repelled more voters than they attracted given the large concentration of Hispanics in Nevada. More problematic, the Angle campaign devoted little attention to the basics of winning electoral politics: securing a voter database in a timely fashion, synchronizing ground operations and messaging, or insuring that moderate and establishment Republicans were supportive of her candidacy or would at least refrain from publically backing her opponent.

In contrast, Reid and his campaign's effort was textbook. Working years in advance to tilt the playing field and shape the opposition candidate pool allowed Reid to overcome significant macro-level headwinds and his high personal negatives. Reid understood that because of the context in which he was running and his unpopularity, his only path to victory was to make Sharron Angle a less appealing choice. By the time voters went to the polls, the Reid campaign's internal polling indicated that Angle's unfavorable ratings were above 55 percent.[44] She ended up with 45 percent of the vote. Reid's campaign melded old-school party building with technical sophistication, precisely articulated messaging, and voter targeting at a level never before seen in Nevada. Angle, hindered by a weak state party organization, a divided and diminished party in the electorate, and a campaign organization at odds with itself, was never in a position to drive the campaign's dynamics. As a consequence, Reid's victory and Angle's defeat were largely individual, as Republicans won the two other high-profile contests on the ballot in Nevada in 2010: the governorship and the 3rd District.[45]

Within Nevada, the race was revealing on a number of fronts. Most notably, it is often said of Nevada politics that regardless of the candidates, the establishment wins. Never has it been so clear who the state's establishment was and how their interests were so closely tied to Harry Reid. Instead of operating behind the scenes, the race's stakes and uncertainty obligated establishment figures to publically support the Senate Majority Leader. Lining up behind Reid were not only most of the state's prominent politicians of both parties, but also diametrically opposed interests. Thus, in a span of a few days the Nevada Mining Association, wanting to insure that the protector of the General Mining Act of 1872 would maintain his perch, and the Sierra Club, fearing that a loss of the Senate's strongest advocate for alternative energy might doom prospects for realigning the nation's energy policy, both endorsed Reid. In a similar vein, executives of the world's largest gaming corporations continually upped their ante in support of Reid, while organized labor leaders cajoled rank-and-file union members into the voting booth.

For her part, Angle never reached out to the establishment. Instead, she wore the establishment's antipathy as a badge of honor that insured, win or lose, that she would be a viable entity within the Tea Party movement moving forward. Perhaps the most telling event of the campaign occurred on Election Night when the establishment-backed Republican gubernatorial candidate Brain Sandoval held his victory party miles from Angle's. Sandoval's primary victory party was also the site of Republican Reno Mayor Bob Cashell's notorious characterization of Angle that "she's wild … And with the wild ideas she has we would never get anything done"; this became a staple of Reid's late television and radio ads.[46]

For some of the GOP establishment that crossed party lines, retribution was swift. The endorsement of Reid by Bill Raggio cost the longest serving member of the Nevada Legislature his leadership position in the Nevada Senate. Raggio would subsequently leave public life despite having two years left in his term. Other casualties were the publisher, Sherman Fredrick, and editor, Thomas Mitchell, of the *Las Vegas Review-Journal*, the state's largest newspaper, who were removed from their positions after the election. While no official reason for the shake-up was given, it was not difficult to infer that the paper's flawed polling that consistently showed Angle in the lead and helped to fuel the storyline of an impending Reid defeat and the two's incessant editorial rants against Reid might have had something to do with their demotions.

The campaign also revealed much about the changing nature of Nevada. On the one hand, the race in a gaming dependent state where prostitution is legal (in its rural counties) featured two tee-totaling candidates—one a Mormon and the other an Evangelical social conservative—who accentuated their rural Nevada roots. On the other hand, the election demonstrated the near deterministic effect of Nevada's two urban centers on statewide electoral outcomes. Moreover, while exit polls suggested that Angle carried the white vote by a significant margin, white voters constituted just 70 percent of the electorate. In contrast, Reid dominated Angle among African Americans (78 percent to 11 percent), Asians (79 percent to 19 percent), and Hispanics (68 percent to 30 percent). Thus, while the Angle campaign mocked Reid's election-ending campaign events in Las Vegas' ethnic enclaves[47] as a sign of weakness, a more appropriate description might have been a thank you tour by the Senate Majority Leader. Most significantly, Hispanics increased their share of the electorate, and recruitment and support by the Nevada Democratic Party for open state legislative races resulted in Hispanic candidates winning six Assembly and two Senate seats in the Nevada Legislature. Thus, as Nevada becomes more diverse, its population more densely concentrated, and the state's Republicans continue to rely on a shrinking white, rural base and purge the moderates from their ranks, without a figure of comparable skill, vision, and will as Harry Reid, 2010 may have been the GOP's last best chance in the Silver State for quite some time.

Notes

*   I am thankful for the input and suggestions of Eric Herzik, Ciara Mathews, Laurel Fee, Bill Harrison, Jeri Taylor-Swade, Andres Ramirez, and Dina Titus.
1. Brian Haynes, "Census: Clark County Population Increase Leads Nevada's Growth," *Las Vegas Review Journal*, February 24, 2011, http://www.lvrj.com/news/census-clark-county-population-increase-leads-nevada-s-growth-116867598.html (accessed February 24, 2011).
2. U.S. Department of Labor, Bureau of Labor Statistics, *Union Membership in Nevada – 2009* (Washington, D.C.: Department of Labor, 2010) http://www.bls.gov/ro9/unionnv.pdf (accessed February 24. 2011).
3. Nevada Department of Employment, Training and Rehabilitation. Research and Analysis Bureau, *Nevada's Occupational Employment Statistics* (Carson City, NV: Nevada Department of Employment, Training and Rehabilitation, 2009) https://www.nevadaworkforce.com/admin/uploadedPublications/2759_OES_2009.pdf (accessed February 24, 2011).

4. Nevada Department of Employment, Training and Rehabilitation. Research and Analysis Bureau, *Nevada's Occupational Employment Statistics* (Carson City, NV: Nevada Department of Employment, Training and Rehabilitation, 2009) https://www.nevadaworkforce.com/admin/uploadedPublications/2759_OES_2009.pdf (accessed February 24, 2011).

5. Sensing that Nevada Democrats were likely to gain a competitive advantage from the early caucus, the Nevada Republican Party hastily moved its nominating event to coincide with the Democratic event. However, the Republican event was hindered by two factors. First, because of the strong contingency of Mormons within the Nevada Republican ranks, most of the GOP candidates bypassed the event fearing that Mitt Romney would dominate. Second, the caucuses consisted of non-binding straw polls that were then followed by the selection of delegates to the party's state convention. This arrangement would prove problematic as the 2008 state Republican convention was over-run by Ron Paul (TX 14th) supporters who felt that their candidate was not given his due in Nevada. This led the state party chair, Sue Lowden, to suspend the convention as she lost control of the proceedings; actions that would earn Lowden the enmity of what would evolve into the state's Tea Party movement and compromise her candidacy for the Republican nomination for the U.S. Senate.

6. In an ironic twist that captures the incestuous nature of Nevada politics, Sandoval would leave the federal bench to run for elective office in 2010. However, instead of running against Harry Reid, Sandoval would run for governor where his Democratic opponent was Rory Reid, the Senator's son. While the presence of two Reids on the ballot was a source of much speculation throughout the 2010 cycle, the storyline fizzled as Rory Reid never gained traction and ended up losing by 12 percent.

7. For an extended discussion of the role of the Tea Party movement in the Nevada Senate race see David F. Damore, "The Tea Party Angle in the Nevada Senate Race," in *Stuck in the Middle to Lose: Tea Party Effects on 2010 Senate Elections*, eds. Will Miller and Jeremy Walling (Lanham, MD: Lexington Books, 2011).

8. Steve Friess, "Harry Reid's Final Trick," *The Daily Beast*, October 13, 2010, http://www.thedailybeast.com/blogs-and-stories/2010-10-13/nevadas-close-election-harry-reids-last-stand/ (accessed December 1, 2010).

9. Nevada is a difficult state to poll because of its transient population, high concentration of non-English speakers, and large number of cell-phone-only residents. As a consequence, public polling in Nevada is poor and was particularly bad during the 2010 cycle (see, J. Patrick Coolican, "Polling Hasn't Changed with the Electorate," *Las Vegas Sun*, November 4, 2010). Regardless of the firm doing the polling (all public polling in Nevada is done by out-of-state firms), there was a consistent Republican bias. The end result was the polling helped to fuel perceptions that the race was closer than it was. Interestingly, the polling done by the Angle campaign eschewed the notion that Republican turnout would surge and oversampled Democrats based on the assumption that the Reid campaign would be able to turn out the vote even in a down Democratic cycle.

10. David R. Mayhew, *Congress: The Electoral Connection*, 2nd ed., (New Haven, CT: Yale University Press, 1974).

11. http://www.lvrj.com/hottopics/politics/polls/may_2009_3_polls.html (accessed March 4, 2011).

12. Ibid.

13. Mark Mellman and Jim Margolis, "Harry Reid: Withstanding the Wave," PollingReport.com, November 15, 2010, http://www.pollingreport.com/a2010nv.htm (accessed December 1, 2010).

14. The Reid campaign archived Angle's original Web page and re-launched it under the domain name therealsharronangle.com to undercut attempts by Angle to reshape her image post-primary.

15. Shira Toeplitz, "Angle's Campaign Sank Candidate," Politco.com, November 21, 2010, http://www.politico.com/news/stories/1110/45463.html (accessed December 1, 2010).

16. Perhaps the comments that most undercut Angle's message and which became a staple of Reid's advertisements was: "People ask me, what are you going to do to develop jobs in your State? ... well that's not my job as a U.S. Senator." Reid also got mileage out of Angle's claim that she would not have intervened as the Senate Majority Leader had to keep credit flowing to complete the MGM Resorts International City Center project and preserve 22,000 jobs.

17. Despite lacking evidence to corroborate their claims, many Nevada conservatives contended that Ashjian was a Reid operative who had been inserted into the race to divide the GOP vote. Beyond press releases and Web advertisements, however, Ashjian's campaign was non-existent. He did reap substantial media attention from unsuccessful legal challenges by conservatives seeking to remove him from the ballot.

18. Jon Ralston, "Angle: 'I'm Not Sure I Can Win' if Ashjian's in, Nat'l GOPers 'Have Lost Their Principles,' Need to 'Leave Me Alone,'" *Las Vegas Sun*, October 3, 2010, http://www.lasvegassun.com/blogs/ralstons-flash/2010/oct/03/angle-im-not-sure-i-can-win-if-ashjians-natl-goper/ (accessed February 24, 2011).

19. Eric Kleefeld, "Angle: Reporters Should Only 'Ask the Questions We Want to Answer,'" TalkingPointsMemo.com, August 3, 2010, http://tpmdc.talkingpoints-memo.com/2010/08/angle-on-the-press-only-ask-the-questions-we-want-to-answer-video.php (accessed February 24, 2011).

20. Never comfortable with the retail aspects of politics, Reid was infamous for making poorly worded comments such as calling President Bush a liar during a visit to a local elementary school, offering that Kristen Gillibrand (D-NY) was the "hottest member" of the Senate, and suggesting that Barack Obama's presidential bid would be helped because he is "light-skinned" and has "no Negro dialect, unless he wanted to have one" (see John Heilemann and Mark Halperin, *Game Change: Obama and the Clintons, McCain and Palin, and the Race of a Lifetime* (New York: Harper, 2010)).

21. The facts on the ground in Nevada were quite different from the Angle campaign's portrayal of the immigration issue. A report issued by the Pew Hispanic Center in September of 2010 estimated that between 2009 and 2010 Nevada had lost 50,000 unauthorized immigrants (see, Jeffrey S. Passell and D'Vera Cohen, *U.S. Unauthorized Immigration Flows Are Down Sharply Since Mid-Decade*, (Washington, D.C.: Pew Hispanic Center, 2010)).

22. http://www.youtube.com/watch?v=tb-zZM9-vB0 (accessed March 4, 2011).

23. Mellman and Margolis, "Harry Reid: Withstanding the Wave."

24. "Total Raised and Spent: 2010 Race: Nevada Senate," Center for Responsive Politics, http://www.opensecrets.org/races/summary.php?id=NVS2&cycle=2010 (accessed February 21, 2011).

25. "Candidate Fundraising and Non-Candidate Spending in House Races – 2010," Campaign Finance Institute, http://www.cfinst.org/data/2010Election_NonCandidate_House.aspx (accessed February 21, 2011).

26. See the Center for Responsive Politics' "Outside Spending" page, http://www.opensecrets.org/outsidespending/index.php (accessed February 21, 2011). In some instances, The Center's Web site includes multiple listings for the same organizations. The data reported here collapse these multiple entries so that there is one entry for each organization. The summaries reported in Table 2.3 only include spending for the general election campaign.

27. Manu Raju, "Karl Rove bets big against Harry Reid," Politico.com, September 15, 2010, http://www.politico.com/news/stories/0910/42180.html (accessed December 9. 2010).

28. Data taken from the Sunlight Foundation, http://sunlightfoundation.com/.

29. Mellman and Margolis, "Harry Reid: Withstanding the Wave."

30. Jon Ralston, "Angle to Hispanic Children: 'Some of You Look a Little More Asian to Me'," *Las Vegas Sun*, October 18, 2010, http://www.lasvegassun.com/blogs/ralstons-flash/2010/oct/18/angle-hispanic-children-some-you-look-little-more-/ (accessed February 24, 2011).

31. Huma Khan, "Sharron Angle's Campaign Denounces 'Don't Vote' Ad in Nevada; Backer Linked to the GOP," ABCNews.com, October 20, 2010, http://abcnews.go.com/Politics/vote-2010-election-vote-ad-nevada-targeting-hispanics/story?id=11927768 (accessed February 24, 2011).

32. Mellman and Margolis, "Harry Reid: Withstanding the Wave."

33. In Nevada, as elsewhere, there was disappointment in the Latino community that a unified Democratic government had not passed comprehensive immigration reform. Reid hoped to mollify concerns that legislative inaction would dampen Latino turnout by attempting to amend the DREAM (Development, Relief and Education for Alien Minors) Act, which would ease the path to citizenship, military service, and college for illegal immigrants who graduated from high school, to the Defense Authorization and Appropriations legislation during the fall.

34. Jon Ralston, "Angle Campaign Attorney: Reid 'Intends to Steal this Election if He Can't Win It Outright'," *Las Vegas Sun*, October 26, 2010, http://www.lasvegassun.com/blogs/ralstons-flash/2010/oct/26/angle-campaign-attorney-reid/ (accessed January 22, 2011).

35. The joint appearance with John McCain was the source of tension within the Angle campaign as her intimates were loath to have her appear alongside McCain given McCain's history of straying from conservative orthodoxy. It was not until McCain was en route to Las Vegas that Angle finally agreed to appear with him on stage (see Toeplitz, "Angle's Campaign Sank Candidate").

36. See, for example, http://www.youtube.com/watch?v=VvcG-blt3pg (accessed March 4, 2011).

37. Eric Kleefeld, "Angle to Reporter: I'll Answer Questions 'When I'm The Senator'," TalkingPointsMemo.com, October 29, 2010, http://tpmdc.talkingpointsmemo.com/2010/10/angle-to-reporter-ill-answer-questions-when-im-the-senator-video.php# (accessed February 24, 2011).

38. Mellman and Margolis, "Harry Reid: Withstanding the Wave."

39. Angus Campbell, "Surge and Decline: A Study of Electoral Change," *Public Opinion Quarterly*, vol. 24, no. 3 (Summer 1960), pp. 397–418.

40. While unions in Nevada are a strong component of the Democratic coalition, union enthusiasm was dampened by the economic downturn and the unwillingness of the Democratic controlled Congress to move organized labor's top legislative priority: the Employee Free Choice Act (which came to be known as "card check" and would ease union organization). To facilitate union turnout, buses were parked outside Strip properties to transport members to the polls. These tactics drew complaints of illegal coordination between the Reid campaign, the management of casino giant Harrah's (now, Caesars Entertainment), and union leaders (see, Elizabeth Crum, "Harrah's Puts Squeeze on Employees to Vote in Pro-Reid Effort," *The National Review*, November 2, 2010, http://www.nationalreview.com/battle10/251906/collusion-harrahs-bosses-put-squeeze-employees-vote-reid-elizabeth-crum (accessed December 2, 2010).

41. See David F. Damore, "The Tea Party Angle in the Nevada Senate Race."

42. David F. Damore, Mallory M. Waters, and Shaun Bowler, "Unhappy, Uninformed, or Uninterested? Understanding 'None of the Above' Voting," *Political Research Quaterly* (forthcoming).

43. Gary C. Jacobson, "The Effects of Campaign Spending in Congressional Elections," *American Political Science Review*, vol. 72 (1978), pp. 469–491.

44. Mellman and Margolis, "Harry Reid: Withstanding the Wave."

45. Republicans won the Nevada governor's race handily and the swing House seat (the 3rd District) by less than 2,000 votes. The Republican incumbent lieutenant governor also won reelection. However, despite the favorability of the 2010 electoral environment, the GOP gave the Democratic Party's two rising stars, Secretary of State Ross Miller and Attorney General Catherine Cortez-Masto, passes as their Republican opponents featured a combined three arrests. The Democratic incumbent treasurer and controller also won reelection and the Republicans made no inroads into what is arguably the state's most influential body, the Clark County Commission, where the Democrats maintained their control of all seven seats. Lastly, despite a large number of open seats for the state legislature, the GOP picked up two Assembly and one Senate seat—all of which were located in the contested 3rd Congressional District.

46. Benjamin Spillman, "Political Eye: Republican Angle Delivers Deal-Closer TV Ad Democrat Reid Sticks with Commercials Painting Angle as Too Extreme." *Las Vegas Review-Journal*, November 1, 2010, http://www.lvrj.com/news/republican-delivers-deal-closer-tv-ad-106431458.html (accessed February 21, 2011).

47. See, Jerry L. Simich and Thomas C. Wright, eds., *The People's of Las Vegas: One City, Many Faces* (Reno: University of Nevada Press, 2005).

3 Edwards vs. Flores in Texas' Seventeenth Congressional District
The Perfect Storm

Victoria A. Farrar-Myers and Daniel Davis Sledge

I can swim against the stream and have done so repeatedly, but I can't swim against a tidal wave.

—Representative Chet Edwards, November 3, 2010[1]

The term "The Perfect Storm" is typically used to describe a devastating 1991 storm that produced 30-foot waves and winds up to 80 knots in the northern Atlantic, and was popularized in a book and motion picture of the same name. As a meteorological event, "[i]t was an unprecedented set of circumstances"[2] that combined atmospheric changes with the residual effects of a hurricane and "that struck with a fierceness that took residents [of New England] by total surprise."[3] In many ways, Democrat Chet Edwards faced a "Perfect Storm" of his own in his reelection campaign in the 2010 congressional election.

Edwards faced the residual effects of a Republican-drawn redistricting plan earlier in the decade that left him representing one of the most Republican-leaning congressional districts in the nation (the district has a R+20 rating from the *Cook Political Report*[4]); in fact, 67 percent of the voters in Texas' 17th District voted for Republican candidate John McCain in the 2008 presidential election.[5] Changes in the political atmosphere in the nation left incumbents generally and Democrats particularly, especially those tied to President Barack Obama, exposed to an angry voting public. These macro-level political dynamics not only shaped the 2010 midterm elections throughout the nation (see Chapter 1), but played a substantial role with the 17th District as well.

Within the district, a Republican candidate emerged who was well-positioned to take advantage of the partisan leanings within the district, including a motivated Tea Party willing to work to elect a candidate it supported. Although most observers believed that the contest for Edwards' seat in 2010 would be competitive, when the results from Election Night came in, Edwards suffered a surprising 25-point loss to a political newcomer, Bill Flores. Much like the meteorological perfect storm, "all of the contributing factors [came] together at just the right time" to end Chet Edwards' 20-year career in the House of Representatives.[6]

The Seventeenth District

Texas' 17th District occupies a vast swath of Central Texas, stretching south-east from the growing suburbs of Fort Worth across the Blackland Prairies and Post Oak Savannah regions to the Brazos valley situated as close as 60 miles northwest of Houston. Once overwhelmingly rural, the area's population is now approximately 65 percent urban. It is centered in three areas: suburban and exurban Johnson County, Waco, and Bryan-College Station.

Johnson County, in the far northwest of the district, is economically inte-grated with the Dallas-Fort Worth Metroplex. The county's population grew by 23.8 percent between 2000 and 2009, from 126,811 to nearly 157,000 people. From 12 percent of the population in 2000, Johnson County's Hispanic popu-lation grew to 16.9 percent of the population in 2009. [7] Near the geographic center of the 17th District is Waco, a city of slightly more than 120,000 peo-ple on the banks of the Brazos River.[8] In the decades following the Civil War, Waco was both an important point of passage for cattle being driven north along the Chisholm Trail and the location of one of the nation's largest inland cotton markets. The city is home to Baylor University, a conservatively-minded Baptist school with nearly 15,000 students.[9] Just outside of town, in 1993, the Federal Bureau of Investigation and the Bureau of Alcohol Tobacco and Fire-arms engaged in an ultimately tragic 51-day standoff with David Koresh's Branch Davidians.[10] The adjoining towns of Bryan and College Station, near the south-eastern corner of the district, are home to a combined total of more than 140,000 people.[11] College Station boasts Texas A&M University, another institution of higher education with an even larger student body of 49,000.[12] Although the 17th District is predominantly white (68.1 percent), the district has a substantial and growing Hispanic population, which now comprises 18.5 percent of district residents. Another 9.7 percent of the population is black. [13]

From the end of Reconstruction through the 1960s, the area that now com-prises the 17th District was staunchly Democratic, dominated by the production of cotton and populated largely by rural "yellow dog" Democrats.[14] In the last 30 years, however, the partisan tide has shifted substantially. Although Texas' most recent Democratic Governor, Ann Richards, hailed from Waco, the 17th Dis-trict voted overwhelmingly for Republican presidential candidate John McCain in 2008 and before him for President George W. Bush (Bush received 70 percent of the vote in 2004), whose Crawford ranch lies within the district.[15] Given declining levels of white partisan identification with the Democrats, Hispanics are emerging as an increasingly crucial voting group. Although Hispanics gen-erally are viewed as identifying more with the Democratic Party, others believe that, in the words of Bill Flores, who is of Hispanic heritage himself, "Hispanic values align very well with conservative Republican values."[16]

Political Boundaries of the 17th District

The district's current lines are the product of Texas' controversial 2003 redis-tricting, a process spearheaded by then-Congressman and Republican Majority

Leader Tom DeLay (R-TX). Until the 1960s and 70s, Republicans were a rare commodity in Texas. Gaining strength first in urban areas with significant levels of northern-born residents, such as Dallas and Houston, Republicans captured their first statewide office since Reconstruction when Republican John Tower won election to the United States Senate in a 1961 special election.[17]

Republicans began to represent a meaningful statewide threat to Democratic dominance of Texas politics during the 1970s, and the last time the state voted for a Democratic presidential candidate was for Jimmy Carter in 1976. Although the tide had turned at the presidential level, a trend reinforced by the popularity of Ronald Reagan, Democrats remained capable of winning elections at the local level. As recently as 2002, Democrats retained a 17 to 15 seat majority in the state's congressional delegation.

The electoral strength of the Democrats, however, had been greatly enhanced by the party's ongoing control of the state legislature. In 1991, the Democratic legislature, faced with mounting Republican strength in the state, drew district boundaries that packed together large Republican majorities, creating safe Democratic seats that Texas Republicans argued were unrepresentative of political currents within the state.[18] In 2001, when population growth led to a two-seat gain in Texas' congressional delegation, the legislature failed to reach agreement on new district boundaries. A panel of federal judges created a map based largely on the 1991 boundaries, which resulted in a majority Democratic House delegation being elected in 2002.[19]

In the same election, however, Texas Republicans gained a majority in the state legislature for the first time since Reconstruction. Spurred on by DeLay, the new Republican legislature began to consider the possibility of an unprecedented second post-census redistricting, aimed explicitly at creating a Republican majority in the state's congressional delegation. "What is at stake here," DeLay argued in 2003, "is the most effective and accurate representation for Texas. Republicans are the majority in both Washington and in Austin and in the state of Texas, and are best able to deliver on Texans' priorities and represent their beliefs."[20]

As the Texas House of Representatives prepared to vote on the DeLay-backed redistricting plan, upwards of fifty Democratic members fled to Oklahoma to ensure that the quorum necessary for passing the bill could not be established. Gathering together at a Holiday Inn 30 miles beyond the Texas-Oklahoma border, "the Democratic lawmakers said they would not return until the redistricting bill was scrapped."[21]

Although this tactic proved initially successful, the Republican legislature ultimately succeeded in passing its redistricting plan, which was later approved, with slight modifications, by the Department of Justice and the United States Supreme Court.[22] The central focus of the plan was to defeat the state's ten Anglo Democratic representatives, heirs to the state's long-standing Democratic heritage.

Among those was Representative Chet Edwards, the Democrat first elected to represent the Waco-based 11th Congressional District in 1990. Long represented by Democrats, the district was, outside of Waco and surrounding

McLennan County, largely rural and agricultural. The exception was the district's other center of population and activity, the United States Army's massive Ft. Hood base, the largest military installation in the nation. From his first term in Congress, Edwards' position as a member of the House Armed Services Committee, support for military issues, and capacity to bring in money to Ft. Hood had proven a source of strength within the district.[23]

The 2003 Republican redistricting placed Edwards in a perilous position. His Waco home was placed within the redesigned 17th District, which now included the conservative south Fort Worth suburbs and Bryan-College Station. The electoral weight of Waco, Edwards' longtime base, was substantially diminished. The new 17th District included only two counties, McLennan and Bosque, from Edwards' old 11th District. In a potentially devastating blow, the new 17th District did not include Ft. Hood, whose military constituency Edwards had successfully cultivated since his election in 1990.[24] At the time, Edwards' career in the House of Representatives appeared as if it would soon come to an end.

In 2004, however, Edwards managed to win the seat in the new 17th District, narrowly carrying it with 51 percent of the vote. Other Anglo Democrats were not so lucky: "Of the ten Democrats who were targeted [by the redistricting plan], five were defeated, one resigned, and another switched parties."[25] Representing one of the most Republican districts in the nation, Edwards continued to win reelection through the end of the decade, long after his predicted demise, and after Tom DeLay had been forced from his position as House Majority Leader and indicted by a Texas grand jury on corruption charges related to his prominent role in state politics.[26]

Incumbent Chet Edwards: Among the Last of a Dying Breed of Democrats

A moderate southern Democrat representing a conservative Republican district, Chet Edwards has long been viewed as among the last of a dying breed. Born and raised in Corpus Christi, on the Texas Gulf Coast, Edwards attended Texas A&M University. In 1978, Edwards campaigned for the seat of retiring Central Texas Democratic Congressman Olin Teague, for whom he had worked as an aide. Then-Democrat Phil Gramm, the future Republican Senator from Texas and Edwards' economics professor at A&M, ultimately won the seat.[27]

After attending Harvard Business School and then serving in the Texas state Senate throughout the 1980s, Edwards won election to the U.S. House from the Waco-based 11th District in 1990. The House Speaker at the time, Tom Foley (D-WA), gave Edwards his predecessor's seat on the House Armed Services committee.[28] Over the course of the next decade, Edwards established himself as an effective retail politician, adept at retaining a hold on the increasingly Republican district and well-known for his ability to bring home the bacon in the form of defense dollars for Ft. Hood.

Following the DeLay-sponsored redistricting of 2003, Edwards proved surprisingly nimble, courting enough support to win in a largely new district, stripped of Ft. Hood and with a new constituency of 400,000 voters who had never seen his name on a ballot.[29] In 2006, when Democrats gained control of the House, Edwards became Chairman of the House Military Construction and Veterans Affairs Appropriations Subcommittee, a useful position given the strength of veterans as a voting bloc in the district and importance of the large V.A. Hospital in Waco to the community.[30]

In 2008, Edwards' ability to win elections in the conservative 17th District helped to put him on the short list of potential Democratic vice presidential candidates. Nancy Pelosi (D-CA), a longtime friend and House Speaker at the time, appeared to be pushing then-Senator Barack Obama to consider Edwards, who she praised as "one of the finest people I've ever served with." Edwards, Pelosi said in an interview with *Newsweek*, "is a person that many of us think would be a good person to have in the mix."[31]

Though he was ultimately not chosen, Edwards established an evident, and widely reported, rapport with the future president. "I come out of this experience," he told *Time* in 2008 of his brush with the vice presidential nomination, "with tremendous respect for Barack's integrity and his values and his personal decency."[32] During the first year of Obama's presidency, Edwards supported the president on 90 percent of the bills on which Obama took a position. His willingness to back Obama, and in particular his decision to vote in favor of Obama's economic stimulus package (the American Reinvestment and Recovery Act), would later prove an electoral liability. As Edwards acknowledged during the final month of the 2010 election, his support for the stimulus "may cost me votes. It may cost me an election. But it was the right thing to do."[33]

Although sometimes portrayed as a "conservative Democrat," Edwards' voting record can best be described as moderate, if at times slightly left of center (see Table 3.1). His career record of support for issues favored by the American Conservative Union (ACU) stood at 29.55 percent in 2010, placing him above the 20 percent cut-off for the ACU's "liberal" designation, but far short of the 80 percent cut-off for ACU's "conservative" designation. In 2009, the first year of the Obama presidency, however, Edwards voted in line with the ACU only 16 percent of the time, placing him solidly within the liberal camp. In 2010, similarly, he scored a 17 percent. As one would expect, the Americans for Democratic Action (ADA) found that Edwards voted as a liberal 75 percent of the time during 2009.

Although the highest percentage of important votes on which Edwards had supported the position taken by President George W. Bush was 60 percent in 2006, his presidential support score dropped to 11 percent in 2007. On the other hand, Edwards supported positions taken by President Barack Obama 90 percent of the time in 2009. In the same year, Edwards voted with the majority of the Democratic caucus 95 percent of the time, lending credibility to the charge that, rather than being an independent voice, he was closely aligned with President Obama and the Democratic leadership in Congress.

As the 2010 election began to loom, however, Edwards noticeably attempted to pivot away from his early support for Obama. In November of 2009, Edwards

Table 3.1 Congressional Vote Scores for Chet Edwards, 1991–2010

Year	American Conservative Union	Americans for Democratic Action	Party Unity	Presidential Support
2010	17%	55%	87%	74%
2009	16%	75%	95%	90%
2008	8%	80%	97%	22%
2007	12%	85%	92%	11%
2006	68%	55%	66%	60%
2005	36%	85%	75%	52%
2004	48%	65%	73%	50%
2003	44%	80%	76%	46%
2002	36%	75%	76%	47%
2001	40%	80%	72%	47%
2000	8%	80%	84%	78%
1999	8%	85%	80%	79%
1998	8%	90%	84%	81%
1997	28%	60%	78%	73%
1996	20%	60%	72%	72%
1995	25%	45%	63%	69%
1994	38%	45%	74%	82%
1993	33%	35%	75%	82%
1992	40%	55%	75%	43%
1991	35%	40%	78%	41%

Source: CQ's Politics in America (Washington, DC: Congressional Quarterly, Inc., 2010 and 2000); The American Conservative Union (http://www.conservative.org); Americans for Democratic Action (http://www.adaction.org); and Congressional Quarterly's vote studies (2009: http://innovation.cqpolitics.com/media/vote_study_2009; and 2010: http://innovation.cq.com/media/vote_study_2010).

was one of thirty-nine Democrats to vote against the House version of the president's health care reform bill (Patient Protection and Affordable Care Act of 2010). In March, 2010, he again voted against the final version of the bill, "despite a personal plea from President Barack Obama."[34] Once Speaker Pelosi's pick for the vice presidency, Edwards appeared increasingly eager to distance himself from her and from the president. Indeed, his party unity score dropped to 87, having been as high as 97 and 95, respectively, the previous two years, and his presidential support score dropped to 74 in 2010.

Republican Challenger Bill Flores: The Businessman Runs for Congress

When he announced his candidacy, Republican Bill Flores had little-to-no name recognition in the 17th District. Having moved into the district only in 2008, he was viewed by some as a carpetbagger, perhaps recruited to challenge Edwards by the national Republican Party.[35] In explaining the rationale behind his run for Congress, Flores sounded much like the businessman he was describing a repositioning of his own personal brand:

> I ultimately decided that I needed to try to find a way to get away from my business, and to take what this country has done for me and reinvest my time and, if necessary some of our capital, some of our money, to run for Congress so I can go up there and help make a difference and help go back to what our Founding Fathers envisioned about limited government and fiscal responsibility and adhering to the Constitution.[36]

After graduating from Texas A&M University, Flores spent nearly 30 years in the business world, much of it in oil and gas-related industries. After serving as chief financial officer for several companies, his business career culminated in helping form and serving as president and CEO of Phoenix Exploration Company, an oil and gas exploration company operating in the Gulf of Mexico. Flores retired from and sold his interests in Phoenix Exploration to run for Congress.

His prior political experience was limited to being an appointed commissioner to the Texas Real Estate Commission, but he believed that his business background would serve him well as a member of Congress. Flores' campaign highlighted his success in business, maintaining that "Bill helped create more than 500 AMERICAN jobs with AMERICAN companies that helped and produced much needed AMERICAN energy resources to help fuel our economy" and "His entire career has been spent balancing budgets, meeting payrolls, and ensuring his companies were focused on producing a good product or service that was better and delivered more effectively than the competition."[37]

Flores won a plurality of votes over four other candidates in the 2010 Republican primary, and then beat 2008 Republican congressional candidate Rob Curnock in a run-off election.[38] Along with complaints about his recent move into the 17th, Flores received criticism from some local party officials and conservative bloggers for not being a true conservative and, worse yet for Texas Republicans, a RINO (Republican in Name Only).[39] Nevertheless, Flores was able to successfully brand himself publicly as a limited-government conservative, an image that resonated particularly well with Tea Party voters in the 17th District.[40]

Money Flows in the 17th District Like the Brazos River[41]

Chet Edwards had a history of successful campaign fundraising, particularly after the redistricting in 2003. In the three election cycles from 2004 to 2008,

Table 3.2 Campaign Finance Data for Texas' 17th Congressional District Campaigns, 2004–2010

Election year	Disbursements		Receipts		Vote Percent	
	Edwards (D)	Opponent (R)	Edwards (D)	Opponent (R)	Edwards (D)	Opponent (R)
2010	$3,841,632	$3,309,747	$3,686,768	$3,353,665	36.6	61.8
2008	$2,114,653	$109,335	$2,267,333	$110,597	53	46
2006	$3,138,215	$2,515,527	$3,194,165	$2,589,364	59	39
2004	$2,664,661	$2,562,877	$2,628,693	$2,586,253	51	47

Sources: 2010 election results: New York Times (http://elections.nytimes.com/2010/results/new-hampshire); all other data: http://www.opensecrets.org (accessed February 15, 2011).

Edwards raised on average $2,696,730 per cycle; an amount well above the average House member. His funds came nearly equally from individual contributions ($1,337,081 per cycle average for 2004 to 2008) and Political Action Committees or PACs ($1,253,834 per cycle on average). Edwards' fundraising prowess continued in the 2010 election cycle as well, raising $2,313,468 from individual contributions and $1,331,740 from PACs for his race against Flores (see Table 3.2).

In 2008, Rob Curnock showed that even a poorly funded Republican challenger could fare well against Edwards. Raising only $110,597 and receiving little to no support from the national Republican Party, Curnock managed to attract 47 percent of the vote. Nevertheless, given the anticipated national visibility of Edwards' reelection campaign, plus his past history to survive in the Republican-leaning district, many observers believed going into the 2010 election season that Edwards' Republican challenger would need to be well financed.

As noted above, Flores indicated that he was willing to invest his own capital to run for Congress—and he certainly did. Flores contributed $1,436,227 toward his campaign, 44 percent of his overall funding. Early Republican critics believed that Flores' ability to self-finance his campaign was one of the reasons that the national Republican Party recruited him to run for Edwards' seat.[42] Although Flores' own financial contributions were used to seed his campaign, he proved capable of raising additional money from outside sources, ultimately receiving $1,522,395 in individual contributions. He received an additional $297,897 from various PACs, most notably from the energy and finance industries.[43]

The 17th District race also garnered the attention of the national parties. The Democratic Congressional Campaign Committee (DCCC) made $627,003 in independent expenditures in the district for the race, while the Republican (RNCC) countered with $475,645 in independent expenditures itself. Most interesting, though, is the timing of the parties' expenditures.[44] The DCCC undertook a $500,000 advertising blitz during the final week of the campaign; meanwhile, the GOP spent much of its money upfront in the campaign and actually cancelled all of its planned television time in the district leading up to the election. Democrats proclaimed that the withdrawal represented a sign that the national Republican Party was giving up on Flores. Flores and the GOP countered, however, that the move actually reflected Flores' strong position heading into the election and allowed the national party to spend its resources on other campaigns.

Another reason that the GOP may have felt comfortable in not spending funds late in the race was that outside groups had become active in attacking Edwards, including a $150,000 television ad campaign in mid-to-late October funded by American Crossroads, a conservative 527 political organization created under the provision of the tax code for which it is named. American Crossroads is connected to former Republican political operative Karl Rove. All in all, three key conservative groups ran advertisements and spent significant funds in the Edwards-Flores race, most of which was used to actively oppose Edwards rather than to promote Flores (by comparison, only one liberal-leaning group made any independent expenditures in the district for a grand total of $1,127). American Crossroads, for example, expended a total of $164,086 in the 17th District. This group received $7,000,000 of its funding from Texan Bob Perry, who contributed $4.45 million to Swift Boat groups in 2004. American Crossroads was one of the largest spenders in the nation among non-party outside groups, and the funds spent opposing Edwards was the group's 8th largest expenditure with respect to a congressman (25th largest if Senators are included).[45]

The American Future Fund (AFF) spent $251,301, which represented approximately 3.4 percent of the $7,387,918 total independent expenditures, communication costs and coordinated expenses that AFF incurred in connection with the 2010 midterm election.[46] This was the 14th largest total that AFF spent in opposition to any candidate. AFF characterizes itself as "a multi-state issues advocacy group designed to effectively communicate conservative and free market ideals,"[47] while critics claimed that AFF violated campaign finance laws by failing to register as a political committee.[48]

The third active outside group, Ending Spending Fund, added $71,334 to the amount of outside groups' funds spent in the Edwards-Flores race.[49] This conservative group spent funds on only three House races (the group's largest and only other expenditures were in opposition to Harry Reid's senatorial campaign in Nevada (see Chapter 2)), yet included Edwards within its narrow list of Democrats. The $486,719 these three groups spent in the 17th District significantly narrowed the $734,931 total advantage that Edwards had when combining the funds raised by each candidate and the amount spent by the national and state parties.

The Campaign: The Shifting Tide

Heading into the 2010 election season, analysts believed that Edwards would be in for a competitive race. An analysis by the *Cook Political Report* during the week of the Texas primaries in March 2010 listed the 17th District among 58 races then viewed as either a "Lean" or a "Toss-Up," but two things stand out about the district in this analysis. First, Edwards represented the most

Republican-leaning district of all the races in the Cook analysis.[50] Second, despite the widely recognized conservative nature of the district, the *Cook Report* still characterized the election as leaning in Edwards' favor. Such was the reputation that Edwards had built up in the district and among political analysts. Despite being in a district intentionally designed to favor Republican candidates, Edwards had always managed to survive in the district and many expected him to do so again. Edwards, in the words of one scholar, "is a good retail campaigner and works the district assiduously between elections."[51]

Nevertheless, Edwards' seat was clearly at the top of the list of those the GOP wanted to win in the 2010 election, and early indications showed that Edwards would face a tight race. Shortly after Flores secured the Republican nomination in his April run-off against Curnock, a public opinion poll of 400 likely voters conducted by a Republican consulting firm found that Flores held a 52 percent to 41 percent advantage over Edwards. The Edwards campaign dismissed the results from "the partisan poll" as "wishful thinking."[52] About the same time, however, the *Cook Political Report* downgraded Edwards' chances from "Lean Democratic" to "Democratic Toss Up," thus perhaps providing more independent and objective evidence than the Republican poll.

In many ways, the Flores campaign seems comparable to the approach that some Democratic challengers used against incumbent Republicans in the 2008 election: tie an otherwise popular incumbent to the unpopular president and policies of the incumbent's party disfavored in the district.[53] In this case, the Flores and Republican strategy was to nationalize the campaign by portraying Edwards as having close ties with President Barack Obama and Democratic Speaker of the House Nancy Pelosi. Obama was an obvious focus; his approval rating in Texas stood at less than 40 percent.[54] Tying Edwards to Speaker Pelosi was just as critical a strategy for Flores and the Republican Party. As Flores noted as early as June 2010, "If you go to almost any grass-roots event and you mention the speaker's name … you will get a huge response from the audience."[55] One early ad run by the National Republican Congressional Committee (NRCC) demonstrates the efficiency by which they were able to tie Edwards to party leaders and policies that were unpopular in the district:

> Chet Edwards calls himself independent. And when he went to Congress 20 years ago, maybe that was true. But now Chet Edwards votes with Nancy Pelosi 96 percent of the time. He backed Obama's failed stimulus plan that cost 800 billion dollars. Spent billions to bail out Wall Street banks, and billions more to bail out auto makers. Chet Edwards, after 20 years, he's not independent.[56]

Edwards sought to establish and maintain distance from Obama and Pelosi politically, particularly touting his votes to oppose Obama's health care legislation despite receiving a personal call from Obama aboard Air Force One requesting the congressman's vote.[57] Among the reasons Edwards cited for voting against the bill was the opposition among his constituents.[58] Attempting to counter the strategy of the Flores campaign and the GOP, the Edwards campaign ran ads detailing the congressman's "Stand":

> When President Obama and Nancy Pelosi pressured Chet Edwards, Chet stood up to them and voted no against their trillion dollar health care bill, and no to Cap and Trade. Chet votes with the conservative Chamber of Commerce sixty-seven percent of the time. And when Washington liberals wanted to take away our guns, Chet said no. That's why the National Rifle Association has endorsed Chet Edwards over Bill Flores.[59]

Over the years, Edwards' voting record in Congress has been called independent, moderate, and even conservative by some. Along with the backing of the National Rifle Association, Edwards garnered endorsements from the Texas Farm Bureau, the Veterans of Foreign Wars, and major newspapers such as the *Dallas Morning News*, the *Fort Worth Star-Telegram*, and the *Bryan-College Station Eagle*. In large part, this backing was based on his lengthy record of constituent service for the district and his perceived independence from the national Democratic Party.

Hoping to draw attention to his strengths and away from his association with Democratic leaders, Edwards ran ads touting his constituent service, such as obtaining federal funding for Texas A&M University, increasing the availability of federal loan guarantees to support the expansion of a nuclear power plant in the district, and especially his well-known efforts for veterans. Although his ability to bring federal money into the district had long been viewed as an electoral asset in the district, the fact that Governor Rick Perry easily carried the district in 2010 while running a campaign that highlighted his willingness to reject "federal dollars with strings attached"[60] suggests that Edwards' ability to bring money back to the district might have had lesser appeal in 2010 than previous election years. Moreover, despite Edwards' efforts to remind voters how closely aligned he has been with the district, Flores' and the GOP's efforts to tie the congressman to Obama and Pelosi ultimately gained traction with district voters and proved to be a lasting and predominant theme of the campaign.

Edwards also sought to shift the focus of the campaign to put Flores on the defensive, although one early attempt to do so backfired on the congressman's campaign. In September 2010, the Edwards campaign ran an advertisement stating that "an oil company [Flores] helped run laid off over 3,000 workers and then paid off its top executives with millions." The *Austin American-Statesman*, through its PoliFact Texas Web site, investigated the facts surrounding the basis for the claim and rated Edwards' claim as being "false."[61] The Flores campaign responded by running ads claiming "The Austin newspaper says Congressman Edwards' attacks on Bill Flores are false. Edwards is not telling the truth about Bill Flores."[62] Ultimately, criticism of the Edwards campaign's ad from newspapers such as the *American-Statesman* and the *Bryan-College Station Eagle* damaged Edwards and resonated more in the district than Edwards' message in the first place.[63]

The Incoming Wave

As the campaign moved forward, evidence started to mount that the tide had shifted in Flores' favor. In September, the Flores campaign released a public opinion poll showing that Flores held a 19-point advantage over Edwards. The Edwards campaign responded by releasing their own internal polling numbers, which showed the congressman down only 4 points, but trending upward.[64] On October 8, 2010, the *Cook Political Report* shifted the Edwards-Flores race from "Democratic Toss-Up" to "Lean Republican." Most significantly, though, *The Hill* published the results of the only independent poll released during the campaign showing that Flores held a 52 percent to 40 percent advantage with only 7 percent of likely voters undecided. The poll itself became a newsworthy item within the district as it provided objective, non-partisan evidence of the size of the surging wave against which Edwards was swimming.

If Edwards could find any solace in *The Hill*'s poll result, it was that the poll was already a week old when released and that it would not capture any swings in the voters' minds that might occur in the few weeks before the election.[65] In these last few weeks of the campaign, Flores made several gaffes that some observers believed might provide the lift that Edwards needed to ride out the storm. For example, responding to a question about Social Security in a television interview, Flores appeared to suggest support for altering the program: "I'd have to look at what the actual economics are. I'm not philosophically opposed to raising the retirement age." Flores later called the reporter and claimed that he had a headache that caused him to misspeak on the subject, and requested the interview not be run (the TV station ran the interview anyway). His campaign subsequently issued a statement from Flores that he opposed raising the retirement age.[66]

The "headache" gaffe followed on the heels of a story from the *Dallas Morning News* that Flores led a company out of bankruptcy proceedings in which the company was allowed to avoid a $7.5 million debt to the U.S. government. In addition, Flores made other misstatements and political missteps throughout the year, at one point saying that he would support privatizing veterans' health care. While any one may not seem significant in itself, the collection of events provided the basis for aggressive advertising by Edwards and the DCCC in the final weeks of the campaign. One DCCC ad, in particular, attacked Flores for his bankrupt company receiving what amounted to a federal bailout. As noted above, just as the DCCC was ramping up its campaign advertising, the GOP withdrew its ads in the 17th District race—thus fueling the speculation that Flores' gaffes might ultimately pave the way for an Edwards' victory.

The Republican decision, however, came less than a week after American Crossroads and Ending Spending Fund spent a combined $230,000 on advertising in opposition to Edwards. Advertising by outside groups picked up on the theme of trying to connect Edwards with national Democratic leaders. One American Crossroads ad interspersed video clips of Edwards promoting Obama while he was running for president with voice-overs and graphics regarding the effect of Obama's policies on Texas:

> Edwards (video dated 9/25/08): It does make a difference, in your day to day lives, who is in the Oval Office.
>
> Announcer: A failed stimulus. [Graphic: FAILED $814 Billion "Stimulus"]
>
> Edwards (video dated 2/24/08): Senator Obama wins on his ultimate message....
>
> Announcer: Millions left unemployed. [Graphic: MILLIONS LEFT UNEM-PLOYED. "Texas jobless rate … at 8.2%" — AP, 8/20/10]
>
> Edwards (video dated 3/3/08): … message of real change …
>
> Announcer: Trillions of dollars in new taxes, reckless spending, and massive debt. [Graphic: RECKLESS SPENDING. "Budget deficit at $1.3 Trillion" — Reuters, 8/19/10]
>
> Edwards (video dated 8/26/08): Let's carry Texas for Barack Obama and Joe Biden.
>
> Announcer: Oh really, Congressman. Working for Obama doesn't work for Texas. [Graphic: Picture of Chet Edwards with Barack Obama in the background]

In addition to furthering Flores' campaign message, the American Crossroads ad proved to be a very effective motivational tool among Tea Party voters. Bill Flores actively courted support from Tea Party voters throughout the campaign. He spoke at Tea Party events, both within the district and in the Dallas-Fort Worth Metroplex just outside the district. Tea Party groups, in return, assisted Flores campaign efforts such as organizing phone banks and promoting Flores at Tea Party events. The Texas Tea Party Patriots even organized a road rally on September 11, 2010, with a caravan of cars driving from Burleson in the north end of the district to Waco, where Flores spoke at an event. By Election Day, Flores was clearly aligned with the Tea Party.

As noted in Chapter 1, the Tea Party movement impacted elections throughout the nation. Unlike in other states, though, where the Tea Party movement sometimes seemed at odds with the Republican establishment, in Texas the Tea Party is more closely aligned with state Republican leaders. For example, Governor Rick Perry was particularly adept at gaining support from the Tea Party, which helped propel him to a victory over Senator Kay Bailey Hutchinson in the Republican Primary and then over former Houston Mayor Bill White in the general election.

The Texas Tea Party movement focuses on "the strength of grassroots organization powered by activism and civic responsibility at a local level." It seeks "to attract, educate, organize, and mobilize our fellow citizens to secure public policy consistent with our three core values of Fiscal Responsibility, Constitutionally Limited Government and Free Markets," which are "derived from the Declaration of Independence, the Constitution of the United States of America, [and] the Bill Of Rights as explained in the Federalist Papers."[67] These core values—fiscal responsibility, limited government, and free markets—as well as the adherence to the Founding Fathers' principles lay at the heart of the brand of conservatism that Bill Flores established for his campaign.[68] The combination of Flores' alignment with the Tea Party movement, the proximity of the state Republican Party and the Tea Party in Texas and the 17th District, and the infusion of spending by outside groups promoting issues that were consistent with Flores' campaign strategy created a powerful dynamic that worked in Flores' favor.

Support from the Tea Party was reinforced by local Republican Party organizations, which worked to identify and mobilize potential voters. According to one local GOP party official interviewed for this chapter who chose to remain anonymous, efforts to target potential swing voters began with a survey of five issues in the summer prior to the election. Based upon this information, a list was created from which the party could use micro-targeting techniques (e.g., targeted mailings, phone banks, social media) to mobilize these voters to get involved in the race. Micro-targeting was a strategy taken from Karl Rove's playbook for winning the ground game in elections, and it proved to be an effective component of retail politics that was part of Flores' campaign.

The Crest of the Wave

As early voting began in the seventeen-day period before November 2, during which time registered voters may cast their ballot, all indications were that Flores would defeat the incumbent Edwards. To be victorious, though, Flores had to break the voting patterns that emerged over the prior three election cycles and led to Edwards' victories in 2004, 2006, and 2008. The key component of these patterns entailed Edwards winning solidly in McLennan County (the largest in the district and where Edwards' home of Waco is situated) and carrying Brazos County (the second largest county and home of both Edwards' and Flores' alma mater, Texas A&M University) and Hill County (fifth largest) to offset losses in the northernmost counties, particularly Johnson and Hood Counties (the third and fourth largest respectively). Another component entailed Edwards performing better in the aggregate in the seven remaining small counties as compared to the five largest. Although the small counties make up less than 15 percent of the vote on average, Edwards' previous victory margins were buttressed by his performance in these areas.[69]

A clue as to how Bill Flores beat Chet Edwards may lie in analysis of the vote from the 17th District (see Table 3.3). Perhaps the most telling finding stemming from this data is just how thoroughly successful Flores was throughout the district. Overall, Edwards received just under 17 percent less in 2010 compared to his 2004–2008 average.

Table 3.3 Vote Totals in Texas' 17th Congressional District by County, 2004–2010

County	2004–2008 Average			2010 Election			Variance: 2010 from 2004–2008		
	Edwards	Republican	County %	Edwards	Flores	County %	Edwards Variance	Republican Variance	County %Variance
North									
Hood	38.34	59.78	8.62	23.41	74.64	9.18	−14.93	14.86	0.56
Johnson	42.82	55.10	19.07	26.31	71.35	17.88	−16.52	16.25	−1.19
Somervell	46.84	51.36	1.41	34.65	63.14	1.57	−12.19	11.77	0.15
Total: North	**41.69**	**56.30**	**29.10**	**25.83**	**71.96**	**28.63**	**−15.86**	**15.6**	**−0.48**
Central									
Bosque	54.29	44.28	3.16	33.59	63.92	3.41	−20.71	19.64	0.26
Hill	55.49	43.11	5.32	37.14	60.78	5.15	−18.36	17.67	−0.16
McLennan	62.62	36.59	32.05	46.90	52.04	31.39	−15.72	15.46	−0.66
Limestone*	63.66	35.34	1.48	44.86	53.95	1.56	−18.81	18.61	0.08
Robertson*	70.83	28.41	1.99	53.07	45.69	2.10	−17.76	17.28	0.11
Total: Central	**61.57**	**37.52**	**44.00**	**44.93**	**53.77**	**43.61**	**−16.64**	**16.25**	**−0.37**
South									
Madison	55.65	42.99	1.60	35.40	62.72	1.82	−20.25	19.73	0.15
Brazos	53.06	45.04	21.41	34.39	64.17	21.84	−18.67	19.13	0.44
Grimes	53.38	44.89	3.25	35.05	62.85	3.50	−18.33	17.96	0.25
Burleson*	55.53	43.17	0.59	33.53	66.18	0.60	−22.00	23.01	0.01
Total: South	**53.31**	**44.85**	**26.90**	**34.52**	**63.95**	**27.76**	**−18.79**	**19.10**	**0.85**
Total: Overall	**53.56**	**44.96**	**100.00**	**36.57**	**61.80**	**100.00**	**−16.99**	**16.84**	**—**

Source: Compiled by authors from data available at the Texas Secretary of State Web site, http://www.sos.state.tx.us/elections/historical/index.shtml.
Notes: The 17th District contains only portions of Limestone, Robertson, and Burleson Counties. Vote percentages for minor candidates are not shown but are included in the calculations used in determining the values in the above table.

When the vote totals are examined, no single or specific set of factors jumps out to explain these results. In terms of vote percentages, Edwards lost about as much in McLennan (–15.72 percent), Brazos (–18.67 percent), and Hood Counties (–18.36 percent) as he did in the northern part of the district (–15.86 percent overall for the three counties in the north). The same holds true for vote reductions in large counties (–16.75 percent) and small counties (–18.68 percent). Nor was the election determined simply because Edwards failed to win his home county (McLennan) and the county of Texas A&M (Brazos County), which combined make up more than half of the votes in the district. Even if Edwards received his historic averages for these two counties, he would have garnered only 45.6 percent of the vote; Edwards would have needed to win at historical levels in the four largest counties (including Johnson and Hood) in order for him to beat Flores. Neither was the election determined as a result of voters in any particular region either increasing their turnout or failing to show up at the polls at historic levels. The percentage of voters from each county remained consistent in 2010 with historical totals.

These vote totals lead to the question of what caused the wave that washed Edwards' 20-year career in Congress away and how was Flores able to so handily ride the crest of the wave to Washington. As with "The Perfect Storm" a number of factors coalesced to fuel Flores' surprisingly large margin of victory. Of all the factors discussed above, the two key ones underlying Flores' victory were:

- the delayed effects of the redistricting in 2003 that resulted in Democrat Edwards representing a predominantly Republican district as well as the strength of the GOP in the district; and
- the presence and track record of national Democratic Party leaders who were unpopular in the district and the success of Flores, the Republican Party, and outside groups in framing the election to be about Edwards' connection to liberal Obama and Pelosi rather than be about independent/moderate/conservative Edwards' service to the district.

Other factors discussed above contributing to Flores' victory include:

- a district full of voters angry about Democratic policies (even Edwards admitted that the pre-election polls did not fully capture the extent to which angry voters would be motivated to vote[70]), including an active Tea Party movement that was able to pursue interests aligned with the Republican Party in Texas and other outside groups involved in the election;
- an adequately financed Republican candidate who had the active support of the Republican Party; and
- the presence of outside groups willing to fund independent expenditures with messages that seemed to reinforce Flores' themes in the campaign, particularly in the crucial last few weeks of the campaign.

In each of Edwards' prior elections in the 17th District, at least one of these contributing factors was missing. The fact that the Republicans held a significant partisan advantage in the district, a necessary component leading to Flores' victory, was not sufficient on its own to lead to Edwards defeat. Edwards' personal appeal and success within the district, whether derived from his conservative/independent voting record, his constituent service particularly for veterans, his experience and/or an incumbency effect, manage to outweigh the strong Republican make-up of the district.

To get a sense of how powerful these factors played in Edwards' prior election and even to some degree in the 2010 vote, consider the *Cook Political Report's* rating of the 17th District as an R+20. This rating means that in the 2004 and 2008 presidential elections, the district performed at 20 percentage points more Republican than the nation as a whole. Between 2004 and 2008, Chet Edwards received more votes than anyone might have expected given the Republican-leaning nature of the 17th District (see Table 3.4). Edwards outperformed what otherwise would have been predicted with the R+20 rating by 20.4 percent in 2004, 22.2 percent in 2006, 15.5 percent in 2008, and even 8.2 percent in his losing effort in 2010.

A common campaign tactic that challengers often take is to try to paint the incumbent as having "gone Washington" and to be out of touch with the district. Where 2010 was different from prior years was that the Flores campaign could take advantage of the two-year track record of a Democratic-controlled national government. From 2004 to 2008, the predominant national political figure was Republican president and Texan George W. Bush, thus making it difficult to tie Democrat Edwards to the policies of the Bush's administration. Obama and Pelosi, though, provided excellent foils for the Republicans in the 17th District, and their advertising strategy successfully turned the election in the district, and what would typically be a local affair, into a referendum on national policies.

To this end, voters were not choosing between the experienced and skilled legislator who has taken care of the district and the political novice prone to gaffes, but instead were choosing between a lieutenant in Obama's and Pelosi's

Table 3.4 Predicted and Actual Vote Percentages in Texas' 17th Congressional District Based on PVI Rating, 2004–2010

Election Year	National GOP %	17th District GOP Predicted % (based on R+20)	Edwards Predicted %	Edwards Actual %	Variance: Actual to Predicted
2010	51.6%	71.6%	28.4%	36.6%	8.2%
2008	42.5%	62.5%	37.5%	53.0%	15.5%
2006	44.1%	64.1%	35.9%	58.1%	22.2%
2004	49.2%	69.2%	30.8%	51.2%	20.4%

Source: Compiled by the authors using the *Cook Political Report's* R+20 rating for the Texas' 17th District.

liberal policies that threatened the nation and the conservative who was going to fight to protect Texan values. Once the contest was framed along these lines, all that Flores needed to do was to ensure he won the ground game, which he did through a mix of retail politics to take advantage of the perceived enthusiasm gap favoring Republican candidates, seeking the support of Tea Party activists who wanted to join the fight against Obama and Pelosi, and leveraging the independent expenditures of outside groups.

Following the election, Edwards was given several opportunities to reflect on his years of public service. In an interview with his hometown *Waco Tribune*, Edwards clearly relished his service to veterans stating, "If we've made a difference for one soldier, one veteran, one family, then it was worth every effort," and adding "If we had done nothing but [writing the John David Fry Law, which gives college scholarships to children of fallen soldiers], it would've been worth all the years that citizens of this district have given me to work for them."[71] At an event at the Bipartisan Policy Center, however, Edwards noted the irony of being "labeled a Pelosi-Obama Democrat even though 'I voted with Bush on TARP [the Troubled Asset Relief Program] and with that liberal Chamber of Congress on stimulus [the American Reinvestment and Recovery Act]'."[72] In the dichotomy of these reflections—the juxtaposition of Edwards' commitment to his constituents against the loss of the election on the basis of national politics—may lie the true lesson that can be drawn from the 2010 midterm election in the Texas 17th Congressional District: All politics may seem local, but even local politics can be driven by national affairs.

Notes

1. Morgan Smith, "Edwards Won't Rule Out Future Public Service," *The Texas Tribune*, http://www.texastribune.org/texas-politics/2010-general-election/edwards-wont-rule-out-future-public-service/ (accessed January 3, 2011).
2. "NOAA Meteorologist Bob Case, The Man Who Named The Perfect Storm," http://www.noaanews.noaa.gov/stories/s444.htm (accessed January 3, 2011).
3. Gail McCarthy, "Storm Blindsides Cape Ann," *Gloucester Times*, http://www.gloucestertimes.com/andreagail/x645305784/Storm-Blindsides-Cape-Ann (accessed January 3, 2011).
4. For a description of Cook's PVI rating, see "Glossary of Terms," http://www.cook-political.com/node/1905 (accessed January 9, 2011).
5. Texas has a semi-open voter registration system. As a result, data on the percentage of Republican voters in the district is not readily available.
6. "NOAA Meteorologist Bob Case, The Man Who Named The Perfect Storm."
7. "State and County Quickfacts, Data Derived from Population Estimates, Census of Population and Housing, Small Area Income and Poverty Estimates, State and County Housing Unit Estimates, County Business Patterns, Nonemployer Statistics, Economic Census, Survey of Business Owners, Building Permits, Consolidated Federal Funds Report," U.S. Census Bureau, 2010, http://quickfacts.census.gov/qfd/states/48/48251.html; "Census 2000 Summary File 1, Matrices P1, P3, P4, P8, P9, P12, P13, P,17, P18, P19, P20, P23, P27, P28, P33, Pct5, Pct8, Pct11, Pct15, H1, H3, H4, H5, H11, and H12," http://factfinder.census.gov/servlet/QTTable?_bm=n&_lang=en&qr_name=DEC_2000_SF1_U_DP1&ds_name=DEC_2000_SF1_U&geo_id=05000US48251 (accessed March 9, 2011).

8. U.S. Census Bureau, "State and County Quickfacts."
9. Baylor University Web site, *Baylor Sets Records with Overall Enrollment, Freshman Class; Regents Set 2011-2012 Tuition and Fees*, http://www.baylor.edu/pr/news.php?action=story&story=79379 (accessed March 9, 2011).
10. See Sam Howe Verhovek, "5 Years after Waco Standoff, the Spirit of Koresh Lingers," *New York Times*, April 19, 1998, http://www.nytimes.com/1998/04/19/us/5-years-after-waco-standoff-the-spirit-of-koresh-lingers.html (accessed March 10, 2011).
11. U.S. Census Bureau, "State and County Quickfacts."
12. Office of Institutional Studies and Planning, "Texas A&M Enrollment Profile, Fall 2010," http://www.tamu.edu/oisp/student-reports/enrollment-profile-fall-2010-certified.pdf (accessed March 9, 2011).
13. Demographic data on the 17th District from the *New York Times*, "Election 2010, Texas 17th District Profile," http://elections.nytimes.com/2010/house/texas/17?scp=1&sq=texas%17th%20district&st=cse (accessed March 9, 2011).
14. This term dates to the 1928 election when some Democratic southerners were angry with Senator Tom Heflin (D-AL), who decided to back the Republican presidential candidate. These exasperated southerners remarked they would "vote for a Democrat even if he were a yellow dog."
15. Michal Barone with Richard E. Cohen, *The Almanac of American Politics, 2010* (Washington, D.C.: National Journal, 2010), p. 1452.
16. "Bill Flores: Hispanics and the Republican Party," http://www.youtube.com/watch?v=bTqeAY9VHB4 (accessed January 22, 2011). See also Kenneth Winneg and Kathleen Hall Jamieson, "Party Identification in the 2009 Presidential Election," *Presidential Studies Quarterly*, vol. 40 (2010), pp. 247–263 (citing an increase in Hispanic identification with the Democratic Party in the 2008 presidential election); David Dutwin, Mollyann Brodie, Melissa Herrmann, and Rebecca Levin, "Latinos and Political Party Affiliation." *Hispanic Journal of Behavioral Sciences*, vol. 27 (2005), pp. 135–160 (analyzing the characteristics associated with Hispanic and Latinos who identify themselves as Republicans versus Democrats); Pew Hispanic Center and Pew Forum on Religion & Public Life, *Changing Faiths: Latinos and the Transformation of American Religion*, 2007, http://pewforum.org/uploaded-files/Topics/Demographics/hispanics-religion-07-final-mar08.pdf (accessed January 22, 2011) (see Chapter 8: Party Identification and Ideology).
17. See Earl Black and Merle Black, *The Rise of Southern Republicans* (Cambridge, MA: The Belknap Press of Harvard University Press, 2002), p. 88.
18. Beth Donovan Bob Benenson, Dave Kaplan, Charles Mahtesian, and Laura Adshead, "Redistricting: Partisans Try to Shape the Maps to Gain Control in the '90s," *CQ Weekly*, December 21, 1991.
19. Mary Clare Jalanick, "Redistricting: Court-Ordered Remap Aids Texas Incumbents," *CQ Weekly*, November 17, 2001.
20. David Barboza with Carl Hulse, "Texas' Republicans Fume; Democrats Remain Awol," *New York Times*, Section A, p. 17, May 14 2003.
21. Ibid.
22. Linda Greenhouse, "Justices Uphold Most Remapping in Texas by G.O.P," *New York Times*, June 29 2006.
23. See Patricia Kilday Hart, "Between the Lines," *Texas Monthly*, January, 2011; Karen Tumulty, "Chet Edwards: The Veep Who Wasn't," *Time*, August 27, 2008.
24. For maps of showing the various district lines throughout Texas before, during, and after the redistricting battle, see http://www.sourcewatch.org/index.php?title=2003_Texas_congressional_redistricting (accessed March 10, 2011).
25. Hart, "Between the Lines."
26. DeLay was subsequently convicted on the charges in November 2010.

27. Cohen, *The Almanac of American Politics, 2010*; Tumulty, "Chet Edwards: The Veep Who Wasn't."; "New Member: Chet Edwards, D-Texas (11)," *CQ Weekly*, January 12, 1991.

28. "New Member: Chet Edwards, D-Texas (11)."

29. Bob Benenson, "Survivor of Texas Remap Urges Tougher Tactics," *CQ Weekly*, February 7, 2005.

30. "Chet Edwards of Texas Seen as Another Possible Running Mate for Obama," *New York Times*, August 22, 2008, http://www.nytimes.com/2008/08/22/world/americas/22iht-veep.5.15561282.html (accesseed March 10, 2011).

31. Tumulty, "Chet Edwards: The Veep Who Wasn't"; Richard S. Dunham, "VP Talk Sparks Interest in Waco's Rep. Edwards," *Houston Chronicle*, June 25, 2008, http://www.chron.com/disp/story.mpl/front/5854183.html (accessed March 10, 2011); Michael Isikoff, "Veepstakes: A New Name," *Newsweek*, August 2, 2008, http://www.newsweek.com/2008/08/01/veepstakes-a-new-name.html (accessed March 10, 2011).

32. Tumulty, "Chet Edwards: The Veep Who Wasn't."

33. Tom Benning, "Longtime U.S. Rep. Chet Edwards Admits He's Trailing in U.S. House District 17 Re-Election Bid," *Dallas Morning News*, October 5, 2010, http://www.dallasnews.com/news/community-news/dallas/headlines/20101004-Long-time-U-S-Rep-3954.ece (accessed March 10, 2011).

34. Todd J. Gillman, "Rep. Chet Edwards digs in on 'no' vote despite call barrage." *Dallas Morning News*, March 18, 2010, http://www.dallasnews.com/news/politics/state-politics/20100318-Rep-Chet-Edwards-digs-in-7275.ece (accessed March 9, 2011).

35. "The Texas 17th and the NRCC," RedState.com, http://www.redstate.com/cmw/2009/12/24/the-texas-17th-and-the-nrcc/ (accessed January 3, 2011); Timothy Delasandro, "Washington's Handpicked 'Ringer' (NRCC Inserts Soros-connected Democrat into TX Rep Primary," FreeRepublic.com, December 21, 2009, http://www.freerepublic.com/focus/news/2412230/posts?page=51 (accessed January 3, 2011). Delasandro was one of the four other candidates that Flores defeated in the Republican primary.

36. "Bill Flores: Selling Phoenix to Run for Congress," http://www.youtube.com/watch?v=ZpWIh1EZ8ik (accessed January 3, 2011).

37. "About," http://www.billfloresforcongress.com/about (accessed January 3, 2011).

38. In the Republican primary, Flores (21,479 votes; 33.04%) led Curnock (18,679 votes; 28.73%), David McIntyre (11,870 votes; 18.26%), Chuck Wilson (9,853 votes; 15.15%), and Timothy Delasandro (3,119 votes; 4.79%). In the run-off, Flores (21,913 votes; 65.13%) defeated Curnock (11,730 votes; 34.86%). Vote totals obtained from the Texas Secretary of State at http://elections.sos.state.tx.us/elchist.exe (accessed January 22, 2011).

39. Reportedly the Hood County Republican Party Chair and the former Johnson County Republican Party Chair openly referred to Flores as a "RINO," although they later denied doing so. Kristopher Cowles, "District 17 County GOP Chair: I Will Bite My Lip and Pull the Level for RINO Bill Flores, Chet Edwards is Satan," http://www.kristofercowles.com/blog/2010/07/district-17-county-gop-chair-i-will-bite-my-lip-and-pull-the-lever-for-rino-bill-flores-chet-edwards-is-satan/ (accessed January 3, 2011). The primary evidence offered up by bloggers to substantiate that Flores was a RINO or even a Democrat were (1) voting records showed that Flores voted in the Democratic primary in 2008; and (2) Flores' Phoenix Exploration was funded in part by well-known liberal George Soros. On a related point, however, an examination by the authors of publicly available data on Flores' campaign contributions shows a history of contributions to Republican candidates, including President George W. Bush, former Arkansas governor and GOP presidential candidate Mike Huckabee, Texas Senator John Cornyn, and Tom DeLay.

40. The *Houston Chronicle* described Flores as "Politically, he's a down-the-line conservative." See "Meet Texas' New Congressmen: Bill Flores," *Houston Chronicle*, http://blogs.chron.com/txpotomac/2010/11/bill_flores_unseats_longstandi.html (accessed January 3, 2011).

41. The Brazos River is the largest river within the state and runs through much of Texas' 17th Congressional District.

42. Delasandro, "Washington's Handpicked 'Ringer.'"

43. For data on Flores' campaign funding sources, see http://www.opensecrets.org/politicians/summary.php?cid=N00031545&newMem=Y (accessed January 3, 2011)

44. "Outside Spending; Texas District 17," Center for Responsive Politics, http://www.opensecrets.org/races/indexp.php?cycle=2010&id=TX17 (accessed March 10, 2011).

45. On expenditures by American Crossroads, see "American Crossroads Recipients, 2010," Center for Responsive Politics, http://www.opensecrets.org/outsidespending/recips.php?cmte=C00487363&cycle=2010 (accessed January 3, 2011).

46. On expenditures by American Future Fund, see "American Future Fund Recipients, 2010," Open Secrets Web site, at http://www.opensecrets.org/outsidespending/recips.php?cmte=American+Future+Fund&cycle=2010 (accessed March 11, 2011).

47. See "About Us," American Future Fund, http://americanfuturefund.com/about-us (accessed January 22, 2011).

48. "Watchdogs to FEC: American Future Fund Appears to Be Violating Campaign Finance Law," *Public Citizen*, http://www.citizen.org/pressroom/pressroomredirect.cfm?ID=3206 (accessed January 22, 2011).

49. "Outside Spending; Texas District 17," Center for Responsive Politics.

50. See "2010 Competitive House Race Chart – March 4, 2010," http://www.cookpolitical.com/charts/house/competitive_2010-03-04_12-34-57.php (accessed January 6, 2011). Overall the 17th District ranked as the 19th most Republican-leaning district in the nation, and tied with Mississippi's 4th District as the most Republican-leaning district represented by a Democratic congressman. See the *Cook Political Report*'s "Partisan Voting Index Districts of the 111th Congress," http://www.cookpolitical.com/sites/default/files/pvivalue.pdf (accessed January 6, 2011).

51. Cal Jillson, quoted in Hilary Hylton, "Texas' 17th Congressional District: Chet Edwards vs. Bill Flores," *Time*, November 1, 2010, http://www.time.com/time/specials/packages/article/0,28804,2019138_2019132_2028678,00.html (accessed January 22, 2011).

52. Tom Benning, "Chet Edwards trails Bill Flores, according to new GOP poll," *Dallas Morning News*, May 10, 2010, http://trailblazersblog.dallasnews.com/archives/2010/05/chet-edwards-trails-bill-flore.html (accessed March 10, 2011).

53. See, for example, Victoria A. Farrar-Myers, "Defending Principles against a Tsunami: Shays vs. Himes in Connecticut's Fourth Congressional District," in *Cases in Congressional Campaigns: Incumbents Playing Defense*, eds. Randall E. Adkins and David A. Dulio, (New York: Routledge, 2010), 75–92. In the Shays-Himes race, despite Shays' history of independence from the national Republican Party in Congress, Himes' campaign was able to depict Shays as being politically aligned with President Bush and presidential candidate John McCain.

54. For example, in early October 2010, Obama's public approval rating in Texas was 39 percent; "Texas Governor: Perry (R) Opens Double-Digit Lead Over White (D)," http://www.rasmussenreports.com/public_content/politics/elections/election_2010/election_2010_governor_elections/texas/texas_governor_perry_r_opens_double_digit_lead_over_white_d (accessed January 22, 2011).

55. Karen Tumulty, "Conservatives Use Pelosi as Face of Liberalism in Campaign Ads," *Washington Post*, June 1, 2010, http://www.washingtonpost.com/wp-dyn/content/article/2010/06/30/AR2010063005328.html (accessed January 7, 2011).

56. "Chet Edwards, He's Not Independent," http://www.youtube.com/watch?v=ivtOTDXiqSg (accessed January 7, 2011).
57. Dave Michaels, "Despite Plea from Obama, Chet Edwards Again Votes 'No' on Health Bill," *Dallas Morning News*, March 15, 2010, http://trailblazersblog.dallas-news.com/archives/2010/03/chet-edwards-again-votes-no-on.html (accessed January 7, 2011).
58. Michaels, "Despite Plea from Obama, Chet Edwards Again Votes "No" on Health Bill."
59. Chet Edwards Campaign, "Stand." Text reprinted at Sam Stein. "Rep. Chet Edwards Touts His Opposition to Obama, Pelosi In New Ad," HuffingtonPost.com, http://www.huffingtonpost.com/2010/09/17/rep-chet-edwards-touts-hi_n_720976.html (accessed January 7, 2011).
60. Rick Perry Campaign, "10th Amendment," http://www.youtube.com/watch?v=MbV8AUvOEWI (accessed March 9, 2011).
61. "Chet Edwards Says Republican Challenger Bill Flores Helped Run a Company That Laid off over 3,000 Workers, Then Paid Millions to Executives," http://www.politifact.com/texas/statements/2010/sep/15/chet-edwards/chet-edwards-says-republican-challenger-bill-flore/ (accessed January 8, 2011). The basis for Edwards' claim stemmed from Flores serving as senior vice president and chief financial officer for Western Atlas when the company merged into Baker Hughes in 1998. Following the merger, Baker Hughes laid off a number of people due to "redundancies" created by the merger, but was also in the process of laying off other workers as a result of an economic downturn. Ultimately, the American-Statesman concluded that Flores did not "help run" Baker Hughes following the merger, thus leading to its "False" rating for Edwards' claim.
62. Bill Flores Campaign, "Austin Paper," http://www.youtube.com/watch?v=DEZF3eAOaUk (accessed January 8, 2011).
63. The *Eagle* described the implication the ad made as "wrong." "U.S. Representative Chet Edwards, Democrat vs. Bill Flores, Republican," http://www.theeagle.com/opinions/Eagle-recommendations-for-Congress—College-Station-Council-and (accessed January 8, 2011).
64. "Texas' 17th Congressional District: Chet Edwards vs. Bill Flores," *Time*, November 1, 2010, http://www.time.com/time/specials/packages/article/0,28804,2019138_2019132_2028678,00.html (accessed January 22, 2011); "Chet Edwards in Tight Race with Challenger Bill Flores (Memorandum from Bennett, Petts & Normington)," http://media.graytvinc.com/documents/PollFindings10-7.pdf (accessed January 22, 2011).
65. Matthew Watkins, "Poll Puts Flores in Lead." *Bryan-College Station Eagle*, October 28, 2010, http://www.theeagle.com/brazospolitics/Poll-puts-Flores-in-lead (accessed January 22, 2011).
66. Melanie Mason, "Bill Flores backs away from saying he's not opposed to raising Social Security retirement age," *Dallas Morning News*, October 15, 2010, http://www.dallasnews.com/news/politics/state-politics/20101015-Bill-Flores-backs-away-from-saying-55.ece (accessed March 10, 2011).
67. "Tea Party Patriots Mission Statement and Core Values," http://www.teapartypatriots.org/Mission.aspx (accessed January 9, 2011).
68. For example, Flores' statement of beliefs on his campaign Web site included statements like "The 17th Congressional district deserves a Representative who will take a leadership role to do the following: Stop the big government expansion of Nancy Pelosi and Barack Obama, and further the ideals of our Founding Fathers by putting forward more common sense, limited government solutions for the challenges facing our nation" and "With your support, we will build a movement to reclaim this district and deliver limited government representation, which will

help rebuild our economy, stop government expansion, and protect our nation."
See http://www.billfloresforcongress.com/beliefs (accessed January 9, 2011).

69. For analysis of the historical voting trends in the 17th District, see Steve Fullhart, "How District 17 Has Been Won," KTBX.com, November 1, 2000. http://www.kbtx.com/home/headlines/How_District_17_Has_Been_Won_106422913.html (accessed January 9, 2011).

70. Morgan Smith, "Edwards Won't Rule Out Future Public Service." *Texas Tribune*, November 3, 2010, http://www.texastribune.org/texas-politics/2010-general-election/edwards-wont-rule-out-future-public-service/ (accessed January 22, 2011).

71. "Rep. Chet Edwards Reflects on His Political Career," KCEN.com, http://www.centraltexasnow.com/Global/story.asp?S=13442422 (accessed January 9, 2011).

72. Eleanor Clift, "The 'Former Member' Club: Defeated Politicians Can Only Reflect on Losses, Cling to Their Principles," *Newsweek*, December 17, 2010, (http://www.newsweek.com/2010/12/17/congress-reflects-on-the-year-what-went-wrong.html) (accessed January 9, 2011).

4 Boxer vs. Fiorina in California's Senate Race

The Wave Stopped at the Sierra Nevada

Casey B. K. Dominguez

Into the last weeks of October, 2010, the *Cook Political Report* still rated the California U.S. Senate race a tossup.[1] With a Republican tide rising around the country, and a liberal incumbent Democrat, Barbara Boxer, polling below 50 percent, the GOP's chances of winning control of the Senate depended on winning races like this one. The challenger, Republican Carly Fiorina, formerly the CEO of the technology firm Hewlett-Packard, was a good candidate, an outsider with business and economic credentials and ties to Republican heavyweights. She was aided by conservative and Republican outside groups that spent millions of dollars to attack Senator Boxer during the last weeks of the campaign, but to no avail. Barbara Boxer defeated her credible, well-financed Republican challenger by ten points on Election Night. That she did so, even in a national Republican landslide, speaks to the liberal tendencies of voters in California and to the ongoing strategic problem faced by a conservative Republican Party in the state. Democrats won up and down the ballot in California in November, buoyed by strong Democratic voter registration and the popularity of the president and the policies he championed.

Outcomes like this one always raise the question of whether the campaign, in the end, mattered at all. Scholarly research shows that voters are creatures of habit, and largely decide who to vote for based on party affiliation, moderated by their perceptions of the economy. Research also shows, however, that campaigns do affect races at the margins, which is where many elections are decided.[2] If the campaign indeed mattered in California, and the experts' uncertainty about the outcome until votes were counted indicated that it probably did, then the story to be told here is one about the degree to which each campaign effectively appealed to the median voter in the state. With 20-20 hindsight, it is evident that the Boxer campaign did everything right, and that the Fiorina campaign made a couple of important strategic mistakes. The Boxer campaign effectively attacked Fiorina's experience at HP, neutralizing the Republican advantage on the issue of the economy. Fiorina also positioned herself to the right of the median California voter on some high-profile issues, including abortion and the environment, allowing Boxer to play her strongest hand. It is not possible to know whether, if the Fiorina campaign had not had to compete in a contested Republican primary, had positioned her further to the left on the environment, or had more effectively defined her biography, she could have beaten Boxer, but it is likely that a different campaign could have come closer to beating Boxer in a wave election like 2010.

California in 2010

By the numbers, California would appear to be solidly Democratic. On Election Night in 2010, Democrats won every statewide office, including the U.S. Senate seat and the governor's office. In 2008, President Obama won 62 percent of the two-party vote. Both U.S. Senators are Democrats, and both have been re-elected since 1992. Of its 53 representatives in the 111th Congress, 34 (65 percent) were Democrats. In voter registration, Democrats have a 13-point advantage over Republicans, with 44 percent of voters registering as Democrats, 31 percent registering as Republicans, and 20 percent registering as "Decline to State."[3] These Democratic successes are driven in part by an ongoing growth in the non-white population, who are more likely to register as Democrats or decline-to-state voters than as Republicans.[4]

The state of California has undergone an internal electoral realignment in the last two decades. Whereas the major partisan divide in the state used to be between Northern (Democratic) and Southern (Republican) California, the movement of white, blue collar workers to the exurbs and to the Central Valley, and the immigration of high-tech, educated, and low-skilled minority workers to the coast has left the state with a partisan divide right down the middle. In the twenty counties that touch either the Pacific Ocean or San Francisco Bay, registered Democrats outnumber registered Republicans by 2.3 million voters (44 percent to 31 percent). In the rest of the state, Republicans outnumber Democrats by 60,000 voters (40 percent to 39 percent). The problem facing the Republican Party is that the coastal counties are home to 71 percent of the state's registered voters.[5] Even in the old Republican heartland of Orange and San Diego counties, registered Republicans outnumber registered Democrats by only 187,000, out of a total of more than 3 million registered voters.

In addition to registering with and voting for the Democrats more often than not, majorities of California voters also favor policy positions associated with the Democratic Party. In over 12 years of polling by the Field Poll, a nonpartisan organization that has polled Californians on public policy since 1947, more than 66 percent of Californians have consistently supported abortion rights[6], and increasingly support gay marriage as well.[7] The vast majority of voters (81 percent in one 2007 poll) say that global warming is a somewhat or very serious problem.[8] Even in the face of serious budget problems, majorities of respondents to a March, 2010, Field Poll said they preferred to keep funding levels high for almost every state program, including funding for public schools and universities, health care, welfare, child care, law enforcement, and roads. Small majorities supported spending cuts for prisons and parks.[9]

The political environment in California, however, is complex. Although socially liberal in some respects, some more conservative tendencies are also present. For example, Californians voted to ban gay marriage in 2008, and opinions remain divided on the issue today. Californians also tend to support "tough on crime" policies like the death penalty and the "three-strikes and you're out" law that sends felons to prison for life after a third offense. A plurality of Californians supports Arizona's controversial immigration law,[10] even though Latinos make up 37 percent of the state's population.[11] Majorities have also supported tougher border control and increased deportations of illegal immigrants, at the same time that they have supported a path to citizenship for some.[12] On economic issues, Californians have a long history of opposing tax increases (while simultaneously preferring robust public services). Going back to the Proposition 13 property tax revolt of 1978, California voters have often rejected policies to make it easier to raise taxes, contributing to a serious and recurring annual budget impasse in Sacramento. So the anti-tax, tough-on-crime, and even anti-illegal immigrant policy positions espoused by the some in Republican Party are not necessarily losing issue positions with the California electorate.

One indicator of the potentially competitive partisan environment is that Republicans have held the governorship of California for 22 of the last 30 years, including the period from 2003 to 2010. The most recent Republican governor, however, has not always pursued orthodox party policies, and has built his legacy around some core Democratic Party issues. Governor Arnold Schwarzenegger, a former bodybuilder and movie star, was first elected in a 2003 special election at the time of the recall of his Democratic predecessor, Gray Davis. He was elected from a nonpartisan ballot that included more than 100 names. Schwarzenegger began his term in office leveraging his personal popularity against the Democratic power structure by supporting ballot initiatives that threatened the power of unions (major supporters of the Democratic Party). All of those initiatives were defeated, and in response, Schwarzenegger tacked to the center. In 2005 and 2006 he moved outside of the Republican Party mainstream to take aggressive action to combat climate change. In 2005, he signed an executive order calling on the state to reduce carbon emissions levels to 1990 levels by 2050, and in fall 2006 he signed a measure which capped statewide carbon emissions at 1990 levels by 2020.[13] That year, he also supported ballot initiatives that would issue bonds to pay for public works, and declared his support for a path to citizenship for some illegal immigrants. Delegates to the state party convention and Republican activists opposed these positions, but in an otherwise bad year for the Republican Party, they supported Schwarzenegger over his Democratic opponent.[14] He was reelected that fall with 56 percent of the vote.

Republican candidates for statewide office must fight against a strong headwind of party identification and liberal policy preferences held by members of the electorate. Schwarzenegger's experience highlights one potentially successful strategy for Republicans in California: Embrace your inner RINO (Republican in Name Only). This strategy was probably available to Schwarzenegger to a degree that it would not be for other Republicans because in order to win office initially, he did not have to position himself to the right to win over conservative primary election voters. In addition, he had the resources to compete without the enthusiastic support of the Republican base in the state.

While it is impossible to know whether a Republican senate nominee who ran to the center could have defeated Barbara Boxer in 2010, Carly Fiorina's failure to do so her raises that question. As discussed below, Fiorina rejected the Schwarzenegger model and ran as a more traditional and orthodox Republican. To the degree that issue positioning and the campaign effects it creates have any impact on elections over and above party identification, Fiorina's decision to position herself as a mainstream Republican probably hurt her chances of winning the election.

In 2010, Californians, like Americans generally (see Chapter 1), were extremely dissatisfied with the direction in which the country and the state were headed. California was actually worse off than the nation as a whole, as unemployment exceeded 12 percent in the state throughout the year, while hovering around or below 10 percent nationally. Voters knew the situation was grim. From March, 2009 to October, 2010, three separate Field Polls recorded more than 90 percent of respondents describing the economic conditions as "bad times." Nearly everyone was concerned about unemployment: 89 percent of respondents said that unemployment in the state was "very serious" and 10 percent said it was "somewhat serious."[15] In September, 55 percent of Californians thought the United States was on the wrong track.[16] Opinions about California and its governing officials were even less enthusiastic. About 80 percent thought the state was on the wrong track[17]; Governor Schwarzenegger's job approval ratings hung in the low 20s throughout the year; and in September, the state legislature's approval reached an all-time low of 10 percent.[18] In short, California was experiencing some of the same political tides that were building across the nation.

On the other hand, Californians differed from the rest of the country in that majorities of survey respondents in the state persistently approved of President Obama's job performance. Even as the rest of the country grew less enthusiastic about his performance during 2009 and early 2010, Californians still generally supported both the president and his policies. In October, he still had a job approval rating of 53 percent in the state, while it hovered in the mid-40s in the nationwide Gallup surveys. In June 2010, 58 percent of Californians said that they approved of the new health care law (the Patient Protection and Affordable Care Act of 2010) or said it was just a first step and more changes were needed, while only 34 percent felt the law should be reversed.[19]

It should also be noted that midterm elections in California are busy affairs. In 2010, in addition to deciding who to vote for in their congressional district race and the U.S. Senate race, the voters in California also had to decide who would hold each of eight statewide offices (including the governorship), and how to vote on nine separate statewide initiatives, as well as how to vote in local races for both elected office and ballot initiatives. Statewide ballot initiatives included an effort to roll back the state's stringent greenhouse gas emissions law (which lost) and an initiative to legalize the cultivation and possession of marijuana (which also lost). The governor's race, in particular, was a high profile one, pitting long-time Democratic politician Jerry Brown against former E-Bay CEO Meg Whitman. Whitman spent more than $100 million of her own money on advertising in that race. So in addition to wooing voters, both Boxer and Fiorina faced the considerable obstacle of catching their attention in a cacophonous political environment.

The Incumbent: Senator Barbara Boxer

Senator Boxer was first elected to the U.S. Senate in 1992, in the so-called "Year of the Woman." That year, there were two Senate races in California, as fellow Democrat Dianne Feinstein ran to fill the last two years of the Senate seat vacated by newly-elected Republican governor Pete Wilson, and Boxer ran in the open-seat election to replace retiring Democratic Senator Alan Cranston. Californians elected both, and have continued to re-elect them since. Prior to winning that election, Boxer served on the Marin County Board of Supervisors (1976–1982) and then represented Marin County in the U.S. House of Representatives for ten years. In 1992, she defeated conservative Republican radio and TV commentator Bruce Herschensohn, in a highly ideological race. She won then, despite having written 143 bad checks at the House bank (a scandal that caused many incumbents to lose that year), due to her formidable campaigning and fundraising skills, and perhaps in part due to the presence of the more moderate Feinstein and Bill Clinton on the ticket.

The *Almanac of American Politics* calls Boxer "perhaps the personification of the feminist left."[20] Boxer has always ranked among the most liberal members of the Senate, averaging an Americans for Democratic Action score of 95 percent over her three terms in office (see Table 4.1). She voted to oppose the resolution authorizing the Iraq war in 2003 and has been one of the staunchest supporters of abortion rights and the environment. It would be hard to say that she moderated her positions to win reelection, given that her American Conservative Union (ACU) score in 2009 was 0, and her ADA score 100, although she did champion bipartisan efforts to improve airline security, including allowing pilots to carry firearms, after the terrorist attacks of September 11, 2001. Boxer also always voted in near lock-step with her party; she has had a party unity score below 95 only four times in her career, and has always opposed Republican presidents and supported Democrats, including overwhelming support for President Obama during his first term in office (see Table 4.1).

More importantly, her most prominent appearances in the news during the last Congress related to controversial climate change legislation. As chair of the Senate Environment and Public Works committee, Boxer shepherded the American Clean Energy and Security Act of 2009 (which came to be known as the cap-and-trade bill) to the floor of the Senate, over the unanimous objection of committee Republicans. Given the action the state had already taken under its Republican governor on the issue of climate change, her work on that bill was probably more an asset than a liability to her at home. Though Californians

Table 4.1 Congressional Vote Scores for Barbara Boxer, 1993–2010

Year	American Conservative Union	Americans for Democratic Action	Party Unity	Presidential Support
2010	0%	95%	97%	98%
2009	0%	100%	97%	96%
2008	4%	95%	99%	30%
2007	4%	80%	97%	34%
2006	8%	95%	97%	47%
2005	12%	100%	99%	30%
2004	4%	95%	96%	65%
2003	10%	95%	99%	44%
2002	5%	90%	95%	65%
2001	0%	95%	98%	64%
2000	4%	85%	100%	92%
1999	4%	100%	97%	84%
1998	4%	95%	88%	85%
1997	0%	100%	95%	89%
1996	5%	100%	94%	88%
1995	0%	100%	93%	85%
1994	0%	95%	91%	85%
1993	8%	90%	95%	91%

Source: CQ's *Politics in America* (Washington, DC: Congressional Quarterly, Inc., 2010 and 2000); The American Conservative Union (http://www.conservative.org); Americans for Democratic Action (http://www.adaction.org); and Congressional Quarterly's vote studies (2009: http://innovation.cqpolitics.com/media/vote_study_2009; and 2010: http://innovation.cq.com/media/vote_study_2010).

dislike taxes, and take a hard line against criminals, they are staunch supporters of the environment. In July 2010, one poll showed that four out of five Californians favored more stringent restrictions on carbon emissions from automakers, industrial sources, and utilities.[21]

Boxer is known more for her willingness to fight on principle than for her willingness to craft bipartisan compromise, opening her to charges that she cannot claim credit for the passage of major pieces of legislation, while at the same time giving her a strong base of liberal allies to help her raise money and win elections.[22] This strategy has not made her an unpopular figure in the state. From 1995 through March of 2010, greater numbers of poll respondents rated Boxer favorably than rated her unfavorably. In late 2009, however, her favorability ratings dipped below 50 percent, signifying a potential vulnerability in the coming election.[23]

Given the somewhat divided opinions of Californians on major issues, her persistent advocacy for liberal positions opened her to criticism that she is too extreme to represent the state. In particular, her support for government programs and higher taxes make her vulnerable in a state whose voters like services, but do not like the taxes that pay for them. Boxer's Republican opponents in her last two reelection campaigns, however, were unsuccessful in making that argument persuasively to voters. Among other shortcomings, neither was well-financed or supported by the national party.[24] For instance, in 2004, Boxer spent $15.9 million compared to Republican Bill Jones' $6.7 million. During her first reelection campaign, in 1998, she spent $13 million, compared to Republican Matt Fong's $10 million. In 2010, however, Boxer again had a large funding advantage as she raised and spent over $29 million, compared to Carly Fiorina's $21.4 (see Table 4.2). Money is an especially important factor in California state-wide races because the size of the state often requires campaigning heavily on television in very expensive media markets. Without sufficient resources it is difficult if not impossible to win.

Conventional wisdom held that if a good candidate, with enough money, were to make the "she's too liberal" case to California voters, Boxer could be defeated. Fiorina seemed to be a candidate in that mold. As 2010 wore on, surveys showed that the November electorate might skew to the advantage of Republicans and made Boxer's ouster seem more plausible.[25]

The Challenger: Carly Fiorina

Carly Fiorina declared her candidacy in November of 2009. She had never held elective office before, and was best known for her leadership of the technology firm Hewlett-Packard (HP) from 1999 to 2005. As CEO, she presided over a merger between HP and Compaq that made it the largest technology company in the world. During her tenure, HP doubled its revenues, in part due to cost-cutting measures that included outsourcing 33,000 jobs.[26] In 2004, *Forbes* magazine named her the tenth most powerful woman in the world, and the most powerful

Table 4.2 Campaign Finance Data for California's Senate Campaigns, 2004 & 2010

Candidate and year	Disbursements	Receipts	Vote percentage
2010			
Barbara Boxer (D)	$29,537,696	$29,331,108	52.2
Carly Fiorina (R)	$21,484,825	$21,521,397	42.2
2004			
Barbara Boxer (D)	$15,979,210	$16,658,496	58
Bill Jones (R)	$6,674,083	$6,714,449	38

Source: 2010 election results: *New York Times*, http://elections.nytimes.com/2010/results/california; all other data: Center for Responsive Politics, http://www.opensecrets.org (accessed February 15, 2011).

woman in business.[27] She left the firm in 2005 after a public falling-out with the directors, and received a large ($21 million) severance package.

Though she had worked her way up from receptionist to CEO, Fiorina had largely stayed out of politics (on occasion even neglecting to vote) until she became a high-profile supporter of 2008 Republican presidential nominee John McCain. Campaigning alongside and as a surrogate for McCain, she offered him credibility on economic issues, helping to answer questions from early primary voters about the subprime mortgage crisis,[28] and later helping the campaign on multiple fronts—raising money, helping McCain appeal to women voters, and appearing regularly as a campaign surrogate on national television news programs.[29] She stepped back from the campaign after saying, in response to a reporter's questions, that neither Sarah Palin nor John McCain was qualified to run a company like HP. Other than her involvement with the national Republican campaign in 2008, she was a newcomer to California politics. On the other hand, her business credentials, ties to national Republicans, and her deep pockets made her a potentially serious challenger to Boxer right from the start.

The Republican Primary

Fiorina was not the only Republican in the field. Both former U.S. Representative Tom Campbell and State Assemblyman Chuck DeVore also sought the nomination. Campbell was a much more familiar face in California politics. He had served as a member of Congress for ten years and was the Republican challenger to Senator Dianne Feinstein in 2000. More recently, he served as Governor Schwarzenegger's finance director, and also served as the Dean of the Haas School of Business at UC Berkeley and as a member of Stanford's law faculty. Pro-choice and pro-gay marriage, he had a reputation as a budget hawk while serving in the U.S. House, and was probably better positioned than either Carly Fiorina or Barbara Boxer to represent median voter opinion in California. Campbell also recently endorsed a state budget compromise that included some tax increases, making him a prominent outlier in the California Republican Party, where nearly all elected California Republicans have signed pledges never to vote for tax increases of any kind. DeVore, a businessman, declared his candidacy in early 2009 and aggressively courted Republican Party activists, including the College Republicans.

Throughout early 2010, the better-known Campbell had the edge in the polls. In January, he led Fiorina 30 percent to 25 percent among likely Republican primary voters.[30] In March, he maintained leads over Fiorina (by 6 points) and DeVore (by 19 points), and was the only Republican who, polls showed, could beat Boxer among likely November voters.[31]

Fiorina's advantage in campaign funds and better campaign strategy allowed her to defeat Campbell and DeVore in the June 8 primary. First, she simply outspent both of her opponents. Campbell spent $3.1 million, and DeVore spent $2.7 million, while Fiorina raised and spent more than $9 million through June 30 (partially financed by loaning her campaign $5.5 million).[32] She also strategically positioned herself to the right of Campbell, interfering with DeVore's appeal to conservatives, by focusing her attacks on Campbell's support for tax increases. One Web ad that received local[33] and national notoriety called Campbell a "Fiscal Conservative in Name Only" and compared him visually to a wolf in sheep's clothing with comically glowing red eyes.[34]

Since she did not have a prior record holding office, Fiorina's primary campaign defined many of her public issue positions for the first time. She announced that she was pro-life due to personal experiences, and that she had voted for Proposition 8 (which had banned gay marriage in the state). She expressed strong support for gun rights, saying in a May 6 debate that people on the "no-fly" list should be able to buy guns. Like her Republican opponents, she expressed support for Arizona's new tough-on-illegal-immigration law.[35] Fiorina also said that she reserved the right to "question the science" behind global warming, and that the Endangered Species Act hurt California families by restricting water availability. Even after the BP oil spill off of the coast of Louisiana had made the position unpopular in environment-friendly California,[36] Fiorina expressed support for oil drilling off of the California coast. She received and advertised an endorsement from former Republican vice presidential nominee Sarah Palin. This combination of positioning on the issues and her financial advantage enabled her to win the Republican primary, receiving 56 percent of the statewide vote to Campbell's 22 percent and DeVore's 19 percent. Unfortunately, these positions were a potential obstacle to winning the general election given the difference between the primary and general electorates in the state.

Campaign Strategy

Both Barbara Boxer and Carly Fiorina employed remarkably similar strategies. Each tried to place blame on the other (and those like her) for the poor economy, each attacked the other more often than she offered positive messages, and each tried to portray the other as "too extreme for California."

Not surprisingly, the number one issue in the campaign was the economy, and unemployment in particular. A main theme on both sides of the campaign concerned who, precisely, was responsible for the high unemployment in the state and the nation. From her first statement as a candidate, Fiorina evoked a traditional Republican argument: that the high unemployment rate was due to the drag on the economy caused by a bloated, over-regulating public sector. In an op-ed column published the day she announced her candidacy, she wrote, "Washington must show the discipline to cut spending and create policies that encourage and empower businesses to put people back to work."[37] Her ads, "Failure,"[38] "Day,"[39] and "Crushed"[40] repeatedly attacked Boxer for supporting "a trillion dollars in wasteful spending" and "a trillion dollars in tax increases," that killed small business and caused "Californians [to] pay the price" in lost jobs. Fiorina stayed on message in public appearances as well. In the first debate, she echoed her own argument that "To create jobs, we need to make sure … our entrepreneurs are freed from strangling regulation and freed from taxation."[41] In the second debate, she reminded voters of her charge that in Boxer's "28 years in Washington, D.C., has done nothing to curb spending and everything to vote to increase spending."[42]

Boxer's counter-attack blamed high unemployment not on the public sector, but on the private sector, and seemed to neutralize what could have been an out-party (Republican) advantage. Her ads made the implicit argument that corporate CEOs (like Fiorina) caused job losses in the United States and in California by shipping jobs overseas. Several of her ads specifically criticized Fiorina for outsourcing jobs, while enjoying a CEO lifestyle during her time at HP. "Workers" featured former HP employees describing being laid off, and saying things like, "I was supposed to retire there," and "we even had to train our replacements." That particular ad ended with the tagline, "Fiorina never cared about our jobs. Not then, and not now."[43] The ads contrasted the laid-off workers' testimonies with descriptions of Fiorina's pay and severance packages from HP and her "five corporate jets." Boxer reiterated the point in the first debate, saying that Fiorina "made her name as CEO of Hewlett-Packard, laying thousands and thousands of workers off, shipping jobs overseas, making no sacrifice while she was doing it and taking $100 million. I don't think we need those Wall Street values right now."[44] Tying Fiorina to unpopular rich corporate executives, and to outsourcing, both hurt Fiorina's image in the public mind, and perhaps more importantly, offered an alternative explanation for the high unemployment that voters were so concerned about. It is certainly as easy to understand how outsourcing leads to unemployment as it is to understand how government regulations do.

Other Issues

Throughout the general election campaign, and indeed, beginning with her first primary ad, Fiorina was on the offensive against Boxer. Some ads, like those noted above, focused on the economy, and tied Boxer to liberal tax-spend-and-regulate policies in Washington. Fiorina went further, however, charging that Boxer was soft on defense, arrogant, and ineffective.

Her entry in the "soft on terror" category was an ad criticizing statements Boxer made relating climate change to national security. In that ad, "Safe," Fiorina touted her national security credentials (she had served as an advisor to the CIA), and faced the camera saying in an incredulous tone that, "Terrorism kills, and Barbara Boxer's worried about the weather." That ad, while appropriate to the Republican primary, actually aired in the closing days of the primary race, which she had already locked up. Because it minimized the importance of climate change as an issue, it was a strange entry to a general election race in a state as committed to the environment as California. In addition to leveling a charge against Boxer, it also seemed to be a sign of her decision not to "come back to the middle" to woo general election voters, at least on the issue of the environment.

Fiorina attacked Boxer for being "arrogant" several times; first in a Web ad in which Boxer's head grew so large that she floated across the country like a hot-air balloon,[45] and later in a television ad drawing on a real incident. In the balloon ad, the disembodied voice charges, as Boxer's giant head crashes through the Capitol dome, "Soon her elitist self image grew so that it overwhelmed the capital and drifted west. Westward, to tell us all how to live our lives. Why our hard earned money should go to her to spend. She quit working for us and worked only for herself." In the second incarnation, "Sir," the Fiorina campaign played a clip from a controversial encounter between Senator Boxer and a military general at an Environment and Public Works Committee hearing, in which she asks that the general call her "Senator" instead of "ma'am."[46] This ad again raised the theme that Boxer, the liberal, was contemptuous of the military, and therefore, implicitly soft on terror. Both tapped into the standard conservative charges against liberals that they look down on regular people and seek to control them.

Fiorina made her play for the middle by levying the charge that Boxer was an ineffective legislator because she was so ideologically extreme. In her first day on the campaign, she said, "Barbara Boxer has been a senator for almost 18 years. During that time, she's only gotten three laws enacted—naming a river in Virginia, a courthouse in Fresno, and bringing bridge repair money to the Bay Area, where she is from. One piece of real work in 18 years isn't much of a track record."[47] Her last ad before Election Day, "Bickering," quoted the *San Francisco Chronicle,* which criticized Boxer and wrote that Californians "deserve a senator who is effective, willing to reach across party lines." Fiorina then promised to "oppose my party if needed."[48]

To counter those charges, Boxer ran positive ads describing her legislative accomplishments, including bringing a new veterans medical facility to California.[49] She also emphasized her support for green technology by featuring a solar panels factory and declaring her support for small business.[50] As she did on the economy, Boxer counterattacked on the extremism front as well, and in mid-October released the ad, "Out of Touch."[51] That ad highlighted Fiorina's positions on oil drilling, abortion, and guns. It also made the standard Democratic charge that Fiorina would, if elected, slash Social Security and Medicare. It concluded with the lines, "No wonder Fiorina is endorsed by Sarah Palin. Carly Fiorina: Just too extreme for California." The ad came out shortly after a statewide poll showed that 58 percent of Californians (including 69 percent of nonpartisans) had a negative view of the former vice presidential candidate.[52]

Boxer also benefitted from President Obama's popularity in the state. Californians voted for the president by an overwhelming 24 point margin in 2008, and from January to October 2010, Obama's job approval in the state only fell from 56 percent to 53 percent.[53] His job approval rating was predictably higher among Democrats and lower among Republicans, but among the key nonpartisan voters, it closely paralleled the statewide average. The president was popular enough that he not only attended a rally at the University of Southern California with Boxer in the closing weeks of the campaign, but also made get-out-the-vote (GOTV) radio ads that ran on her behalf.[54]

The campaign itself, perhaps as intended by Fiorina, turned out to be largely a referendum on Senator Boxer's record and style of representation. A late September poll indicated that 67 percent of Boxer supporters were voting for her rather than against her opponent, and 65 percent of Fiorina supporters were voting against Barbara Boxer rather than for Fiorina.[55] It is notable that throughout the campaign, neither candidate ran many biographical ads. This was unsurprising for Boxer, who had already represented the state for 18 years, but perhaps strange for Fiorina, who began the year largely unknown to voters.[56] It is possible that the dearth of positive biographical ads explains why Fiorina's favorability ratings never significantly outweighed her unfavorability ratings. Even as additional voters developed an opinion of her as the year progressed, a roughly equal number of poll respondents reported unfavorable/favorable opinions of her. The high water mark for her favorability/unfavorability ratio was in July, when 34 percent of voters reported a favorable impression of her, while 29 percent reported an unfavorable impression of her. At that point 37 percent had no opinion. Even in late October, 42 percent rated her favorably, and 42 percent rated her unfavorably. Since voters are more likely to vote for a candidate toward whom they have positive feelings, having unfavorability ratings so high is generally considered a big problem for a candidate, especially a challenger. The evenness between Fiorina's favorability and unfavorability ratings was certainly equally due to the fact that she faced both primary and general election opponents, and was the focus of negative ads throughout the campaign. Boxer also faced a year's worth of attack ads, but since she was much better known to begin with, opinions about her were probably a lot less malleable by a campaign.

Boxer did not poll above 50 percent during the whole of 2010 (see Fig. 4.1).[57] Polls during the course of the campaign showed a tight race in the spring and

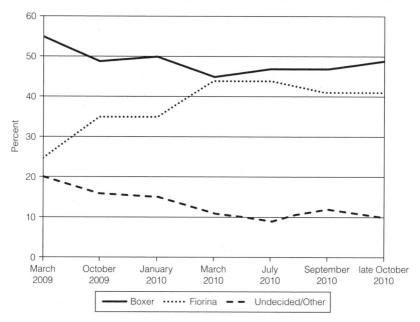

Figure 4.1 Boxer vs. Fiorina Polling Results, 2009–2010.
Source: Field Poll, various dates.

into the summer, although Boxer never lost her lead in the Field Poll. The tightened polls in the spring coincided with an increase in Boxer's unfavorability/favorability ratio, and with similarly tight polls in the other races on the statewide ballot, and with a decline in the president's approval ratings. They also coincided with heightened press coverage and advertising in the Republican primary race(s). As soon as Boxer began television advertising in the fall, her lead opened up.

Both candidates were able to air television ads throughout September and October, although Boxer's bigger campaign war-chest gave her an important financial advantage. She began 2010 with more than $7.2 million in the bank, and as of June 30 had $11.3 million cash on hand. As noted, Fiorina won the primary in part due to her financial advantage over her opponents, but the primary took its toll on her campaign. By June 30 she had less than $1 million cash on hand (see Table 4.3). Going into the general election, Fiorina was at a sizeable funding disadvantage. Boxer was able to spend more than $20 million between July 1 and the election, whereas Fiorina's disbursements during that time period totaled only about $13 million.

The Boxer campaign (and others) always believed that it was a possibility that Fiorina would spend her own money on the general election the way that she had during the primary campaign, and the way Whitman did in the governor's race.[58] For whatever reason, aside from the $5 million she spent to help win the primary, and a $1 million loan (which was repaid) towards the end of the campaign, that did not happen.[59] It is hard to know whether spending more of her own money would have helped Fiorina—on the same ballot, Former E-Bay CEO Meg Whitman spent a record-breaking $160 million of her own money for the honor of losing to Democrat Jerry Brown by 13 points.[60] Despite Boxer's fundraising advantage, the financial playing field was nearly level, when taking into account the spending from the parties and from outside groups.

The Impact of Outside Parties and Groups

The closeness of the polls and the potential for a liberal stalwart in the Senate to be defeated combined to encourage a number of outside groups, including the national party committees, to intervene in the race. Overall outside spending in both the primary and general election totaled $21.1 million.[61] Including the national parties, Fiorina benefitted from $14 million in outside spending, while Boxer benefitted from just $7.1 million.

The National Republican Senatorial Committee (NRSC) spent the most money on the Republican side, allocating $7.5 million to the state. The NRSC spent two-thirds of that in support of Fiorina, and the rest on ads and other activities opposing Barbara Boxer. This investment was quite a bit more than what the Democratic Senatorial Campaign Committee (DSCC) put into the race ($4.8 million). The next biggest player was the U.S. Chamber of Commerce, which spent $4.9 million on electioneering communications in opposition to Senator Boxer. Other pro-Republican groups (including National Right

Table 4.3 Boxer and Fiorina Campaign Receipts and Disbursements by Reporting Period, 2009–2010

Reporting Period	Barbara Boxer			Carly Fiorina		
	Receipts	Disbursements	Ending Cash	Receipts	Disbursements	Ending Cash
Beginning Cash as of September 30, 2009			$6,351,514.37			$0.00
2009 Year End (October 1–December 31)	$1,858,669.61	$951,151.50	$7,259,032.48	$3,584,133.66	$830,517.56	$2,753,616.10
2010 April Quarterly (1 January–31 March)	$2,469,967.47	$994,763.14	$8,734,236.81	$1,710,688.45	$1,657,417.00	$2,806,887.55
2010 Pre-primary (1 April–19 May)	$2,036,303.40	$1,094,222.06	$9,676,318.15	$2,061,814.15	$4,248,240.92	$620,460.78
2010 July Quarterly (20 May–30 June)	$2,568,387.67	$917,556.63	$11,327,149.19	$3,291,771.88	$2,959,446.38	$952,786.28
2010 October Quarterly (1 July–30 September)	$6,257,135.48	$11,074,522.84	$6,509,761.83	$5,860,312.62	$4,994,145.48	$1,818,953.42
2010 Pre-general (1 October–13 October)	$1,104,768.07	$5,340,604.18	$2,273,925.72	$1,426,887.26	$1,974,290.02	$1,271,550.66
2010 Post-general (14 October–22 November)	$3,059,414.42	$4,504,934.63	$828,405.51	$4,770,012.93	$5,971,845.67	$69,717.92
Total	**$19,354,646.12**	**$24,877,754.98**		**$22,705,620.95**	**$22,635,903.03**	

Source: Compiled from candidate reports to the Federal Election Commission, Form 3, Lines 23, 24, 26, and 27, various dates.

to Life, the National Rifle Association, Susan B. Anthony List, Freedomworks, and others) spent an additional $2.4 million. Liberal non-party spending was led by EMILY's List/Women Vote!, which spent $1.1 million. Others, including Planned Parenthood, NARAL, unions, Moveon.org, and the League of Conservation Voters, spent an additional $1.2 million.

The biggest spenders (the national parties, the Chamber of Commerce, and EMILY's list) devoted their money to "independent expenditures" on television advertisements that closely followed the themes of both campaigns. The Chamber of Commerce reiterated the Republican/Fiorina argument about the economy, reminding voters of Boxer's "143 bad checks" in the 1992 House bank scandal, and then charging her with voting to raise taxes and killing jobs. The ad closes with the line, "Tell Boxer to stop killing jobs."[62] The NRSC repeated the same theme, saying, "If we vote for Barbara Boxer, nothing will change. She'll continue to vote for higher taxes. Job Crushing Policies.... Boxer will continue to be ... self serving, ineffective, more of the same."[63] With ads like these, so similar to the themes in the Fiorina campaign's own ads, it was hard for voters to notice the Boxer campaign's fundraising advantage.

Other groups also stuck closely to the campaign's own messages. EMILY's list did the Boxer campaign the favor of specifically counterattacking against the "arrogance" charge that Fiorina had leveled against Boxer. In their silent ad, white words flash on a black screen, reading in part, "It was a reign of terror at HP with Carly in charge ... Fired thousands. Tanked a tech company. Took the money and ran. We know who's really arrogant, and voters will too."[64]

The other high profile issues on which the two candidates disagreed, especially abortion and guns, also prompted outside groups to support either Boxer or Fiorina, although these generally involved smaller dollar amounts. It is important to remember that although TV is still the most important and expensive campaign medium, there are others as well. According to FEC reports, other outside spenders bought radio ads (National Right to Life PAC, National Rifle Association, Planned Parenthood/Protecting Choice), Web/search engine ads (Restore America's Vote PAC, Susan B. Anthony List), and Facebook ads (NARAL, Restore America's Voice PAC). They also paid for consultants (Feminist Majority), bus tours (California Nurses' Association), phone banking (Planned Parenthood), robocalls (National Organization for Marriage, Planned Parenthood) and door hangers (FreedomWorks, South Bay AFL-CIO Labor Council).

When the spending by the candidates' campaigns, the parties, and all outside groups is tallied, the two sides come out roughly even, $33.6 million spent on the Republican side and $34.1 million spent on the Democratic side. The net effect of all of this outside spending was probably to help Fiorina stay competitive.

Analysis

On Election Night, Boxer won handily in the twenty coastal counties, receiving 60 percent of the vote there, while Fiorina won overall in the interior of the state, with 55 percent of the vote.[65] This reflects the split in the state described above. The overall vote was not close, however, because so many more votes were cast in the coastal counties (71 percent of the state's registered voters live there). In total, Boxer received 52 percent to Fiorina's 42 percent. Boxer's margin was very similar to her performance against Fong in 1998 (53 percent of the vote), and it was below her 57.7 percent win over Jones in 2004. For all of the preceding discussion about campaign dynamics and issue positioning, it must be noted that Boxer received a percentage of the statewide vote that was very similar to the percentages received by other Democrats on the ballot. In the gubernatorial race, Democrat Jerry Brown beat Republican Meg Whitman 54 percent to 41 percent; in the Lieutenant Governor's race, the Democrat won 50 percent to 39 percent; and in the Secretary of State's race, the Democrat won, 53 percent to 38 percent. California voters chose Democrats, up and down the ballot, almost regardless of the merits of any candidate's campaign.

According to exit polls,[66] Fiorina won a plurality of the Independent vote, 46 percent to 42 percent. This is a lower level of "Independent" voter support for Republicans than was found in the national level House race exit poll, where 56 percent of Independents indicated support for House Republicans. Predictably, Democrats preferred Boxer, 88 percent to 9 percent, and Republicans voted for Fiorina, 87 percent to 10 percent. The problem for Fiorina, and other Republicans in California, is that Democrats made up (according to exit polls) 42 percent of the electorate, while Republicans made up only 31 percent, and independents 27 percent. In other words, the Democratic registration advantage held, and splitting the independent vote was just not enough to get the Republican candidate close to the finish line. To win, Fiorina needed to win a much larger percent of independents, and at least some Democratic registrants, which is difficult to do running as a mainstream Republican in California.

In some respects, Fiorina ran the perfect campaign against Boxer. It highlighted all of the facets of her performance in office that Californians might not like—her lack of major legislative accomplishments, her votes for higher taxes, and her reputation for being "too liberal." Boxer, however, ran a *more* perfect campaign against Fiorina. Boxer's counterattacks were especially well-crafted. Fiorina's record of laying off workers while at HP was a heavy albatross in a bad economy, especially given the unpopularity of Wall Street and corporate executives after the 2008 bank bailouts (the Troubled Asset Relief Program, or TARP). Boxer's ads highlighting Fiorina's HP experiences undermined her credentials to hold office while simultaneously offering a narrative about the private sector causes of the bad economy that effectively neutralized any vulnerability Boxer might have had regarding unemployment, which was the biggest issue in the election. Fiorina's positions, which were strengthened in her competitive primary race, were also exploited effectively by the Boxer campaign. Boxer seized on the issue positions where Fiorina was most outside of the California mainstream—on the environment, abortion, and guns, and used both ads and public statements to highlight them. Her attacks made it difficult for Fiorina to appeal to moderate voters, and to make a persuasive argument that Boxer was more extreme than she was.

California Republicans continue to grapple with the classic problem of first having to satisfy an extreme primary electorate and then trying to satisfy a more moderate general electorate. They failed to solve that problem in 2010. Republicans were aware of the danger of nominating Fiorina. In every hypothetical general election match-up throughout the primary season, the more moderate Campbell out-performed Fiorina against Boxer in trial-heat polls, even after it was clear Campbell would lose the primary. Fiorina was arguably the best representative of the Republican Party of those in the primary field. Her nomination and her well-funded mainstream Republican campaign failed to put a Republican representing California in the United States Senate. The national mood probably could not have been more favorable to a Republican candidate than it was in 2010, so this election result should cause some soul-searching among California Republicans. They will have to evaluate whether their real problem in winning statewide office is the specific strategic choices made by the Fiorina campaign, or whether their real problem is nominating candidates with mainstream Republican positions on issues that may just be too conservative for California voters.

Notes

1. Mike Zapler, "Control of U.S. Senate Could Be Decided in California," *San Jose Mercury News*, October 22, 2010.
2. See, for example, Thomas Holbrook, "Campaigns, national conditions and U.S. Presidential Elections," *American Journal of Political Science*, vol. 38, pp. 973–998; and Lynn Vavreck, *The Message Matters: The economy and Presidential Campaigns* (Princeton, NJ: Princeton University Press 2009).
3. "2010 Statement of The Vote," California Secretary of State, http://www.sos.ca.gov/elections/sov/2010-general/ (accessed March 14, 2011).
4. Field Poll, Release #2309, August, 4, 2009, http://field.com/fieldpollonline/subscribers/Rls2309.pdf (accessed March 9, 2011).
5. Calculated by the author from data made available by the California Secretary of State. "Voter Registration Statistics By County, Report of Registration As of October 18, 2010." http://www.sos.ca.gov/elections/sov/2010-general/02-county-voter-reg-stats-by-county.pdf (accessed March 9, 2011).
6. Field Poll, Release #2350, July 21, 2010, http://field.com/fieldpollonline/subscribers/Rls2350.pdf (accessed March 9, 2011).
7. Field Poll, Release #2349, July 20, 2010, http://field.com/fieldpollonline/subscribers/Rls2349.pdf (accessed March 9, 2011).
8. Field Poll, Release #2230, April 12, 2007, http://field.com/fieldpollonline/subscribers/Rls2230.pdf (accessed March 9, 2011).
9. Field Poll, Release # 2335, March 24, 2010, http://field.com/fieldpollonline/subscribers/Rls2335.pdf
10. Field Poll, Release #2348, July 16, 2010, http://field.com/fieldpollonline/subscribers/Rls2348.pdf
11. U.S. Census 2009 Quickfacts, http://quickfacts.census.gov/qfd/states/06000.html (accessed March 9, 2011).
12. Field Poll, Release #2229, April 10, 2007, http://field.com/fieldpollonline/subscribers/Rls2229.pdf (accessed March 9, 2011).
13. Samantha Young, "Schwarzenegger Signs Global Warming Bill," *Washington Post*, September 27, 2006.

14. Laura Mecoy, "Republicans upbeat at state convention; They like their chances of winning governorship and two or three other top state positions," *Sacramento Bee*, August 19, 2006.
15. Field Poll, Release #2360, October 5, 2010, http://field.com/fieldpollonline/subscribers/Rls2360.pdf (accessed March 9, 2011).
16. Field Poll, Release #2358, September 29, 2010, http://field.com/fieldpollonline/subscribers/Rls2358.pdf (accessed March 9, 2011).
17. Field Poll, Release #2357, September 28, 2010, http://field.com/fieldpollonline/subscribers/Rls2357.pdf (accessed March 9, 2011).
18. Field Poll, Release #2357.
19. Field Poll, Release #2336, June 3, 2010, http://field.com/fieldpollonline/subscribers/Rls2336.pdf (accessed March 9, 2011).
20. Michael Barone and Richard E. Cohen, *The Almanac of American Politics* (Washington, D.C.: National Journal 2008), 162.
21. Mark Baldassare, Dean Bonner, Sonja Petek and Nicole Willcoxon, "PPIC Statewide Survey: Californians and the Environment," http://www.ppic.org/content/pubs/survey/S_710MBS.pdf, (accessed March 9, 2011)
22. For a recent journalistic profile, see, Mike Zapler, "Boxer an Aggressive, at Times Antagonistic, Presence in the Courtly Senate," *San Jose Mercury News*, October 10, 2010.
23. Field Poll, Release #2363, October 29, 2010, http://field.com/fieldpollonline/subscribers/Rls2363.pdf (accessed March 9, 2011).
24. For more detail, see Michael Barone and Richard E. Cohen, *The Almanac of American Politics* (Washington, D.C.: National Journal, 2008).
25. Field Poll, Release #2366, November 2, 2010, http://www.field.com/fieldpollonline/subscribers/Rls2366.pdf (accessed March 9, 2011).
26. Mike Zapler, "A Reality Check on TV Ads By Senate Candidates Boxer and Fiorina," *San Jose Mercury News*, October 28, 2010.
27. Elizabeth MacDonald and Chana R. Schoenberger, "The World's 100 Most Powerful Women," *Forbes*, August 20, 2004, http://www.forbes.com/2004/08/18/04powomland.html (accessed March 9, 2011).
28. Elisabeth Bumiller, "Once a Thorn, McCain now Courts a Wary Party," *New York Times* February 4, 2008.
29. Elisabeth Bumiller, "Ousted Executive Provides a Feminine Face to the McCain Campaign," *New York Times* June 6, 2008.
30. Field Poll, Release #2322, January 21, 2010, http://field.com/fieldpollonline/subscribers/Rls2322.pdf (accessed March 9, 2011).
31. Field Poll, Release #2331, March 18, 2010, http://field.com/fieldpollonline/subscribers/Rls2331.pdf (accessed March 9, 2011).
32. Opensecrets.org and Judy Lin, "Enterprise: Fiorina Faces Fundraising Challenge," *Associated Press*, July 12, 2010.
33. Mike Zapler, "It's a Sheep. It's a Demon. It's… Tom Campbell?" *San Jose Mercury News*, February 4, 2010; and Dena Bunis, "Demonic Sheep Join State's Political Menagerie," *Orange County Register*, February 6, 2010.
34. http://www.youtube.com/watch?v=KRY7wBuCcBY (accessed March 9, 2011).
35. Mike Zapler, "California GOP Senate Candidates Get Scrappy at Their Only Face to Face Debate," *San Jose Mercury News*, May 7, 2010.
36. A poll in May showed that 48 percent of Californians opposed new oil drilling, while only 41 percent favored it. "In Reversal, California Turns Against Offshore Oil Drilling, USC/LATimes Poll Finds," http://latimesblogs.latimes.com/lanow/timesusc-poll/. (accessed March 9, 2011).
37. Carly Fiorina, "Too Few Jobs, Too Much Spending," *Orange County Register*, November 3, 2009.

38. http://www.youtube.com/watch?v=b8XVMU5obkc (accessed March 9, 2011).

39. http://www.youtube.com/watch?v=-mMnPrUh23I (accessed March 9, 2011).

40. http://www.youtube.com/watch?v=as3aiyuRdxA (accessed March 9, 2011).

41. "We Meet at Last," *The Hotline*, September 2, 2010.

42. Mike Zapler, "Fiorina, Boxer Clash in Radio Debate," *San Jose Mercury News*, September 29, 2010.

43. http://www.youtube.com/watch?v=9lg61qIpstY (accessed March 9, 2011).

44. "We Meet at Last," *The Hotline*, September 2, 2010.

45. http://www.youtube.com/watch?v=lJKlc77K5dg (accessed March 9, 2011).

46. http://www.youtube.com/watch?v=2j4RF6cx0SY (accessed March 9, 2011).

47. Carly Fiorina, "Too Few Jobs, Too Much Spending," *Orange County Register*, November 3, 2009.

48. http://www.youtube.com/watch?v=yc1aXp0sGAE (accessed March 9, 2011).

49. http://www.youtube.com/watch?v=fMe1CW1uy5U (accessed March 9, 2011).

50. http://www.youtube.com/watch?v=0YyiTHnaguU (accessed March 9, 2011).

51. http://www.youtube.com/watch?v=C21iWn1sU7o (accessed March 9, 2011).

52. Field Poll, Release #2361, October 6, 2010, http://field.com/fieldpollonline/subscribers/Rls2361.pdf (accessed March 9, 2011).

53. Field Poll, #2358.

54. http://www.youtube.com/watch?v=Sx6J2RfzuDw (accessed March 9, 2011).

55. The Field Poll, Release #2354, September 24, 2010, http://field.com/fieldpollonline/subscribers/Rls2354.pdf (accessed March 9, 2011).

56. In January 2010, 66 percent of Field Poll respondents did not have enough of an opinion of her to rate her favorably or unfavorably. See Field Poll, # 2363, October 29, 2010, http://field.com/fieldpollonline/subscribers/Rls2363.pdf (accessed March 9, 2011).

57. In January, she led Fiorina 50 percent to 35 percent, in March, 45-44, in July 47–44, in September 47–41, and in late October, 49–41. Field Poll, Release #2363, October 29, 2010. http://field.com/fieldpollonline/subscribers/Rls2363.pdf (accessed March 9, 2011).

58. Maeve Reston, "Boxer's Cash is Ahead of Fiorina's Wealth," *Los Angeles Times*, July 16, 2010.

59. Maeve Reston, "Boxer Outraised, Outspent Fiorina; Democrats wrongly feared challenger's wealth would give her an edge," *Los Angeles Times*, December 3, 2010.

60. Jack Chang, "It's Brown Again; Whitman spends a record-smashing $160 million in vain" *Sacramento Bee*, November 3, 2010.

61. All financial information in this section is totaled by the author from data available through The Center for Responsive Politics/Opensecrets.org. The data come from CRP's "Outside Spending" category in the California 2010 Senate race, and includes electioneering communications and independent expenditures. Data accessed January 11, 2011. http://www.opensecrets.org/races/indexp.php?cycle=2010&id=CAS1 (accessed March 9, 2011).

62. http://www.youtube.com/watch?v=jQvid0H9Q78 (accessed March 9, 2011).

63. http://www.youtube.com/watch?v=Py23YTqQThk (accessed March 9, 2011).

64. http://www.youtube.com/watch?v=mkCGshyPTtE (accessed March 9, 2011).

65. Calculated by the author from data made available by the California Secretary of State. "Voter Registration Statistics By County, Report of Registration As of October 18, 2010."

66. All exit poll data from CNN.com, http://www.cnn.com/ELECTION/2010/results/polls/#CAS01p1 (accessed March 9, 2011).

5 Mitchell vs. Schweikert in Arizona's Fifth Congressional District
A Rematch in the Desert

Jennifer A. Steen

Recent history paints a deceptive picture of Arizona's 5th Congressional District. Following its creation in the 2001 round of redistricting, it was won by a Republican twice and a Democrat twice, so a casual observer could reasonably mistake the 5th District for a competitive seat. Swing districts are an excellent context in which to study the effects of congressional campaigns, and rematches, like the one between Harry Mitchell and David Schweikert, even more so because the candidates and district are held constant. A close inspection of the district, however, reveals that the outcome in 2010 was nearly pre-ordained. While campaign strategy and tactics usually matter in all but the least competitive districts, the Democratic incumbent, Harry Mitchell, faced such high hurdles to reelection it is doubtful that any changes to his campaign, large or small, could have changed the outcome. The 5th District is strongly Republican, and the Democratic victory in 2006 was the result of "perfect storm" conditions unlikely ever to be replicated. Harry Mitchell's entry to Congress resulted from an upset, but his departure did not. Rather, the 2010 election can aptly be described as a "course correction."

The 5th Congressional District

The 5th District covers the northeastern portion of the Phoenix-Mesa-Scottsdale metropolitan area in Maricopa County. It is dominated by the affluent, older communities of Scottsdale and Fountain Hills, with the younger, relatively liberal town of Tempe comprising about one-quarter of the district's population. The economic engines of the district are Arizona State University and the travel and tourism industry that revolves around high-end golf resorts and spring-training baseball.

At the close of registration before the 2010 general election, Republicans enjoyed a significant advantage in voter registration, as they outnumbered Democrats 144,639 to 105,106, a margin of 11 percent among all registrants and 16 percent among major-party registrants. Notably, Democrats were also outnumbered by the 120,378 independent registrants. There were also 4,087 minor-party adherents.[1] Consider the Republican advantage in practical terms: even if Democrats turned out to vote at the same rate as Republicans (which they do not), a Democratic candidate would need to win more than two-thirds of the independent and minor-party voters to prevail. While the independent bloc is large enough to swing an election to the Democrats, in reality they rarely do. In 2008, for example, the total number of votes cast for *all* Republican candidates on the ballot in the 5th District (for municipal and county offices, state legislature, state corporation commission, U.S. House and president) was 2,211,383, compared to 1,286,787 won by Democrats. Two years earlier, Republicans garnered 1,640,752 votes district-wide (for all federal, state and local offices), while Democrats received only 1,068,471.[2]

Incumbent Harry Mitchell

Despite the strong Republican leanings of the 5th District, in 2010 it was represented by a Democrat. Representative Harry Mitchell rode his party's wave in 2006, defeating six-term congressman J.D. Hayworth by four percentage points. Given the Republican tilt of the district, Mitchell's margin was impressive, even in a strong Democratic year, and in part reflected Hayworth's deficiencies. Hayworth was closely associated with disgraced lobbyist Jack Abramoff, and a widely cited report by the Center for Responsive Politics, issued in March 2006, identified Hayworth as the "largest single congressional recipient" of contributions from Abramoff and his associates. While several members of Congress donated Abramoff-related campaign contributions to charities, Hayworth defiantly kept his.[3] Adding insult to injury, later that year Hayworth captured the number-four slot on *Radar* magazine's list of "America's Dumbest Congressmen."

Mitchell's victory also indicated his own personal and political qualities, assets that would make him a strong candidate regardless of opponent or national tides. Indeed, as he defeated Hayworth in 2006, Mitchell outpolled all other Democrats on the ballot in the 5th except for Governor Janet Napolitano and Attorney General Terry Goddard, both popular incumbents who faced weak opponents. In fact, no other candidate for office at any level (other than Napolitano and Goddard) received more votes than Harry Mitchell in areas where both appeared on the ballot. Mitchell's intrinsic quality as a candidate stemmed in part from extensive experience in electoral politics. Prior to the 2006 campaign, Mitchell won elections for the Arizona state Senate, mayor of Tempe and Tempe city council. He also served as Arizona Democratic Party Chairman immediately prior to his 2006 congressional bid. Mitchell's long history of service in public office gave him a set of significant advantages: a large base of constituents who were already familiar with his name and his record; a long list of campaign contributors who supported his previous campaigns and thus facilitated early fundraising; an existing network of volunteers that could be re-activated for the congressional race; and prior relationships with important strategic players, like party officials and local interest group leaders, who could direct financial and human resources to his campaign.

Beyond this enumeration of political assets that can be mobilized in a campaign, Mitchell's personal qualities helped him win over new supporters and hold onto old ones. He was a beloved figure in Tempe, where he had taught generations of students at Tempe High School and served as mayor for 14 years, winning with landslides each time. He hailed from an old Tempe family, and the schools, parks and plazas that bear the Mitchell name honor both Harry and his grandfather William Mitchell, a seven-term state legislator.

In Congress, Mitchell aligned himself with conservative Democrats, joining the Blue Dogs and the New Democrat Coalition. Leading up to the 2010 election, Mitchell had the eighth-highest conservative-rating score among Democrats in the House, voting with the conservative position on 40 percent of key votes identified by the American Conservative Union (ACU) in the 2009 session (see Table 5.1). ACU's liberal counterpart, Americans for Democratic Action (ADA), used a different selection of roll-call votes to calculate their ratings, but Mitchell's 2009 ADA score mirrored his ACU score, at 60 percent (eleventh lowest among Democrats). His party unity score in the 110th Congress (2007 and 2008) was 81.9 percent (15th lowest among all Democrats) and in the 111th Congress (2009 and 2010) was just 57.4 percent (8th lowest among Democrats).[4] These scores represent a bit of a shift for Harry Mitchell, as his first two years in the House were much more aligned with his party and reflected a voting record that leaned more to the left.

Mitchell was more loyal to his party's position when it counted most. He voted with the Democratic majority on 88 percent of key votes in the 110th Congress and 80 percent of key votes in the 111th. However, he defected from his party's position on such prominent measures as the auto industry bailout of 2008 and the 2009 energy bill (the American Clean Energy and Security Act). He also voiced support for the Bush-era tax cuts (but did not have an opportunity to vote to extend them). Mitchell was especially active on veterans' issues, assuming the chair of the Oversight and Investigations Subcommittee of the House Committee on Veterans' Affairs as a freshman. His legislative record in the 111th Congress, however, included two major vulnerabilities—his votes for two signature issues of the Obama administration, the health care reform bill (the Patient Protection and Affordable Care Act of 2010) and the stimulus

Table 5.1 Congressional Vote Scores for Harry Mitchell, 2007–2010

Year	American Conservative Union	Americans for Democratic Action	Party Unity	Presidential Support
2010	29%	60%	47%	76%
2009	40%	60%	63%	67%
2008	32%	75%	80%	52%
2007	8%	80%	83%	13%

Source: *CQ's Politics in America* (Washington, DC: Congressional Quarterly, Inc., 2010 and 2000); The American Conservative Union (http://www.conservative.org); Americans for Democratic Action (http://www.adaction.org); and Congressional Quarterly's vote studies (2009: http://innovation.cqpolitics.com/media/vote_study_2009; and 2010: http://innovation.cq.com/media/vote_study_2010).

package (the American Reinvestment and Recovery Act). Mitchell also voted in favor of the second version of the financial industry rescue bill (Troubled Asset Relief Program, or TARP). These votes played a dominant role in David Schweikert's challenge, and one political operative succinctly described the opinions of many other operatives: "Harry [Mitchell] lost the race when he voted for the health care bill."[5]

Challenger David Schweikert

In a rematch of the 2008 election, Mitchell's Republican opponent in 2010 was David Schweikert. Schweikert also fit political scientists' profile of a high quality candidate: he had been elected to the Arizona state legislature in 1990 and served two terms.[6] When he first ran for the 5th District in 2008, however, it had been 16 years since Schweikert's last campaign. After leaving the Arizona House, Schweikert was appointed chairman of the Arizona State Board of Equalization, the state agency that considers appeals of property valuations. From the Board of Equalization Schweikert moved in 2004 to another appointed position related to taxation, chief deputy treasurer for Maricopa County, and later that year was elected County Treasurer without opposition in the general election (Schweikert won the Republican primary that year with 60.4 percent of the vote). The nature of his public positions gave him strong credentials as an expert on finance and taxation issues—although Schweikert did not give these credentials particular emphasis in his campaign messages—but also conferred vulnerabilities. An internal audit of the treasurer's office indicated a number of deficiencies, primarily with respect to record-keeping,[7] which Mitchell portrayed negatively in both 2008 and 2010. In his private life, Schweikert owned Sheridan Equities Holdings, a real estate venture that acquires and manages foreclosed properties.

As a repeat challenger, Schweikert may have been in a stronger position in 2010 than in 2008. As Peverill Squire and Eric Smith explain, "An unsuccessful first campaign may set the stage for success on the second attempt."[8] William Cavala elaborates, referring to Democrat Julian Camacho's 1974 rematch against Congressman Burt Talcott (R-CA), "Rather than having to spend long hours meeting and courting the district's activists and contributors, Camacho would be able to build on the relations established in 1972. The money spent on signs, direct mail, and radio in 1972 had provided some residual name identification and a base of positive support among the district's voters."[9]

On the other hand, empirical analysis of repeat candidacies suggests that the second time is usually no charm. Analyzing congressional candidates from 1960 through 1980, Squire and Smith found that "against incumbents, repeaters fare little better than do first-time challengers. There is no evidence that these repeaters benefit from a previous campaign."[10] The fortunes of repeaters have improved since Squire and Smith's analysis. From 1984 through 2008, 132 congressional candidates re-challenged after losing the general election with 40 percent or more;[11] on average, their vote shares declined by 2.1 points in the second effort, compared to the first.[12] All else being equal, one would thus expect Schweikert to do worse in 2010 than in 2008, although, of course, all else was far from equal.[13]

The Institutional Context: Arizona's Election Calendar

Two distinctive aspects of Arizona's election calendar combined to create a remarkably short campaign season: the late date of the primary election and the long window for casting ballots in the general election through "early voting." Both of these institutional features have the potential to significantly disadvantage challengers in Arizona; however, the lop-sided vote tally suggests that their impact on the outcome in the 5th District was probably minor and certainly not crippling to the challenger, Schweikert, who won a decisive victory.

The August 24 Primary

Given favorable conditions for a Republican challenger in the 5th District, it is not surprising that the Republican primary attracted a number of candidates in addition to David Schweikert, as it had in 2008. In 2010, Schweikert faced primary opposition from businessman Jim Ward and Scottsdale city councilor Susan Bitter Smith. Smith had given Schweikert a tough fight for the 2008 nomination, losing by just 1,021 votes (2.1 percent of the total), and Ward outraised Schweikert in the pre-primary period by $127,399.[14] In the end, Schweikert won a decisive 38 percent of the primary vote; Ward and Smith took 25 and 24 percent, respectively, and the remaining votes were divided among three other candidates. Two weeks before the primary, Schweikert was so confident of his lead that he cut his television and radio buys in half to conserve funds for the general election.[15]

Among the political cognoscenti, it is conventional wisdom that a late primary enhances the already formidable advantages of incumbent officeholders. There are a number of reasons why challengers are handicapped by a late primary: before the general election they have little time to replenish depleted campaign coffers, to recover from wounds inflicted during a vigorous primary and to consolidate support, including financial support, from co-partisans who supported losing primary candidates or stayed neutral in the primary.[16] Arizona held its primary election on August 24, 2010, a mere ten weeks before the general election. Only nine states conferred nominations later, and the delay (compared to other states) had the potential to undermine Schweikert's campaign. Despite his dominance in the GOP primary, Schweikert's general election campaign could not fully launch until the nomination was official. Some strategic players, like campaign contributors and interest groups, were committed to other candidates through the primary, while others stayed neutral pending the outcome.

Consider a comparison between Republican challengers nominated before August 24 and those whose primaries were decided on or after that date. As of August 24, Republican challengers who, like Schweikert, faced opposition for a GOP nomination but who, unlike Schweikert, had already won that nomination had raised an average of $365,975, while those whose nominations were not yet decided raised an average of $271,092.[17] The late primary was a mere inconvenience for Schweikert, who raised $360,477 prior to his nomination, well above the mean among late nominees and in the upper one-third for late and early nominees alike. Given the pattern among similarly-situated candidates, it is plausible that his fundraising was inhibited by the late primary, but of course this did not prove determinative, as Schweikert ultimately won the general election by a comfortable margin.[18]

Early Voting In Arizona

Arizona is one of 33 states that offer so-called early voting and/or no-excuse absentee voting to its residents. Early voting allows voters to cast a ballot before Election Day by visiting an elections office or a satellite location; in Arizona these locations include city halls, churches, community centers, libraries and universities. Arizonans can also vote absentee (i.e., by mail) without providing an excuse for their absence from the polls. Although early voting at a special location is usually distinguished from absentee voting by mail, the two processes are essentially combined in Arizona, as they use the same balloting materials and applications. The only difference is the location and method of submitting the completed ballot.

Early ballots are provided, either by mail or at an early-voting location, 26 days before an election. This is a particularly generous window for in-person early voting, as most states offer early voting for only about two weeks prior to Election Day; no-excuse absentee voting is generally available longer.[19] Arizonans take good advantage of the flexible voting provisions, with more than half of voters statewide casting an early ballot. In Maricopa County, where the 5th District is located, voters requested 866,440 early ballots and returned 665,065 (77 percent), although 117,129 of those ballots were not early at all because they were submitted to a polling place on Election Day.[20] Still, the statewide proportion of votes cast before Election Day was a striking 32 percent. In the 5th District, nearly two-thirds of all votes were cast on early ballots.[21]

There is anecdotal evidence that early voting (or "convenience voting," as political scientist Paul Gronke and his colleagues dub the practice) influences campaigns by shifting the election calendar.[22] Advertising pushes that were traditionally reserved for the last weeks of campaign season now come at the beginning of October or even in September, as campaigns hustle to reach voters with early ballots in hand. While traditional get-out-the-vote efforts take place during the last weekend before Election Day, resources that were once directed to Election Day mobilization now pour into get-out-the-early-vote efforts. The shift is apparent in spending patterns, as candidates in states with convenience voting spend their last campaign dollars earlier than states with more traditional voting regulations (see Figure 5.1 which depicts spending by Republican challengers who had contested primaries, at top, and the Democratic incumbents they faced, at bottom).

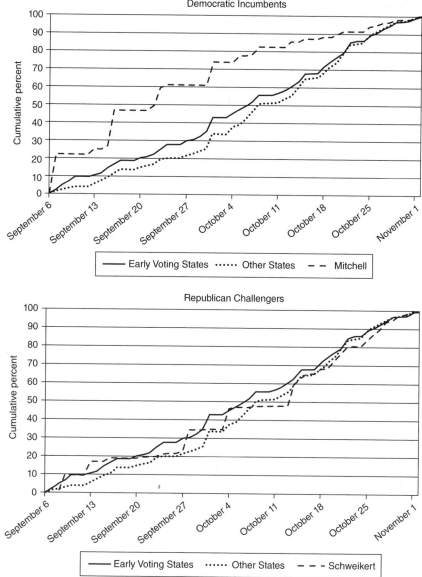

Figure 5.1 Cumulative Spending for Candidates in Early Voting States, Non-early Voting States, and in Arizona's 5th Congressional District, Labor Day through Election Day, 2010. *Source:* Daily disbursements were calculated from Federal Election Commission data. *Note:* Each panel illustrates how candidates allocated their post-Labor Day spending, with candidates in each group further divided by whether or not their states offer early (or no-excuse absentee) voting. The entry for each date is a ratio, with the numerator equal to cumulative spending (by all candidates in the group) since September 6 and the denominator equal to total spending (by the group) between Labor Day and Election Day. The ratio starts at zero for all groups on September 6 (Labor Day), because

Figure 5.1 Continued   no post-Labor Day spending had yet occurred, and rises up to one on Election Day, when all post-Labor Day spending had occurred. For example, by October 6 (four weeks from Election Day), Republican challengers in states with early voting had spent a total of $32.0 million since Labor Day. Those same challengers would ultimately spend a total of $67.0 million from Labor Day through Election Day, so their cumulative spending through October 6 represented 47.7 percent of their total post-Labor Day spending. Their counterparts in states without convenience voting had spent $18.4 million from Labor Day through October 6, 43.7 percent of the total amount they would eventually spend after Labor Day ($42.2 million).

Candidates in early-voting states do indeed spend funds relatively earlier, as among both Republican challengers and Democratic incumbents, the candidates in early-voting states spent larger proportions of their post-Labor Day funds right up until the final days of the campaign, when the candidates from states without early voting finally "caught up." Particularly noteworthy are the lines representing David Schweikert and Harry Mitchell. Mitchell frontloaded his post-Labor Day funds to an even greater degree than his fellow Democratic incumbents in early-voting states. Schweikert, in contrast, appears to have frontloaded to some extent, spending heavily in the first week of the end game, but he also saved about one-third of his total post-Labor Day spending to use in the last two weeks of the election.

Issues: The Climate and the Campaigns

As congressional candidates craft their strategies and messages, they are constrained in very practical ways by the political environment. A candidate can play to his strengths, touting his most significant achievements or credible claims, but this is only effective if those strengths relate to the issues that matter most to the electorate. Alternatively, a candidate can address the voters' top concerns, but this only helps if he compares favorably to the opponent in those areas. If a candidate is either lucky or shrewd, his own agenda dovetails with the voters'. This concept is aptly illustrated by the famous catchphrase posted in the "war room" of Bill Clinton's 1992 campaign: "It's the economy, stupid." In the 1992 presidential campaign, the dismal state of the economy held the top spot among voters' concerns, and President George H.W. Bush had some "'splainin'" to do.

John Petrocik's theory of issue ownership generalizes the implications of "It's the economy, stupid." Petrocik posits that certain issues are "owned" by one of the two major parties, such that the owning party's presidential candidate is presumed to be more likely to "handle" an owned issue well.[23] Subsequent work has extended the theory of issue ownership to congressional elections.[24] The constraints on candidates are implicit in Petrocik's apt statement of the link between issues and campaigns: "A candidate's campaign can be understood as a 'marketing' effort: the goal is to achieve a strategic advantage by making problems which affect *owned issues* the programmatic meaning of the election and the criteria by which voters make their choice."[25] A candidate's ability to succeed in this marketing effort depends on his or her "ownership"—or, more precisely, his or her party's ownership—of salient issues.

Perhaps the most salient issue in Arizona in 2010 was illegal immigration. In April of that year, Arizona captured the national spotlight when it enacted S.B. 1070, a measure related to illegal immigration. Although the provisions of S.B. 1070 largely duplicated federal law, its passage triggered a heated national debate and calls to boycott Arizona, which depends heavily on its travel and tourism industry. The most controversial provision of S.B. 1070 required law enforcement personnel to check immigration status during any official interaction if there were reasonable suspicions that a person was illegally present in Arizona (this provision has been stayed pending a federal lawsuit). The measure was immensely popular among Arizonans when it passed, with one poll finding 64 percent of Arizona voters supported it and 65 percent indicating that the law would be a "very important" factor in determining how they would vote in the next election.[26] After the initial hoopla died down, S.B. 1070 reappeared in headlines in July when the U.S. Department of Justice sued the state of Arizona in federal court, seeking to overturn the law on the basis of the Supremacy Clause of the U.S. Constitution.

Survey data are not publicly available to verify that Republicans "owned" the illegal immigration issue in the minds of voters in the 5th District, or even statewide in Arizona, but the circumstantial case is compelling.[27] Upon its passage, the public champions of S.B. 1070 were Republican state legislators, especially lead sponsor Senator Russell Pearce. Republican Governor Jan Brewer stayed quiet on the issue as it made its way through the legislature, but once she signed the bill she became the face of S.B. 1070 nationally as well as in Arizona. Most prominent Arizona Democrats, including Harry Mitchell, avoided the topic as much as possible, unless they were outspoken opponents of the bill (like Mitchell's House colleague, Representative Raul Grijalva, who was one of the early proponents of an Arizona boycott). Many out-of-state Democrats (including the party's top two national leaders, President Obama and Democratic National Committee Chairman Tim Kaine) voiced opposition to the measure. The level of passion in Democrats' public criticism ranged from Congressman Luis Gutierrez's condemnation of "the serious civil rights catastrophe that Republicans in Arizona are unleashing on immigrants and all Latinos in the state"[28] to Homeland Security Secretary (and former Arizona Governor) Janet Napolitano's statement, "The Arizona immigration law will likely hinder federal law enforcement from carrying out its priorities of detaining and removing dangerous criminal aliens."[29]

Harry Mitchell's position was somewhat obscure: he did not issue an official statement when S.B. 1070 passed but subsequently published an op-ed in the *Arizona Republic* opposing boycotts and urging President Obama not to sue Arizona.[30] When a federal judge enjoined implementation of parts of the law, Mitchell's statement emphasized the importance of border security and the need for immigration reform, offering this qualified endorsement of the original measure: "I believe that if the new state law spurs Washington to act, then it is a good thing."[31]

Given the salience of S.B 1070, the intensity of public opinion, and the Republicans' ownership of the issue in Arizona, it is perhaps surprising that illegal immigration was barely a secondary issue in the 5th Congressional District. In fact, the only reference to illegal immigration in the candidates' own television ads was Schweikert's claim, included among other promises in an introductory ad aired during primary season, that he would "secure our border and defend Arizona laws to stop illegal immigration." Schweikert also ran a 60-second radio spot focusing exclusively on border security, but like the television ad it came out in early summer and did not mention or even allude to Harry Mitchell. In fact, neither ad referred to S.B. 1070 or its provisions; instead they emphasized the pre-emptive issue of border security.

Although Schweikert chose not to highlight illegal immigration and border security, those issues still may have boosted his campaign in a subtle, indirect way, by mobilizing Republican voters. Turnout among Republicans dwarfed that of Democrats in the 5th District, with 69 percent of registered Republicans casting a ballot and only 60.5 percent of registered Democrats.[32] One local observer argued that intense feelings about the new immigration law contributed to higher turnout among Republicans.[33] Survey data do not exist to evaluate this claim empirically, but polls do suggest that the illegal immigration issue generated more light than heat. Voters were clearly much more concerned about the economy and government spending than illegal immigration.

One survey conducted in late summer found that the economy was the most important election issue to 58 percent of likely voters in the 5th District (only 7 percent volunteered illegal immigration as the most important issue).[34] These attitudes persisted through Election Day, when a statewide exit poll indicated that the economy was the most important issue for 66 percent of actual voters. In Arizona, an aspect of the economic situation with particular significance was the housing crisis. The meltdown of the mortgage industry, nosedive of home values, and the surge in foreclosures were felt nationally and received such extensive media attention that even those who were not directly affected personally understood the broader implications for their communities, and Arizona was one of the hardest-hit states. Home values fell by 48 percent from 2005 through 2010, more than any state except Florida and Nevada (the average national decline was 26 percent),[35] and the annual foreclosure rate in the Phoenix-Mesa-Scottsdale metro area was 7.3 percent in 2010 (fourth highest in the nation).

Harry Mitchell attempted to inject the housing crisis into the campaign by framing David Schweikert as one of the bad guys in the housing collapse because of his business acquiring and managing foreclosed properties. Mitchell's campaign devoted one entire advertisement—entitled "Speculator"—to this theme, describing Schweikert as a "predatory real estate speculator" and "foreclosure profiteer."[36] Similar charges were included as one-off's in other Mitchell ads. Much of the heavy lifting on this issue was done by the Arizona Democratic Party and the Democratic Congressional Campaign Committee (DCCC). For example, the Arizona Democratic Party established a Web site devoted to

Schweikert's real estate dealings and produced a 90-second video about "David Schweikert's Vulture Valley."[37] Such a division of labor, with political parties assuming responsibility for negative advertising, is typical of contemporary congressional campaigns.[38]

Mitchell's attacks on Schweikert's business ventures were complemented by criticism of Schweikert's public record. On both fronts, Mitchell attempted to raise doubts about Schweikert's trustworthiness and, with respect to his public service, Schweikert's competence. Several of Mitchell's ads charged Schweikert with "mismanagement" (the title of one ad) of the Maricopa County Treasurer's office, citing an external audit that noted a number of record-keeping lapses and ethics violations. According to the adage, "the best defense is a good offense," and Mitchell's criticism of Schweikert's public record was half of a larger attempt to turn the tables and shift the public's anti-incumbent anger onto Mitchell's opponent. The other half focused on Mitchell's own record, presenting the case for exempting the congressman from such anger. To that end, Mitchell emphasized a signal achievement, his role as the lead sponsor of H.R. 5146, blocking the cost-of-living pay raise members of Congress were to receive in FY 2011. The pay-raise issue was the theme of one Mitchell television ad and was mentioned along with additional credentials in two others. The female narrator of the pay-raise ad advised viewers,

> Harry Mitchell … wrote the bipartisan legislation to block pay raises for politicians. When Congress gave itself a pay raise during these tough times, Harry voted no and donated his to local charities." Then Mitchell himself chimed in, "When you look at the fact that you're in a war, people were struggling economically. And for Congress to get a pay raise? I think that's unconscionable.[39]

Mitchell also touted his moderate credentials with two ads, one emphasizing his endorsement by the U.S. Chamber of Commerce and the other featuring a parade of supportive testimonials from Arizona Republicans. "Mitchell: supports small business tax cuts, endorsed by the Chamber of Commerce for opposing Washington's reckless spending," the narrator informed viewers in the bad grammar typical of political scripts. "Washington can learn a great deal from small businesses, to do more with less," Mitchell himself continued as he spoke directly into the camera.[40]

Mitchell devoted additional advertising resources to his support for military veterans. This may well have been an irresistible tactic, given Mitchell's tenure as chairman of the Oversight and Investigations subcommittee of the House Committee on Veterans' Affairs. Mitchell had a concrete record on this issue, and his campaign messages were reinforced by his congressional activity and news coverage thereof, as well as by constituents' memories of his 2008 campaign (which also emphasized Mitchell's work on veterans' issues). Veterans, however, are not an especially large section of the 5th District population (7.1 percent, ranking 240th out of 435 congressional districts nationally and fifth out of eight in Arizona), nor were veterans' issues near the top of the list of concerns identified by 5th District voters in surveys. These ads did not offer Mitchell nearly the traction he needed to pull ahead of Schweikert.

Schweikert's own message was simpler and conformed largely to the national template for Republican congressional challengers which linked Democratic incumbents to the unpopular Speaker Nancy Pelosi and President Barack Obama. This should not have been an easy task in the 5th District because Mitchell was the only Democratic incumbent endorsed by the U.S. Chamber of Commerce and had a more conservative voting history than other endangered Democrats. Schweikert did charge Mitchell with being a "liberal" but did not harp on an accusation that was not particularly convincing given the totality of Mitchell's record in office. Instead, Schweikert's campaign advertising emphasized the theme of government spending, a special priority for the Tea Party movement, decrying Mitchell's votes for "Obamacare" and "billions for Obama's failed stimulus plan." One ad in heavy rotation focused on Mitchell and Pelosi's joint misdeeds. "Do they know what they have done?" it asked as a picture of the speaker and the 5th district congressman appeared on screen. "Do Harry Mitchell and Nancy Pelosi really understand what they have done to our future? They passed Obama's government-run health care, spent $800 billion on Obama's stimulus plan that failed, leaving America deeply in debt, punishing our grandchildren, mortgaging their future. The damage Harry Mitchell has done must be undone."[41]

These themes were reinforced by advertising by the National Republican Congressional Committee (NRCC) which, like its Democratic counterpart, accentuated the negative.[42] The NRCC's three ads all revolved around the issue of government spending, invoking the names and images of Pelosi and Obama. "Harry Mitchell must think your money grows on trees," the NRCC told television viewers in the Phoenix media market as a rendering of Mitchell jauntily plucked dollar bills from a cartoon tree.[43] A different ad recited Mitchell's sins against taxpayers over a soundtrack of ominous music: "Mitchell voted for the $800 billion stimulus that allowed Wall Street bonuses, and gave millions to dead people and prisoners, a trillion for the government health-care takeover, over a billion to companies that shipped jobs overseas. Harry Mitchell exploded the national debt, and more people are unemployed."[44] It concluded with juxtaposed photos of Mitchell and Pelosi, but instead of naming the speaker used a sneering emphasis strategically. "He, and *she*, have made America poorer and weaker." Schweikert's campaign, like other Republican efforts, was eerily reminiscent of the 1996 congressional campaigns, with "stimulus and Obamacare" substituted for "$270 billion cut in Medicare," Nancy Pelosi taking over the role of bogeyman from Newt Gingrich, and, of course, Democrats on the run instead of Republicans.[45]

The Schweikert team shrewdly—some even said deviously—co-opted one of Mitchell's own campaign mechanisms to cement Mitchell to the unpopular Democratic policies and leaders. Throughout the district, Schweikert supporters erected additions to Mitchell's own roadside signs. Schweikert's appendages were printed in the same font against the same color as Mitchell's own "Harry Mitchell/U.S. Congress" signs, adding unflattering modifiers like "Supports Obamacare" and "Pelosi's Lapdog." (The Schweikert modifiers also included "Hides from Voters" and "Union-Owned," which were negative but off the campaign's dominant theme.) The signs attracted significant news coverage[46] and clearly lingered in voters' minds. Two months after the election it was striking to this author how many local political observers spontaneously mentioned the "Lapdog" and "Obamacare" signs specifically as they reflected on the race.

Mitchell and his staff knew that the 2010 environment was toxic for him. As if responding to an air quality alert, they took their campaign indoors. The Mitchell team organized about 70 house parties, believing that the smaller scale and intimate feeling of gatherings of neighbors would provide a much more hospitable context in which the congressman could plead his case. As Mitchell himself explained later, "The house parties gave me a chance to explain the health care vote," contrasting those quieter events with the "hollering" that went on at his regular congressional town halls.[47] (Similar "hollering" at congressional appearances around the country was well documented in the wake of the health-care debate.[48]) The house parties targeted persuadable voters, independents or Republicans not already identified as Mitchell supporters, and focused on parts of the district where Mitchell was less familiar, especially Scottsdale. The total number of attendees was a fraction of the 5th District electorate, but the Mitchell campaign hoped that the house parties would indirectly influence thousands of voters through word of mouth. It may well have been the best play available given the terrifically challenging context.

Campaign Spending in Arizona's 5th District

The Mitchell and Schweikert campaigns were both well-funded, with Mitchell spending $2.31 million and Schweikert $1.72 million (see Table 5.2). These numbers are remarkably similar to the national average for winning challengers ($1.5 million) and defeated incumbents ($2.2 million).[49] It has been well established that challenger spending tends to be more productive than incumbent spending,[50] so it is not shocking that Schweikert got more bang for his $1.72 million than Mitchell got from his $2.31 million. Indeed, the leading research group studying campaign-finance reminds us that the national pattern, embodied in the 5th District tallies, "is normal: defeated incumbents typically outspend successful challengers by wide margins."[51] This was true in the district four years earlier as well, as Mitchell spent $1.9 million to unseat J.D. Hayworth, who spent $3.0 million in defeat. It may be notable that as an endangered incumbent Mitchell only raised $400,000 more than he had as a rising challenger; however, this increase was close to the norm for Democratic incumbents first elected in the 2006 wave.

There was also considerable spending by political parties and independent groups in the Mitchell/Schweikert contest.[52] Republican Party committees spent slightly more than their Democratic counterparts, but independent groups spent

Table 5.2 Campaign Finance Data for Arizona's 5th Congressional District Campaigns, 2006–2010

Election year	Disbursements		Receipts		Vote Percent	
	Mitchell (D)	Opponent (R)	Mitchell (D)	Opponent (R)	Mitchell (D)	Opponent (R)
2010	$2,308,400	$1,721,364	$2,174,509	$1,732,956	43	52
2008	$2,324,598	$1,416,883	$2,437,569	$1,421,599	53	44
2006	$1,933,184	$3,000,381	$1,954,180	$2,947,388	51	46

Sources: 2010 election results: *New York Times*, http://elections.nytimes.com/2010/results/arizona; all other data: Center for Responsive Politics, http://www.opensecrets.org (accessed February 15, 2011).

more heavily for Mitchell, or, rather, against Schweikert, so outside spending was nearly equal on both sides. In terms of overall reported spending, Mitchell enjoyed a modest advantage with $4.4 million in spending compared to $3.9 million on Schweikert's side (see Table 5.3). The most significant player among the independent groups was the National Education Association, a teachers' union of which Mitchell was a member during his days as a high school teacher, which spent $650,000 for ads criticizing Schweikert's positions on education (plus minor amounts, $11,471, for mail to its own members). Among those opposing Mitchell were two conservative groups, the 60-Plus Association, which spent nearly $400,000 on advertising picking up the themes of Obamacare and

Table 5.3 Summary of Campaign Spending in Arizona's 5th Congressional District, 2010

Spender	Spending for Schweikert	Spending for Mitchell
Candidate's campaign committee	**$1,662,854**	**$2,308,400**
Political party committees		
National political party	$1,145,515	$1,169,957
State political party	$209,029	$1,641
Party committee totals	$1,354,544	$1,171,598
Outside groups		
Supporting the candidate	$186,221	$5,024
Opposing the opponent	$669,035	$946,604
Outside group totals	$855,256	$951,628
Total spending by parties and groups	**$2,209,800**	**$2,123,226**
Total resources deployed	*$3,872,654*	*$4,431,626*

Source: Figures for candidate and party spending from the Center for Responsive Politics (http://www.opensecrets.org). Figures for independent groups combine totals reported by the Center for Responsive Politics with amounts of electioneering communications calculated by the author from reports published by the Federal Election Commission.

government spending, and the Club for Growth, which spent $150,000 on ads emphasizing Mitchell's votes for government spending.[53] The ad by the 60-Plus Association featured three residents of the 5th District who lamented Mitchell's support for "the Obama/Pelosi health care disaster." John Ady of Scottsdale further emphasized a connection to Speaker Pelosi, telling viewers, "Mitchell pretends he's independent, but when we needed him to stand up for us, Mitchell voted with Pelosi."[54]

There is one notable absence from this list. In 2010, the U.S. Chamber of Commerce spent more on federal election campaigns than any other non-party entity. The Chamber got involved in 53 House races, spending an average of $212,000 per race to help its endorsed candidates. Mitchell, despite earning the Chamber's endorsement, was not one of their beneficiaries. It seems unlikely that the Chamber's participation would have changed the outcome—with a funding advantage of nearly $600,000, Mitchell still trailed Schweikert by 10 points at the ballot box—but it is conceivable that Mitchell's defense against the "big spender" charge could have been bolstered by Chamber-sponsored advertising.

Conclusion

The 2010 midterm was a wave election that saw Republicans gain 63 seats, erasing many of the gains the Democrats made in 2006 and 2008. Harry Mitchell was in many ways like a lot of Democrats who were defeated—he had himself been elected in a wave that now seems more like a ripple in comparison to the 2010 election and hoped his moderate positions would help him hold his seat. Mitchell was probably a stronger candidate than many of his fallen classmates given the depth and breadth of his ties to Tempe, but the partisan tilt of his district made his task difficult. In early 2010 it was not yet clear exactly how difficult, as the 5th District tended to appear in the second tier of prognosticators' lists of vulnerable Democrats.

The climate in 2010 grew inarguably more hostile to Democrats as the months passed, especially in Arizona where Republicans made a clean sweep of the statewide constitutional offices and expanded their already large majorities in both legislative chambers. In that environment, Harry Mitchell struggled to deflect anti-incumbent sentiment and to present his credentials as a fiscal moderate. Schweikert's job was much easier. Mitchell's support of health care reform and, perhaps to a lesser extent, the economic stimulus, gave Schweikert a simple, compelling message—Harry Mitchell supported the Obama-Pelosi agenda rather than the interests of the 5th District. Ultimately, the geniality for which Harry Mitchell was widely known was no match for the anger and frustration of the electorate.

Could things have been different? Were there aspects of the campaigns that were determinative? Without the benefit of a window onto parallel universes, it seems that there are two significant decision points in the campaign. The first was the House vote on health care reform in March, the significance of which cannot be understated. Mitchell's support for the castigated "Obamacare" made it easy for David Schweikert to overwrite voters' impression of Mitchell as a moderate who operated independently of party leaders. Undoubtedly, any of the other Republican aspirants would have employed this message, too, but perhaps less effectively, which leads me to the second decision point, the Republican primary on August 24.

Had Republican primary voters made a different selection, there is some chance that Mitchell would have prevailed. Consider a comparison to Arizona's 8th District, in which Democrat Gabrielle Giffords fended off a challenge from Iraq war veteran Jesse Kelly. As the *Arizona Republic* reported, "Newcomer Jesse Kelly's upset victory over former state Sen. Jonathan Paton in Tuesday's Republican primary election for the 8th Congressional District has caused nearly as much jubilation among Democrats as among Kelly's supporters … [Giffords'] allies saw Paton as a more formidable opponent and believe that Kelly's ultraconservative views will turn off moderate swing voters in the general election."[55] Both of the alternatives in the 5th District Republican primary, Jim Ward and Susan Bitter Smith, had significant political shortcomings that would likely have rendered them weaker challengers to Mitchell, although their flaws seem less critical than the extreme positions and temperament of Jesse Kelly. Ward had just recently moved to Arizona, and although the state is replete with newcomers he would have been vulnerable to carpet-bagging charges. Smith, a moderate Republican, would have had a very difficult time motivating conservatives (many of whom blasted her in the blogosphere during the primary). Of course, these vulnerabilities are exactly why this is a "what if?" discussion—neither Smith nor Ward were the Republican nominee, having fallen considerably short of Schweikert's tally in the primary.

A longtime observer of Arizona politics said, "I think Harry's just about the only Democrat who could have won that seat." In 2010, however, he sailed Republican seas against a Republican wind, while challenger David Schweikert was able to take ownership of—daresay by foreclosing on?—the issue of government spending and, by extension, the economy.

Notes

1. Registration numbers were provided by a political operative who compiled them from Maricopa County Elections Division and requested anonymity.
2. This gap is inflated by the number of votes for Republicans in several uncontested elections. Surely if a Democrat had appeared on the ballot for any of those offices, he or she would have received some votes. When the uncontested elections are excluded, Republicans still outpolled Democrats in 2006, 835,769 to 819,591. In 2008, Democrats appear to enjoy a slight edge, when uncontested elections are omitted, receiving 1,190,317 votes to Republicans' 1,170,517. However, this "edge" is also inflated by the exclusion of the uncontested elections, some of which were uncontested because of Republican dominance in the area.
3. Jon Kamman and Billy House, "Hayworth will keep tribal gifts despite scandal," *The Arizona Republic*, December 23, 2005, http://www.azcentral.com/arizonarepublic/news/articles/1223hayworth23.html (accessed January 31, 2011).

4. *Congressional Quarterly* identifies "party unity votes" as roll-call votes in which a majority of Democrats opposed a majority of Republicans. The numerator of the party-unity score is the number of party unity votes in which an individual member voted with his or her party's position and the denominator is the number of party-unity votes in which the member voted. For example, in the 110th Congress, there were 1,097 party-unity votes. Harry Mitchell cast a vote in 1088 of them, voting with the Democrats 891 times and the Republicans 197 times.
5. Interview with the author, January 28, 2011.
6. For a discussion of the conceptualization and measurement of candidate quality, see Jennifer A. Steen, *Self-Financed Candidates in Congressional* Elections (Ann Arbor: University of Michigan Press, 2006), pp. 49–50.
7. Ross L. Tate, Maricopa County Auditor, "Treasurer's Office: A Review of Selected Areas; A Report to the Board of Supervisors" (April 2007).
8. Peverill Squire and Eric R.A.N. Smith, "Repeat Challengers in Congressional Elections,"*American Politics Research*, vol. 12 (1984), no. 1, p. 52.
9. William Cavala, "The Case of the Chicano Challenger: the Sixteenth District in California," in A. Clem, ed., *The Making of Congressmen* (Belmont, CA: Wadsworth, 1976), cited in Squire and Smith, "Repeat Challengers in Congressional Elections." Green and Krasno ("Salvation for the Spendthrift Incumbent: Reestimating the Effects of Campaign Spending in House Elections," *American Journal of Political Science*, vol. 32 (1988), pp. 884–907) adopt similar logic, awarding one point for any previous campaign and a second point for a previous campaign in the same jurisdiction in their eight-point index of challenger quality. Green and Krasno explain that a previous campaign "provides a candidate with the political connection so important to campaigning, as well as the political skills gained by a candidate."
10. Squire and Smith, "Repeat Challengers in Congressional Elections," p. 66.
11. I agree with Squire that challengers who repeat after winning less than 40 percent of the vote in their first outing are likely sacrificial lambs, running only to put a name next to their party's label on the ballot. One should not expect them to do better in the second run because it is not at all clear that they waged serious campaigns the first time out. See also David Canon, "Sacrificial Lambs or Strategic Politicians? Political Amateurs in U.S. House Elections," *American Journal of Political Science*, vol. 37 (1993), no. 4, pp. 1119–41.
12. This difference is statistically significant (p < .001).
13. Repeat challengers fared significantly better than first-time challengers, winning 13.6 percent of their challenges, compared to 9.5 percent for first-time challengers, and taking an average of 42.5 percent of the vote, compared to 39.2 percent for first-timers. These findings suggest that an unsuccessful challenge may not *add* to a candidate's strength, but there is indeed something about second-time candidates that sets them apart from novices.
14. Schweikert made up some of this gap by self-financing $49,000 more than Ward did.
15. Jeremy Duda, "Schweikert says he's wrapped up Arizona's Congressional District 5," *Arizona Capitol Times*, August 13, 2010, http://findarticles.com/p/news-articles/arizona-capitol-times/mi_8079/is_20100813/schweikert-hes-wrapped-arizonas-congressional/ai_n55294689/ (accessed January 24, 2011).
16. Jennifer A. Steen and Jonathan G.S. Koppell, "Primary Timing and Incumbent Reelection," paper presented at the Annual Meeting of the Midwest Political Science Association, Chicago (April 2004).
17. The difference of $94,883 is statistically significant (p < .10, one-tailed).
18. Fundraising totals were calculated from Federal Election Commission data files by adding the amounts of itemized individual contributions through August 24,

itemized political committee contributions through August 24, and unitemized individual contributions through June 30.

19. National Conference of State Legislators, "Absentee and Early Voting," http://www.ncsl.org/default.aspx?tabid=16604 (accessed January 26, 2011); see also the Pew Center on the States' early voting dataset, available at http://www.pewcenteronthestates.org/report_detail.aspx?id=58252 (accessed January 26, 2011).

20. Paul Gronke, "No-excuse absentee ballots, voter ID, and slow counts in Arizona," *Early Voting InformationCenter Blog*, November 29, 2010, http://www.earlyvoting.net/blog/2010/11/no-excuse-absentee-ballots-voter-id-and-slow-counts-arizona (accessed January 26, 2011).

21. The number of these that were submitted early could not be determined by the author.

22. See, for example, CNNPolitics.com, "Early voting: Every day is Election Day," CNN.com. http://www.cnn.com/2008/POLITICS/10/27/early.voting/ (accessed January 26, 2011); and Sean J. Miller and Shane D'Aprile, "Early voting has campaigns scrambling to gain support." *The Hill*, September 29, 2010, http://thehill.com/blogs/ballot-box/house-races/121483-early-voting-has-campaigns-scrambling-to-gain-support (accessed January 26, 2011). In some circumstances it is also appropriate to consider whether early voting mechanisms affect who votes, and thus poses different strategic challenges to candidates than they would face under more restrictive voting systems. This question might be relevant in the 5th District race if Arizona's early-voting rules were new in 2010; however, the Mitchell-Schweikert rematch occurred in the same institutional context as round one. Compositional effects of early voting could only be identified in comparison to similar contests in states without early voting, and such effects would likely be dwarfed by other differences, such as party registration (or affiliation) among the electorate.

23. John R. Petrocik, "Issue Ownership in Presidential Elections, with a 1980 Case Study." *American Journal of Political Science*, vol. 40 (1996), no. 3, pp. 825–850.

24. See, for example, Owen G. Abbe, Jay Goodliffe, Paul S. Herrnson and Kelly D. Patterson, "Agenda Setting in Congressional Elections: The Impact of Issues and Campaigns on Voting Behavior," *Political Research Quarterly*, vol. 56 (2003), no. 4, pp. 419–430.

25. Petrocik, "Issue Ownership in Presidential Elections," p. 828, emphasis added.

26. Rasmussen Reports survey reported April 28, 2010, reported in Polling the Nations.

27. Nationally, opinion was split on which party owned the immigration issue. October surveys by multiple pollsters showed voters tended to trust Republicans more than Democrats, but by small margins that were dwarfed by the number of unsure or indifferent voters.

28. Office of U.S. Rep. Gutierrez, "Congressman Plans Weekend Trip to Arizona to Stand with Latinos and Immigrants in Opposition to State Measure," press release, April 23, 2010. http://www.gutierrez.house.gov/index.php?option=com_content&task=view&id=551&Itemid=55 (accessed January 28, 2011).

29. AZ/DC Blog. "Napolitano: AZ. law will hinder U.S. law enforcement." AZCentral.com, (2010), http://www.azcentral.com/members/Blog/azdc/79267 (accessed January 28, 2011).

30. Harry Mitchell, "Suing Arizona won't fix immigration," *Arizona Republic*, July 2, 2010, http://www.azcentral.com/arizonarepublic/opinions/articles/2010/07/01/20100701mitchell02.html. (accessed January 28, 2011)

31. ABC15.com staff, "Officials, groups react to SB1070 ruling." ABC15.com (2010), http://www.abc15.com/dpp/news/state/arizona-reacts-to-ruling-on-sb1070 (accessed January 26, 2011).

32. These figures were calculated by a political party operative and provided to the author in a confidential personal communication.

33. Gary Grado, "Inside Arizona Politics: SB1070 and GOP voter turnout." ABC15. com, November 1, 2010, http://www.abc15.com/dpp/news/state/inside-arizona-politics:-sb1070-and-gop-voter-turnout (accessed January 28, 2011).

34. Whit Ayres, Jon McHenry and Dan Judy, "The State of the AZ 05 Race," memo (August 31, 2010), available http://americanactionforum.org/files/AAF%20AZ%20 05%20Memo.pdf (accessed January 14, 2011).

35. These figures were calculated from data provided by Zillow, available at http:// www.zillow.com/local-info/. The decline was 47 percent in Fountain Hills, 45 percent in Tempe and 44 percent in Scottsdale, the three cities that constitute most of the 5th District.

36. http://www.youtube.com/watch?v=JNbZh-Kjzsg (accessed March 12, 2011).

37. http://www.youtube.com/watch?v=knPtvQiF4iA (accessed March 12, 2011).

38. David B. Magleby and Kelly D. Patterson, "Conclusion," in *The Battle for Congress: Iraq, Scandal and Campaign Finance in the 2006 Election*, David B. Magleby and Kelly D. Patterson, eds., 224–234 (Boulder, CO: Paradigm Publishers, 2008).

39. http://www.youtube.com/watch?v=xuQYCBGAp8Q (accessed March 12, 2011).

40. http://www.youtube.com/watch?v=gCGcDZZZ9ms (accessed March 12, 2011).

41. http://www.youtube.com/watch?v=_-6YMOdh7-0 (accessed March 12, 2011).

42. In fact, to describe the NRCC advertising as "reinforcing" Schweikert's is a bit misleading because the NRCC's advertising outlays dwarfed Schweikert's. The NRCC reported $1,145,283 in independent expenditures against Harry Mitchell, whereas Schweikert's entire campaign budget was only $1,662,854.

43. http://www.youtube.com/watch?v=aADy0dscyuY (accessed March 12, 2011).

44. http://www.youtube.com/watch?v=9hTqnYtlwR8 (accessed March 12, 2011).

45. For a discussion of the Democrats' Medicare-related ads in 1996, see Deborah Beck, Paul Taylor, Jeffrey Stanger and Douglas Rivlin, "Issue Advocacy Advertising During the 1996 Campaign," Annenberg Public Policy Center Report, September 16, 1997, http://www.annenbergpublicpolicycenter.org/Downloads/Political_Communication/Advertising_Research_1997/REP16.PDF (accessed May 16, 2011); and Anthony Corrado, "Financing the 1996 Election," in *The Election of 1996: Reports and Interpretations*, Gerald M. Pomper, ed., 135–171 (Chatham, NJ: Chatham House, 1997).

46. See, for example, Ari Cohn, "Mitchell, Schweikert race turns ugly," *Ahwatukee Foothills News*, September 7, 2010, http://www.ahwatukee.com/news/article_ ef5f951a-baa1-11df-9519-001cc4c002e0.html (accessed March 8, 2011); Kasie Hunt, "Mitchell laments Obama yard signs," *Politico*, October 14, 2010, http://www.politico.com/news/stories/1010/43565.html (accessed March 8, 2011); MyFoxPhoenix. com, "Campaign Sign States Arizona Congressman is Pelosi's Lap Dog," August 30, 2010, http://www.myfoxphoenix.com/dpp/news/elections/mitchell-schweikert-campaign-sign-lap-dog-08302010 (accessed March 8, 2011); Brian Webb, "Political signs in disguise hit the Valley," abc15.com, August 29, 2010, http://www.abc15. com/dpp/news/region_phoenix_metro/ahwatukee/political-signs-in-disguise-hit-the-valley (accessed March 8, 2011).

47. Harry Mitchell, interview with the author, February 11, 2011, Tempe, Arizona.

48. See, for example, Jeffrey Bell, "Energy Tea: The power of the resurgent conservative populism," *The National Review* (December 7, 2009), available at http://nrd. nationalreview.com/article/?q=ZGE0YTVjNjkyNjAzMjc1ZTFlMTM3NjlkYmM xMmExN2E= (accessed March 11, 2011); K. Borsuk, "Looking to second term, Himes eager to get back to work," *Darien Times*, November 11, 2010, available at http://www.darientimes.com/news/darien-features/local-news/76941-looking-to-second-term-himes-eager-to-get-back-to-work.html (accessed March 11, 2011); FoxNews.com, "Town Halls Having an Impact? White House Bends on Health Care Provision in Face of Discontent," August 16, 2009, available at http://www. foxnews.com/politics/2009/08/16/town-halls-having-impact-white-house-bends-

health-care-provision-face#ixzz1GKPISDWv (accessed March 11, 2011); Alex Pareene, "Watering the tree of liberty," Salon.com, January 10, 2011, http://www.salon.com/news/politics/war_room/2011/01/10/revolutionary_rhetoric   (accessed March 11, 2011).

49. Campaign Finance Institute "Non-Party Spending Doubled in 2010 But Did Not Dictate the Results," press release, November 5, 2010, http://www.cfinst.org/Press/PReleases/10-11-05/Non-Party_Spending_Doubled_But_Did_Not_Dictate_Results.aspx (accessed February 7, 2011).

50. Alan I. Abramowitz, "Incumbency, Campaign Spending, and the Decline of Competition in U.S. Elections," *Journal of Politics* vol. 53 (1991), no. 1, pp. 34–56; Stephen Ansolabehere and Alan Gerber, "The Mismeasure of Campaign Spending," *Journal of Politics* vol. 56 (1994), pp. 1106–18; Green and Krasno, "Salvation for the Spendthrift Incumbent"; Gary Jacobson, "The Effects of Campaigning in House Elections: New Evidence for Old Arguments," *American Journal of Political Science*, vol. 34 (1990), no. 2, pp. 334–362.

51. Campaign Finance Institute, "Non-Party Spending Doubled in 2010."

52. The figures reported in Table 5.3 only include independent expenditures, coordinated expenditures and electioneering communications. The do not include spending on internal communications (such as the NEA mail mentioned below) or any other campaign activity that does not qualify as express advocacy or electioneering. Such activity would include, for example, direct mail distributed by an organization that is not a federal PAC and including a message that does not expressly advocate the election or defeat of a specific candidate.

53. The 60-Plus Association structured their advertising as electioneering communications instead of independent expenditures.

54. http://www.youtube.com/watch?v=XeQiP6vG_Vo (accessed March 12, 2011).

55. Erin Kelly, "Giffords' camp giddy to face Jesse Kelly in general election for Dist. 8 seat," *Arizona Republic*, August 29, 2010, http://www.azcentral.com/news/election/azelections/articles/2010/08/29/20100829republican-gabrielle-giffords-jesse-kelly.html#ixzz1GKA87YV1 (accessed March 10, 2011).

6 Kirk vs. Giannoulias in Illinois' Senate Race
Scandal and Competition to Replace a President

Wayne Steger

Barak Obama's victory in the 2008 presidential election set in motion a series of events that greatly impacted the 2010 midterm elections in Illinois. First, Obama's election to the White House put Democrats in control of the federal government. By unifying government control under one political party, Obama's election contributed to a national context in which Democrats were more easily blamed for the nation's problems. The slow pace of economic recovery, high unemployment, declining home values, and other problems contributed to the declining popularity of Democrats heading into the midterm elections. Also, while unified government gave Democrats opportunities to pursue policies desired by their constituents, pursuing ideologically oriented policies tends to motivate opposition partisans and can erode support among independent voters, which it did during 2009 and 2010. Despite action on issues the Democratic base had clamored for—health care reform and other policies—segments of the Democratic Party base were dissatisfied with the progress on issues like immigration and global warming, as well as the continuation of some Bush policies in the War on Terror. In short, as described in Chapter 1, the national tides were working against the Democrats going into the 2010 midterm elections.

The economic problems that dragged down Democratic support at the national level were even worse in Illinois where unemployment ran a full percentage point higher than the national average in the year leading up to the elections.[1] Federal budget deficits limited Democratic options to hasten the pace of economic recovery at the national level, while the Illinois state government, also under Democratic control, was on the brink of fiscal insolvency. Unified control of Illinois government made Democrats easy targets for blame for a struggling local economy and massive budget deficits. The salience of the weak economy, the financial crisis, the crash of the housing market, and budget deficits were made all the more relevant to the 2010 U.S. Senate race in Illinois by the Democratic nomination of Alexi Giannoulias who was the Illinois State Treasurer *and* who had been the senior loan officer of a bank that collapsed under the weight of bad home mortgages.

In addition to normal political tides, Illinois has its own peculiar tides that ebb and flow with the shifting focus of federal investigations of public corruption. The tides of political scandal shifted away from Republicans and toward the

Democrats in 2010. In the early 2000s, the former Republican Governor George Ryan and numerous associates were convicted of various charges involving the illegal sale of government licenses, contracts, and leases while he was Illinois Secretary of State.[2] The taint of Republican scandals helped Illinois Democrats make gains early in the decade, but the taint of scandal turned against Democrats by 2010. Obama's move from the U.S. Senate to the White House created an opportunity for the Democratic governor of Illinois to appoint a replacement to the vacant seat left by Obama. Governor Rod Blagojevich was arrested in December of 2008 for allegedly trying to sell Barak Obama's Senate seat.[3] The scandal decimated the pool of potential Democratic candidates. It also raised the saliency of candidate character, which became a central issue in the campaign messages of the Republican candidate Mark Kirk and outside groups like Crossroads America, a political organization started by Karl Rove, who had been the architect of George W. Bush's presidential campaigns.

That the 2010 Senate contest was for President Obama's seat gave the race symbolic value for both parties. Illinois was an increasingly "blue state" and voted Democratic in the last five presidential elections. Democrats were elected to both U.S. Senate seats and had won 12 of 19 seats in the U.S. House of Representatives, including three "pick-ups" in the traditionally Republican collar suburbs during the 2006 and 2008 Democratic "wave" elections. In addition, Democrats won all five statewide elected positions and 59 percent and 63 percent of the seats in the Illinois State Assembly and Senate, respectively. While Illinois trended Democratic, the heterogeneity of the Illinois population and the candidate-centric quality of Senate campaigns means that Senate contests in Illinois are competitive. For Republicans, gains in Obama's home state demonstrated the extent of public dissatisfaction with Democrats and helped them win back some seats they lost in the previous elections. For Democrats, holding on to Obama's seat was symbolic, but also important to the party's chances of holding their majority in the Senate. In a race likely to be decided by a few percentage points, national and state tides, candidate character, and the efficacy of the campaigns can affect the outcome. All of these worked against the Democrats in 2010. Republican Mark Kirk defeated Democrat Alexi Giannoulias on Election Day.

The Political Context: The State of Illinois and Illinois Political Parties

Illinois is the state closest to the national averages on demographics, income, and economic sectors.[4] The state is predominantly white with 71.5 percent of the population but there are also sizeable Latino (15.8 percent), African American (14.5 percent), and Asian populations (4.6 percent).[5] A little less than a quarter of the state's population lives in the City of Chicago while almost half of the state's population lives in suburban Cook County and the surrounding collar counties. The remainder lives in small- to medium-sized cities, towns, and rural areas. The state's economy is diversified with manufacturing (e.g., chemical, machinery, and electronics), agriculture (e.g., corn and soybeans), and services (e.g., financial trading and logistics). Manufacturing has declined for the better part of four decades, contributing to declining populations in the City of Chicago and mid-sized cities scattered throughout the state. The suburban population has grown as the economy continues to shift toward education-driven services in finance, technology, logistics and legal services among others.

The state also has considerable geographic and demographic variation in household incomes.[6] Median household income in Cook County is $54,559 while the average median household income of the six collar counties is $77,389—a difference that helps account for the relatively greater Republican appeal in the collar suburbs. The southern-most rural counties are the poorest with a median household income of $35,179. Demographic distributions of income across the state closely mirror national averages with whites, Asians, African Americans, and Latinos having median incomes and poverty rates near national medians for these groups.[7]

The demographic, socio-economic and geographic diversity of Illinois poses two important implications for statewide elections. First, a heterogeneous population means that there are multiple possible winning coalitions that can be formed, so statewide elections usually are competitive. Second, the heterogeneity of the state contributes to political parties that are internally fractured with cross-cutting cleavages on economic and social issues. The Illinois' Democratic and Republican parties mirror the national parties in their internal divisions along economic and social dimensions. Illinois Democrats generally are economically more liberal and the Republicans generally are economically more conservative, with both parties divided internally by social issues that cut across both political parties. The City of Chicago and suburban Cook County are largely liberal on economic and socially issues and are solidly Democratic. The suburbs north of the city, which Mark Kirk represented in the U.S. House, are predominantly economically conservative and socially moderate to liberal. The suburbs to the northwest and west of the city are more affluent and politically tend to be economically and socially conservative. The suburbs to the southwest of the city tend to be more socially conservative but are economically liberal closer to the city and more economically conservative further out. The central and northern rural and small town areas of the state tend to be economically and socially conservative. Downstate Democrats tend to be economically liberal but conservative on social issues like gun control/ownership, abortion, and gay marriage.

Such demographic, economic, and political heterogeneity mean that the coalitions of Illinois political parties are internally diverse and sometimes nominate candidates who have cross-over appeal on social issues. While Republican nominees for statewide offices over the last 20 years tended to be economically conservative, the nominees were also ideologically more varied social issues. Democrats have nominated for statewide office economic liberals who were either socially liberal or socially moderate to conservative. Republicans tend to win statewide offices with economic conservative and socially moderate candidates, while Democrats tend to win with economic and social liberal candidates. Socially conservative Republicans tend not to run well in the wealthy suburbs north of Cook County, while socially moderate Republicans tend not to run well in the rural areas of the state. Socially liberal Democrats tend not to run well in the southern part of the state, while socially conservative Democrats tend not to run well in Cook County.

The Candidates, Messaging, and Liabilities

Although open Senate seats usually attract numerous high quality candidates seeking the major party nominations, the 2010 Democratic and Republican nomination campaigns featured few strong candidates. On the Democratic side of the race, the Blagojevich seat-selling scandal deterred some high quality candidates from running. The pool of quality Republican candidates was also thin because their ranks were reduced by their own scandals and electoral losses earlier in the decade. The result was Democratic and Republican nominees whose vulnerabilities left many voters dissatisfied with their choices.

The Democratic Primary: Scandal Shapes the Race and the Issues

Democratic Governor Rod Blagojevich was already under federal investigation for public corruption when Obama won the presidential election. Under state law, the governor had the authority to appoint a replacement to fill Barak Obama's vacant Senate seat. Obtaining the seat two years ahead of the 2010 election offered an advantage to the appointee since that person could use the office to gain the benefits of incumbency. The appointee would be able to increase his or her name recognition, establish a record in Washington D.C., provide services to constituents, build political networks, and raise funds in advance of the election. A number of prominent Democrats were reported to want the appointment, including members of Congress Jesse Jackson, Jr. (2nd District) and Jan Schakowsky (9th District). Blagojevich also considered State Senate Majority Leader Emil Jones and Attorney General Lisa Madigan, whose father was the State Assembly Majority Leader and the Illinois State Democratic Party chair. Reports indicated that President Obama wanted his friend and presidential advisor, Valerie Jarrett, appointed to the seat. Blagojevich, however, wanted something in return for the appointment. Wiretap tapes played at his trial indicate that he wanted a well-paying job, campaign contributions, or an appointment to a Cabinet position or an Ambassadorship. Blagojevich was heard on wiretap at his trial saying, "I've got this thing and it's [expletive] golden … And I'm not just giving it up for [expletive] nothing."[8] Blagojevich was caught on tape making contemptuous comments about the president-elect's unwillingness to offer something, saying, "but they're not willing to give me anything except appreciation. [Expletive] them!"[9] Blagojevich even considered appointing himself to the position, saying on tape, "And if I don't get what I want and I'm not satisfied with it, then I'll just take the Senate seat myself."[10] On December 9, 2008, the Federal Bureau of Investigation (FBI) arrested Blagojevich to stop what an FBI spokesperson called a "corruption crime spree."[11] The Blagojevich scandal stretched from December of 2008 through the entire 2010 campaign.[12]

The scandal had major effects on the Democratic nomination contest. First, none of the Democrats revealed as candidates in FBI documents would seek the Democratic nomination.[13] That robbed the Democrats of some of their strongest candidates. Second, Blagojevich's eventual appointee was so tainted that the Democrats lost any advantage incumbency might have offered. Before he was impeached in January of 2009, Blagojevich made a surprise appointment by naming Roland Burris to the position. Burris was an African-American politician and former Illinois attorney general. Burris, however, was not a strong candidate and he previously failed in three attempts to gain the Democratic nomination for governor. According to one poll, Burris' 14 percent approval rating at the beginning of 2010 was the lowest ever recorded for a Senator.[14] Burris also faced a criminal investigation and a Senate ethics investigation for possible perjury stemming from promises he may have made to Blagojevich.[15] In light of the ethics investigation, his own unpopularity, and his inability to raise funds, Burris decided not to seek election in 2010. In addition to knocking out potentially strong Democratic candidates, the scandal also affected the Democratic nomination race by raising the saliency of integrity as a major candidate character issue.

Candidate character was a central campaign issue in the Democratic nomination campaign. The main Democratic candidates were Alexi Giannoulias, the Illinois State Treasurer and a friend of Barak Obama, and David Hoffman, a "reformer" who had served as Inspector General for the City of Chicago and who had clashed with Mayor Richard M. Daley over patronage and other procedures. Other candidates included Cheryl Jackson, president of the Urban League who had the potential to divide the party base of the Democratic primary because of her potential to draw African-American votes.

Hoffman attacked Giannoulias for mismanagement of a state college savings fund as well as for his role as the senior loan officer at his family's bank. Broadway Bank was rumored to be in financial difficulty owing to a large portfolio of failed home loans that were made when Giannoulias was the bank's senior loan officer. Hoffman, however, could not overcome the fact that he was relatively unknown outside of Chicago and underfunded compared to Giannoulias. With better name recognition, more party establishment endorsements, and more money, Giannoulias maintained a double digit lead in polls, though polls showed the race narrowing toward the end of the campaign.[16] On February 2, Giannoulias won a weak plurality of the primary vote taking 38.9 percent compared to 33.7 percent and 19.8 percent for Hoffman and Jackson, respectively.[17] The bruising attacks on Giannoulias character were a harbinger of what was to come when he faced a much better funded opponent in the general election campaign.

Democrat Alexi Giannoulias was elected as the Illinois State Treasurer in 2006 at age 30. He played basketball for Boston University and professionally in Greece, and was known as one of a small group of people who played basketball with Barak Obama while Obama was still in Illinois. In addition to having

the support of President Obama, Giannoulias was endorsed by core constituencies of the Democratic Party including pro-choice, environmental, and gay
rights groups. Giannoulias entered office during the public corruption trial of
former Republican Governor George Ryan and sought to build a reputation as
a reformer. He introduced ethics reforms prohibiting the state treasurer from
accepting campaign contributions from employees, banks, and other contractors with the office.[18] He also ran on his record as treasurer for saving jobs by
pressuring Wells Fargo to stop liquidation of a clothier, working with banks to
provide small businesses get access to credit, his promotion of "green" practices
through record keeping at the state treasury, and his overhaul of Illinois' state
college savings program.[19]

  Though he had already demonstrated his ability to win a state-wide election,
Giannoulias was saddled with baggage. Giannoulias was the treasurer of a state
government that was billions in debt and six months behind on payments to
state contractors and vendors who delivered state services. He was also tied to
Blagojevich through his family. His father had contributed $10,000 to Blagojev-
ich's reelection fund in 2008, and Blagojevich had appointed Alexi's brother to
a paid state board position. Giannoulias had supervised Illinois' college savings
fund that suffered losses in the financial crisis of 2008. In addition, Giannoulias
was the senior loan officer at Broadway Bank during the mid-2000s when the
bank made a large number of home loans that eventually went into default. The
bank also gave loans to convicted felons with mob ties—loans that were not
repaid.[20] Giannoulias' family's bank collapsed in the spring of 2010, costing the
Federal Deposit Insurance Corporation $390 million.[21] The bank failure tied
Giannoulias to the financial crisis of 2008–2009, and made him a personification of millionaire bankers who left taxpayers with the bills for risky decisions.
All of these liabilities were exploited by Republicans during the general election.

The Republican Primary: A Fractured Party with Few Quality Candidates

On the Republican side, five-term U.S. Representative Mark Kirk (10th District) sought the nomination against an unknown and inexperienced candidate
field. Illustrating the thinking of a strategic politician, Kirk delayed entering the
Republican nomination race until Democratic Attorney General Lisa Madigan
opted not to run.[22] Madigan was widely considered as a prohibitive favorite for
either governor or the U.S. Senate seat given her own popularity and the support of her father, the state Democratic Party chair. She decided against the
uncertainty of either race and ran for a third term as state attorney general. The
effect was to open the race on the Republican side. "With Lisa Madigan out of
the race, it clearly makes this at least an even, if not a Republican-tilting field,"
said Republican state Senator Kirk Dillard.[23]

  Kirk had few prominent Republican rivals since many Republicans had lost
elections in the aftermath of the George Ryan scandals and the Democratic
waves of 2006 and 2008. There were no Republicans who held statewide elected

office and few Republican members of the U.S. House of Representatives were well known in the Chicago area. Kirk's opponents included an attorney and real estate developer, a former city councilman, a former judge, a college professor, and a perennial candidate in Illinois. Though he was relatively unknown beyond the Chicago area (where his congressional district was located), Kirk had substantial advantages in endorsements, campaign funds, media coverage, and led the polls throughout the Republication nomination campaign.[24]

Kirk had long cultivated an image of a "moderate" Republican with a mixture of economic conservatism and socially more moderate positions. In his five terms in the House, Kirk had an American Conservative Union (ACU) lifetime score of 58—the lowest of all Illinois congressional Republicans in the 2000s.[25] Kirk also was adept at shifting his positions during his career. He began his congressional career in 2001 as a moderate but moved to the right in the election year of 2002, as seen by his relatively high ACU score in that year (see Table 6.1). He then moved toward more moderate positions—as evidence by a series of lower scores—as George W. Bush and the national Republican Party became more unpopular. Often characterized as too liberal for the Republican base, Kirk moved to the right in his voting in 2009 during the primary campaign. After the primary was over, Kirk reverted to a moderate voting record in 2010. The Americans for Democratic Action (ADA) scores show a similar tracking in which Kirk trended more moderate through 2008 before going more conservative in 2009 (see Table 6.1). Kirk also showed independence from his party while serving in the U.S. House. He started his congressional career siding with the

Table 6.1 Congressional Vote Scores for Mark Kirk, 2001–2010

Year	American Conservative Union	Americans for Democratic Action	Party Unity	Presidential Support
2010	62.5%	10%	76%	50%
2009	72%	35%	78%	59%
2008	48%	55%	73%	53%
2007	40%	40%	70%	41%
2006	54%	45%	79%	80%
2005	36%	30%	80%	67%
2004	63%	45%	84%	63%
2003	63%	10%	87%	81%
2002	76%	20%	85%	85%
2001	48%	25%	85%	74%

Source: CQ's *Politics in America* (Washington, DC: Congressional Quarterly, Inc., 2010 and 2000); The American Conservative Union (http://www.conservative.org); Americans for Democratic Action (http://www.adaction.org); and Congressional Quarterly's vote studies (2009: http://innovation.cqpolitics.com/media/vote_study_2009; and 2010: http://innovation.cq.com/media/vote_study_2010).

Republican delegation in the House 84 percent to 87 percent of the time from 2001 to 2004. Thereafter, he showed increasing independence, voting less frequently with his party in Congress (see Table 6.1). Unlike the vast majority of other House Republicans at the time, Kirk supported Barak Obama in 2009 and 2010 about as much as he supported George W. Bush in 2007 and 2008. In a year of Tea Party activism, Kirk stood out as a Republican going against the tide of conservatism in Republican nomination campaigns.

A big question about Kirk's candidacy was how well he would appeal to socially conservative Republicans. Republican nominations in past elections featured bitter fights between social conservatives and moderates. Perennial candidate Andy Martin created a stir in the campaign with allegations that Mark Kirk was gay, something that Kirk denied but the accusation raised the salience of Kirk's moderate positions on social issues including abortion and gun control. The question remained as to how enthusiastically social conservatives would embrace a socially moderate Republican candidate with a pro-environment, pro-choice record and who had supported Barak Obama as often as he had supported George W. Bush. In the end, Kirk won 56.6 percent of the primary vote compared to 19.3 percent for his closest rival.

The General Election Campaign

The general election thus featured candidates with starkly different positions on nationally salient issues. The campaign appeared to be framed as a choice between supporting Obama and the Democratic agenda versus supporting the Republican opposition. Candidate character, however, played as prominently as the candidates' issue positions.

The contrasts between the candidates were stark. Giannoulias supported Obama's economic stimulus package (the American Reinvestment and Recovery Act). Kirk voted against it. Giannoulias supported extending the Bush era tax cuts for all but the wealthiest 2 percent of Americans. Kirk supported extending the tax cuts for all Americans.[26] Giannoulias supported unions (including the Employee Free Choice Act, which came to be known as "card check") and extending unemployment benefits. Kirk voted against both in Congress.[27] Giannoulias also supported a number of other Democratic issues including Obama's health care bill (the Patient Protection and Affordable Care Act of 2010), emphasizing those aspects of the bill that were relatively more popular like eliminating limits on pre-existing conditions and prescription drug provisions. On immigration, he supported securing the borders and providing a path to citizenship for illegal immigrants, especially the DREAM Act (Development, Relief and Education for Alien Minors) which would give citizenship to immigrant children who grew up in the United States and graduated from college or served in the U.S. military.[28] On foreign policy, Giannoulias supported a plan to draw down troop numbers in Afghanistan and Iraq as well as taking a tougher line on trade relations with China.[29] He offered a number of promises to deal with federal budget deficits including pay-as-you-go budgeting (which Mark Kirk voted against), reforming earmarks (which Kirk used as a member of Congress), clos-ing corporate tax loopholes, stronger enforcement of tax collection, reducing some aspects of defense spending, and other more vague promises. Giannoulias emphasized job creation by small businesses and sought to portray Republican Mark Kirk as a tool of Wall Street and as a creature of Washington D.C.[30]

While his moderate positions on social and environmental issues were problematic during the primary phase of the campaign, those positions helped Mark Kirk in the general election. During the campaign, Kirk emphasized fiscal conservatism, his support for low taxes, a strong defense, expertise on foreign policy, and a hard line against terrorism and Iran, but moderate views on the environment and social issues. Kirk had a long record of supporting tax cuts and opposing tax increases in the House. During the recession in 2008–2009, Kirk hewed a complex position on the economy, urging FBI investigation of unethical behavior by corporate leaders during the financial meltdown of 2008, while supporting the Bush administration bailout of the financial sector (the Troubled Asset Relief Program, or TARP). Most of his messaging on jobs and the economy emphasized lower taxes, modernizing infrastructure, and support for free trade.[31] Kirk was a Republican who espoused fiscal conservatism while pursuing federal funding of local projects. His campaign beyond the Chicago area emphasized his support for ethanol subsidies, rural infrastructure, and tax cuts. Giannoulias' campaign was almost silent on issues salient to rural areas. Kirk's voting record on defense and national security was conservative; he was a Commander in the U.S. Naval Reserve Intelligence Office and touted his record during the Gulf War of 1991, the Kosovo intervention in the 1990s, and Afghanistan. He expressed a hard line on terrorism, Iran, and Iraq in the Middle East. Exaggerations of his military record, however, became a major "character" issue in the 2010 campaign (see below).

Kirk demonstrated his ability to dance between positions on energy, abortion, and the environment. As a congressman, Kirk backed a mixture of liberal and conservative positions on energy supplies—supporting both alternative energy and expanded oil drilling, for example. He supported the American Clean Energy and Security Act of 2009, which came to be known as the cap-and-trade bill. It was disliked by many Republicans, and Kirk announced during the pri-mary campaign that he would vote against it if elected Senator.[32] Kirk supported gun control, but did not advertise that in his campaign (nor did Democrats). He also took a centrist position on abortion by supporting rules bringing restrictive amendments to the House floor, but then voting against those measures on roll call votes.[33]

The Money Campaign: Candidates, Parties, Outside Groups, and Attack Ads

While fundraising is often identified as a critical factor in explaining congres-sional campaign success,[34] money is a necessary but not sufficient condition for winning congressional elections. Money allows candidates to compete for votes by enabling them to make their case before voters, but money cannot ensure that voters will like what they read, hear, or see. Money matters most when there is a financial imbalance between the candidates—when one candidate has a greater ability to communicate with voters and tell them why he or she should be elected rather than the opposing candidate. A major imbalance in fundraising existed in recent Illinois Senate elections. The winning candidate in the last three Illinois Senate elections raised over $13 million. The losing candidates in 2004 and 2006 were massively outspent and easily defeated by the winners (see Table 6.2). Candidate spending in the 2010 election which was more balanced, which is both a result and a cause of a competitive race.

In the 2010 Illinois Senate race, both candidates were well funded though Mark Kirk had a substantial financial advantage over Alexi Giannoulias (see Table 6.3). Kirk raised over 42 percent more money than Giannoulias—which translated into a substantial advantage in campaign advertising. Kirk's advantage in money during the general election was even greater since Giannoulias spent more for the Democratic nomination in which he faced a strong challenge from David Hoffman (see Table 6.3). Kirk was essentially unopposed in the Republican primary allowing him to keep his funds in reserve for the general election. He outspent Giannoulias by almost two to one in the final six weeks of the campaign.

Kirk began running ads attacking Giannoulias within days of the close of the Democratic primary. His attack ads hit Giannoulias for his role in his family's failed bank, ties to Blagojevich, and his record as state treasurer, particularly in regard to financial losses by the state's college savings program. Kirk also ran ads touting his record as an "independent" Republican with emphasis on his record for supporting tax cuts, defense spending, national security, veterans' benefits, environmental regulations, and education.[35]

Table 6.2 Campaign Finance Data for Illinois' Senate Campaigns, 2004–2010

Candidate and year	Disbursements	Receipts	Vote percentage
2010			
Mark Kirk (R)	$14,079,356	$14,305,287	48.0
Alexi Giannoulias (D)	$9,926,766	$10,020,307	46.4
2006			
Dick Durbin (D)	$13,112,372	$11,317,550	67
Steve Sauerberg (R)	$1,112,838	$1,117,161	29
2004			
Barack Obama (D)	$14,371,464	$14,964,184	70
Alan Keyes (R)	$2,664,471	$2,803,878	27

Source: 2010 election results: *New York Times*, http://elections.nytimes.com/2010/results/illinois; all other data: Center for Responsive Politics http://www.opensecrets.org (accessed February 15, 2011).

Table 6.3 Kirk and Giannoulias Campaign Receipts and Disbursements by Reporting Period, 2009–2010

Reporting Period	Mark Kirk			Alexi Giannoulias		
	Receipts	Disbursements	Ending Cash	Receipts	Disbursements	Ending Cash
Beginning Cash as of September 30, 2009			$2,293,758.90			$2,429,549.22
2009 Year End						
(1 October–31 December)	$1,864,687.29	$981,863.45	$3,176,582.74	$528,439.60	$2,066,630.27	$891,358.55
2010 April Quarterly						
(14 January–31 March)	$1,881,072.50	$2,041,711.71	$3,015,943.53	$1,206,466.66	$876,196.31	$1,221,628.90
2010 July Quarterly						
(1 April–30 June)	$2,317,555.63	$1,386,971.80	$3,946,527.36	$900,663.79	$1,097,235.79	$1,025,056.90
2010 October Quarterly						
(1 July–30 September)	$3,127,569.91	$2,667,715.88	$4,406,381.39	$2,329,585.37	$2,186,970.60	$1,167,671.67
2010 Pre-general						
(1 October–13 October)	$696,688.57	$2,791,342.87	$2,311,727.09	$390,534.68	$1,066,222.20	$491,984.15
2010 Post-general						
(14 October –22 November)	$1,542,101.64	$3,027,224.31	$826,604.42	$1,613,226.21	$1,989,383.48	$115,826.88
Total	**$11,429,675.54**	**$12,896,830.02**		**$6,968,916.31**	**$9,282,638.65**	

Source: Compiled from candidate reports to the Federal Election Commission, Form 3, Lines 23, 24, 26, and 27, various dates.
Note: The 2009 Year End Report for Mark Kirk represents the Pre-Primary reporting period from October 1, 2009 to January 13, 2010.

While Kirk had an advantage in candidate spending, Giannoulias benefitted from relatively greater national and state party spending (see Table 6.4). The Illinois Democrat Party (IDP) and the Democratic Senate Campaign Committee (DSCC) spent over $9 million on the race supporting Giannoulias and especially in opposing Kirk. That is compared with $5.6 million spent by the Republican National Committee (RNC) and Republican National Senate Committee (RNSC) in support of Kirk and opposed to Giannoulias. Combined, candidate and party spending made the race incredibly even in terms of spending. The Republicans outspent the Democrats by a thin margin—$19,769,014 to $19,202,822. Overall, both sides had roughly equal resources to communicate their messages and explain to voters why their candidate should be elected and not the other.

The various party organizations spent their funds differently. The IDP spent most of its money on the ground war, emphasizing voter mobilization and turnout, which is something that helped candidates up and down the ticket. Democrats recruited more than 20,000 volunteers for get-out-the-vote efforts, operating out of 191 staging locations in the closing days of the race.[36] The IDP State Chair, Michael Madigan, was rumored to be far more concerned with winning the governor's race than winning the Senate race.[37] Differences in grassroots mobilization of voters may have contributed to a small vote difference for the two headline Democratic candidates, but not enough to account for the differences in the Democratic governor and Senate candidates' vote shares.[38] In contrast to the state IDP, the national party committees the DSCC, the NRSC and the RNC were active in this race, spending mostly on television advertising. There was variation in spending strategy even across these party organizations. The DSCC spent 70 percent of its funds opposing Mark Kirk, while the NRSC spent almost 60 percent of its funds in support of Mark Kirk and only 40 percent opposing Giannoulias. To a large extent, negative advertising was used to mobilize the party base, which matters tremendously in midterm elections in which independents are a relatively small part of the voting electorate.

The national Republicans got involved in the race early. The day after the Illinois Democratic primary concluded, the RNSC began airing a hard hitting "Tony Soprano" ad linking Giannoulias to a $15.4 million loan by Broadway Bank, when Giannoulias was senior loan officer, to a convicted mobster.[39] The loan was never repaid and contributed to the bank's financial collapse. The ad also linked Giannoulias to Rod Blagojevich and to Tony Rezko, a convicted Democratic fundraiser who had close ties to Blagojevich and to Barak Obama. The NRSC's supportive ads touted Kirk's record as a "fiscal conservative" and his record of voting for tax cuts in the U.S. House.[40] The NRSC ads also repeatedly attacked Giannoulias as risky and reckless, characterizing him as a "mob banker," as having made bad investment decisions with Illinois college savings program, and as a "Blagojevich crony."[41] The DSCC started airing ads in September, about six months after the NRSC began airing ads. DSCC ads attacked Kirk as a Washington insider, his congressional votes against extensions of unemployment benefits, and his votes against a number of bills benefitting vet-

Table 6.4 State and National Political Party Spending in Illinois' Senate Race, 2010

Democratic Committees	*Supported Giannoulias*	*Opposed Kirk*	*Total*
Democratic Party of Illinois/10th District	$5	$5	$10
Democratic Party of Illinois	$847,000	$0	$847,000
Democratic Senatorial Campaign Committee (DSCC)	$2,496,526	$5,932,520	$8,429,046
Total	**$3,343,531**	**$5,932,525**	**$9,276,056**
Republican Committees	*Supported Kirk*	*Opposed Giannoulias*	*Total*
National Republican Senatorial Committee (NRSC)	$3,377,303	$2,312,060	$5,689,363
Republican National Committee	$295	$0	$295
Total	**$3,377,598**	**$2,312,060**	**$5,689,658**

Source: Center for Responsive Politics, http://www.opensecrets.org/outsidespending/index.php (accessed February 28, 2011).

erans. The NRSC responded to these DSCC attack ads by supporting Kirk's military record and voting record on veteran's bills.[42]

Alexi Giannoulias and Democratic Party organizations sought to make the election about an insider—a five-term member of Congress—versus an outsider. The Giannoulias campaign and the DSCC focused on Kirk's support for tax cuts for the rich and his opposition to extending unemployment benefits, Obama's economic stimulus package, the health care bill as well as Kirk's exaggerations of his service in the U.S. Naval Reserves. The DSCC ads generally attacked Mark Kirk as a Washington insider, an ironic choice of messaging given the source as a Washington, D.C. operation. The approach of attacking Kirk as the insider had limited credibility, however, since Kirk's reputation as an "independent" Republican was well-established. Giannoulias' attacks on this front also had a hollow feel since he was the nominee of the party-in-power and a friend of Obama. The Democratic national party ads hitting Kirk on issues and character, however, appear to have been more effective. The DSCC ran frequent ads noting that Kirk voted against extending unemployment benefits while voting for congressional pay raises.[43] The DSCC also attacked Kirk for supporting tax cuts for the rich and contributing to the massive federal budget deficit.[44]

The DSCC also ran ads featuring military veterans attacking Kirk for his distortions of his military record and his votes against combat bonuses and job training for veterans.[45] During the campaign, Kirk was forced to admit to a series of embellishments of his record in the U.S. Naval Reserve. He stated in speeches that he was a veteran of Operation Desert Storm in the first Gulf War when he had actually served stateside during the conflict; that he had won the Navy's award for intelligence officer of the year for his service during the Kosovo engagement in the 1990s when the award had actually been given to his unit for meritorious service; that he had come under fire while flying reconnaissance missions over Iraq in 2000 when records showed that no such attacks had occurred; that he had served in Operation Iraqi Freedom in 2003 when he had actually served stateside; and that he had been deployed to Afghanistan when he had only visited Afghanistan as a part of a congressional mission and not in his capacity as an officer in the Naval Reserve.[46] These attacks were particularly damaging to Kirk who touted his military expertise and frequently appeared in his ads wearing his Naval Unit cap. A *Chicago Tribune*/WGN poll in late September indicated that the attacks on Kirk's embellishments were effective, as 35 percent of voters identified Giannoulias as the more honest and trustworthy candidate while 30 percent identified Kirk.[47]

While political party and candidate money made the race competitive from a campaign spending standpoint, the spending by outside groups aligned with the parties tipped the scales decidedly in favor of Kirk (see Table 6.5). The various groups supporting Kirk and attacking Giannoulias spent $9,474,980. The groups supporting Giannoulias and attacking Kirk spent only $1,203,946. Giannoulias' groups were a mixture of groups that typically support Democratic candidates, including unions, environmental, pro-choice, and liberal ideological groups. Kirk was backed by doctors, businesses, the U.S. Chamber of Commerce, and especially Crossroads Grassroots Policy Strategies (GPS) and American Crossroads—two political organizations founded with help from former Bush administration official Karl Rove. These groups spent over $5.5 million attacking Giannoulias—all in the last month of the campaign.[48]

The two Crossroads groups ran similar ads attacking Giannoulias for loaning millions to convicted mob figures, for taking a multimillion dollar "fishy tax dodge" for losses when his family bank collapsed, and for "squandering money families saved for college" while overseeing the Illinois college savings program as the Illinois state treasurer. Though the American Crossroads and Crossroads GPS ads were identified as deceptive by one fact-checking organization, the ads were omnipresent on Illinois television during the final month of the campaign.[49] Further, the ads ran largely without countervailing messages from the Democrats.[50] Rather than rebut the charges of the ads, the Giannoulias campaign attacked the source of the ads, attacking Kirk as the beneficiary of secret cash by undisclosed corporate donors as a result of the *Citizens United* decision. In the second debate between the candidates in October of 2010, Giannoulias mentioned Karl Rove nine times as he criticized the Republicans for their campaign.[51] The Chamber of Commerce and Crossroads GPS were organized under the tax code as 501(c)4 social welfare groups, which meant that they did not have to disclose the source of their spending. It is doubtful that a "that's unfair" argument had as much impact as did ads directly attacking Giannoulias' character.

Overall, campaign spending and advertising favored Kirk. He raised and spent more than Giannoulias, while Giannoulias benefitted from relatively greater spending by political party committees. Spending by outside groups, however, was decidedly against Giannoulias with Republican-leaning groups spending

Table 6.5 Spending by Outside Groups in Illinois' Senate Race, 2010

Republican-leaning Outside Groups	Supported Kirk	Opposed Giannoulias	Total
Crossroads Grassroots Policy Strategies		$4,479,605	$4,479,605
U.S. Chamber of Commerce			$1,682,856
American Crossroads		$1,127,231	$1,127,231
New Prosperity Foundation	$427,017	$579,290	$1,006,307
American Action Network		$659,909	$659,909
American Society of Anesthesiologists	$152,300		$152,300
American Hospital Association	$123,500		$123,500
Illinois Chamber of Commerce	$107,500		$107,500
American College of Surgeons Prof Association	$90,030		$90,030
Trust in Small Business	$23,236		$23,236
Revere America	$10,012		$10,012
National Right to Life		$9,994	$9,994
Illinois Right to Life	$2,500		$2,500
Total	**$936,095**	**$6,856,029**	**$9,474,980**

Democratic-leaning Outside Groups	Supported Giannoulias	Opposed Kirk	Total
AFL-CIO	$4,613	$1,742	$6,355
America's Voice	$9,433		$9,433
American Association for Justice	$517		$517
American Federation of Teachers	$89,550	$21,789	$111,339
Human Rights Campaign	$85		$85
Laborers Union	$8,399		$8,399
League of Conservation Voters Action Fund		$74,000	$74,000
League of Conservation Voters, Inc.	$126,328		$126,328
Moveon.org	$2,181	$62,232	$64,413
NARAL Pro-Choice America	$278		$556
National Association of Letter Carriers	$8,913		$8,913
National Education Association	$60,216		$60,216
People for the American Way	$937		$937
Sierra Club	$10		$10
The Advocacy Fund	$28,992	$11,325	$40,317
Working for Us PAC		$692,128	$692,128
Total	**$340,452**	**$863,494**	**$1,203,946**

Source: Center for Responsive Government, http://www.opensecrets.org/outsidespending/index. php (accessed February 28, 2011).

millions on ads in the final month of the campaign. Most of the campaign ads during the final month were attack ads, particularly those by the non-candidate groups. Most of the money spent by the candidates on campaign ads were positive ads that featured their policy strengths, or comparative ads that emphasized candidate strengths while attacking the other's record. The ads by party committees and outside groups, however, were overwhelmingly negative ads attacking the personal character of the candidates.[52]

Senate campaigns typically are candidate-centered with the media and voters looking at the candidate and his or her character as much as they do policies. The candidates' character, and specifically, their experience, integrity, and trustworthiness became central features of both candidates' campaign advertisements and especially in advertising aired by outside groups like the American Crossroads, Crossroads GPS, and the Chamber of Commerce. The impact of character ads can be seen in the timing of ads and polling during the campaign. Kirk and NRSC ads started running in February and March of 2010 attacking Giannoulias' role as senior loan officer in his family's Broadway Bank. Giannoulias' polling numbers hit their nadir in April of 2010 when Broadway Bank failed. Giannoulias' support was relatively soft among Democrats and independent voters in various polls, compared to Kirk who retained relatively strong support from Republicans. Kirk's support in polls started to slide a bit in August and September when Democrats started running ads hitting Kirk for his exaggerations of his military record. Kirk, however, rebounded as the RNSC started running ads defending Kirk's record and support for the military and Kirk took the strategy of confessing to "having misspoken." Polls over the last two months of the campaign indicated a race too close to call (see Figure 6.1).

It appears that both candidates' vulnerabilities softened their support, as voters had negative views of both candidates. As noted above, a *WGN/Chicago Tribune* poll from October showed that neither candidate was particularly trustworthy.[53] The same *Tribune* poll found that 23 percent of respondents had a favorable view of Kirk compared to 32 percent with an unfavorable view. Giannoulias was viewed favorably by 31 percent of respondents and unfavorably by 31 percent. These feelings were also clear on Election Day as neither candidate would muster a majority of the general election vote. Kirk won the race with 48.2 percent of the vote compared to Giannoulias' 46.3 percent. If anything, Kirk's vote totals were surprising given the net favorability rating of –9 percent he had in the October poll compared to Giannoulias.

Analysis of the Vote

The 2010 elections illustrate the complexities of the political nature of Illinois as well as macro- and micro-political factors quite nicely. Republicans won the U.S. Senate seat and two other statewide offices while Democrats won the governor's race and two other state-wide offices. The Republican gubernatorial candidate Bill Brady was a social conservative while the Senate candidate Mark Kirk was a social moderate. The headline candidates on the Democratic ticket were

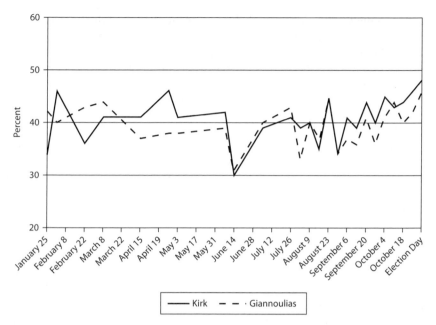

Figure 6.1 Senate Candidate Support in Illinois' Senate Campaign, 2010.
Source: All polls are of registered voters. Figures are based on polls sponsored by *The Chicago Tribune*, CNN/Time; FOX News/POR-Rasmussen, Public Policy Polling, R2000/ Daily Kos, Rasmussen Reports, Suffolk University, Southern Illinois University, and WeAskAmerica. Data were obtained from Real Clear Politics, http://www.realclear-politics.com/epolls/2010/senate/il/illinois_senate_giannoulias_vs_kirk-1092.html#polls (retrieved January 6, 2011).

economic and social liberals. In the Senate race, Republican Mark Kirk beat Democrat Alexi Giannoulias by 59,220 votes, for a margin of victory of about 1.5 percent of all votes cast in the Senate election.[54] In the governor's race, Democrat Pat Quinn beat Republican Bill Brady by 31,834 votes for a winning margin of less than eight tenths of one percent of all votes cast. There was a 91,054 vote swing in the two races—indicating that a small but critical segment voters cast ballots differently in the two races.[55] Brady's socially conservative positions appear to have hurt him in the vote rich counties around Chicago while helping him in the vote thin rural counties.

Giannoulias won Chicago and Cook County by 456,722 votes and the counties around East St. Louis by a combined 513 votes. Kirk won the remaining 98 counties by a margin of 516,455 votes. The Democratic gubernatorial candidate ran slightly ahead of Giannoulias in Cook County and the surrounding collar counties with 16,946 more votes than Giannoulias. Kirk ran ahead of Brady in Cook County and the five most populous collar counties by a margin of 71,098 votes. Brady ran ahead of Kirk in 45 of 54 of the most rural counties, but gained only 5,310 more votes than Kirk in these areas. The two Republican candidates were divided by only 468 votes in the remaining 42 counties. Cook County and the surrounding suburbs divide along economic lines, but generally are more socially moderate than the rural central and the southern regions of the state. While we cannot know the reasoning of voters who split their ballots using aggregate, county-level vote returns, the distribution does suggest that the different social positions of the Republican candidates. Of course, social issues were not the only factor that affected voters' decisions. There also are several other factors that could account for the difference including the effects of candidate personality and campaign effects that affect voter turnout and vote choice.

It should be noted that Third Party candidates also had differential affects on the races. First, the Green and Libertarian candidates received 69,724 more votes in the Senate race than did the Green and Libertarian candidates in the Governor's race—despite the fact that 26,409 more people voted in the governor's race. This may reflect the relative unpopularity of both the Democratic and Republican Senate candidates. Interestingly, the Libertarian Senate candidate drew more votes than the Libertarian gubernatorial candidate—hurting Kirk more than Brady. The Green candidate in the Senate race attracted 17,158 more votes than the Green candidate in the governor's race—hurting Giannoulias more than Quinn but not enough to have changed the outcome even if we assume the Democrat would have received those votes in absence of a Green Party candidate. So the effects of these third party candidates could not explain why Kirk won and Brady lost (or that Quinn won and Giannoulias lost). The candidate who probably did have some effect on the gubernatorial race but not the Senate race was independent candidate Scott Lee Cohen. Cohen won the Democratic primary for Lt. Governor, but withdrew from that contest after revelations that he had been arrested for domestic abuse.[56] Cohen later decided to run as an independent candidate in the Governor's race. Cohen, however, appears to have taken votes from both candidates. Cohen received almost identical shares of the vote in counties won by Republicans as he did in counties won by Democrats.[57] Because there were almost 50 percent more votes cast in counties Republicans won, Cohen pulled a larger number of votes in Republican counties (80,876) than in Democratic counties (54,829). Thus, it is possible that Cohen hurt Republican Brady more than Democrat Pat Qinn. It would explain why Brady trailed Kirk in more counties and gained 65,313 fewer votes than Kirk overall, despite the Libertarian candidate doing better in the senate race than in the governor's race.

Conclusions

After Barak Obama's landslide victory in 2008, no one really thought that his vacancy in the Senate would result in Republicans picking up that seat in the 2010 midterm elections. National tides were running strongly in favor of Democrats in 2008. Illinois leaned strongly Democratic and Obama had just won the state with more than 62 percent of the presidential vote. Republicans lacked depth in their pool of quality candidates while the Democratic pool was deep. Those things changed within a month of Election Day 2008. The incumbent governor tried to exchange appointment to the seat for his own gain, resulting in an appointee who could not be expected to win the election, a shrinking of the Democratic field as quality candidates shied away from the controversial seat, and the Democrats nominated a candidate with some serious baggage. Alexi Giannoulias went from financial wizard, Obama friend, and state treasurer to being "a mob banker" whose family bank closed under the weight of home mortgage defaults, Illinois state investments lost value in the financial crisis of 2008 and 2009. An extraordinary investment by Republican leaning groups, most notably the Chamber of Commerce, Crossroads America, and Crossroads GPS exploited Giannoulias' vulnerabilities in a massive advertising barrage. Not even personal campaigning by Barak Obama could save the seat from Republicans in 2010. Yet, the race remained competitive throughout. The Republicans nominated a candidate who would be exposed by Democrats as a serial resume embellisher who was trusted even less than the maligned Democrat. Neither candidate won a majority of the vote. While not changing the outcome, Green and Libertarian Party candidates gained more votes than normal as they provided dissatisfied voters an alternative to the two major parties.

Tides come and go. National and state tides benefitted Democrats in 2006 and 2008 but flowed to the advantage of Republicans in 2010. The effects of those tides can be stemmed or exploited. The Illinois Senate race of 2010 indicate that candidate character, money, and messaging matter in Senate elections. A different Democratic nominee with a reputation for integrity, a reform agenda, and the advantages of incumbency may well have held the seat for the Democrats. A corrupt governor's arrest, impeachment, and conviction robbed Democrats of their chance to hold the seat. Still, Republicans *almost* missed their golden opportunity by nominating their own flawed candidate, but they had few options in a state where the talent pool was thinned by a previous round of corruption scandals and convictions. H. L. Menken may have had Illinois in mind when he said, "democracy is the theory that the common people know what they want, and deserve to get it good and hard." Perhaps it is a reflection on the state of politics in America that Illinois is the "most average" state in the Union.

Notes

1. Illinois Department of Employment Security, "Local Area Unemployment Statistics," December 2010, http://www.ides.state.il.us/ (accessed January 28, 2011).
2. Republican Governor George Ryan opted not to run for reelection in 2002 while facing a federal investigation. Ryan, his chief of staff, and 76 others were convicted or plead guilty to various charges between 2003 and 2006.
3. Blagojevich has yet to be convicted on those specific charges. At the time of this chapter, Rod Blagojevich is awaiting retrial on various charges relating to public corruption.
4. "How Average is Your State," *Associated Press*, http://hosted.ap.org/specials/interactives/wdc/average_state/index.html?SITE=AP (accessed March 17, 2011).
5. "U.S. Census Bureau Delivers Illinois' 2010 Census Population Totals, Including First Look at Race and Hispanic Origin Data for Legislative Redistricting," U.S.

Census Bureau, http://www.census.gov/newsroom/releases/archives/2010_census/cb11-cn31.html

6. Data on county level income come from the U.S. Census Bureau's American Community Survey, 2010, www.quickfacts.census.gov/gfd/states/17000.html (accessed March 17, 2011).

7. "Illinois: Median Household Income, by State and Race/Ethnicity, 2006–2008," U.S. Census Bureau, http://www.statehealthfacts.org/profileind.jsp?rep=35&cat=15&rgn=15 (accessed February 26, 2011); and "U.S. Census Bureau Delivers Illinois' 2010 Census Population Totals."

8. Michael Tarm and Mike Robinson, "Rod Blagojevich trial: Infamous 'golden' comment on display." *Associated Press*, June 30, 2010.

9. http://www.thesmokinggun.com/documents/crime/obama-senate-seat-sale (accessed January 25, 2011).

10. Ibid.

11. "Feds: Governor tried to 'auction' Obama's seat," MSNBC.com, December 9, 2008, http://www.msnbc.msn.com/id/28139155/ns/politics/ (accessed February 14, 2011).

12. Although Blagojevich was convicted on one of 24 federal charges in August of 2010, the scandal continued because the federal prosecutor announced they would seek a second trial. Blagojevich was convicted of lying to the FBI while the jury deadlocked on the remaining 23 counts, which included racketeering conspiracy, wire fraud, extortion, extortion conspiracy, attempted extortion, and lying to federal agents pertaining to his efforts to sell the appointment to Obama's Senate seat. Other charges included trying to extort owners of the *Chicago Tribune*, extorting the director of a Children's Hospital for a $50,000 campaign contribution in return for releasing state funds, and seeking graft in the form of campaign contributions from companies and individuals who received state contracts or appointments to state jobs.

13. The one Democratic candidate mentioned in federal papers who was not likely affected by the scandal was Lisa Madigan, who Blagojevich was critical of and wanted to get rid of as a potential political rival.

14. *Public Policy Polling*, Jan. 28 2010, http://www.publicpolicypolling.com/pdf/PPP_Release_Ill_128.pdf (accessed January 25, 2011).

15. No perjury charges were filed, and the Senate Ethics Committee suspended the investigation for lack of evidence.

16. "IL US Senate - D Primary," http://www.ourcampaigns.com/RaceDetail.html?RaceID=165489 (accessed February 30, 2011).

17. Illinois State Board of Elections, http://www.elections.il.gov/ (accessed January 17, 2011).

18. http://www.treasurer.il.gov/news/press-releases/2007/PR8aJan2007.htm (accessed November 8, 2010).

19. "About Alexi," http://www.alexiforillinois.com (accessed January 4, 2011).

20. Rick Pearson, "Tribune poll: Giannoulias, Kirk locked in tight U.S. Senate race," *Chicago Tribune*, October 1, 2010, http://newsblogs.chicagotribune.com/clout_st/2010/10/tribune-poll-giannoulias-kirk-locked-in-tight-us-senate-race.html (accessed January 4 2011).

21. "FDIC: Broadway Bank Failed Because of Real Estate Loans, Bad Management," MyFoxChicago.com, http://www.myfoxchicago.com/dpp/news/metro/fdic-broadway-bank-real-estate-loans-report-alexi-giannoulias-20101116 (accessed February 26, 2011).

22. Rick Pearson, "Illinois political floodgates open after Madigan passes on governor, Senate bids," *Chicago Tribune*, July 9, 2009, http://newsblogs.chicagotribune.com/clout_st/2009/07/illinois-political-floodgates-open-after-madigan-passes-on-governor-senate-bids.html (accessed March 8, 2011).

23. Ibid.

24. "IL US Senate - R Primary," http://www.ourcampaigns.com/RaceDetail.html?Race ID=504417 (accessed February 24, 2011).
25. "2010 U.S. House Votes," American Conservative Union, http://www.conserva-tive.org/ratings/ratingsarchive/2010/2010HouseRatings.htm#IL (accessed March 17, 2011).
26. "Federal Budget," http://www.alexiforillinois.com/issues/federalbudget (accessed January 26, 2011).
27. "Supporting American Workers," http://www.alexiforillinois.com/issues/support-ing-american-workers (accessed January 25, 2011).
28. http: //www.alexiforillinois.com (accessed January 4, 2011).
29. Ibid. Both Kirk and Giannoulias expressed strong support for Israel and its right to defend itself.
30. Ibid.
31. http://www.kirkforsenate.com/ (accessed February 15, 2011).
32. Christopher Wills, "Kirk talks trade, Giannoulias talks environment," *Bloom-ington-Normal Pantagraph*,August 30, 2010, http://www.pantagraph.com/news/state-and-regional/illinois/article_853f5bcc-b4a5-11df-ad02-001cc4c03286.html (accessed March 17, 2011).
33. Wayne Steger, "Running Scared from the Hill and at Home," in *Cases in Congres-sional Campaigns: Incumbents Playing Defense*, eds. Randall E. Adkins and David A. Dulio (New York: Routledge, 2010), pp. 60–74.
34. Gary C. Jacobson, *The Politics of Congressional Elections*, 3rd ed. (New York: Harper-Collins, 1992); Paul Herrnson, *Congressional Elections: Campaigning at Home and in Washington*, 2nd ed. (Washington D.C.: CQ Press, 1997).
35. "IL US Senate - D Primary."
36. Christopher Weber, Democrats Hope High Voter Turnout Will Boost Odds in Some Races," *Politics Daily*, http://www.politicsdaily.com/2010/11/01/democrats-hope-high-voter-turnout-will-boost-odds-in-some-races/ (accessed March 1, 2011).
37. Giannoulias had defeated Madigan's preferred candidate in the 2006 Democratic primary for state treasurer. The more important consideration, however, was that Madigan needed to retain the governorship for the Democratic Party in order to control congressional and state redistricting after the 2010 Census.
38. The Democratic candidates were separated by only 2,087 votes in Cook County, the county with the greatest Democratic Party organizational presence and effort.
39. "In Attack Ad, Republicans Tie Illinois Dem Candidate to Mob," FoxNews.com, http://www.foxnews.com/politics/2010/02/04/attack-ad-republicans-tie-illinois-dem-candidate-mob/ (accessed February 28, 2011).
40. "Kirk Launches New Ad Highlighting His Mainstream Illinois Values," NRSC, http://www.nrsc.org/kirk-launches-new-ad-highlighting-his-mainstream-illinois-values (accessed February 18, 2011).
41. Ibid.
42. "Response To DSCC's Illinois Ad Attacking Mark Kirk's Military Service," NRSC, http://www.nrsc.org/response-to-dsccs-illinois-ad-attacking-mark-kirks-military-service (accessed February 28, 2011).
43. Video can be seen at: http://www.realclearpolitics.com/articles/2010/09/22/dscc_attacks_kirk_on_jobs_107266.html (accessed February 25,2011).
44. Video can be seen at: http://www.realclearpolitics.com/video/2010/10/27/il-sen_dscc_ad_who_did_mark_kirk_stand_up_for_not_us.html (accessed February 28, 2011).
45. Video can be seen at: http://tpmdc.talkingpointsmemo.com/2010/10/dscc-ad-mark-kirk-didnt-tell-the-truth-about-his-military-record-video.php (accessed January 4, 2011).
46. Todd Lighty, John Chase, and Rick Pearson, "Kirk accepts responsibility for series of 'mistakes' on military resume," *Chicago Tribune*, June 4, 2010, http://newsblogs.

chicagotribune.com/clout_st/2010/06/kirk-accepts-responsibility-for-series-of-mistakes-on-military-resume.html (accessed February 25, 2011).

47. Bruce Drake, "Illinois Senate Race Turning on 'Who Do You Trust (Less)?'" PoliticsDaily.com, http://www.politicsdaily.com/2010/10/02/illinois-senate-race-turning-on-who-do-you-trust-less/ (accessed February 23, 2011).

48. Adam Doster, "American Crossroads Loves Kirk," ProgressIllinois.com, http://www.progressillinois.com/quick-hits/content/2010/10/05/american-crossroads-loves-kirk (accessed February 20, 2011).

49. The *Chicago Tribune* and *Political Correction.org* found that Giannoulias was in law school rather than at the bank when the loans were made to convicted mobsters; that the tax deductions for the losses were legitimate; and that Oppenheimer Fund decisions rather than Giannoulias were responsible for the losses in the Bright Start college fund. For a summary, see, "Crossroads GPS Stretches The Truth, Outright Lies To Smear Giannoulias," at http://politicalcorrection.org/adcheck/201010250032 (accessed March 1, 2011).

50. Ibid.

51. Lynn Sweet, Kirk, Giannoulias Spar in Illinois Senate Debate, but No Knockout Blows," PoliticsDaily.com, http://www.politicsdaily.com/2010/10/20/kirk-giannoulias-spar-in-illinois-senate-debate-but-no-knockou/ (accessed March 2, 2011).

52. A sample of attack ads on both sides include: "Alexi Giannoulias: He'd Make Tony Soprano Proud," https://www.youtube.com/watch?v=VP8ruoFSxoY (NRSC ad); "Alexi Giannoulias: Not Responsible and Not Ready," https://www.youtube.com/watch?v=eocJHtBVLyI (Illinois Republican Party ad); "Alexi Giannoulias, Broadway Bank, Democrat, Crook," https://www.youtube.com/watch?v=4YHwXf_-tm8 (Illinois Republican Party); "Illinois 'Driver Error' TV30," http://www.youtube.com/watch?v=M-iBXHJ1L-8&feature=player_embedded#at=17 (Crossroads GPS and American Crossroads); "The Problem-Alexi Giannoulias," https://www.youtube.com/watch?v=kvQgDm4VkXo (Committee for Truth in Politics); "The Problem is Mark Kirk," https://www.youtube.com/watch?v=OGy2heAZlyc (DSCC ad); "Mark Kirk: Beholden to Special Interests," https://www.youtube.com/watch?v=tnVBe2_ODfw (Giannoulias campaign); and "Mark Kirk, Connect the Dots," https://www.youtube.com/watch?v=R2QDwfPTxLw (MoveOn.org).

53. Rick Pearson, "Tribune poll: Giannoulias, Kirk locked in tight U.S. Senate race," *Chicago Tribune*, October 1, 2010, http://newsblogs.chicagotribune.com/clout_st/2010/10/tribune-poll-giannoulias-kirk-locked-in-tight-us-senate-race.html (accessed January 4, 2011).

54. All vote calculations are based on the official results according to the Illinois State Board of Elections, http://www.elections.il.gov/ (accessed January 25, 2011).

55. There were 26,409 more votes cast in the governor's race than in the Senate race, indicating that a net of at least 60,000 voters split their ballots between the two races.

56. Cohen was alleged to have held a knife to his ex-girlfriend's throat during a dispute. It was later revealed that his ex-girlfriend had once been arrested for prostitution. Cohen's ex-wife had accused him in divorce papers of using anabolic steroids, having fits of rage and of trying to force him on her sexually. Chicago Sun Times. Feb. 7, 2010. http://blogs.suntimes.com/sweet/2010/02/scott_lee_cohen_not_fit_to_ser.html, Retrieved on Jan. 6, 2011.

57. Democratic counties are those won by the Democratic senate and gubernatorial candidates, while Republican counties are those won by Republicans in both races. No counties split these races. Overall, about 40 percent of the votes cast in the governor's race were cast in Democratic counties while almost 60 percent of votes cast were in Republican won counties.

7   Bass vs. Kuster in New Hampshire's Second Congressional District

Riding the Wave to a Comeback

Dante J. Scala and Andrew E. Smith

While 2010 was lauded as the third straight "change" election in American politics, in New Hampshire's 2nd Congressional District, the agent of change was unclear. The two-term incumbent, Democrat Paul Hodes, left the seat open in pursuit of the U.S. Senate. The Democratic nominee in the 2nd District, Ann McLane Kuster, faced the challenge of presenting herself as someone who could bring about the kind of change the voters wanted, while effectively representing the party in power in Washington. Her Republican opponent, Charlie Bass, had the burden of being a familiar face to voters after serving as the district's representative for a dozen years before being defeated by Hodes in 2006. The district, in short, was a test case as to whether the wave of 2010 was anti-incumbent, or simply anti-Democrat.[1]

Several dynamics in this race made this an open question. After easily defeating a well-funded opponent in a mid-September primary, Kuster's campaign possessed a formidable array of resources, including strong fundraising. The Democrat also had a campaign operation that was well regarded by allies and opponents alike, along with the support of the national party. Bass, in contrast, lagged in fundraising and failed to win 50 percent of the vote in a primary against poorly-funded opponents. Last but not least, the political geography of this district that borders Vermont tilted significantly in the Democrat's direction. In the final weeks, fellow partisans and neutral observers alike saw Kuster as the party's best chance to salvage a victory in a difficult cycle. On Election Night, however, any organizational or geographical advantages Kuster may have possessed were outweighed by the broader dynamics in play in this "wave" election. Charlie Bass may have been the quasi-incumbent in the race, but more importantly in 2010, he was the Republican.

New Hampshire's 2nd District

The 2nd Congressional District encompasses the western and northern two-thirds of New Hampshire. This expansive area borders Vermont to the west, Quebec to the north, and Massachusetts to the south. With such a large geographic area, the 2nd District is quite heterogeneous on several levels. It includes the state's second largest city, Nashua, as well as the capital city of Concord and the growing suburbs of greater Boston such as Salem, Windham, and Pelham. About half of the district is rural, including college towns such as Keene (home of Keene State College), Hanover (where Dartmouth College is located) and Plymouth (home to Plymouth State University); former mill towns such as Lebanon, Berlin, Claremont, and Franklin; and a host of small to very small communities. The 2nd District includes the beautiful tourist regions of the White Mountains, the Great North Woods, and Mount Monadnock, perhaps the most frequently climbed mountain in the world. Major industries include BAE Systems, the British aerospace and military manufacturer in Nashua; Dartmouth-Hitchcock Medical Center and related medical technology businesses in Hanover and Lebanon; and the state government in Concord.

The 2nd District has grown in size through redistricting. In recent decades, the population of New Hampshire has become increasingly concentrated in the southeastern corner of the state, necessitating a geographic downsizing of the 1st Congressional District located in that part of New Hampshire. While heterogeneous in geography, the people of the 2nd district are rather homogeneous. They are overwhelmingly white (95 percent), relatively older (the median age is 40), highly educated (33 percent of adults 25 and older have a bachelor's degree or higher), and relatively affluent (the median household income was $61,544, and only 7.4 percent of all people were in poverty in 2009).[2] Interestingly, while 95 percent of district residents were born in the United States, less than half of all adults were born in New Hampshire.[3]

The Politics of the 2nd District

Republican strength in the 2nd District belies the old trope that the migration of Massachusetts voters across New Hampshire's southern border moved the Granite State in a Democratic direction. Nowadays, a key cache of Republican voters live in the district's suburban towns along the Interstate 93 corridor on the Massachusetts border, in places such as Atkinson, Litchfield, Pelham, Salem, and Windham. These border towns, with their distinctive culture and economy, almost form a district within the district.[4] Democrats often refer to this part of the district as the "Bermuda Triangle"; it is a place where Democratic candidates disappear. This growing pool of voters presents a challenge to candidates. While they live in New Hampshire, their jobs often take them on lengthy commutes beyond the state's borders, and tend to get their news from media outlets outside the state. It is relatively difficult to communicate with voters along the border, and much more expensive, in part because they reside within the reach of the Boston television media market, and in part because their lengthy commutes mean less time spent talking with neighbors in their local communities. In addition, the decline in circulation of local newspapers make earned media less valuable; many of those voters who read a newspaper might well pick up the *Boston Globe*, rather than the *Nashua Telegraph*.[5]

North and west of this cluster of border towns are areas much friendlier to Democrats. The state capitol of Concord, about half an hour north from the

New Hampshire border, has a decided Democratic tilt. In addition, counties bordering Vermont, such as Cheshire and Grafton, contain college towns where Keene State College (Keene) and Dartmouth College (Hanover) are located. Also around Dartmouth, increasing numbers of highly educated professionals work at institutions such as the Dartmouth-Hitchcock Medical Center and related medical technology companies. Moreover, large numbers of wealthy easterners, who also tend to support Democrats, have long had summer and retirement homes in the area. On the other hand, the former paper mill towns of Berlin and Gorham in the state's North Woods, once strongly Democratic working-class areas, have lost influence as their populations have dwindled.

As a whole, New Hampshire's 2nd District has been trending Democratic for decades, consistently voting more strongly for the Democratic candidate for President since 1992 than has New Hampshire's 1st District.[6] Indeed, the *Cook Political Report*, headed by political analyst and election handicapper Charlie Cook, lists the 2nd District's Partisan Voter Index (PVI) as D+2. Despite the Democratic trend, Republican Charlie Bass held the 2nd District's seat for most of the past two decades, after defeating freshman Democrat Dick Swett in 1994, in another GOP wave year when the Republicans regained control of the U.S. House of Representatives for the first time in four decades. In succeeding cycles, Bass consolidated his hold on the district, winning reelection by ever increasing margins, from 7 percentage points in 1996 to 20 percentage points in 2004 during a period when Democratic presidential candidates carried the district by an average of 8 percentage points. In large part due to his pro-choice position on abortion, Bass had cultivated a reputation as a moderate Republican, the only type of Republican who could hold a district such as this.

Party identification in the district also trended Democratic during the 1990s. At the turn of the century, Republicans held a slight lead of 41 percent to 38 percent in party identification, but this soon eroded as the wars in Iraq and Afghanistan dragged on (see Figure 7.1). The breaking point for Bass came in 2006, however. Twelve years earlier, he entered the House as part of the new Republican majority; he departed the House in another "sea change" election that restored Democrats to the majority. During the 2006 election cycle, Democrats held, on average, a 10-point advantage (46 percent to 36 percent) in party identification over Republicans. Bass' communications director, Scott Tranchemontagne, recalled what Bass had told him about the sour atmosphere in the district that election season. When the candidate went to a campaign event, past Republican supporters approached him, "and they'd be kind of sheepish or they'd be looking down, and they'd say, 'Hey Charlie, great to see you, good luck.'" The body language of those supporters told another story: "We love you as a guy, but we may not be voting for you."[7]

The 2006 election resulted in New Hampshire Democrats winning both U.S. House seats, the governorship, control of both the State House and Senate, and four of the five executive council seats. This marked the first time since 1874 that Democrats held the governorship and both houses of the legislature. Even as the election slipped away from him, Bass' personal support among voters of

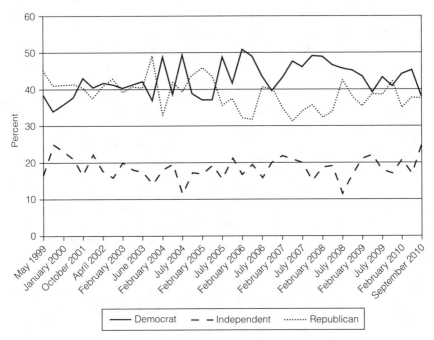

Figure 7.1 Party Identification in New Hampshire's 2nd Congressional District, May 1999–September 2010.
Source: UNH Survey Center polls, various dates.

his district remained relatively strong. His net favorability rating a month before the election was a healthy +21 percent, with 48 percent of district residents saying they had a favorable opinion of him. Bass' problem was not that voters soured on him in 2006, it was that they soured on Republicans as a whole. In fact, Bass' defeat appeared to signal the end of an endangered species in American politics: the New England Republican. After Election Night in 2006, there was only one New England Republican left in the House of Representatives, Christopher Shays of Connecticut, who went on to lose his seat in the subsequent "wave" election of 2008.

Party identification, however, is not a stable indicator and does fluctuate with events. In 2008, Barack Obama carried the district with 56 percent of the vote, and Paul Hodes easily won a second term in Congress. The very next year, however, there was a slight falling off in Democratic identification among the district's voters, and a small increase in Republican identification. By September 2010, partisan identification was even at 38 percent—a parity that was striking, given the clear Democratic tilt of the district. On the ground, Bass could tell the difference. As told by his communications director, Scott Tranchemontagne:

> He said everybody's body language was so different. They were glad to see him again. They were thrilled that he was running again. They went out of their way to tell him that they're behind him 100 percent. They asked him

how they could help. He said it was just like a complete 180 [from 2006]. That's what a change in environment can do for you, because he was the same guy, the exact same guy, with the exact same record, as he was in 2006.[8]

The Republican Primary: Bass Resurfaces

Upon announcing his entrance into the race for his old seat in February 2010, Bass commented on members of the so-called "Tea Party," a loose affiliation of conservatives who had taken on mainstream Republicans in a number of GOP primaries nationwide. "I love them," he said. "God bless every single one of them. Their agenda is exactly the same as mine."[9] Bass' expression of devotion prompted the editorial board of the *Concord Monitor* to scoff:

> One of the basic rules of Republican politics is "run to the right" in the primary and "move to the middle" for the general election. But Charlie Bass, our Charlie Bass, a tea-partier? You gotta be kidding ... It's impossible to characterize Tea Party members accurately, since the ad hoc party has no real platform, at least one all its incarnations agree with. Many of its members appear to believe, however, that the country is going to Hell in a handbasket and some sort of revolution is called for. Does Charlie? Who knows? Bass was once a moderate Republican in the Walter Peterson, Susan McLane mold, but what is Charlie now?[10]

Bass entered the race for the Republican nomination for his old seat with name recognition far superior to his main rivals, former talk show host Jennifer Horn and former State Representative Bob Guida. It was Bass' well-known reputation as a moderate "Main Street" Republican, however, which was viewed as a potential stumbling block to his comeback.

By 2010, the Democratic waves of 2006 and 2008 were long since receded and a Republican wave was breaking on New Hampshire. Curiously, Bass was less popular in 2010 than he was in 2006. By fall of 2010, his favorability rating dropped to 36 percent and his net favorability rating stood at a very weak +2 percent (see Figure 7.2). A major reason for the decline from 2006 to 2010 was that the very thing that made Bass a successful Republican in a marginally Democratic district—that he was perceived as a moderate to liberal Republican—hurt him in a year that favored more conservative Republican candidates. From fall of 2006 to the fall of 2010, Bass' net favorability dropped by more than half among Republicans (from +57 percent to +27) and among conservatives (from +49 percent to +20).

During his time in office, Bass was a pro-choice Republican who sometimes cast votes against the majority of his party on issues such as the ban on same-sex marriages, and drilling in the Arctic National Wildlife Refuge. His tendency to vote against his party increased as he served longer in the House and resulted in relatively low party unity scores. He also often voted against President Bush's

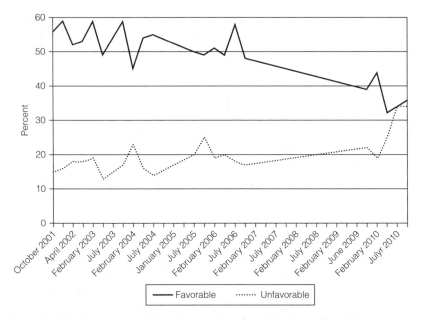

Figure 7.2 Charlie Bass Favorability Ratings, October 2001–September 2010.
Source: UNH Survey Center polls, various dates.

position on issues, as seen in low presidential support scores (see Table 7.1). A similar pattern can be seen in ratings from the American Conservative Union (ACU) and Americans for Democratic Action (ADA). In 2006, for example, the ACU issued Bass a score of 56, down from 80 in 2002; ADA scored him at 40, up from 20 in 2003. In his time out of office, Bass headed up the Republican Main Street Partnership, a moderate Republican lobbying group in Washington. Bass' brand of Republicanism was once quite common in New Hampshire, and indeed across New England, including Jeb Bradley, Bass' former colleague from New Hampshire's 1st District (who also lost in 2006), Chris Shays from Connecticut's 4th District (who lost in 2008), U.S. Senators Olympia Snowe and Susan Collins (ME), Scott Brown (MA), and Jim Jeffords (VT) who left the GOP in 2001. Bass seemed a good fit for a New Hampshire Republican electorate that is moderate to liberal on social issues, yet fiscally conservative. A clear indicator of how New Hampshire Republicans are moderate on social issues was seen during the 2008 Republican presidential primary; voters were more pro-choice than were Americans as a whole.[11]

Overall, 2010 was a year in which Republicans, nationwide and in New Hampshire, did not seem satisfied with the status quo in their party. As Bass contended for the nomination, a larger battle erupted statewide, as social conservative Ovide Lamontagne surged forward to challenge establishment favorite Kelly Ayotte for the GOP nomination to the U.S. Senate. Similarly, in Delaware, longtime moderate Republican Mike Castle was upended in his primary

Table 7.1 Congressional Vote Scores for Charlie Bass, 1995–2006

Year	American Conservative Union	Americans for Democratic Action	Party Unity	Presidential Support
2006	56%	40%	82%	72%
2005	58%	25%	87%	67%
2004	56%	45%	85%	68%
2003	64%	20%	91%	78%
2002	80%	15%	85%	82%
2001	60%	25%	85%	79%
2000	75%	20%	85%	34%
1999	68%	20%	83%	27%
1998	63%	10%	78%	33%
1997	80%	15%	87%	39%
1996	100%	0%	91%	34%
1995	72%	15%	90%	25%

Source: CQ's *Politics in America* (Washington, DC: Congressional Quarterly, Inc., 2010 and 2000); The American Conservative Union (http://www.conservative.org); Americans for Democratic Action (http://www.adaction.org); and Congressional Quarterly's vote studies (2009: http://innovation.cqpolitics.com/media/vote_study_2009; and 2010: http://innovation.cq.com/media/vote_study_2010).

by a conservative challenger with national Tea Party support. Given Bass' reputation as a moderate, the former incumbent seemed vulnerable to an upset by a conservative competitor, but an especially dangerous challenger never appeared.

While the media portrayed Bass as a moderate trying to ingratiate himself with the Tea Party, the Bass campaign was confident that, in fact, the candidate was in sync with these conservatives on the fiscal issues that mattered most to them. In its advertising during the primary, the campaign stressed Bass as a tax-fighting fiscal conservative. According to Tranchemontagne:

> So we always felt that we would get the so-called … Tea Party support by really hammering this idea that Charlie is the strong fiscal conservative that they are looking for … I always felt that their number one focus was stopping this out-of-control spending and reversing the growth of government. And for those two issues, we had a very strong message for Charlie to tell.[12]

In part, this happened because neither of Bass' challengers was able to gain a monopoly on the opposition to his candidacy. The best known Republican to challenge Bass was the 2008 Republican nominee for the 2nd District seat, Jennifer Horn, a conservative radio host from Nashua. Horn's 2008 campaign, her first run for office, was a mild success. She defeated a mediocre field of candidates, including a state senator, to win the nomination. She was touted by some as the Granite State version of Sarah Palin, but ultimately carried less than 45 percent of the vote against incumbent Democrat Paul Hodes in another strong year for Democrats. Two years later, despite her 2008 run, Horn was still largely unknown in the 2nd District. In the last poll before the September 14 primary, only 21 percent of 2nd District residents held a favorable opinion of Horn; 11 percent had an unfavorable opinion of her, while the remaining two-thirds did not know enough about her to say or were neutral. The third significant Republican candidate, conservative State Representative Bob Guida, hailed from a small town in Grafton County and was even less known than Horn. Moreover, neither of Bass' challengers spent more than $200,000 in their bid for the nomination.

Faced with two weak opponents and seeing favorable polling data, the Bass campaign felt it was in a "pretty comfortable position" and conserved resources accordingly.[13] Through the primary, the campaign only spent half a million dollars for the year to date. This left some in the media with the perception that Bass was "cruising" and taking the race for granted.[14] The media's perceptions were reinforced by Bass' performance on the night of the primary. The former House member defeated Horn by fewer than 10 percentage points, 42 percent to 35 percent; Guida, despite poor name recognition and little funding, won 17 percent of the vote. Bass' campaign made a decision during the run-up to the primary, said Tranchemontagne, to deploy staff with an eye toward the general election campaign, which was expected to be difficult, given the nature of the district and the strength of either of the Democratic contenders, Ann McLane Kuster and Katrina Swett. "I kept telling reporters, off the record … this is not going to be a landslide, either way, this is going to be a field goal game. And it was."[15]

The Democratic Primary: Kuster Rolls

While Bass' primary was fairly low-key, two women—one new to running for office, the other a former congressional candidate—competed fiercely for the Democratic Party nomination. Ann McLane Kuster had not run for office before, but spent a lifetime around politics. Her mother was a Republican state senator, her father was once mayor of Concord, and her grandfather started one of the state's largest and most prestigious law firms. As an attorney and lobbyist, she worked on several state campaigns and was well known to Democratic Party insiders. Katrina Swett was also very familiar to politics. Her husband, Dick, held the 2nd District seat for one term until Bass defeated him in 1994, and her father was Tom Lantos, the longtime congressman from San Francisco. Swett herself challenged Charlie Bass in 2002, only to lose by 16 points to the then four-term incumbent.

As the race for the nomination began, Swett was somewhat better known to voters of the 2nd District than Kuster, but struggled against her rival among the progressive activist core of the party. Early on Kuster backed Barack Obama in the 2008 presidential primary contest, and was thought to represent the more progressive wing of the party. Swett, who supported Connecticut Senator Joe

Lieberman for president in 2004, was viewed as a more moderate candidate, in the style of the Democratic Leadership Council (DLC).[16] In May 2010, the progressive blog Blue Hampshire issued an endorsement of Kuster: "in addition to her strongly progressive views," said the editors and contributing writers, "Ann Kuster also has the clearest path to victory in the fall."[17]

When Kuster hired Colin Van Ostern, a veteran of several campaigns in New Hampshire, to manage her campaign in 2009, she was in the process of building an organization from scratch. At the time, Van Ostern recalled, Kuster had raised just under $200,000 from a base of fewer than 500 donors; Swett, in contrast, carried over approximately $900,000 from an aborted U.S. Senate campaign in 2008. "We really started with her Rolodex, and her life's relationships, and her ideas for the country, and her time. And that's it," said Van Ostern.[18] Kuster's contact list was an extensive one, based on a lifetime of connections that she and her family had made in the Granite State. While almost unknown to voters, she was a familiar face in New Hampshire's elite circles, based on her work in the state capital, as well as her participation on various non-profit boards. To build a network of volunteers, Kuster used the time-honored New Hampshire tradition of house parties, attending more than 100 around the district during the campaign.

While Kuster gained the allegiance of progressive activists in the 2nd District, Van Ostern stressed that the candidate had a goal of attracting a broad spectrum of voters. Although the primary was often depicted as an ideological battle, Van Ostern noted that Kuster's television advertisements were devoid of references to ideology, as were most of the campaign's communications. Both candidates spent money on advertisements showcasing their attention to jobs and the economy. On other issues, however, the candidates displayed clear differences. Abortion rights advocates such as Emily's List and the NARAL Pro-Choice America PAC backed Kuster over Swett, who favored restrictions on abortion in the past. Kuster also took a more liberal stance on the wars in Iraq and Afghanistan; indeed, on the latter, Kuster criticized President Obama's escalation of operations. The blog Blue Hampshire admiringly noted that Kuster "supports the public option [to be included in health care reform], the Employee Free Choice Act, non-punitive immigration reform, and environmental regulation. Not only does she want to repeal Don't Ask Don't Tell, she wants to repeal DOMA [the Defense of Marriage Act], and she worked to help bring marriage equality to New Hampshire."[19] In terms of defining the primary contest, however, the Kuster campaign aimed to avoid framing the race as a contest over who was the most progressive candidate.[20] Kuster was able to draw not only Obama supporters from the 2008 primaries, said campaign manager Van Ostern, but also Hillary Clinton supporters.

For her part, Swett attempted to define her opponent as a political insider whose views were too far left to attract mainstream voters in a general election. Her campaign dwelled on the fact that Kuster had worked as a lobbyist, particularly for the pharmaceutical industry. In a televised debate the week before the primary, Swett asked her opponent:

Annie, you have cast yourself as the very, very progressive candidate and have been warmly supported by the far-left progressive movement. In a year when everyone understands that the country is moving back toward the center and away from the more left, progressive point of view, if you were to become the nominee, would you try to distance yourself from your own positions?[21]

At this point, however, Swett's campaign seemed all but lost. Ten days out, Kuster enjoyed a lead of some 20 points, but her campaign decided not to reduce its ad buys and save the money for the general campaign. The campaign made this decision in part because of the uncertainties of a low-turnout primary, but also because "winning big actually was more important than just winning," in part to impress the Democratic Congressional Campaign Committee (DCCC) and independent groups that Kuster was worthy of notice (and financial assistance) in the general election.[22] Ultimately, Kuster won the primary with 71 percent of the vote, a performance that gained the campaign a windfall of positive press. A worrisome omen of the race to come, however, was the Democratic primary turnout in the district. It totaled less than 36,000, compared to nearly 67,000 votes in the GOP primary. In short, Democratic turnout was just 55 percent of Republican turnout. Surely, the disparity was due in part to the competitive Republican primary race for the U.S. Senate nomination between Kelly Ayotte and Ovide Lamontagne. In retrospect, however, it also may have been a sign of an enthusiasm gap between partisan supporters, a gap that became increasingly evident as the general election approached.

The General Election Campaign

After the September 14 primary, just six weeks remained until the November 2 election. The morning after, Kuster and her campaign could look back with justifiable pride at their accomplishments. In the past year, Kuster transformed from a political unknown to the party's nominee, defeating a much better recognized adversary. Kuster's organization proved to be top-notch, a fact her opponents recognized. "Annie showed from early on that she had a great team around her that knew what they were doing," said Tranchemontagne, Bass' communication director.

Even though Kuster had a strong campaign organization (an important micropolitical factor), the larger political environment proved daunting to the Democrat. Nationally, unemployment hovered around 10 percent, President Obama's approval ratings were below 50 percent, and Republicans enjoyed a significant advantage on the generic Congressional ballot (see Chapter 1). The Democrats' House majority appeared doomed. Moreover, the DCCC was confronted with a massive triage effort to save whatever incumbents they could. Their counterpart, the National Republican Congressional Committee (NRCC), pursued Democratic incumbents aggressively, and an armada of independent groups followed suit, dwarfing those allied with the Democrats.

Inside the Granite State, the political dynamics were not any better. Top-of-ticket help was scarce, as Democratic Governor John Lynch, seeking a record fourth consecutive term, faced his most difficult reelection bid amid fierce opposition. Lynch was in far better shape, however, than Paul Hodes, the Democratic occupant of the 2nd District seat at the time. The congressman faced a double-digit deficit to former Attorney General Kelly Ayotte in their bid to replace Judd Gregg (R) in the U.S. Senate, and had little hope of serious assistance from outside sources. All this meant that Kuster would have to win the race on her own without help from fellow Democrats at the top of the ticket. The Kuster campaign was strong enough to succeed, estimated campaign manager Van Ostern, even in a down year for Democrats. What was unknown was how bad the environment would be by Election Day.

Messaging

Like the rest of the country, the overriding issue in New Hampshire was the state of the economy. In a University of New Hampshire survey one month before the election 47 percent of 2nd District adults said the economy/jobs was the most important issue facing the state followed by the state budget (16 percent). Concerns about jobs and the economy had been the most important problem since the fall of 2008 and budget concerns took the second spot in early 2009. While health care was only mentioned by 2 percent of district residents as the most important problem facing the state, there was considerable animosity toward the health reform legislation passed earlier in 2010 (Patient Protection and Affordable Care Act of 2010)—49 percent of 2nd District residents said they opposed the health reform bill while only 39 percent supported it.[23]

Typically in midterm elections, the president's party is rewarded at the ballot box during good economic times and takes the blame during bad times. Faced with this environment, the Kuster campaign thought they saw a strategy that would lead to victory on Election Day. In short, they wanted to make Charlie Bass the incumbent and tie him to policies that were perceived to have failed while portraying Kuster as a political newcomer who was not responsible for what had happened in the past. Though Kuster was obviously a Democrat, she was able to avoid the dilemma incumbent Democrats faced, as to whether to embrace the legislative accomplishments of the first two years of the Obama administration, or to downplay and distance themselves from them. According to campaign manager Van Ostern, every ad her campaign ran in the general election was a contrast ad, which helped them lay out Kuster's proposed policies, but also tell voters why they should not send Bass back to Congress.[24] To make their case, the campaign highlighted votes the former incumbent had cast during his time in Congress. One such ad stated that Bass raised his pay as a congressman and cut veterans' benefits.[25] Another ad, and an example of the Kuster campaign drawing contrasts in their messaging, focused on job creation.

In an ad titled "Whoa," Kuster attacked Bass for voting for bills that made it easier to send jobs overseas:

Bass: For every single job that's outsourced in America—two new jobs are created. [Concord Debate, 10/14/2010]

Announcer: Whoa. Charlie Bass thinks outsourcing jobs is good for New Hampshire? No wonder Bass voted to give China special trade privileges. And for tax breaks that encourage shipping jobs overseas.

Kuster: I'm Annie Kuster and I approved this message because my priorities are right here. Close tax loopholes for corporations that ship jobs overseas … And make New Hampshire the hub of clean energy to create new jobs, now. [26]

And in "Get Real," Kuster argued for retargeting tax incentives to create jobs.

Announcer: Brian got up every day. Worked hard. The same job for 13 years. So when the mills shut down and jobs moved to China, it was devastating.

Kuster: I'm Annie Kuster, and enough is enough.

Announcer: Kuster's plan? End tax breaks for companies that ship jobs overseas. Provide tax incentives to small business and companies that create jobs here at home.

Kuster: I'm Annie Kuster, and I approved this message because it's time to get real about jobs.[27]

In both cases, Kuster stayed away from defending the performance of the House of Representatives (which was led by liberal Nancy Pelosi (D-CA)), and concentrated on drawing contrasts on taxation, an issue typically owned by Republican candidates.[28] In all, the Kuster campaign emphasized that the candidate had never run for office before, and that she would be an agent of change in Congress.

While Kuster grappled with presenting herself as something new even though she was part of the party in power, Charlie Bass wrestled with how a six-term former incumbent could be perceived as a valid agent of change. Bass, like many GOP candidates across the country, tried to take advantage of the political environment that favored the GOP. Specifically, the Bass campaign attacked the policies pursued by the leadership of the Democratic Party, and President Obama and Speaker Pelosi in particular. For instance, an early advertisement depicted Bass as the "change we need," and the candidate who would be able to stop the Obama-Pelosi agenda:

How do we change Washington? Send a fighter with experience. Someone we know: Charlie Bass. Fiscal conservative. A record of cutting taxes, cutting wasteful spending. Bass will fight Pelosi's trillion-dollar deficits, and work to repeal and reform Obama's government takeover of health care. Charlie Bass has the experience we need to change Washington now. That's the change we need in Congress. [29]

Other Bass ads tied his opponent to Obama and Pelosi, even though she had not been in Congress to participate in policy making the prior two years, and argued that Kuster's "new approach" was more of the same Obama-Pelosi agenda. If anything, the campaign went further and argued Kuster represented a set of policy positions to the left of the Democratic leadership. One ad cited the country's higher unemployment and exploding deficits, and displayed Kuster alongside Obama and Pelosi, with the headline "More of the Same."[30] In their "New Approach?" ad, the Bass campaign focused on Kuster's support for a "public option" in a national health care plan, labeling it "a government takeover of health care more extreme than Obama-care."[31] In all, the Bass campaign bet heavily on the theory that "who she was and what she stood for ... was probably the weakest link of her campaign. Just too left, too liberal, and the opposite of change."[32] Looking back on his rival's campaign strategy, Colin Van Ostern stated that the essence of the Bass message was ultimately effective: "She's a Democrat. Democrats are the problem."[33]

Campaign Finance

Ann Kuster proved to be a potent fundraiser, ultimately accumulating $2.5 million, twice that of her opponent (see Table 7.2). This was not a position Charlie Bass was familiar with, having outraised or been near parity with his past opponents in House races. Bass started out 2010 behind in cash on hand compared to Kuster and never caught up. In fact, he was out-raised and out-spent in each reporting period during 2010 (see Table 7.3). Much of this reflects the two campaigns' different approaches to the end of their primary campaign. During the summer months and through the primary, Kuster spent nearly three times what Bass did. The strategy of spending heavily during the last few weeks of the primary, in order to "win big," while Bass conserved resources resulted in Kuster actually being behind in cash on hand going into the general election (at the end of September Bass had over $370,000 while Kuster had just shy of $360,000). Kuster out-spent Bass again during October, but Bass had enough funds to compete.

Both Kuster and Bass succeeded in drawing independent expenditures from outside groups. All told, the 2nd District was one of the ten most attractive districts for outside spending. Outside groups spent almost $2.5 million on Kuster's behalf and almost $2 million on Bass' behalf. Most of the support came in the form of advertisements opposing the two candidates. The DCCC led the charge, spending almost $1 million against the Republican and the NRCC spent more than $500,000, of which almost $425,000 was in opposition to the Democrat.[34] Like Kuster, the DCCC also highlighted Bass' past voting record in Congress. In one ad, the DCCC noted Bass' votes to increase the national debt and raise

Table 7.2 Campaign Finance Data for New Hampshire's 2nd Congressional District Campaigns, 2002–2010

Election year	Disbursements		Receipts		Vote Percent	
	Bass (R)	Opponent (D)	Bass (R)	Opponent (D)	Bass (R)	Opponent (D)
2010	$1,249,005	$2,486,894	$1,242,838	$2,506,615	48.3	46.8
2006	$1,538,323	$1,528,729	$1,228,541	$1,237,271	46	53
2004	$717,749	$465,062	$740,299	$467,164	59	38
2002	$886,765	$1,457,913	$906,760	$1,492,259	57	41

Source: 2010 election results: New York Times, http://elections.nytimes.com/2010/results/new-hampshire; all other data: Center for Responsive Politics, http://www.opensecrets.org (accessed February 15, 2011).

Note: 2008 is omitted because Charlie Bass did not run.

Table 7.3 Bass and Kuster Receipts and Disbursements by Reporting Period, 2009–2010

Reporting Period	Charlie Bass			Ann Kuster		
	Receipts	Disbursements	Ending Cash	Receipts	Disbursements	Ending Cash
Beginning Cash as of September 30, 2009			$36,187.93			$260,034.06
2009 Year End						
(1 October–31 December)	$147,622.73	$22,237.76	$161,572.90	$207,827.76	$78,720.86	$389,140.96
2010 April Quarterly						
(1 January–31 March)	$153,255.62	$50,137.51	$264,691.01	$290,337.98	$116,445.71	$563,033.23
2010 July Quarterly						
(1 April–30 June)	$178,749.20	$72,540.79	$370,899.42	$316,619.58	$134,634.50	$745,018.31
2010 Pre-primary						
(1 July–25 August)	$57,190.00	$116,268.62	$311,820.80	$224,221.00	$518,109.32	$451,129.99
2010 October Quarterly						
(26 August–30 September)	$306,593.10	$245,354.28	$373,059.62	$456,570.18	$550,505.76	$357,194.41
2010 Pre-general						
(1 October–13 October)	$116,276.95	$289,243.84	$200,092.73	$204,236.43	$305,185.54	$256,245.30
2010 Post-general						
(14 October–22 November)	$259,696.10	$436,270.35	$23,518.48	$255,507.50	$592,578.09	$36,461.73
Total	**$1,219,383.70**	**$1,232,053.15**		**$2,157,714.78**	**$2,381,287.11**	

Source: Compiled from candidate reports to the Federal Election Commission, Form 3, Lines 23, 24, 26, and 27, various dates.

congressional pay, concluding, "Charlie Bass wants a second chance in Washington. Sorry, Charlie, once was more than enough."[35]

Another group, the America's Family First Action Fund, spent $675,000 on Kuster's behalf, all of it in opposition to Bass. Unlike Kuster, however, Bass' leading source of outside support was not his Hill Committee, the NRCC, but an allied group, Revere America, which spent $750,000 opposing Kuster. In addition, the U.S. Chamber of Commerce spent almost $150,000 to assist the Republican.[36]

The fact that both campaigns were well funded meant that they had sufficient resources to wage a spirited campaign. This was the case all the way to Election Day as the Bass and Kuster campaigns ran extensive ads in New Hampshire and the Kuster campaign, as well as outside groups that supported both candidates, were on expensive Boston stations as well.

Endgame Dynamics

Soon after the September primary, Ann McLane Kuster appeared to be resisting the national Republican wave. University of New Hampshire Survey Center polling indicated that the Democrat rapidly closed the gap with Bass and even surged ahead of him in October (see Figure 7.3). This is possibly because of the large funding advantage Kuster enjoyed which allowed her to spend money that helped increase her name recognition and spread her message, even though much of it was focused on her primary opponent. Unlike Paul Hodes in 2006,

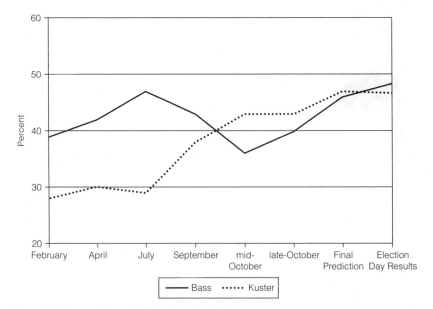

Figure 7.3 Bass vs. Kuster Polling Results, 2010.
Source: UNH Survey Center polls, various dates.
Note: Data before Election Day represent likely voters in the 2nd District.

however, Kuster was not able to pull away from Bass, and the race appeared too close to call in the week before the election.

Throughout the year, Charlie Bass' campaign operation was discounted, especially compared to Kuster's organization, which had performed so impressively in the primary season. His campaign vigorously disagreed with this perception, claiming that the efforts of candidate and campaign, especially on get-out-the-vote activities, were strong: "We would get knocked around in the press by certain pundits for running a so-called lackadaisical campaign, when we were busting our butts, behind the scenes, doing the things that we knew had to be done to win the general."[37] Reliable data on such groundwork is hard to obtain, making it difficult to show evidence of a robust field operation. It may not have mattered, however. Republicans were after all more excited to vote than Democrats in 2010, so they did not have to work as hard as Democrats to get their voters to the polls. In short, any differential between the rival campaign operations was outweighed by the Republican wave that swept New Hampshire and the country.

The 2010 electoral environment certainly favored Republicans, and Republican voters were more enthusiastic about the election than were Democrats. An October WMUR-TV/University of New Hampshire Survey Center poll showed that 45 percent of the district's Republican likely voters said they were very interested in the election, compared to 35 percent of Democratic likely voters; 78 percent of Republican likely voters said they would definitely vote, compared to just 68 percent of Democratic likely voters; and 60 percent of Republican likely voters said they were excited about the outcome of the November elections, compared to just 46 percent of Democratic likely voters.[38]

Turnout was an important key to this election, just as it had been in 2006. On Election Day 2010, Republicans went to the polls in high numbers while Democrats largely stayed home. When Bass last won in 2004, the final electorate in the district consisted of 39 percent core Democrats, 37 percent core Republicans and 24 percent swing voters. In 2010, the electorate was remarkably similar—39 percent core Democrats, 36 percent core Republicans, and 24 percent swing voters (see Figure 7.4). In comparison, in the elections of 2006 and 2008 participation by core Democrats swelled to 47 and 48 percent of the electorate, respectively; core Republicans turned out at only a rate of 26 percent in 2006 and 31 percent in 2008. These were insurmountable turnout margins for even a well-known and well-liked Republican such as Bass in 2006; Horn had no chance in 2008. Simply, the same Democrats who elected Paul Hodes in 2006 and 2008, as well as Democratic majorities in New Hampshire's state House and Senate, did not turn out in 2010. Among core Republicans in the final pre-election poll, Bass led Kuster by an expected 84 percent to 2 percent margin. Similarly, Kuster led Bass among core Democrats by 89 percent to 2 percent. Among the critical 24 percent of the electorate who were swing voters, Bass held a narrow 34 percent to 29 percent lead.[39]

On Election Night, the 2nd District race was the last major race in the Granite State to be called by the media. By the time Charlie Bass was declared the

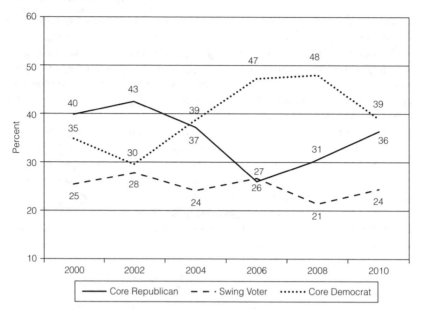

Figure 7.4 Voter Turnout of Core Partisans in New Hampshire's 2nd Congressional District, 2000–2010.
Source: UNH Survey Center final pre-election polls, various dates.

winner, the startling dimensions of the Republican landslide were becoming apparent. At the top of the ticket, Democratic Governor John Lynch survived (beating John Stephen 53 percent to 45 percent), but Paul Hodes failed to carry even 40 percent of the vote against Republican Kelly Ayotte in the U.S. Senate race.[40] Farther down the ticket, Republicans rolled up veto-proof majorities in both chambers of the state legislature, wiping out years of Democratic gains in a single evening. Despite all this, Kuster trailed by a relatively close margin throughout the night. Ultimately, though, it was the "district within a district," the vote-rich Republican towns on the Massachusetts border, that overwhelmed Kuster's support in Democratic strongholds elsewhere in the district. In historic swing areas, such as Merrimack County, Bass carried prosperous towns such as Bow. All in all, the six-term former incumbent won a seventh term by a margin of fewer than 4,000 out of nearly 225,000 votes cast, by a margin of 48.3 percent to 46.8 percent.[41]

Looking Ahead to 2012

New Hampshire Democrats swept nearly every major elected office in the state in 2006. Four years later, Republicans won by even larger majorities in the Granite State. An easy but fundamentally incorrect lesson that can be drawn from recent elections is that the New Hampshire electorate is swinging wildly between partisan and ideological extremes. This, however, flies in the face of more than 50 years of political science data (beginning with *The American Voter*[42]) indicating that most people in America pay little attention to politics and consistently vote their partisan leanings. A much simpler explanation for recent swings is that New Hampshire is relatively evenly balanced between Republicans and Democrats. That does not mean, however, that both sides turn out to vote at equal rates on every Election Day. Both 2006 and 2010 clearly demonstrate what happens when one party is energized and the other is depressed—energized people (be they excited or angry) go to the polls, while dejected or disappointed people stay home.

In the 2nd District, Charlie Bass was both the victim and the beneficiary of such disparities in partisan enthusiasm during his congressional career. In 2006, Democrats were angry with the Bush administration, particularly about the ongoing war in Iraq, while Republicans were depressed about the legislative and foreign policy activities of the administration and saw no reason to go out and vote for Republicans whom they felt had lost their way. As a result, Bass' ability to hold a Democratic-tilting district disappeared virtually overnight. Just four years later, Bass' party had been re-energized by anger against the Obama administration, particularly its inability to improve the economy while expanding the scope of the federal government. Republicans enthusiastically came out to vote against any Democratic candidate, while Democrats, depressed about the state of the economy and without any partisan opponent to blame, stayed home. As campaign manager Van Ostern noted, the campaign anticipated Kuster would not be at as big of a disadvantage as other Democrats, but those hopes were dashed: "We thought the anti-incumbency sentiment was likely to be stronger than the anti-Democratic sentiment. It would be a close call, but that is part of what the contest would be about. And ultimately we were wrong … Our race was a pretty good test as to whether people were more upset at Democrats, or more upset at politicians."[43]

The Kuster campaign may have been wrong—but just barely so. In a terrible year for New Hampshire Democrats, Kuster still managed to carry 47 percent of the vote, the second-best Democratic performance in a major race behind Governor Lynch. Republicans may well continue their Granite State resurgence in 2012. It is a reasonable expectation, however, that Democrats in New Hampshire's 2nd District will return to the polls in greater numbers during a presidential election year (and when Obama, who won the state by just under 10 points in 2008, will be on the ballot again). Ann Kuster might reasonably consider her performance in 2010 a floor, not a ceiling; this was possibly a factor in her decision to run atain in 2012 which she announced only 5 months after her defeat. For Charlie Bass, the concern is that in a presidential election year, the enthusiasm gap in his favor might well narrow significantly, if not disappear altogether. In such a situation, the Democratic tilt of the district might well manifest itself more clearly. After all, in a year that so strongly favored Republicans, he was unable to earn the votes of a majority of the citizens from his district. This is a clear signal of vulnerability, even for a moderate Republican in a slightly Democratic district. Democrats, including Ann Kuster, will be trying hard to knock off Charlie Bass the next time around.

Notes

1. Interview with Kuster campaign manager Colin Van Ostern, December 28, 2010.
2. U.S. Census Bureau, 2005–2009 American Community Survey 5-Year Estimates, http://www.census.gov/acs/www (accessed March 12, 2011).
3. Ibid.
4. Van Ostern interview.
5. Ibid.
6. Michael Barone, and Richard Cohen, *The Almanac of American Politics, 2010* (Washington, D.C.: National Journal, 2010).
7. Interview with Bass communications director Scott Tranchemontagne, January 21, 2011.
8. Ibid.
9. Quoted in *Concord Monitor*, "Is Bass truly steeped in Tea Party agenda?," February 10, 2010, http://www.concordmonitor.com/article/is-bass-truly-steeped-in-tea-party-agenda (accessed February 25, 2011).
10. Ibid.
11. UNH Survey Center/WMUR Poll, March 27–April 2, 2007 (Likely NH GOP Primary Voters). Abortion should be: legal in any circumstance (29 percent), legal under certain circumstances (50 percent), illegal in all circumstances (14 percent), don't know (7 percent). Gallup Poll, May 10–13, 2007 (all U.S. adults). Abortion should be: legal in any circumstance, (26 percent), legal under certain circumstances (55 percent), illegal in all circumstances (18 percent), don't know (1 percent).
12. Tranchemontagne interview.
13. Ibid.
14. Ibid.
15. Ibid.
16. After he lost a race for U.S. Senate in 1996, Dick Swett was appointed Ambassador to Denmark by another DLC Democrat, President Bill Clinton.
17. "Blue Hampshire Endorses Ann McLane Kuster," BlueHampshire.com, May 20, 2010, http://www.bluehampshire.com/diary/9986/blue-hampshire-endorses-ann-mclane-kuster (accessed February 25, 2011).
18. Van Ostern interview.
19. "Blue Hampshire Endorses Ann McLane Kuster."
20. Van Ostern interview.
21. Karen Langley, "Swett: Kuster stands at far left," *Concord Monitor*, September 9, 2010, http://www.concordmonitor.com/article/215670/swett-kuster-stands-at-far-left (accessed February 25, 2011).
22. Van Ostern interview.
23. WMUR / Granite State Poll press releases, October 1 and 4, 2010. http://www.unh.edu/survey-center/news/pdf/gsp2010_fall_govapp100110.pdf; http://www.unh.edu/survey-center/news/pdf/gsp2010_fall_presapp100410.pdf (accessed March 12, 2011).
24. Van Ostern interview.
25. http://www.realclearpolitics.com/video/2010/10/13/nh-2_kuster_working_for_new_hampshire.html (accessed March 12, 2011).
26. http://www.bluehampshire.com/diary/11204/kuster-rips-into-bass-defense-of-outsourcing (accessed March 12, 2011).
27. Ibid.

28. John R. Petrocik. "Issue ownership in presidential elections, with a 1980 case study," *American Journal of Political Science*, vol. 40 (1996), pp. 825–50.
29. http://www.votebass.com/videos/ (accessed March 12, 2011).
30. Ibid.
31. Ibid.
32. Tranchemontagne interview.
33. Van Ostern interview.
34. Center for Responsive Politics, "New Hampshire District 02: Outside Spending," http://www.opensecrets.org/races/indexp.php?cycle=2010&id=NH02   (accessed February 25, 2011).
35. http://www.youtube.com/watch?v=_E_w6OHrtnk&playnext=1&list=PL961C550F 8D32E097; also see http://www.youtube.com/user/DCCC2010#p/search (accessed March 10, 2011).
36. Center for Responsive Politics, "New Hampshire District 02: Outside Spending."
37. Tranchemontagne interview.
38. UNH Survey Center, WMUR / UNH 2010 New Hampshire Election Poll, October 20, 2010, http://www.unh.edu/survey-center/news/pdf/e2010_interest102010. pdf (accessed March 12, 2011).
39. UNH Survey Center, WMUR / UNH 2010 New Hampshire Election Poll, October 27–31, 2010, http://www.unh.edu/survey-center/news/pdf/e2010_house103110. pdf (accessed March 12, 2011).
40. By the end of the election season, Hodes had become such a liability to the Democratic ticket that the Bass campaign ran an advertisement linking Kuster to the U.S. Senate candidate in Hodes' home district.
41. Minor party and independent candidates earned roughly 5 percent of the vote. An independent candidate, Tim vanBlommesteyn, won 2.8 percent of the vote; Libertarian Howard Wilson, 2.1 percent.
42. Angus Campbell, Phillip E. Converse, Warren E. Miller, and Donald E. Stokes, *The American Voter* (Chicago: University of Chicago Press, 1960).
43. Van Ostern interview.

8 Rubio vs. Crist vs. Meek in Florida's Senate Race
Coming Out of Nowhere

Seth C. McKee and Stephen C. Craig

It began with a hug. On February 10, 2009, three weeks after being inaugurated as the 44th President of the United States, Barack Obama made a trip to Fort Myers, Florida. With one of the worst foreclosure rates in the country combined with huge electoral significance in presidential politics, the Sunshine State was an ideal setting for President Obama to "go public" in seeking support for his newly proposed economic stimulus plan. Curiously, because in contemporary American politics the major political parties have grown increasingly ideologically polarized, Republican Governor Charlie Crist was not only present in Fort Myers to greet the president (a gesture expected of a governor), but he also warmly embraced him. This show of affection was symbolic of the reason why, less than two years later, Crist would fail to win a U.S. Senate seat that had once appeared to be his for the asking. "The Hug" came to be viewed as much more than an act of kindness. Instead, it was deftly framed by opponents within his party as a sign of the governor's embrace of the policies of the Obama administration—and more specifically, policies which, by November 2010, had become so politically toxic that a Senate victory for a once-popular sitting governor was out of reach.

The Senate race in Florida is a story about timing. For one candidate, Charlie Crist, the timing could not have been worse; for another, former state House Speaker Marco Rubio, the timing surely could not have been better. Florida is the nation's largest electoral bellwether. It holds this important position because in statewide elections, the roughly even balance of Democratic and Republican voters is buffered by a substantial and growing segment of political independents whose votes shift in response to short-term conditions and, in the process, determine the outcome of most statewide elections. The "tides of consent"[1] created by these short-term forces swept Democrats into office in 2006 and 2008 but, by Election Day 2010, had moved sharply in the other direction and grown into an even larger GOP wave. Such a turnaround illustrates very clearly that what political independents give can quickly be taken away. So it was for Charlie Crist, a lifelong Republican whose election as governor was one of the few success stories for his party in 2006, but whose attempt to capture the center four years later by shedding his party label ironically helped to ensure his defeat as independent voters in Florida moved to the right and embraced Marco Rubio, a dashing young politician who proved the perfect vessel for ushering in the Republican wave.

The Setting of Florida Politics

Since 1948, Florida has supported the winning presidential candidate on all but two occasions (John F. Kennedy in 1960 and Bill Clinton in 1992). Starting in 1992, however, the state became a bona fide battleground in the race for the White House with neither party able to win the state consistently or with many votes to spare. George W. Bush captured the largest share of the two-party vote during this period with 52.5 percent in 2004, four years after the controversial "virtual tie" of 2000[2] when a margin of 537 votes sent Bush to the White House in the first place. As for U.S. Senate races, Democrats and Republicans have each won four of the contests held since 1988; split Senate delegations are the rule and not the exception in recent Florida politics.

To understand what happened in 2010, one must consider Florida's unique context and how this environment interacted with the prevailing national political milieu. Although once a member of the erstwhile Confederacy, by the late 1940s, in *Southern Politics in State and Nation*, political scientist V. O. Key correctly observed that Florida was different. "[I]t occasionally gives a faintly tropical rebel yell, but otherwise it is a world of its own."[3] Two characteristics set Florida apart from the rest of the American South: population growth and population change.[4]

Over the last 70 years the rate of population growth in Florida has been unlike the rest of the nation and even the South in general. Florida was the least populated southern state in 1940, but is now the second largest in the region (trailing only Texas) and the fourth most populous overall (right behind New York). From 1940 to 1990, Florida's decennial population growth (45 percent) soared well above the regional (16 percent) and national average (13 percent); indeed, between 1950 and 1960, the number of Florida residents grew by an astonishing 79 percent.[5] By 2000, however, the rest of the South had almost caught up with Florida, and the economic decline that occurred over the next decade left the state lying close to the regional average.

Compared with other southern states, both Florida and Texas have a lower percentage of African-American residents and a higher proportion of Hispanics.[6] Yet Florida differs from its Lone Star counterpart in two important (for our purposes) respects: its dramatic population increase took place over a much shorter period of time; and whereas Texas and most other southern states lean predominantly Republican in both state and national politics, Florida is the largest presidential swing state. Its battleground classification is intriguing because, similar to the rest of the South, the Florida GOP now has the upper hand in U.S. House, state legislative, and most statewide contests.[7] It is in elections for president and U.S. Senate where Florida has become an electoral barometer.

Although Florida's population growth rate since 1940 is remarkable, the changing *composition* of its electorate is what truly sets the state apart and contributes greatly to its electoral volatility. As Carver and Fiedler put it, "The Sunshine State is, in fact, less a part of any region than it is composed of the parts of many regions. The reason for this peculiarity is simple: newcomers."[8] Political historian David Colburn summed it up nicely when he noted that "[b]etween 1940 and 1980, Florida gradually abandoned its southern past and its racial traditions and became a place where the northern and southern regions of the Western Hemisphere intersected culturally, socially, and economically."[9]

An important factor in the make-up of the Sunshine State is the number of residents born outside the state. Decade after decade Florida stands out from other southern states, and the nation as a whole, because of its unusually large percentage of residents born somewhere else (66 percent in 2008 vs. 44 percent in the South and 41 percent nationally). Florida is composed largely of immigrants who come not just from northern and other southern states, but from Mexico, the Caribbean, Latin America, and points beyond.[10] To be sure, the compositional change within the Florida electorate has varied in both degree and in kind from one part of the state to the next. For instance, central Florida has experienced an influx of Puerto Ricans; south Florida has welcomed Latinos of various stripes, plus many Haitians and Yankees from the northeast (especially New York, New Jersey, and Connecticut); midwesterners have long been drawn disproportionately to the west coast; and the least amount of in-migration has taken place in the Florida panhandle from Pensacola in the west across to Jacksonville in the east.[11]

It is this perpetual influx of immigrants that accounts for the competitiveness and instability in presidential and senatorial elections. Prior to the 1960s, Florida was very much a southern state with respect to its politics being dominated by the Democratic Party,[12] but northern in-migration after World War II established Republican toeholds in certain areas of the state (most notably St. Petersburg) where outsiders succeeded in growing the local GOP.[13] More recently, there has been a reversal in the partisan influence of in-migrants, with northerners more likely to be Democratic than their native Florida counterparts. In addition, north Florida, the historical stronghold of the Democratic Party, is now the most reliably Republican section of the state due to generational change among its large native white population.[14]

South Florida has witnessed perhaps the greatest change in its electoral composition because so many new residents come from other countries. Cubans are overwhelmingly concentrated in Miami-Dade County, but outside of this Republican-leaning group (especially among older voters[15]) most newcomers tend to favor the Democrats. Finally, the middle section of the state, roughly tracking Interstate-4 (the "I-4 Corridor") from Tampa Bay on the west coast to Daytona Beach in the east (and running through Orlando in the middle), has a very diverse population of suburban communities that exhibit a high degree of political independence and typically have held the key to victory in recent statewide elections.[16]

It is this complicated mixture of residents that explains the unsettled nature of Florida politics, providing the state with what at times appears to be a bad case of political amnesia; that is, many a candidate has won a statewide contest only to be thrown out of office, sometimes resoundingly, in their initial reelection bid. The setting of Florida politics is a place where terms like "[d]eracination and displacement"[17] and a "crowd" rather than a "community"[18] best characterize the electoral environment. Even in the late 1940s, V. O. Key observed of Florida that "[f]lux, fluidity, uncertainty in human relations are the rule.... [T]here is plausibly a relation between a diverse, recently transplanted population and a mutable politics."[19]

Changes in the population composition of the state have had important political consequences. This can be seen in the data on Florida voters' self-identified party affiliation from 1986 to 2010 (see Table 8.1). Two points deserve emphasis. First, Republican loyalty has reached parity with Democratic support (and in fact exceeded it, at least slightly, for much of the past decade). Second, the percentage of political independents has risen to nearly the thirty percent mark—and because Democrats and Republicans essentially cancel each other out, it is the nonaffiliated Florida voter who is the kingmaker in contemporary

Table 8.1 Party Affiliation of Florida Voters, 1986–2010

Election	Democrats	Independents	Republicans
2010	36%	29%	36%
2008	38%	26%	35%
2006	37%	22%	41%
2004	38%	21%	41%
2002	39%	18%	43%
2000	41%	20%	39%
1998	38%	22%	41%
1996	40%	21%	40%
1994	39%	20%	41%
1992	42%	20%	38%
1990	38%	22%	40%
1988	39%	18%	43%
1986	44%	21%	36%
2010–1986	–8%	+8%	0%

Source: With the exception of the 2010 data, which were retrieved from the CNN web site (www.cnn.com/ELECTION/2010/results/polls/#val=FLS01p1), all the data on the previous twelve general elections (1986–2008) were retrieved and calculated by the authors from the Inter-university Consortium for Political and Social Research (www.icpsr.umich.edu). Data for 1986 and 1988 data are from the *CBS-New York Times* exit polls. Data for 1990 and 1992 data are from the *Voter Research and Surveys* exit polls. Data for 1994–2002 data are from the *Voter News Service* exit polls. Data for 2004–2010 data are from the *National Election Pool* exit polls. All data on Florida voters come from a national survey except in 2002 when they come from a state survey;

Note: Due to rounding, data in any given year may not sum exactly to 100 percent. All data were weighted.

statewide political contests. This group can be extremely fickle, as its voting behavior in 2008 and 2010 makes abundantly clear.

The Impact of National Conditions in the Florida Senate Race

Retrospective voting is a common behavior for a large segment of the American electorate. Because politics can be complicated, voters often use shortcuts in their decision-making,[20] and past performance is an important guide for many people in deciding how to cast their ballots on Election Day. Simply put, to vote retrospectively means to assess the state of political affairs and determine whether the party in office should continue receiving support or be cast aside in favor of candidates from the opposition party.[21] Thus, retrospective voters are basically asking the party in power, "What have you done for me lately?" An unpopular war or declining economy are the kinds of salient conditions that can have a large effect on how individuals vote—especially independents, who are by definition not loyal to a particular party. Independents can be thought of as "scorekeepers"[22] and, when the party in power does not appear to be doing a good job of dealing with the problems that people care about, politically unaffiliated voters will exhibit the greatest shift in their political support in the next election.[23]

Retrospective voting has been rampant in the past three election cycles. Initially, the public mood favored Democrats as voters exhibited dissatisfaction with the Iraq War in 2006[24] and then continued to turn against the GOP in 2008 because of the declining state of the economy and the financial crisis that arose during the final months of the Bush presidency.[25] In 2010, however, independents moved strongly against the Democrats and in favor of Republican Party candidates (see Chapter 1). With power comes responsibility—and as the economy struggled to regain its footing, unemployment remained high, a controversial health care law (the Patient Protection and Affordable Care Act of 2010) was enacted, and the advent of the so-called Tea Party movement became the most prominent (though by no means the only) manifestation of a growing opposition to the Obama administration and his Democratic congressional majority.[26]

Midterm elections are rarely kind to the president's party and thus losing House seats is almost a given (see Chapter 1). For many voters, their retrospective political evaluations turn midterm elections into referendums on presidential performance—and the verdict rendered in those referendums is usually, to a greater or lesser degree, unfavorable. This was clearly the case in 2006 and 2010. Exit poll data show, for example, that among the 54 percent of voters nationwide in 2006 who indicated that their vote was about the president, just 18 percent cast a ballot in support of President Bush while 36 percent voted against the president.[27]

Similarly, among Florida Senate voters in 2010, 58 percent agreed that their vote was about the president; of these, 24 percent gave a "thumbs up" to President Obama while 34 percent said their vote was meant to express opposition to the president.[28] In this historic three-candidate race, Democrat Kendrick Meek won a majority of votes cast as an expression of support for President Obama (54 percent) and, not surprisingly, Tea Party-backed Republican Marco Rubio took a whopping 88 percent of the votes cast as an expression of opposition to the president. Interestingly, among the 40 percent of Florida Senate voters who said that President Obama was not a factor in their decision, a plurality (43 percent) supported Independent Charlie Crist.

Between 2008 and 2010, changing national conditions swung the political pendulum from Democratic to Republican. This relatively abrupt shift in political support was on full display among the Florida electorate,[29] whose large independent population led the way. As we will show, voter opinion on most of the elements that dominated the political environment in 2010 broke in favor of the Republican Party—a sharp reversal from 2008, when Democrats were the beneficiaries of short-term conditions. In particular, independent voting behavior in Florida reflected the changing state of American politics generally. The 52 percent of Florida independents who backed Barack Obama in 2008 helped deliver the state's electoral votes into the Democratic column. In 2010, independent voters reversed course as 51 percent supported Republican Senate candidate Marco Rubio, thereby assuring victory for a vocal critic of the Obama administration.

The Candidates

The 2010 election was unprecedented largely because it was the first time the Sunshine State experienced a U.S. Senate race in which there were three qualified and plausible candidates for voters to choose from: 44-year-old Democrat Kendrick Meek, 54-year-old Independent Charlie Crist, and 39-year-old Republican Marco Rubio. The demographic profiles of the three candidates speak directly to Florida's tremendous racial and ethnic diversity: "a prominent African American (Meek), Cuban American (Rubio), and the grandson of a Greek immigrant (Crist)."[30] Not only were the candidates physically distinct, they were also philosophically differentiable, staking out positions across the ideological spectrum: Meek the liberal, Crist the centrist, and Rubio the conservative. In this section, we provide information on the backgrounds of these candidates.

The Democrat: Kendrick Meek

Before seeking his party's Senate nomination, Kendrick Meek represented the Miami-based 17th Congressional District where he was first elected in 2002; he previously served in the Florida House of Representatives (1994–1998) and Florida Senate (1998–2002). Kendrick succeeded his mother, Carrie Meek, who had represented the 17th District since 1992, when it was newly created as a majority-black district following the 1990 Census.[31] Considered an effective legislator and a rising Democratic star, Meek was moving up in the congressional ranks and landed a seat on the prestigious House Ways and Means Committee in 2007.[32]

On December 2, 2008, Republican U.S. Senator Mel Martinez announced that he would not seek reelection,[33] and just over a month later (on January 13, 2009), Meek became the first major-party contender to declare his candidacy for the soon-to-be-open seat. His path to the Democratic nomination seemed clear until a political gadfly with deep pockets showed up to make the primary interesting if ultimately not very competitive. Political novice Jeff Greene was a California expatriate who had Mike Tyson as the best man in his wedding (a really unfortunate fact for people in need of a voting shortcut), an erstwhile Republican, and a billionaire who made his fortune betting that the housing market would tank.[34] Greene poured over $20 million of his own money into his primary campaign.[35] Unfortunately for Greene, the earned media exposure he received was mostly negative and arguably on the mark in casting him as both mercurial and unfit for political office. By contrast, Meek benefited from media coverage that portrayed him as being more qualified and more serious, and solid performances in a series of candidate debates solidified his frontrunner status.

As primary day neared, Greene's unexpectedly strong showing in some media polls proved to be ephemeral.

> Three weeks ahead of the August 24 primary, Greene still had a 10-point lead, but that lead evaporated as Meek's ads aired and Presidents Barack Obama and Bill Clinton came to Democratic vote-rich South Florida to campaign on his behalf. Meek surged and handily beat Greene for the Democratic nomination despite being outspent by Greene by 5-to-1.[36]

Even though no African American had represented a southern state in the Senate since the end of Reconstruction, the most daunting hurdle for Meek as he looked ahead to the fall campaign was perhaps his positions on the issues. Simply put, Meek was an unabashed liberal in a centrist to right-leaning state that tilted even further toward the conservative end of the spectrum since giving its electoral votes to Barack Obama two years earlier.

The Independent: Charlie Crist

By 2010, Republican Governor Charlie Crist was an established Florida politician whose record of holding elected office dated back to 1992 when he won a seat in the Florida Senate. He remained in the state legislature through 1998, a year in which he was drubbed by incumbent Democrat Bob Graham in his first bid for the U.S. Senate.[37] After that defeat, Crist was elected education commissioner (in 2000), attorney general (in 2002) and finally governor (in 2006). In his race for the state's top executive, Crist won an open-seat contest (Republican Jeb Bush was term limited) against Democratic Congressman Jim Davis (11th District) by a margin of 52 percent to 45 percent, in a year that otherwise proved favorable to Democrats in the Sunshine State and the nation as a whole. As a candidate "on the statewide ballot in four of five elections between 1998 and 2006,"[38] Crist presumably benefited from almost universal name recognition in the state as he vacated the governorship for another run at the U.S. Senate in 2010.

Political analysts described Charlie Crist "as an ambitious, media-savvy pol, always sporting a healthy tan and blessed with retail campaigning skills."[39] To those observers who have seen Crist up close, the man who grew up in St. Petersburg, Florida, seems to have an extraordinary trait that normally redounds to his advantage on the campaign trail: an ability to place himself consistently near the center of voter opinion in the state. Indeed, we suspect that Anthony Downs, who articulated the so-called "median voter theory," would be impressed by Crist's skill at taking positions that resemble where most Florida voters stand on a range of issues.[40] In representational terms, he is not a "trustee" but rather the quintessential "delegate" politician[41]—that is, Charlie Crist aims to please his constituents and has usually been very adept at doing so. Referring to himself as "The People's Governor," Crist bought into a characterization that nicely captured the strong populist streak defining both his campaigning and governing philosophy.[42] He has never been an ideologue, choosing instead to move with the political winds.

It was not surprising, then, that Republican Governor Crist gave such a warm welcome to the hugely popular and newly elected President Obama in early 2009, when the political climate still shined brightly on the Democratic Party. In the end, the winds of change in 2010 ultimately proved unmanageable for Charlie Crist. Whereas in most election cycles it was possible to build a political majority by shifting to the center, in 2010 the center was not where the votes were; they had shifted back to the right, and with them went most of the political independents from whom Crist had hoped to draw support.

Charlie Crist officially announced his candidacy for the Republican Senate nomination on May 12, 2009, declaring that "I want to serve where I can serve the people of my state the very best, and I believe that to be in the United States Senate."[43] Exactly a week before and with markedly less media fanfare, former Florida House Speaker Marco Rubio also declared his intention to seek the Republican nomination. Although Rubio was widely considered more conservative, Crist was quickly endorsed by the National Republican Senatorial Committee.[44]

That simple fact speaks volumes about the 2010 elections. On the Republican side of the aisle, being part of the establishment proved electorally fatal to several GOP politicians around the country who were ousted by more conservative primary opponents carrying the fervor and backing of the Tea Party movement (e.g., Nevada U.S. Senate candidate Sharron Angle, see Chapter 2; and Delaware U.S. Senate candidate Christine O'Donnell). Rubio was one of these insurgent Republican candidates, and his message was superbly tailored to the right-leaning Florida electorate. On the other hand, unlike the aforementioned examples of Tea Party-endorsed candidates (and others, including successful Kentucky Republican Senate candidate Rand Paul), Rubio never said he was *of* the Tea Party, but that he was *allied with* the movement. This may seem like a trivial distinction, but it reveals Rubio's political acumen—allowing him more legislative flexibility should he win the election. After all, Rubio was by no means a political outsider; rather, he was a political insider with outsider backing.

The Republican: Marco Rubio

Marco Rubio was born in Miami, Florida, to Cuban exiles who escaped the Castro regime. His father worked as a bartender and his mother as a hotel house-keeper. His family moved to Las Vegas, Nevada, when Rubio was eight, but after several years they returned to Miami. From 2000 to 2008, Rubio was a member of the Florida House of Representatives where he shot up the leadership ranks serving successively as majority whip, majority leader, and finally as speaker of the House from 2006 to 2008.[45] Given such a promising career path, Rubio's decision to run for the U.S. Senate came from out of nowhere—especially given that Crist appeared almost unbeatable. Rubio's timing proved to be perfect. An appropriate analogy might be Bill Clinton's seemingly quixotic decision to run for president in 1992. In the summer of 1991, President George H. W. Bush enjoyed extraordinarily high job approval numbers based largely on his handling of the Persian Gulf War against Iraq. Rapidly coming to the surface, however, was voter discontent over the state of the economy. Clinton succeeded in tapping into voters' concerns regarding what became the most important issue in the 1992 presidential campaign. Likewise, at the time Rubio announced his Senate bid, Crist's approval was high and early polls projected him as winning the Republican nomination in a landslide. Similar to President Bush in 1992, conditions in 2010 were rapidly turning against Crist and in favor of the conservative politics of Marco Rubio.[46]

The General Election Campaign

The general election campaign began unofficially on Thursday, April 29, 2010, a typical warm and sunny afternoon in St. Petersburg's Straub Park, when Charlie Crist announced his decision to seek election to the U.S. Senate as a candidate with no party affiliation. Opening with a statement about how the current two-party system in Washington was broken because of the inability of politicians to reach bipartisan solutions, Crist went on to frame the choices facing Florida voters: "If you want somebody on the right or you want somebody on the left you have the former speaker, Rubio, or the congressman, Meek. If you want somebody who has common sense, who puts the will of the people first, who wants to fight for the people first, now you've got Charlie Crist. You have a choice."[47]

Of course, political expediency dictated Crist's decision to change his voter registration from Republican to no party affiliation and to declare his independent Senate bid, because it was now a virtual certainty that he would lose the August 24th Republican primary to Marco Rubio. As the political climate shifted to the right over the previous winter and into spring, media polling left little doubt that Rubio had not only overtaken Crist—but that his lead was actually growing among likely primary voters. Thus, for Crist to have any chance at all, he needed to cut ties with his lifelong party and assemble a coalition of Democratic defectors, political independents, and disgruntled Republicans.

The 2010 Florida Senate general election campaign can be denoted as two sequential stages: from early May to mid-August and from mid-August to November (see Figure 8.1).[48] Although Rubio had the lead prior to Crist's announcement that he was running as an Independent, the governor's support was given a significant boost by his decision to leave the Republican Party. In fact, during the first phase of the campaign Crist either had the lead or was in a dead heat with Rubio, indicating his apparent viability after renouncing the GOP. For all intents and purposes, however, Crist's resurgence turned out to be illusory. It was a reflection, first, of the excitement (in some quarters) generated by his decision and, second, of the fact that he received a great deal of media coverage focused on this event from late spring through mid-summer.[49] As it happens, summer is a bad time for any candidate to peak because many voters, especially independents, pay little heed to politics during the "dog days"—a period when people tend to be preoccupied with other things. It is not so much that polls conducted early in the campaign season are inaccurate, but rather that they fail to capture the fully formed impressions of citizens who often do not make up their minds until later.[50]

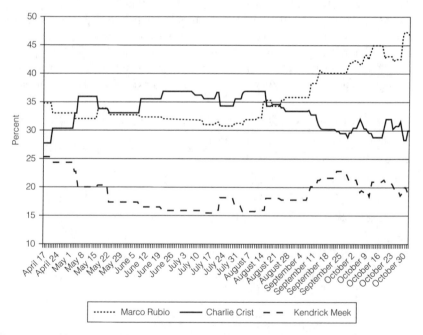

Figure 8.1 Rubio vs. Crist vs. Meek Polling Averages, 2010.
Source: Data compiled by the authors from Real Clear Politics, http://www.realclear-politics.com/epolls/2010/senate/fl/florida_senate_rubio_vs_meek_vs_crist-1456.html (accessed March 9, 2011).

So, we find that by the latter half of August, Rubio once again overtook Crist and began to build what would soon become a sizable lead over the incumbent governor. Unfortunately for Democrat Kendrick Meek, his greatest level of support occurred at the start of the time series in April (25.3 percent from April 17–25). His campaign never really gained traction, hardly surprising given Meek's party affiliation and issue stands in an election cycle that smiled upon the Republican Party. Reflective of his overall lack of standing with voters was the difficulty Meek had in raising money: his campaign was financially strapped from the start and ultimately spent just $9.2 million. At first glance that seems like a lot, but not compared with $13.6 million for Crist and $21.6 million for Rubio (see Table 8.2).[51] Over the last three Florida Senate contests (2004, 2006, and 2010), only Republican Katherine Harris in 2006 spent less money than Kendrick Meek did in 2010; Meek was also the only Senate candidate to spend more funds than he raised. Making matters worse, the media basically framed the race as a two-man contest. As a result, even though Rubio had a much larger campaign war chest, Crist was universally recognized by voters and garnered large amounts of earned media coverage, while Meek was more or less written off as a hopeless case (and the coverage he did get was not always helpful; see below).

From late August to Election Day, the Republican wave continued to build, lifting Rubio higher and higher in the polls. A core function of campaigns is to remind partisans of why they are Democrats or Republicans; responding to these cues, most partisans who might at one time have considered defecting from their traditional loyalties end up "returning home" and backing their party's candidates.[52] This was the case for Florida Republicans in 2010, but it was not true of Florida Democrats. As we will show in the next section, Democrats were

Table 8.2 Campaign Finance Data for Florida's Senate Campaigns, 2004–2010

Candidate and year	Disbursements	Receipts	Vote percentage
2010			
Marco Rubio (R)	$21,638,315	$21,748,330	48.9
Charlie Crist (I)	$13,608,676	$13,680,424	29.7
Kendrick B. Meek (D)	$9,243,904	$8,877,378	20.2
2006			
Bill Nelson (D)	$16,718,881	$18,031,681	60.3
Katherine Harris (R)	$8,659,232	$8,666,803	38.1
2004			
Mel Martinez (R)	$12,445,089	$12,463,752	49.4
Betty Castor (D)	$11,421,863	$11,601,990	48.3

Source: Election data are from the Florida Department of State, Division of Elections; all other data: Center for Responsive Politics, http://www.opensecrets.org (accessed February 15, 2011).

divided between Meek and Crist. Although we do not test this expectation here, there is evidence suggesting many Democratic identifiers preferred Meek, but instead voted for Crist because they thought he had a chance to win and Meek did not.[53] It should also be noted that independent voters did *not* align with the Independent candidate. When there is a strong partisan tide as in 2010, independents will invariably show the greatest movement in its direction;[54] accordingly, Republican Marco Rubio and not Independent Charlie Crist was the main beneficiary of the independent vote.

Compared to the rancorous campaign for Florida governor between Democrat Alex Sink and Republican Rick Scott, the Senate race was downright civil and on many occasions quite jocular, as evident in a number of exchanges that occurred over the course of six televised debates. To be sure, there were moments when candidates went on the attack, particularly in the case of Crist who criticized Rubio for his alleged personal use of GOP campaign money.[55] Further, it seemed as though there was no end to the political mileage Meek and Rubio sought to rack up by attacking Crist for abandoning his party and making him appear inauthentic and not credible with respect to his stances on a range of issues (gay adoption, abortion, health care reform). Overall, though, with Crist's sunny demeanor and the similarly favorable dispositions of Meek and Rubio, one of the nation's most watched campaigns was anything but overtly nasty and bitter. This is true despite perhaps the only serious bit of drama, which transpired during the week leading up to the election.

It was a case of "he said, he said," making it unclear what exactly happened. News broke that while former President Bill Clinton was campaigning on behalf of Kendrick Meek, he allegedly encouraged Meek to bow out so that Crist might have a chance to defeat Rubio. The story was huge, but Clinton and Meek both denied that the conversation ever took place; indeed, the Democratic nominee accused Crist of fabricating the whole thing in a last desperate attempt to climb back into the race.[56] Regardless of what was said, polling data suggest that it was too late in the game for this event to alter the election outcome—Rubio was simply too far ahead (see Figure 10.1). When all the votes were tallied, Rubio ended up with 48.9 percent, Crist took 29.7 percent, and Meek finished a distant third with 20.2 percent. Perhaps even more impressive is the geographic breadth of Rubio's support. Out of Florida's 67 counties, Rubio won a plurality of votes in 62; Crist captured the most votes in four (Broward, Leon, Palm Beach, and Pinellas—his home county); and Meek managed to secure the most votes in "only one—Gadsden—the state's lone majority black county."[57]

Voting Behavior in the 2010 Florida Senate Election

In understanding the voting behavior of an electorate, it is important to examine the fundamental characteristics of voters as well as their attitudes about political conditions prevailing at the time of an election. Using exit poll data from the 2010 Florida Senate race, it is possible to assess how both *enduring* and *transitory* factors help to shape vote choice. More specifically, we can examine

172 Seth C. McKee and Stephen C. Craig

the relationships between voter characteristics and candidate preferences (see Table 8.3), and the degree to which people's opinions on the short-term issues that pervaded the 2010 election corresponded with their Senate vote (see Table 8.4). These data illustrate, first and foremost, how an advantage on short-term issues allowed Marco Rubio to register a convincing victory in a three-candidate race that initially looked like it might turn out very differently.

Of twenty-six categories of voters shown in Table 8.3, the exit poll data indicate that Rubio won at least a plurality in nineteen (including the largest categories such as whites, married people, and those ages 45 and over). Rubio also tied Crist among two other groups (unmarried voters and urban residents).[58] Rubio trailed the governor, though not by much, among individuals with a postgraduate education (42 percent to 40 percent) and those who called themselves political moderates (41 percent to 36 percent)—and finished in third place behind both Meek and Crist only among groups that constitute the political base of the Democratic Party: African Americans (just 11 percent of the electorate in 2010, they gave 4 percent of their votes to Rubio), liberals (19 percent of the electorate, 10 percent of whom voted for Rubio), and Democratic identifiers (36 percent of the electorate, 8 percent of whom supported the Republican nominee).

Closer examination reveals other interesting patterns that mirror political cleavages evident in the nation as a whole. For example, men were more likely than women to support Rubio—a partisan gender gap that has existed since the 1980s in American politics, though the Republican tenor of this election year is evident in the fact that Rubio even won a plurality (44 percent) among women. Rubio's 4 percent support among blacks was unusually low, but explicable (we would assume) by the fact that his positions on salient issues were anathema to the bulk of the African-American electorate, and that Crist (with 21 percent of black votes) likely siphoned off support from some blacks who might otherwise have considered voting Republican in 2010.[59] In addition to these relationships and the tendencies noted in the previous paragraph, we also see from the exit poll data that Rubio fared better among middle- and upper-income voters and, oddly enough (because this group tends to be relatively less affluent), among citizens with no more than a high-school education. Finally, it is consistent with recent voting proclivities both in Florida and nationwide that the Senate vote was correlated with population density, that is, Rubio did much better in the more spacious suburban and rural communities than in the state's largest cities.

The effects of political ideology and party identification are also of particular interest (see the last two variables in Table 8.3). Where Rubio captured just 10 percent of the one out of five Florida voters who called themselves liberals, he took a respectable share of the moderate vote (42 percent of the electorate, 36 percent of whom supported Rubio) and dominated among the almost equal number of self-identified conservatives (with 82 percent). Reflecting the pull of partisan loyalties, Rubio received a paltry 8 percent from Democratic identifiers (who split more or less equally for Meek and Crist), a resounding 87 percent from Republicans—and, in the most telling statistic of all, 51 percent from independents (compared with 38 percent for Crist, 10 percent for Meek).

Table 8.3 Voter Characteristics and Senate Preferences in Florida, 2010

Voter Characteristics (% of the electorate)	Meek (D)	Crist (I)	Rubio (R)
Sex			
Male (45%)	17	28	55
Female (55%)	22	33	44
Race			
White (74%)	12	33	55
Black (11%)	74	21	4
Hispanic (12%)	20	25	55
Age			
18–29 (8%)	31	33	36
30–44 (17%)	23	29	47
45–64 (39%)	19	30	51
65 and older (35%)	17	33	50
Income			
Less than $50,000 (45%)	26	31	42
$50,000 or more (55%)	15	30	55
Education			
High School Graduate (20%)	22	24	53
Some College (31%)	19	31	50
College Graduate (32%)	18	31	50
Postgraduate (14%)	17	42	40
Marital Status			
Married (62%)	16	27	56
Unmarried (38%)	27	36	36
Size of Place			
Urban (26%)	25	37	37
Suburban (59%)	19	30	50
Rural (16%)	13	25	61
Ideology			
Liberal (19%)	37	52	10
Moderate (42%)	23	41	36
Conservative (39%)	7	10	82
Party Identification			
Democrat (36%)	47	44	8
Republican (36%)	1	12	87
Independent (29%)	10	38	51

Source: All data are from the National Election Pool exit poll for the Florida U.S. Senate and are available from CNN, www.cnn.com/ELECTION/2010/results/polls/#val=FLS01p1 (accessed March 8, 2011)

Note: N = 3,185 total respondents.

Table 8.4 Opinion of Political Conditions and Senate Preferences in Florida, 2010

Short-Term Opinions (% of electorate)	Meek (D)	Crist (I)	Rubio (R)
How Obama is Handling his Job as President			
Approve (45%)	41	50	8
Disapprove (54%)	2	16	82
Opinion of Government			
Government should do more (36%)	34	46	20
Government doing too much (57%)	10	20	70
Opinion of Federal Government			
Satisfied/Enthusiastic (28%)	37	48	15
Angry/Dissatisfied (70%)	12	23	64
Opinion of Tea Party Movement			
Support (40%)	3	10	86
Neutral (24%)	20	35	44
Oppose (32%)	39	55	6
Most Important Issue Facing Country Today			
Economy (69%)	19	31	50
Health Care (16%)	24	32	44
Highest Priority for Next Congress			
Cutting Taxes (18%)	11	14	74
Reducing Deficit (34%)	12	23	64
Spending to Create Jobs (43%)	31	42	27
Stimulus Package Has ...			
Helped Economy (33%)	42	49	9
Hurt Economy (34%)	2	11	86
Made No Difference (30%)	16	32	51
U.S. Economy Is In ...			
Normal Downturn (24%)	32	42	26
Long-Term Decline (73%)	15	26	58
What Should Congress Do with new Health Care Law?			
Expand It (29%)	40	47	12
Leave It As Is (19%)	30	44	25
Repeal It (45%)	2	13	85
Want U.S. Senate Controlled By ...			
Democrats (40%)	46	46	8
Republicans (46%)	3	10	87
Country Is Going In ...			
Right Direction (36%)	44	47	9
Wrong Track (61%)	7	21	72

Source: All data are from the National Election Pool exit poll for the Florida U.S. Senate and are available from CNN, www.cnn.com/ELECTION/2010/results/polls/#val=FLS01p1 (accessed March 8, 2011)

Note: N = 3,185 total respondents.

Even more impressive than Rubio's performance among different voter demographics was his strong performance with respect to voter opinions on the issues and broad themes that dominated the 2010 election (see Table 8.4). In short, Rubio was the candidate for the political season. Recall that Rubio won 49 percent of the total Florida U.S. Senate vote. On ten of the eleven exit poll questions examined here, the plurality (or in some cases majority) of voters registered support for Rubio that exceeded his share of the overall vote. For example, the Republican nominee won 82 percent of the vote from those (54 percent) who disapproved of President Obama's job performance, 64 percent from those (70 percent) who expressed anger or dissatisfaction with the federal government, 50 percent from those (69 percent) who named the economy as the nation's most important issue, 85 percent from those (45 percent) who wanted to repeal the new health care law, and so on. The one exception to this pattern occurred among the plurality (43 percent) who said that "spending to create jobs" should be the highest priority for the next Congress (Rubio took just 27 percent from this group, compared with 42 percent for Crist and 31 percent for Meek).

Among Florida voters in 2010, the common thread is the palpable negativity and pessimism regarding the political status quo—and the extent to which those sentiments contributed to Rubio's victory in the senate race. While the Republican nominee fared poorly among those who were satisfied with the way things were going, such individuals constituted a distinct minority of the 2010 electorate. For instance, 40 percent of Florida voters supported the Tea Party movement and 86 percent of them backed Rubio. For the much larger number of citizens who disapproved of President Obama, felt the government was doing (and spending) too much, viewed the U.S. economy as being in long-term decline, and generally wanted a conservative change of policy direction, Marco Rubio was viewed as a welcome agent of change.[60]

Conclusion

In 2010, the decision of a sitting Florida governor to seek election to the U.S. Senate by disavowing his Republican affiliation and running as an Independent, sent shockwaves throughout the state and across the nation. In keeping with his centrist record and governing philosophy, Charlie Crist welcomed President Obama to the Sunshine State at a time when the newly elected Democratic president was still basking in the glow of his honeymoon and aggressively promoting an economic stimulus plan designed to put the brakes on a downward spiraling economy. Crist strongly supported using federal dollars to soften Florida's economic woes, but his decision to do so (and to do so with such apparent enthusiasm) would ultimately force him out of the Republican Party. In an age of highly polarized partisan elites, Crist's bipartisan overture was deemed sacrilege by the GOP faithful and Marco Rubio emerged as the defender of conservative values and the leading opponent of the Democratic agenda emanating from Washington.

Exit poll data in 2008 revealed that 62 percent of Florida presidential voters considered the economy to be the nation's most important issue; 56 percent of these individuals cast a vote for Democrat Barack Obama. In the 2010 exit poll, 69 percent of Florida voters selected the economy as the most important issue— and in a three-way Senate race, 50 percent of them supported Republican Marco Rubio. It is truly remarkable how fast things can change. More than any other issue, the economy has dominated the last two election cycles and, as Charlie Crist found out, being "wrong" on this one not only forced him to leave his party but left him without enough support from political independents, most of whom ended up riding the Republican wave in November. Ironically, Independent Charlie Crist failed to win the Florida U.S. Senate race because independents turned against him. With an economic recovery failing to materialize, many of these voters shifted their support to the GOP in the hopes that it could get the results Democrats had failed to deliver.

In contemporary American politics, volatility is a cardinal feature of recent elections.[61] At the national level, the two major parties are so evenly balanced that the shift of a relatively small number of political independents often determines which party wins the next majority.[62] Indeed, recent developments in Florida politics signal a perpetuation of electoral instability. In March, 2011, Crist's successor, Republican Governor Rick Scott, stood firm in rejecting $2.4 billion in federal dollars that would be used to build a high-speed rail line between the cities of Tampa and Orlando. This decision (one suspects it will be the first of many) stirred up bipartisan opposition in the state legislature, and generated strong criticism from Democratic U.S. Senator Bill Nelson, who will stand for reelection in 2012.

If the recent past is a harbinger of the future, another Republican wave in 2012 is unlikely. To the contrary, we suspect that it may turn out to be a reasonably good year for Democrats at least as long as the economy in Florida and around the country show signs of recovery. If this happens, then the state's substantial population of political independents will almost certainly shift in the direction of both Nelson and other Democratic candidates. If Senator Nelson, in particular, is fortunate to draw another Republican purist challenger as he did in 2006 (former Secretary of State Katherine Harris), then it should surprise no one if this opponent ends up falling on his or her ideological sword.

Notes

1. James A. Stimson, *Tides of Consent: How Public Opinion Shapes American Politics* (Cambridge: Cambridge University Press, 2004).
2. James W. Ceaser and Andrew E. Busch, *The Perfect Tie: The True Story of the 2000 Presidential Election* (Lanham, MD: Rowman & Littlefield, 2001).
3. V.O. Key, Jr., *Southern Politics in State and Nation* (New York: Knopf, 1949), p. 83.
4. We define the South as the eleven ex-Confederate states (Alabama, Arkansas, Florida, Georgia, Louisiana, Mississippi, North Carolina, South Carolina, Tennessee, Texas, and Virginia), and all remaining states as the non-South.

5. In this section all of the data on population growth and birth location were compiled by the authors from online sources made available by the U.S. Census Bureau.

6. Of the eleven southern states Texas ranks last in its percentage of African Americans and first in its proportion of Hispanics; in contrast, Florida ranks second in its Latino percentage and second to last in its proportion of African Americans (Seth C. McKee, *Republican Ascendancy in Southern U.S. House Elections* (Boulder, CO: Westview Press, 2010)).

7. Stephen C. Craig and Roger Austin, "Elections and Partisan Change in Florida," in *Politics and Government in Florida*, 3rd ed., ed. J. Edwin Benton (Gainesville, FL: University Press of Florida, 2008), pp. 48–79; Danny Hayes and Seth C. McKee, "Toward A One-Party South?" *American Politics Research*, vol. 36 (2008), no. 1, pp. 3–32. The geographic concentration of Florida Democrats greatly advantages the GOP in district-based contests. "By 2008, more than 60 percent of the state's Democrats lived in only ten metropolitan counties; 80 percent lived in just twenty counties" (Michael J. Scicchitano and Richard K. Scher, "Florida: Political Change, 1950–2008," in *The New Politics of the Old South: An Introduction to Southern Politics*, 4th ed., eds. Charles S. Bullock III and Mark J. Rozell (Lanham, MD: Rowman & Littlefield, 2010), pp. 245–266). As meticulously analyzed by Chen and Rodden (Jowei Chen and Jonathan Rodden, "Tobler's Law, Urbanization, and Electoral Bias: Why Compact, Contiguous Districts are Bad for the Democrats," Unpublished Manuscript, 2009) and explained by Scicchitano and Scher (p. 250), "for congressional and state legislative races—determined by districts—it will be hard for them to achieve a majority of the congressional delegation or of either chamber of the state legislature. There are simply too many Democrats in too few places to expect otherwise."

8. Joan Carver and Tom Fiedler, "Florida: A Volatile National Microcosm," in *Southern Politics in the 1990s*, ed. Alexander P. Lamis (Baton Rouge, LA: Louisiana State University Press, 1999), p. 343.

9. David R. Colburn, *From Yellow Dog Democrats to Red State Republicans: Florida and its Politics since 1940* (Gainesville, FL: University Press of Florida, 2007), p. 3.

10. Scicchitano and Scher, "Florida: Political Change, 1950–2008."

11. James G. Gimpel and Jason E. Schuknecht, *Patchwork Nation: Sectionalism and Political Change in American Politics* (Ann Arbor: University of Michigan Press, 2004).

12. Key, *Southern Politics in State and Nation*.

13. Suzanne L. Parker, "Shifting Party Tides in Florida: Where Have All the Democrats Gone?" in *The South's New Politics: Realignment and Dealignment*, eds. Robert H. Swansbrough and David M. Brodsky, pp. 22–37 (Columbia, SC: University of South Carolina Press, 1988).

14. Gimpel and Schuknecht, *Patchwork Nation*.

15. Benjamin G. Bishin and Casey A. Klofstad, "The Political Attitudes and Behavior of Cuban Americans: Why Won't Little Havana Turn Blue?" (Unpublished Manuscript, 2011).

16. Susan A. MacManus, "Florida Overview: Ten Media Markets—One Powerful State," in *Florida's Politics: Ten Media Markets, One Powerful State*, eds. Kevin A. Hill, Susan A. MacManus, and Dario Moreno (Tallahassee, FL: Florida Institute of Government, 2004), pp. 1–64.

17. Stephen J. Whitfield, "Florida's Fudged Identity," *Florida Historical Quarterly*, vol. 71 (1993), no. 4, p. 430.

18. Lance deHaven-Smith, *The Florida Voter* (Tallahassee, FL: Florida Institute of Government, 1995).

19. Key, *Southern Politics in State and Nation*, p. 86.

20. Samuel L. Popkin, *The Reasoning Voter: Communication and Persuasion in Presidential Campaigns* (Chicago: University of Chicago Press, 1991).
21. Morris P. Fiorina, *Retrospective Voting in American National Elections* (New Haven, CT: Yale University Press, 1981); V. O. Key Jr., *The Responsible Electorate: Rationality in Presidential Voting, 1936–1960* (Cambridge, MA: Belknap Press of Harvard University Press, 1966).
22. Stimson, *Tides of Consent.*
23. The opposite is also true, of course: When conditions are favorable, most independents can be expected to support keeping the majority party in power.
24. Gary C. Jacobson, *The Politics of Congressional Elections* (New York: Pearson Longman, 2009).
25. Paul R. Abramson, John H. Aldrich, and David W. Rohde, *Change and Continuity in the 2008 Elections* (Washington, D.C.: CQ Press, 2010).
26. Susan A. MacManus, "Florida: A Plummeting Economy, Tea Parties, and Palin Give GOP a Clean Sweep," in *Key States, High Stakes,* ed. Charles S. Bullock III (Lanham, MD: Rowman & Littlefield, forthcoming).
27. Jacobson, *The Politics of Congressional Elections,* p. 205.
28. These data are from the 2010 National Election Pool exit poll on Florida U.S. Senate voters (http://www.cnn.com/ELECTION/2010/results/polls/#val=FLS01p1; accessed March 15, 2011).
29. As mentioned throughout this book, voter enthusiasm is an indicator of which party's supporters are more motivated to vote, whether in favor of or against candidates. The enthusiasm gap benefited Democrats in 2008, but in 2010 Republicans were much more energized. Election data from Florida speak to this change in partisan mobilization. Early voting is a good proxy for gauging voter enthusiasm and Michael P. McDonald's early voting statistics (his Web site is: http://elections.gmu.edu/voter_turnout.htm) on Florida are revealing: Among early voters, 45.6 percent in 2008 were registered Democrats and 37.3 percent were registered Republicans; by contrast, the early voting numbers in 2010 were 36.5 percent registered Democrats and 49.2 percent registered Republicans.
30. Susan A. MacManus, "Florida: A 'Red Tide' Beaches All Democrats Running Statewide; U.S. Senate and Gubernatorial Races Highly Nationalized," in *Pendulum Swing,* ed. Larry J. Sabato (New York: Pearson Longman, 2012), p. 7 [draft chapter].
31. In terms of racial composition, the 17th had the largest percentage (56 percent) of African Americans among congressional districts in Florida. The district was also 25 percent Hispanic and Meek ran unopposed in all four of his U.S. House contests (Barone and Cohen, *The Almanac of American Politics 2010* (Washington, D.C. National Journal, 2009)).
32. Meek was not without blemish. He was caught up in a low-grade scandal involving his mother, who after leaving Congress received payments from a developer she had lobbied to build a pharmaceutical park in her son's district. Michael Barone and Richard E. Cohen, *The Almanac of American Politics 2010.*
33. On August 7, 2009, Martinez announced his resignation effective as soon as a replacement could be appointed. Governor Crist selected George Lemieux, his chief of staff, "to fill the vacancy (in essence, a placeholder) [convincing] many observers Crist would run for the Senate" (MacManus, "Florida: A 'Red Tide' Beaches All Democrats Running Statewide," p. 4). The observers were obviously correct on that score.
34. See http://www.dailyfinance.com/story/real-estate/from-profiteer-to-politician-billionaire-jeff-greene-races-for/19485569 (accessed March 15, 2011).
35. MacManus, "Florida: A 'Red Tide' Beaches All Democrats Running Statewide."
36. Ibid., p. 6. Out of 918,273 Democratic senatorial primary votes, Meek won 57.5 percent to Greene's 31 percent (and two minor candidates won the remaining

11.4 percent). Election data here and throughout the chapter are from the Florida Department of State, Division of Elections.
37. Craig and Austin, "Elections and Partisan Change in Florida"; Stephen C. Craig and James G. Kane, "Nelson Defeats McCollum in Florida's Senate Race," in *The Roads to Congress 2000*, eds. Sunil Ahuja and Robert Dewhirst (Belmont, CA: Wadsworth, 2002), pp. 165–179.
38. Barone and Cohen. *The Almanac of American Politics 2010*, p. 346.
39. Ibid., p. 346.
40. The median voter theory proposes that politicians will maximize their vote shares by taking issue positions close to those preferred by the median (middle) voter. Anthony Downs, *An Economic Theory of Democracy* (New York: Harper, 1957); see also: Duncan Black, "On the Rationale of Group Decision-making." *Journal of Political Economy*, vol. 56 (1948), no. 1, pp. 23–34.
41. Delegates take positions that reflect the preferences of their constituents, while trustees rely upon their own judgment in determining what course of action is in the best interests of those whom they represent. See Roger H. Davidson, Walter J. Oleszek, and Frances E. Lee, *Congress and Its Members*, 12th ed. (Washington, D.C.: CQ Press, 2010).
42. The *St. Petersburg Times* published an excellent feature on Crist, highlighting his political style and making explicit note of how often he used the word "people" in his rhetoric (see "The Progress of a 'People' Person," by Alex Leary and Caryn Baird (May 30, 2010, pp. 1P, 6P)).
43. MacManus, "Florida: A 'Red Tide' Beaches All Democrats Running Statewide," p. 4.
44. Barone and Cohen. *The Almanac of American Politics 2010*, p. 346.
45. These biographical facts were taken from Rubio's U.S. Senate Web site, http://www/rubio.senate.gov/public/index.cfm/about?p=biography (accessed March 10, 2011).
46. Against two obscure opponents, Rubio won 84.6 percent of the 1,264,442 votes cast in the Republican Senate primary.
47. Quoted in Adam C. Smith and Beth Reinhard, "Charlie Crist, I-Florida, has long slog to Nov. 2," *St. Petersburg Times*, April 30, 2010, p. 10A.
48. See http://www.realclearpolitics.com/. The results here are very reliable because each data point represents an average across multiple polls for each day of the campaign. Note, however, that there are several consecutive days when the numbers do not change because no new polls have been administered; this accounts for the stair-step patterns observed in the figure.
49. This provided voters with a somewhat one-sided information flow; John R. Zaller, *The Nature and Origins of Mass Opinion* (New York: Cambridge University Press, 1992).
50. Stimson, *Tides of Consent.*
51. Data are from the Center for Responsive Politics, http://www.opensecrets.org (accessed February 15, 2011).
52. Bernard R. Berelson, Paul F. Lazarsfeld, and William N. McPhee, *Voting: A Study of Opinion Formation in a Presidential Campaign* (Chicago: University of Chicago Press, 1954).
53. M. V. Hood III and Seth C. McKee, "Strategic Voting in the 2010 Florida Senate Election" (Unpublished Manuscript, 2011).
54. John R. Petrocik and Scott W. Desposato, "Incumbency and Short-Term Influences on Voters," *Political Research Quarterly*, vol. 57 (2004), no. 3, pp. 363–373; Stimson, *Tides of Consent.*
55. The Florida Republican Party was under a cloud during the 2010 campaign because of various financially related corruption scandals. For example, state GOP chairman Jim Greer was forced to vacate his post because of financial indiscretions, and

Charlie Crist had trouble accounting for the sources of monies he used to pay for a Walt Disney World vacation.
56. See Beth Reinhard, Michael Van Sickler, and Aaron Sharockman, "Full Day of: No he Didn't, Yes he Did," *St. Petersburg Times*, October 30, 2010, p. 1A.
57. MacManus, "Florida: A 'Red Tide' Beaches All Democrats Running Statewide," p. 7.
58. For each category listed under a particular variable (e.g., there are three of these for race: white, black, and Hispanic), the table shows the percentage of voters who fell into that category (e.g., 74 percent were white, 11 percent were black, and 12 percent were Hispanic). This information lets us know the relative size of each group in the voting electorate and, when we also consider how they cast their ballots, it is apparent which groups played the largest role in determining the election outcome.
59. Crist managed to win 18 percent of the black vote when he ran for governor in 2006, "an unusually high figure for a Republican" (Barone and Cohen, *The Almanac of American Politics 2010*, p. 346).
60. The exit poll asked voters what is the "candidate quality that mattered most to you?" A plurality of voters (34 percent) chose "understands people," and 52 percent of this group voted for Rubio (vs. 25 percent for Meek and 22 percent for Crist). A close second (33 percent) was the quality "can bring change"—and 61 percent of people giving this answer voted for Rubio (vs. 18 percent for Meek and 20 percent for Crist). Only 16 percent of voters selected "experience," and Crist took 54 percent among these voters (vs. 15 percent for Meek and 30 percent for Rubio).
61. Abramson, Aldrich, and Rohde, *Change and Continuity in the 2008 Elections*.
62. Earl Black and Merle Black, *Divided America: The Ferocious Power Struggle in American Politics* (New York: Simon & Schuster, 2007).

9 Marshall vs. Scott in Georgia's Eighth Congressional District

The Power of Incumbency Fails

Charles S. Bullock, III and Karen P. Owen

In this monumental election that saw Republicans gain 63 seats in the House of Representatives, the most vulnerable Democrats represented districts where their conservative constituents preferred Republican presidential candidates. Jim Marshall of Georgia's 8th District was one of these Democrats. Many of these candidates managed to retain their seats by balancing demands from their party's leadership that sought their votes for controversial policies against a tendency of their constituents to support Republicans. Increasingly, they confronted a Hobson's choice: try to curry favor with Nancy Pelosi and risk rejection back home; or ignore her demands to stand with the Democratic leadership in facing down the united Republicans and possibly forfeit promotion to a better committee, become a subcommittee chair, or obtain that coveted project for the district.

Some of the savvier Democrats from marginal districts anticipated the potential for problems, even in the afterglow of Obama's election, and ignored calls from their leaders to fall in behind the agenda of the new president and the House Speaker. Wary Democrats may have remembered the fate of Marjorie Margolis-Mezvinsky, who, in 1994, won a suburban Philadelphia district that Republicans had held for 76 years. She made herself a one-term member of the House when she ignored her campaign promise to oppose a tax increase and voted for the Clinton deficit reduction package.[1]

Among marginal congressional Democrats, the onset of the Obama administration bore an eerie resemblance to the beginning of the Clinton administration. Both new presidents embraced policy positions designed to please the liberal components of their electoral coalitions. Moderate and conservative Democrats in Congress looked on in dismay as their party pushed programs that would not play well in a congressional district where a majority voted for John McCain for president while simultaneously sending a Democrat to the House. Beginning with the first day of the 111th Congress, Democrats from marginal districts had to cast votes that they knew might come back to haunt them. The first roll call of the new session elected the Speaker and Democrats lined up behind liberal Nancy Pelosi. As the session progressed, their leadership called for support of the administration's stimulus package (the American Reinvestment and Recovery Act) and its major environmental initiative, the American Clean Energy and

Security Act of 2009 (or what came to be known as the cap-and-trade bill). Later the signature accomplishment of the Obama administration, its health care bill (the Patient Protection and Affordable Care Act of 2010) came up for a vote. Time and again, Democrats from districts that preferred McCain to Obama had to confront their party's whips' entreaties that they save their president from public humiliation. By November 2010, marginal Democrats like Jim Marshall were struggling to retain their seats. In the end, Marshall was among those swept out by the Republican tide—even though he voted against the Obama health care legislation and cap-and-trade. Seeking his fifth term, Marshall could not survive the midterm drop off in Democratic turnout coupled with a Republican electorate energized in opposition to Marshall's support for the Troubled Asset Relief Program (TARP) and the stimulus bill.

Georgia's 8th District

The district Marshall initially won in 2002 ran east to west across the middle of the state. After Republicans took control of the state legislature in 2005, they redrew the congressional map to restore the 8th District to its earlier north-south alignment. Consequently in 2006, 44.7 percent of the voting age population was new to the district. Republicans sought to make the new district more hospitable for their party but did not go to the extreme that Texas Republicans had a couple of years earlier when redesigning their state (see Chapter 3).[2] Had Republicans split more counties—for example, had they shifted much of Macon's black population into the 2nd District and replaced it with whites – they could have defeated Marshall in 2006.[3] In 2010 the 8th District started one county north of the Florida border, went through Macon, and had its northern terminus in counties on the southeast corner of the Atlanta metropolitan area.

I-75 ties the 8th District together. Cordele, at the southern end, bills itself as the Watermelon Capital of the World while nearby autumn fields spew forth peanuts. The population concentration lies along the fall line that bisects Georgia in an arc curving northeast from Columbus to Macon and on to Augusta. Macon, the state's sixth largest city, has about one-seventh of the district's population. The second largest city, Warner Robins, just south of Macon, has about 60,000 residents. The 8th District includes four of the five counties in the Macon metropolitan area, but its most rapid growth has come at the northern end anchored in the southeast corner of the booming Atlanta metropolitan area. During the first six years of the 21st century, Newton County, the northernmost in the 8th District, was the 11th fastest growing county in the nation. In 2010, about one-sixth of the vote came from the metro Atlanta counties while one-third came from the metropolitan Macon.

Robins Air Force Base in Warner Robins serves as a jobs magnet. The base has approximately 20,000 workers, with civilians constituting two-thirds of the work force. Civilian workers come from many counties in middle Georgia. The economic significance of the base means that the district representative needs to secure appointment to the Armed Services Committee, where Marshall served throughout his House career. By having seats on Armed Services and Agriculture, Marshall managed to represent two key district industries and also could connect with the rural southern end of the district and the more urbanized middle portion.

Macon, the district's largest city, has not flourished in recent decades. Its population peaked at 122,000 in 1980. It has subsequently declined by about a quarter and has lost jobs as industry, including a major cigarette plant and textile manufacturers, has pulled out of the city. With the Atlanta airport just an hour north of Macon, the city has also experienced reductions in air service. Like other Georgia counties that have core cities, Bibb County consistently supports Democratic candidates up and down the ballot.

Much of what makes Georgia's 8th District so competitive is the fact that African Americans make up 33 percent of the population. In recent years, Republicans have held every state Senate district that was less than 30 percent African American and Democrats have held districts more than 30 percent African American (with one exception).[4] In the 2002 election when Georgia elected the first Republican governor in more than 130 years, Sonny Perdue won 107 of the 110 counties that were less than 30 percent black. To survive in 2010, Jim Marshall needed to maintain strong turnout in the African-American community and win the support of a sizable minority of the white electorate.

District Politics

During Jim Marshall's tenure in the House, Georgia grew increasingly more Republican. Throughout his career, however, he oscillated between narrow midterm victories and comfortable presidential year successes. When first elected in 2002, Marshall eked out a 51 percent to 49 percent victory over Commissioner Calder Clay of Bibb County (which is home to Macon). That year, Republicans won the governorship and defeated Democratic incumbent Senator Max Cleland. They also took control of the state Senate for the first time in more than a century in 2002. Two years later, following imposition of a court redistricting plan, Republicans expanded their share of the Senate seats and won control of the state House. Increased turnout in the 2004 presidential election, however, boosted Marshall's margin of victory to 63 percent even as the district's presidential vote slipped from 42 percent for Al Gore to 39 percent for John Kerry. Democrats did well nationally in 2006 gaining 30 U.S. House seats. That Democratic tide barely lapped at Georgia's shore where Marshall held on to his seat with a margin of 1,752 votes as he turned back a bid by former U.S. Representative Mac Collins. Marshall's narrow reelection win coincided with Republican victories for the positions of lieutenant governor and secretary of state. In 2008, Republicans won Georgia's Electoral College vote for a fourth consecutive time and the sixth time in the previous seven elections (Bill Clinton managed a 13,714-vote plurality win in 1992). The pendulum swung again and Marshall defeated retired General Rick Goddard more handily taking 57 percent of the vote in the process.

The battle in the 8th District was not unlike those in many competitive districts, especially those where Democratic incumbents fell, in terms of the issues that were front and center for voters. In these competitive races, challengers focused on the incumbent's voting record in keeping with one of those maxims of politics: voters do not hire challengers, but they may fire incumbents. In 2010, Jim Marshall had to defend his vote to make Nancy Pelosi Speaker, and those on controversial policies such as the stimulus package and to bail out Wall Street (TARP). Marshall, however, tried to put his opponent on the defensive for a vote and comment he made about illegal aliens.

The Incumbent Jim Marshall

Jim Marshall might seem like a poor fit for a largely rural Georgia district. Born in Ithaca, New York, he received his undergraduate education at Princeton before earning a law degree at Boston University. Marshall came to Georgia to join the law faculty at Mercer University and left academia in 1995 to serve as Macon's mayor. The element in his background with which district residents could most readily identify involved his military ties. The district has a long tradition of representation by congressional leaders in the sphere of national defense. It includes the home of Sam Nunn (1972–1997), who, while in the Senate, was the chamber's leading national defense expert and chair of the Armed Services Committee. Furthermore, nine of the counties were represented by Representative Carl Vinson who chaired the House Naval Affairs Committee from 1931 until 1947 when it was combined with the Military Affairs Committee to create the Armed Services Committee. Vinson chaired the Armed Services committee or served as ranking minority member from 1947 until 1965. Marshall's father and grandfather had served as Army generals. Marshall, who initially dropped out of college, joined the army, was wounded while a platoon leader in Vietnam, and received two bronze stars.

Marshall, a very savvy politician, recognized the competitiveness of the 8th District, as well as the important racial divisions that exist. Knowing whites in his district tend to be Republican, he maintained one of the most conservative voting records among House Democrats. On the ratings scheme developed by the *National Journal*, Marshall ranked as the fourth most conservative Democratic in 2009. His support scores, as calculated by the American Conservative Union and Americans for Democratic Action, varied rather wildly over his first seven years in office, but they generally reflected a more conservative record than most Democrats (see Table 9.1). As he gained experience, Marshall's ACU scores increased, peaking at 72 percent in 2007 before declining and averaging only 30 percent in 2008–2009. His support for the roll calls selected by the ADA hovered between 50 and 70 percent except for 2006, his most conservative year when it plummeted to 35 percent.[5]

Marshall gave relatively low support to his party leadership, voting against it more than a quarter of the time in his first year. His support for his party dropped in the next few years, although he became more loyal after Demo-

Table 9.1 Congressional Vote Scores for Jim Marshall, 2003–2010

Year	American Conservative Union	Americans for Democratic Action	Party Unity	Presidential Support
2010	48%	35%	72%	67%
2009	32%	50%	79%	75%
2008	28%	70%	83%	33%
2007	61%	60%	75%	37%
2006	72%	35%	65%	65%
2005	46%	70%	67%	59%
2004	48%	55%	69%	53%
2003	24%	70%	73%	53%

Source: CQ's *Politics in America* (Washington, DC: Congressional Quarterly, Inc., 2010 and 2000); The American Conservative Union (http://www.conservative.org); Americans for Democratic Action (http://www.adaction.org); and Congressional Quarterly vote studies (2009: http://innovation.cqpolitics.com/media/vote_study_2009; and 2010: http://innovation.cq.com/media/vote_study_2010).

crats took control of the House in 2007. He also distinguished himself from liberal Democrats, supporting President Bush more often than not through 2006. Marshall supported President Obama only slightly more than he had supported President Bush prior to 2007. He voted against the signature item of the Obama first term, the health care bill and opposed the cap-and-trade bill. On the other hand, he supported the Obama stimulus plan and in late 2008 voted for the Bush administration's Troubled Assets Relief Program (TARP).

In spite of his very conservative record for a Democrat, Marshall was still in the ideological center for the entire House and he recognized that over his first seven years his voting record placed him right in the middle of the liberal-conservative continuum.[6] In the Georgia delegation, Marshall stood well to the right of the four African-American members and only slightly more conservative than another white Democrat, John Barrow. Marshall, however, was far to the left of the delegation's Republican members. In 2009, Georgia's seven Republicans had an average *National Journal* composite conservative score of 90.4 compared with Marshall's 55.[7]

The Challenger Austin Scott

His close victories in previous midterm contests suggested that 2010 would be a challenge for Marshall. The challenge became much stiffer when seven-term state Representative Austin Scott adjusted his ambitions and withdrew from the gubernatorial contest, where he was making little headway, and declared his intent to run for the 8th District's seat. Scott, an insurance agent, campaigned as a conservative small business owner. He jumped into a primary that already had two Republican contestants. Despite his late entry, Scott had far more experience than his competitors and won nomination without a costly and divisive runoff.[8]

When Scott was first elected to the Georgia House in 1996, Democrats still dominated southern Georgia. Only one other rural district in the southwest quadrant of the state sent a Republican to the state House. At that time, other than Scott's the only state House district with a Republican representative in the current 8th Congressional District was an urban one in Macon. No Republican represented any portion of southwest Georgia in the state Senate.

Austin Scott got to the state legislature by defeating Henry Bostick, an attorney seeking his seventh consecutive term, but who had previously served in the House during the 1970s. The 1992 redistricting plan gave the district a Republican tilt, and it had begun voting for statewide GOP candidates. As in his 2010 congressional bid, Scott had the advantage of youth when he challenged Bostick. Scott won that race and became the chamber's youngest member at 27 years of age. Scott attributes his win to a televised debate ten days before the election in which he demonstrated a command of the issues and convinced voters that the district needed new leadership. He won the state legislative seat without much assistance from the state GOP.

He quickly made the district a safe one and faced no Democratic challenger until 2006. Some thought that when Democrats redrew the maps following the 2000 census in an audacious gerrymander,[9] Scott would become a victim. The new maps paired most Republican legislators (in an attempt to make them run against each other) but Scott escaped, probably because no nearby districts had Republican legislators with whom to pair him and his Democratic cousin who represented an adjoining district retired. Scott did draw a Democratic challenger in 2006 and 2008 but won both years with about 54 percent of the vote.

During his state House service Scott demonstrated a degree of independence. In 2001, Scott was one of the few rural Republicans to join with urban legislators, both black and white Democrats, who voted to change Georgia's flag to remove the St. Andrew's cross due to its similarity to the flag of the Confederacy during the Civil War. After Republicans took control of the House, Scott and only four other Republicans ignored the House speaker's call for them to vote to override a gubernatorial veto. The Speaker's deal making to line up votes offended Scott.[10] The future member of Congress felt so strongly about the issue that he offered to resign his committee chair.

The Campaign

The 8th District race included the kind of charge and counter-charge dynamic that has become common in U.S. House campaigns. Scott quickly put the incumbent on the defensive, attacking him for the votes he had cast for unpopular Obama programs and repeatedly linking Marshall and Nancy Pelosi. Marshall, recognizing the unpopularity of the Democratic brand in 2010, denounced Pelosi and emphasized instances in which he had voted against the national Democratic Party in order to take the more conservative stands popular in the district.

Although the Tea Party had little visibility, and this contest is not among those identified as one in which the Tea Party had a candidate, Austin Scott articulated concerns of that grassroots movement. Dressed in a work shirt and jeans and leaning on a pickup truck he looked into the camera in one ad and promised to cut taxes, reduce the debt and protect jobs. Scott frequently attacked Marshall for supporting the Obama stimulus bill and castigated the incumbent for supporting the Employee Free Choice Act (also known as "card check," which would make union organizing easier), TARP, and for voting to raise the national debt limit. A common theme in Scott's ads was his promise to fight for jobs. One Scott ad asserted that Marshall "sent nearly two billion tax dollars oversees to create jobs in China."[11]

The challenger and his supporters never passed up an opportunity to link Marshall to Nancy Pelosi and the Democratic leadership, often referring to the incumbent as a "Pelosi-crat." One ad began with citizens chastising the incumbent for false attacks on Scott then transitioned to "False attacks are wrong but Marshall's votes with Nancy Pelosi are worse."[12] The ad continued with a voiceover denouncing Marshall's "vote to bail out Wall Street and for Nancy Pelosi's stimulus bill that sent $18 million to dead people, $4.3 million to prison inmates and spent over a billion on jobs overseas." It concluded with a stern constituent's observation, "Jim Marshall, it's time for you to go!" In another ad Scott accused Marshall of false advertising which Scott characterized as a distraction "to hide his [Marshall's] support for Barack Obama and Nancy Pelosi and job killing taxes, wasteful spending, massive debt and record unemployment."[13]

The National Republican Congressional Committee (NRCC), which invested heavily in Scott, also frequently linked Marshall to Pelosi. One NRCC advertisement portrayed Marshall chauffeuring Pelosi around in a Cadillac convertible as viewers were told that the incumbent had voted with Pelosi 90 percent of the time. The ad further explained that Marshall supported the bail out of financial institutions. In other words, Marshall was looking out for Wall Street but ignored Main Street. Another NRCC ad asked if Nancy Pelosi was right 88 percent of the time, and yet another one conjoined Marshall, Pelosi and his vote to increase the estate tax, also known as the "death" tax. Despite allegations of closeness between Marshall and the Speaker, Scott warned in a debate that as retribution for criticizing Pelosi from the stump, the speaker would boot Marshall off the Armed Services Committee which would hurt Robins Air Force Base, the district's largest employer.[14] The NRCC, did a "The Real Jim Marshall" ad that contrasted what Marshall stood for in the district—lower taxes and characterizing debt as a sin—with behavior in Washington.[15] The NRCC criticized Marshall for voting to increase the death tax and raising the national debt limit by $2 trillion. The American Future Fund, a conservative outside group that ran television ads against 15 Democrats, spent $350,000 to elect Scott with an ad that observed: "Times are hard. Jim Marshall makes them worse."

Marshall fought back stressing his independence and noting that he broke with his party's leaders when he thought them too liberal. In one frequently-aired ad he appeared opening his billfold to remove identification while announcing that "I'm Jim Marshall and here's my driver's license to prove it. Austin Scott seems to think I'm Nancy Pelosi. I do what I think is best for Georgia."[16] After mentioning his support for rural health care, jobs at Robins Air Force Base, and the right to bear arms, Marshall continued, "I voted against Nancy Pelosi's trillion dollar health care bill because we just can't afford it. I approved this message because this is just one reason why I won't support her for Speaker." This triple-edged ad sought to inject humor, showcase Marshall's local values, and head off questions about his preferences for speaker. A second ad began with a shot of 1960s hippies as an announcer observed, "Georgia is a long way from San Francisco and Jim Marshall is a long way from Nancy Pelosi."[17] In another television ad, Marshall vowed, "I'm not going to do what some party leader wants. I'm going to do what's right."[18]

As a rejoinder to the charge that he voted with Pelosi 90 percent of the time, Marshall asserted that he voted the same as Republican leaders 65 percent of the time.[19] He boasted of voting against every budget, favoring a balanced budget, and having worked to achieve $1 trillion in tax cuts. In an attempt to reassure conservative whites, he highlighted endorsements he received from the Chamber of Commerce, National Right to Life, the National Federation of Independent Business, and the National Rifle Association which also put out direct mail on his behalf.[20]

Georgians supported the tough immigration law adopted by Arizona in the spring of 2010. One survey showed 68 percent of adults approved of the law in the Peach State.[21] Until Arizona acted to allow law enforcement officers to check on the immigration status of individuals who they stopped, Georgia may have had the most pronounced stand against illegal immigrants. Marshall sought to undermine Scott's claims of being tough on illegal immigrants by running ads criticizing the challenger's opposition to a 5 percent tax on money wired back to families in Latin America. After pointing out that illegal immigrants cost tax payers when using public services, a snide voice turned Scott's explanation for his vote against him. "Austin Scott said he had 'a moral problem about making illegal immigrants pay [to send money back home].' Mr. Scott, what about the moral problem of illegal immigrants breaking the law?"[22]

Georgia has a long history of legislators providing strong support for the military. Two of the state's most famous senators, Richard Russell and Sam Nunn, chaired the Armed Services Committee and won wide recognition for their expertise on national security issues. Nunn's uncle, U.S. Representative Carl Vinson, served for decades first as the chair of the Naval Affairs Committee and after it merged with the Military Affairs Committee of the new House Armed Services Committee. Marshall ran ads describing his service in Vietnam, medals and inclusion in the Ranger Hall of Fame. Elsewhere, he reminded voters of his efforts to expand Robins Air Force Base.[23]

When Scott accused him of supporting higher taxes, Marshall returned fire with an ad that enumerated tax increases that Scott had supported. Marshall attacked Scott for wanting to re-impose the state sales tax on groceries, increasing taxes on telephone bills, taxing on-line purchases while proposing to eliminate the corporate income tax, and opposing a plan to lower property taxes.[24] Marshall also stressed his record as mayor of Macon where he cut property taxes and balanced the budget.

Polls

Relatively little polling was reported in Georgia's 8th District race and much of what was reported appeared toward the end of the campaign. A Republican poll taken after Scott secured the GOP nomination showed the incumbent ahead, but with less than 50 percent of the vote and with the incumbent's advantage almost within the margin of error (44 percent to 39 percent).[25] In mid-September, a Democratic poll showed Marshall ahead by twelve points, but still with less than half the vote, 48 percent.[26] Marshall's internal polls always showed him ahead.[27] Mark Mellman, Marshall's pollster and a leading Democratic strategist who has worked for Senate Majority Leader Harry Reid (D-NV), then-House Majority Leader Steny Hoyer (D-MD) as well as the Democratic National Committee, conducted the last poll (mid-October) that found the incumbent in the lead with 47 percent, although Scott was now within the margin of error at 44 percent. Marshall released the results to offset media reports of polls which showed him trailing by double digits.[28] The first indication of a Scott lead came in late September with the release of a poll by American Viewpoint, a GOP firm, which showed the challenger up 46 percent to 38 percent. At the same time that Mellman had Marshall leading, Landmark Communications, a Georgia firm with GOP ties, showed Scott with a substantial lead and majority support at 51 percent to 35 percent. Landmark fielded a second poll less than a week before Election Day and it showed little movement during the previous week with Scott maintaining a 53 percent to 39 percent lead. A survey commissioned by *The Hill* between the dates of the two Landmark polls had similar results, Scott ahead 50 percent to 37 percent.[29]

In the Scott campaign's weekly tracking polls in the weeks leading up to the election, Marshall never got more than 38 percent of the vote.[30] Scott's polls were consistent with those appearing in the media.

Campaign Finance

Successful congressional campaigns increasingly rely upon a well-conditioned and productive fundraising machine. Jim Marshall and Austin Scott completely understood the need to raise substantial amounts of money to communicate their messages, and both campaigns raised over $1,000,000. The 8th District's 21 counties stretch into three media markets, including the expensive Atlanta market, and the campaigns invested heavily in TV advertising in each. In addition to the candidates' campaign efforts, outside groups spent hundreds of thousands of dollars on advertising either in support of one candidate or in attacking his opponent. The American Future Fund and other conservatives 527s (a tax-exempt organization named after a section of the United States tax code, 26 U.S.C. § 527) spent at least $1,000,000 promoting Scott and offsetting Marshall's larger war chest.[31]

Jim Marshall raised nearly $1.5 million dollars, 17 percent less than 2008, and 23 percent less in total receipts compared to 2006 (see Table 9.2). He spent $1.8 million, comparable to his spending in the two previous elections. As the incumbent with networks inside the Beltway, Marshall could tap outside financiers. Third quarter financial disclosures revealed that PACs contributed generously to the Marshall campaign, however, Marshall raised over 57 percent of his monies from individual contributions. Community leaders and friends supported the incumbent whom they believed would continue to defend and protect the interests of middle Georgia. Missing from the coalition of Marshall contributors was the national Democratic Party. Marshall commented in a local interview that the Democratic Congressional Campaign Committee (DCCC) "have been pretty good about helping me a bit with fundraising—but I'd be happy to have more help than I've received."[32] *The Hill* reported in late October that the party had invested only $31,000 in Marshall.[33]

In previous elections, the DCCC included Marshall in its "Frontline" program, practically guaranteeing him an influx of campaign funds. In 2010 Marshall was not part of the program because he was deemed a seasoned legislator. The DCCC provided campaign research assistance, but did not buy advertising in the district, claiming that the party could not help Marshall since he was one of the Blue Dogs running against the national Democrats. The DCCC reserved two weeks of slots for television advertising for Marshall but failed to follow through. While the DCCC did not run ads for Marshall it did spend heavily in an unsuccessful bid to reelect Alabama's Bobby Bright who, like Marshall, voted against key components of the Obama program and attacked Pelosi.[34] DCCC support for Bright but not Marshall may have resulted from an assessment that the Alabamian had brighter prospects or Marshall's seniority may put him in a different category where he was expected to self fund while freshman Bright could still get party money.

While the DCCC cut Marshall off, he was one of ten Democrats to benefit from a major ad purchase ($390,030) by the U.S. Chamber of Commerce. The Chamber ad lauded Marshall for opposing the Obama health care bill and appealed to seniors by noting that in opposing Obamacare, Marshall had voted against a bid to strip $500 billion from Medicare.[35] The Chamber typically endorses candidates whose lifetime support for its positions exceeds 70 percent. Marshall scored 73 percent for the first session of the 111th Congress but his cumulative score stood at 63 percent. The Chamber nonetheless made the ad buy because he had opposed health care reform.[36]

Austin Scott, labeled by many political watchers as an "aggressive fundraiser," raised a little more than $1,000,000. He revealed his fundraising prowess by raising 61 percent more than the incumbent in the second and third quarters of 2010 (see Table 9.3). Scott attributed his success to his messages resonating within the district.[37] Hometown connections and local business ties also helped Scott's fundraising. He raised over 75 percent of his monies from individual

Table 9.2 Campaign Finance Data for Georgia's 8th Congressional District Campaigns, 2006–2010

Election year	Disbursements		Receipts		Vote Percent	
	Marshall (D)	Opponent (R)	Marshall (D)	Opponent (R)	Marshall (D)	Opponent (R)
2010	$1,814,549	$1,024,631	$1,496,152	$1,035,300	47.3	52.7
2008	$1,734,540	$1,149,903	$1,816,862	$1,158,989	57	43
2006	$1,813,542	$2,001,059	$1,953,070	$2,088,353	51	50

Source: 2010 election results: New York Times, http://elections.nytimes.com/2010/results/georgia; all other data: Center for Responsive Politics, http://www.opensecrets.org (accessed February 15, 2011).

Table 9.3 Marshall and Scott Receipts and Disbursements by Reporting Period, 2009–2010

Reporting Period	Jim Marshall			Austin Scott		
	Receipts	Disbursements	Cash on Hand	Receipts	Disbursements	Cash on Hand
Beginning Cash as of September 30, 2009			$425,230.10			$0.00
2009 Year End (1 October–31 December)	$83,587.73	$33,506.41	$475,311.42			
2010 April Quarterly (1 January–31 March)	$407,201.95	$32,324.87	$850,188.50			
2010 July Quarterly (1 April–30 June)	$168,824.58	$33,611.68	$985,401.40	$250,989.59	$37,574.12	$213,415.47
2010 October Quarterly (1 July–30 September)	$302,233.37	$449,736.17	$837,898.60	$460,799.48	$322,642.42	$351,572.53
2010 Pre-general (1 October–13 October)	$56,195.44	$292,351.58	$601,742.46	$115,931.50	$240,338.47	$227,165.56
2010 Post-general (14 October–22 November)	$313,225.35	$881,165.78	$33,802.03	$191,429.86	$407,490.13	$11,105.29
Total	**$1,331,268.42**	**$1,722,696.49**		**$1,019,150.43**	**$1,008,045.14**	

Source: Compiled from candidate reports to the Federal Election Commision, Form 3, Lines 23, 24, 26, and 27, various dates.
Note: The 2009 July Quarterly Report for Austin Scott represents the pre-primary reporting period from April 1, 2010 to June 30, 2010. The primary was held on July 20, 2010. Scott did not file a separate July Quarterly Report.

contributions, as he garnered substantial support from district health professionals, lawyers, and small business owners.

Examining the previous 8th District Republican challengers' campaign finances reveals that Scott actually raised less and spent less than each previous contestant (see Table 9.2). Compared to the previous midterm election where former Congressman Mac Collins challenged Marshall, Scott raised 50 percent less. With fewer dollars, however, Scott gained 4 percent points more of the vote total than Collins. Scott won by 10,000 votes even though outspent by almost $800,000. Scott, who is a generation younger than Collins, worked harder than the former incumbent and also benefitted from the anger over Obama administration policy initiatives that increased turnout by 35,000, or 22 percent more than in 2006.

The NRCC pumped money and resources into the Scott campaign. To qualify for NRCC funding, Scott needed polls showing him within five percentage points of the incumbent.[38] When he got that close, the NRCC initiated Scott into its "Young Guns" program, guaranteeing financial support through November, and purchased $130,000 in television advertising. As a favored "Young Gun," Scott benefited from campaign visits by future House speaker John Boehner and Republican National Committee Chairman Michael Steele. Boehner promised that should Scott win, he would get a seat on the Armed Services Committee, which Marshall had served on. By the end of October, the NRCC had reserved "$300,000 in Jim Marshall's district" for advertising.[39] The 8th was one of 32 congressional districts where the NRCC placed targeted robocalls.[40]

Results and Explanations

Austin Scott took 52.7 percent of the votes for a victory margin of 10,520 votes. Of 21 counties wholly or partially in the district, the incumbent carried only four. In 2006, when he struggled to a third term with 50.6 percent, Marshall won ten counties and in his 2008 landslide he carried all but five counties, and in four that he lost he garnered at least 45 percent of the vote. From 2006 to 2010, Marshall experienced an average loss of 5.5 percentage points per county. He continued to dominate Bibb County in 2010, the district's most populous county where he had served as mayor and which gave him an 11,000-vote margin. His other wins came in two small counties near Bibb and in Baldwin County, only part of which lies in the 8th District. Scott did especially well in the southern part of the district, the area he comes from. The results show a hint of the "friends and neighbors" politics that V. O. Key observed in southern elections almost three generations ago.[41]

One reason for Marshall's defeat is that the Democratic brand has become increasingly unappealing to white voters in Georgia. In recent years, most southern elections have seen a racial chasm with blacks giving more than 90 percent of their support to the Democratic nominee while most whites support the Republican. This pattern also appears in the 8th District. Ecological inference estimates that Marshall got 99 percent of the black vote; in homogeneously black precincts Marshall got 96 percent of the vote.[42] Scott won 68 percent of the non-black vote based on ecological inference and 77 percent of the votes cast in 47 homogeneously white precincts. A Landmark Communications poll just before the election showed Scott with 71 percent of the white vote. Marshall almost certainly did better with white voters than the top of the Democratic ticket since the Democratic nominee for governor managed only 42 percent of the 8th District vote.[43]

Just over half (51.5 percent) of African American registered to vote turned out in 2010, compared to 55.6 percent of other racial groups.[44] African Americans voted at slightly lower rates than they registered to vote, casting 31.3 percent of the votes while constituting 33.0 percent of all registrants in the district. Non-blacks also turned out at higher rates than blacks.[45] When Marshall won 57 percent in 2008, 78.3 percent of the black registrants cast ballots, and blacks participated at higher rates than they registered as they cast 33.8 percent of all ballots while constituting 33.1 percent of the registrants. The narrow escape of 2006 occurred when blacks cast 24.9 percent of the votes based on a turnout rate of 42.4 percent compared with 53.6 percent of the remainder of the electorate. Marshall's 2010 defeat and narrow escapes in 2002 and 2006 were partially due to lower black turnout in midterms. The other contributor to Marshall's defeat came from substantially less support from white voters.

Athletic coaches sometimes see an advantage in winning close contests. They boast that their team neither panics nor collapses when hard pressed or actually behind because, based on past experience, they expect to pull out a victory. Marshall's narrow victories in 2002 and 2006 may have not had the positive effect that coaches posit. Reporters and the Scott campaign perceive that Marshall did not take Scott seriously until too late. Reporters in the district with whom we spoke believe that early polls showing Marshall with a comfortable lead gave the incumbent a false confidence so that he waited too long before answering charges Scott repeatedly hurled linking the incumbent to Nancy Pelosi and unpopular Democratic programs. Perhaps he was tending to responsibilities in Washington, but reporters commented on Marshall's absence from some early events where a staffer represented him and other times when there was only an empty chair. Marshall's hesitancy allowed Scott to paint the incumbent as a spendthrift liberal who consorted with Nancy Pelosi. Second guessers suggest that Marshall should have run ads during primary season even though he had no challenge within his party.

Early polls showing Marshall well ahead may explain the absence of DCCC support. The DCCC may have thought Marshall in reasonably good shape in a year in which as many as 100 congressional districts appeared on lists of competitive districts. By the time it became clear that Marshall was struggling, the DCCC had many incumbents on life support and assigned low priority to a candidate openly criticizing the speaker. An alternative hypothesis holds that with Marshall trailing the challenger by double digits, the DCCC wrote him off and shifted its efforts westward to the adjoining 2nd District where U.S. Representative Sanford Bishop was locked in a surprisingly tight race. Scott credits Bishop's challenger, who managed 48.6 percent of the vote, with diverting DCCC attention from the 8th district. "Had the 2nd District not become so close, that money might have been used against me," said the newly elected Scott.[46]

Marshall sought to inoculate himself against what proved to be highly unpopular in the district by voting against the Obama health care reform. He published a critique of the legislation and his suggestions for improvement in the conservative publication *National Review Online*.[47] He also stressed that he had never voted for the budget. He had, however, voted for the stimulus package and to raise the debt ceiling, which provided documentation to the Scott campaign's claims that Marshall voted with the national Democratic Party. Scott's general consultant expressed frustration at trying to explain that while Marshall had not voted for budget resolutions, he had voted for most spending bills.[48]

Unlike some defeated incumbents, no one accused Marshall of losing touch with the district. Robins Air Force Base is a major economic engine not just in the district but for middle Georgia. The incumbent used his position on the Armed Services Committee to promote the base. He also attracted support from veterans and his fellow Vietnam Veterans endorsed him again in 2010.

Marshall's reputation as a strong supporter of national defense and travels through the district had previously earned him some support from Republicans, but in 2010 reporters and the Scott campaign believe that GOP support evaporated. "When we were out shaking hands, we found a number of people who had voted for him in the past but were now supporting us."[49] Scott continued, "One of the leading volunteers with my campaign had voted for Marshall in the past." The switch in voter loyalty away from Marshall had already occurred in contests for higher office. The district voted Republican in the two previous presidential elections by landslide proportions. A Landmark Communications poll also captured the district's Republican leanings when it asked: "If the 2010 election were being held today, would you generally vote for the Republican candidate or the Democratic candidate in your area?" Among 763 respondents, 39.9 percent said they would vote only for Republicans and another 21.8 percent would vote "mostly for Republicans."[50] The district gave John McCain 56 percent of its votes.

Of all the opponents he faced since 2002, Austin Scott was probably Jim Marshall's most formidable challenger. Scott displayed a competence that some of his predecessors lacked. Mercer University political scientist Chris Grant described the change as follows: "Marshall looked like he'd be more attentive to district service than did the previous Republican candidates. Austin Scott looked like he could handle constituency service and then when Scott was promised seats on Armed Services and the [Agriculture] committees, voters had fewer concerns about what he could do for the district."[51]

The challenger also had a stronger organization than the incumbent. "Scott had tons of volunteers. He had a strong get-out-the-vote effort." Grant contrasted Marshall with Scott, observing of the incumbent, "The campaign had no volunteers. They didn't want volunteers. All they wanted to do was to try to raise money. That told me that Marshall had given up on the ground game." In contrast Scott's volunteers made 350,000 personal telephone calls seeking support.[52]

Personality may have also played a role. According to Professor Grant, "Jim was not warm and fuzzy. He was not always that friendly ... He is not a glad-hander and somewhat standoffish and people may come away from meeting him with not all that positive a response. He is more like Barack Obama than Bill Clinton. He is very bright and he is not shy about letting you know he is bright." In contrast, a reporter noted Scott's "Hollywood looks" and sincerity. "It is something like the JFK–Richard Nixon comparison. Scott is an attractive young man."[53] A representative for the Scott campaign agreed, "You notice that we put him [Scott] on camera whenever we could because he was connecting so well with the public."[54]

Sensing that Scott's ads linking him with Pelosi might be propelling the challenger's bid, Marshall tried desperately to divorce himself from his party's leader. He vowed not to vote for Pelosi for speaker and to help repeal the health care legislation. The incumbent went on record favoring the extension of *all* of President Bush's tax cuts and sent a letter to Nancy Pelosi urging her to allow the extension to come up for a vote. These actions may have cost Marshall support among Democrats without winning over Republicans.[55] Some Republicans at Robins Air Force Base who had supported Marshall previously may have defected believing that the incumbent's attacks on Pelosi would reduce his ability to protect the base.

Despite the various problems for the incumbent noted above, Jim Marshall might have survived had his district not undergone a major reconfiguration in 2005. Marshall took 54 percent of the vote in the portion of the district he had represented since 2003 but managed only 40 percent of the vote in the area added to the district at the mid-decade redistricting.[56] The redistricting carried out by Republicans hoping to defeat Marshall did not have an immediate effect in 2006 but ultimately paid the dividend the GOP had hoped for.

Tea Party activities commanded center stage in many GOP wins but not in the 8th District. While supporters of the Tea Party movement backed the challenger, none of our interviewees saw the movement as a force in the district. According to one reporter, "Three weeks before the election we were at an event and asked them who the leaders were and what their issues were and they said that they were still trying to figure that out."[57] A person close to the Scott campaign confirmed, "The Tea Party was not very active in this part of the state."

Conclusion

What could Jim Marshall have done to secure reelection? He had a reputation of working the district in the off years and protecting its primary economic force. He compiled one of the most conservative voting records among Democrats. He had sizable cash reserves.

Changes to the political environment leading up to and during 2010 (macro-political factors) endangered conservative southern Democrats. Jim Marshall found himself in a situation akin to that of saber tooth tigers at the end of the last ice age. The victor observed that the incumbent was a victim of "the trade winds of national politics."[58] Unhappiness with the health care reform, the stimulus package and TARP combined to create a toxic brew that crippled those who tasted it—even those like Marshall who sipped tentatively then tried to spit it out. Except in North Carolina, the 2010 elections decimated conservative southern Democrats, a once robust species. Southern Democrats survived the initial changes when Republicans began winning presidential votes because the electorate engaged in a split-level realignment, opting for Democrats for all offices below that of president.[59] As long as Democrats were as conservative as the Republicans who challenged them, many voters stayed with the more familiar party and candidates. Gradually, as conservative incumbents retired, a shift spread down ballot as increasing numbers of voters selected Republicans for Congress and governor.[60] Still later, Republicans began winning majorities in southern legislative chambers. The last refuge of the southern Democrat, local office, is now slipping away with 68 percent of Georgia's newly-elected county commissioners being Republican and with the GOP holding almost as many commission seats as Democrats.[61] The advantages that accompany incumbency enabled some Democrats to continue to win, but now electorates followed their Republican leanings and retained a known, conservative in office.

In a wave election like 2010, however, even the power of incumbency fails. A former Marshall staffer explained, "They weren't voting against Jim. They liked him; he told them the truth. They liked his military background. It's just that the climate was so difficult. They were voting against Obama and Pelosi and the D beside his name."

Notes

1. Burdett A. Loomis and Wendy J. Schiller, *The Contemporary Congress*, 5th ed. (Belmont, CA: Thompson Wadsworth, 2006), pp. 1–3.
2. On the mid-decade Texas redistricting, see Charles S. Bullock, III, *Redistricting: The Most Political Activity in America* (Lanham, MD: Rowman and Littlefield, 2010), pp. 118–120.
3. M. V. Hood, III, and Seth C. McKee, "Trying to Thread the Needle: The Effects of Redistricting in a Georgia Congressional District," *PS: Political Science and Politics*, vol. 42 (2009), pp. 679–687.
4. In 2010 Republicans won a second district that was more than 30 percent black.
5. Having to compete in a newly configured district may explain why Marshall had his most conservative voting record in 2006.
6. Telephone interview with Jim Marshall conducted by Bullock, January 26, 2011.
7. Calculated from scores in the *National Journal* (February 28, 2009), pp. 52–53.
8. Georgia requires that candidates win a majority of the vote in the primary. Otherwise, the top two vote-getters square off in a runoff roughly a month later.
9. On the Georgia redistricting, see Ronald Keith Gaddie and Charles S. Bullock, III, "From *Ashcroft* to *Larios*: Recent Redistricting Lessons from Georgia." *Fordham Urban Law Journal*, vol. 34 (April 2007), pp. 997–1048 and Charles S. Bullock, III,

Redistricting: The Most Political Activity in America (Lanham, MD: Rowman and Littlefield, 2010), Chapter 6.

10. Telephone interview with Scott campaign consultant Mitch Hunter conducted by Bullock, January 10, 2011.

11. "Tired," http://www.youtube.com/watch?v=0haMsuuSNFY

12. "Go," http://www.youtube.com/watch?v=SAgePk3aOgU

13. "Desperate," http://www.youtube.com/watch?v=YlP1PS-bxCA

14. Mike Stucka, "Marshall, Scott Hold Blistering Debate in Perry," *Macon Telegraph*, October 15, 2010, http://www.macon.com/2010/10/15/1303243/marshall-scott-hold-blistering.html (accessed February 11, 2011). Pelosi seemingly forgave endangered Democrats who campaigned against her, telling PBS that "I just want them to win. They know their districts." Katherine Q. Seelye, "For Some Embattled Democrats, Campaign Against Their Leader," *New York Times*, October 17, 2010, http://www.nytimes.com/2010/10/17/us/politics/17pelosi.html (accessed February 11, 2011).

15. "The Real Jim Marshall," http://www.youtube.com/watch?v=WexdBA1faR4.

16. "Jim," http://www.youtube.com/watch?v=A4Gyv43SNBA.

17. "Long Way," http://www.youtube.com/watch?v=dngrecgvv4k.

18. "Politics is Easy," http://www.youtube.com/watch?v=WokL-RHdVl4.

19. The independent OpenCongress calculated that Marshall voted with Pelosi 60.9 percent of the time in 2010; it confirmed that Marshall voted with John Boehner 65.3 percent of the time. Jim Galloway, "Republicans' New Ads Target 27 Dems, Including Rep. Jim Marshall," Georgia Elections News, October 5, 2010, http://blogs.ajc.com/georgia_elections_news/2010/10/05/republicans-new-ads-target-27-dems-including-rep-jim-marshall/ (accessed February 11, 2011).

20. Marshall interview.

21. Jeremey Redmon, "Poll: Most Georgia voters want Arizona-style immigration law here," *Atlanta Journal-Constitution*, July 16, 2010, http://www.ajc.com/news/georgia-politics-elections/poll-most-georgia-voters-572201.html (accessed February 28, 2011).

22. "Whose Burden," http://www.youtube.com/watch?v=hdirJkAoXbI.

23. For example, see "Real Important," http://www.youtube.com/watch?v=2rsXWeDgk2M.

24. "Austin And," http://www.youtube.com/watch?v=08Xi7gURrn4.

25. "GOP Poll Shows Scott in Striking Range of Marshall," *Houston Home Journal*, August 18, 2010, http://blogs.ajc.com/georgia_elections_news/2010/08/17/gop-poll-shows-scott-in-striking-range-of-marshall-in-ga-8/ (accessed February 11, 2011).

26. Tom Baxter, "Marshall Poll Claims He's Up by 12 Points," *Insider Advantage Georgia*, September 21, 2010, http://insidergeorgia.com/restricted/IAG%20Archives_2010_September-December.php (accessed February 11, 2011).

27. Marshall interview.

28. Ibid.

29. "Georgia-08," *The Hill*, October 26, 2010, http://thehill.com/polls/thehill-poll-week-4/125975-district-by-district (accessed February 11, 2011).

30. Hunter interview.

31. Ibid.

32. Bob Keefe, "Marshall distances self from Democrats; If re-elected, he says he won't vote to keep Pelosi in power as speaker," *Atlanta Journal-Constitution*, October 14, 2010, http://www.ajc.com/news/georgia-politics-elections/democratic-u-s-rep-681867.html (accessed February 11, 2011).

33. "Georgia-08," *The Hill*.

34. Jeremy P. Jacobs, "DCCC Spending Big for Disloyal Dems," Hotline On Call, October 8, 2010, http://hotlineoncall.nationaljournal.com/archives/2010/10/dccc_spending_b.php

35. http://www.youtube.com/watch?v=uWKqTWYgcgw.

36. Telephone interview with Moore Hallmark, U.S. Chamber of Commerce Southeastern Regional Director conducted by Bullock, January 28, 2011.

37. Dick Pettys, "Two Congressional Races Boiling in Georgia," *Insider Advantage Georgia*, September 20, 2010, http://insidergeorgia.com/restricted/IAG%20 Archives_2010_September-December.php (accessed February 11, 2011); Shelby G. Spires, "Scott Raises More Cash, But Marshall Has More to Spend," *Macon Telegraph*, October 17, 2010, http://www.macon.com/2010/10/17/1305434/scott-raises-more-cash-but-marshall.html (accessed February 11, 2011).

38. Telephone interview with Representative Austin Scott, conducted by Bullock, December 29, 2010.

39. Steve Visser, "GOP nipping at Blue Dogs' heel. Conservative Democrats must hold off seasoned politicians to keep seats." *Atlanta Journal-Constitution*, October 21, 2010, p. A1.

40. "National GOP Targets Marshall," *Macon Telegraph*, August 14, 2010, http://www.macon.com/2010/08/14/1228736/national-gop-targets-marshall.html (accessed February 11, 2011).

41. V. O. Key, Jr., *Southern Politics in State and Nation* (New York: Knopf, 1949).

42. On ecological inference, see Gary King, *A Solution to the Ecological Inference Problem* (Princeton, NJ: Princeton University Press, 1997). Ecological inference makes use of the method of bounds to estimate turnout and candidate preferences using precinct data on turnout, numbers of registered voters, candidate preferences and the percentage African American. Homogeneous precincts are those in which at least 90 percent of the registered voters are of the same race.

43. Calculations of the 8th District vote for governor made by Dan O'Connor, personal communication December 22, 2010.

44. Georgia is one of five states that collect registration and turnout information on voter ethnicity. The figures in this paragraph were calculated using those data.

45. The 8th District has only 200 registered voters who are not either black or white.

46. Scott interview.

47. Jim Marshall, "Real Health-Care Reform," *National Review Online*, July 15, 2010, http://www.nationalreview.com/articles/243434/real-health-care-reform-jim-marshall (accessed February 11, 2011).

48. Hunter interview. The difference between the budget resolution and appropriations bills was explored in a fact-checking article, "Marshall Voted Against 'Budget Resolutions' but Not Necessarily Federal Spending Bills," *Atlanta Journal-Constitution*, October 11, 2010, http://politifact.com/georgia/statements/2010/oct/11/jim-marshall/marshall-voted-against-budget-resolutions-not-nece/ (accessed February 11, 2011).

49. Scott interview.

50. Landmark Communications poll of October 19, 2010.

51. Telephone interview with Professor Chris Grant conducted by Bullock, January 3, 2011.

52. Scott interview.

53. Telephone interview with Shelby Spires conducted by Bullock, December 27, 2010.

54. Hunter interview.

55. Marshall's pollster, Mark Mellman offered the same caveat. Seelye, "For Some Embattled Democrats, a Campaign against Their Leader."

56. Email from Seth McKee to Bullock, March 8, 2010.

57. Telephone interview with Russell Savage, WMAZ news director by Bullock, December 28, 2010.

58. Scott interview.

59. Charles D. Hadley, "Dual-Partisan Identification in the South," *Journal of Politics*, vol. 47 (February 1985), pp. 254–268.
60. Charles S. Bullock, III, Donna Hoffman and Ronald Keith Gaddie, "Regional Variations in the Realignment of American Politics, 1944–2004," *Social Science Quarterly*, vol. 87 (September 2006), pp. 494–518; Earl Black and Merle Black, *The Rise of Southern Republicans* (Cambridge, MA: Belknap Press, 2002); Seth C. McKee, *Republican Ascendancy* (Boulder, CO: Westview Press, 2010).
61. Personal interview with Ross King, executive director of Associated County Commissioners of Georgia, January 4, 2011, and data supplied by Michele NeSmith at the ACCG.

10 Feingold vs. Johnson in Wisconsin's Senate Race
The Maverick Icon Meets His Match

David T. Canon

In perhaps no other U.S. Senate race were the media-driven aquatic images of Republican candidates "riding the wave" more apt than the contest in Wisconsin between the Democratic incumbent Russ Feingold and his challenger, Ron Johnson. Johnson came out of nowhere to swamp the 18-year incumbent in one of the biggest upsets of the midterm elections.[1] During the last few weeks of the campaign, I received phone calls from reporters all over the country (and even from the largest newspaper in Mexico) who asked the same questions about the Badger State, "What is going on in Wisconsin? Is Feingold really going to lose?"

This chapter will explore what happened in Wisconsin and explain why this highly respected, political independent lost. First, I will review the context of the election in Wisconsin as well as nationally. Next, I will discuss the "virtues and vulnerabilities" of the incumbent and explain the background and characteristics of the challenger. Then, I will analyze the candidates' campaigns—including a discussion of the strategies and tactics the campaigns employed—and the importance of outside groups (especially the Tea Party). This will include a discussion of issues in Wisconsin, and whether either side gained the upper hand in the competition for campaign funds or the ad wars. Finally, this chapter will answer the most basic question, "Why did Johnson win?"

Campaigning in the Badger State

Wisconsin is medium-sized politically competitive state with a voting eligible population of approximately 4.3 million adults, of which 3.4 million are registered voters. About 85 percent of Wisconsin residents are non-Hispanic white and about a third live in rural areas. The largest cities in the state are Milwaukee and Madison, the state capital. The state's economy is based on agriculture, industry, and a small but growing high-tech and biotech sector centered in the Madison area. The manufacturing sector is mostly in the southeastern part of the state, but like the rest of the upper Midwest, many of those jobs have disappeared. For example, late in 2008 General Motors closed its plant in Janesville, which led to the loss of more than 5,000 jobs. The paper industry is still an important part of the economy in the Fox River valley. Overall, the unemployment rate is lower in Wisconsin than the national average, but economic concerns dominated the 2010 elections.

In the 20 years before the 2010 midterms, elections in Wisconsin were very evenly divided between the two parties. Republicans controlled the governor's office for 12 of the 20 years; the U.S. House delegation was divided almost as evenly as possible between 1990 and 2010, with Democrats winning 44 of the races and Republicans 42; Republicans controlled the state Assembly for 14 of the 20 years with two changes in party control, while the state Senate was evenly divided between the two parties (10 years of control for each party), switching party control four times. The Democratic presidential candidate won every election in the state since 1988, but some of the elections were excruciatingly close. In 2000, Al Gore defeated George W. Bush by two-tenths of 1 percent (just over 5,700 votes out of 2.5 million cast) while four years later John Kerry beat Bush by less than four-tenths of 1 percent (just over 11,000 votes out of nearly three million cast). In a departure from this trend, Barack Obama trounced John McCain in 2008 (56 percent to 42 percent), but by 2010 Republicans were poised to make substantial gains in the state. The incumbent governor, Democrat Jim Doyle, decided not to run for a third term (polls suggested that he would have lost) and Republicans recruited some strong candidates for the U.S. House and state legislative races.

As the 2010 election season started, President Obama was somewhat more popular in Wisconsin than he was in the nation as a whole. In addition, the reaction against health care reform (Patient Protection and Affordable Care Act of 2010) and the stimulus bill (the American Reinvestment and Recovery Act) were not as strong as in some parts of the country. On the other hand, the Wisconsin voters who were upset about these issues appeared to be more motivated and energized than Obama's supporters.

At first glance, it appeared that Senator Feingold might survive the Republican tide. First, U.S. Senate races in Wisconsin were relatively immune from the state-wide pattern of close partisan competition. Since 1962, Democrats won every Senate election with the exception of two terms by Bob Kasten from 1981 to 1993. Second, Feingold had established himself as an independent, even a maverick, in a state that embraces such politicians. As a relatively unknown state senator, Russ Feingold crushed two more well-known and better-funded candidates in the 1992 Democratic Senate primary with 70 percent of the vote. He went on to beat Kasten by a 53 percent to 46 percent margin, despite being outspent by more than 2.5 to 1. Feingold used humorous, even quirky, campaign ads to introduce himself to the voters in his first statewide campaign. In one memorable ad he opened a door showing an empty closet and said, "See, no skeletons." In another ad, he showed the back of his left hand with a map that outlined his travels in a state, concluding that he "knows the state of Wisconsin like the back of my hand." His modest means (throughout his Senate career Feingold ranked at or near the bottom of the list of senators' net worth), his direct approach with issues, and his personal integrity resonated with voters. In 1998, Feingold narrowly defeated his challenger U.S. Representative Mark Neumann by 50.5 percent to 48.4 percent. Six years later Feingold cruised to a relatively easy win over businessman Tim Michels (55 percent to 44 percent) in a campaign that featured many of the same themes used by Ron Johnson in 2010.

The Incumbent: Russ Feingold's Virtues and Vulnerabilities

A profile of Senator Feingold noted, "When one senator out of 100 is voting no, odds are good it is Feingold. He doesn't mind being the lone voice of dissent no matter what the issue or the Democratic Party's position."[2] Indeed, by the end of his career, he had voted against his party 887 times, and on 97 of those occasions he was the lone voice of dissent (which was more than any other incumbent senator).[3] In some cases, his opposition was from the left. For instance, Feingold was the lone vote against the USA Patriot Act in 2001; he opposed the Troubled Asset Relief Program (TARP) in 2008, President Obama's troop surge in Afghanistan in 2009, and the Dodd-Frank Wall Street Reform and Consumer Protection Act in 2010 (which nearly led to its defeat). In other cases, he aligned himself with Republicans against his own party in high-profile votes. He angered liberals in 2001 by voting for John Ashcroft as George W. Bush's Attorney General, he was the only Democratic senator to vote against dismissing the articles of impeachment against President Clinton (he later voted against convicting Clinton), and he had a reputation for being one of the strongest fiscal hawks in the Democratic Party. Feingold teamed up with Senator John McCain (R-AZ) and other Republicans to fight against pork barrel spending, he supported the line-item veto, and was a strong proponent of balancing the budget throughout his career. He was also famously frugal with his allocation of tax-payers' money for his Senate staff and office: over his 18-year career, he returned more than $3.2 million of his allotted money to the federal government and also gave back $70,000 in pay raises (when he was first elected, he pledged not to accept any pay raise he received in between elections). Despite these independent positions, Feingold was a solid liberal, as shown by various roll call measures (see Table 10.1). His vote scores from Americans for Democratic Action were consistently at 95 or 100, indicating a strong liberal record. As noted above, however, Feingold was not always a consistent supporter of his party, illustrated by his relatively low party unity scores. In fact, perhaps in anticipation of the need to appeal to more independent voters in the upcoming election, Feingold's party unity scores in 2009 and 2010 were the lowest of his career, while his scores from the American Conservative Union were the highest of his time in the Senate.

Feingold's independent streak got him in trouble with colleagues when he tackled ethics issues such as lobbying restrictions on senators after they leave the Senate, trips paid for by lobbyists, a complete ban on gifts for legislators and staff, automatic pay raises, and most famously, campaign finance reform. Feingold prevailed on most of these issues, much to the chagrin of many senators who would have preferred to leave things the way they were. He had a strong reputation for personal integrity and he demanded that his staff comply with

Table 10.1 Congressional Vote Scores for Russ Feingold, 1993–2010

Year	American Conservative Union	Americans for Democratic Action	Party Unity	Presidential Support
2010	24%	95%	83%	87%
2009	24%	95%	74%	85%
2008	24%	100%	93%	30%
2007	4%	95%	93%	37%
2006	8%	100%	92%	47%
2005	13%	100%	95%	37%
2004	8%	100%	95%	66%
2003	30%	95%	93%	53%
2002	5%	90%	84%	67%
2001	20%	95%	89%	61%
2000	8%	100%	92%	90%
1999	8%	100%	88%	82%
1998	12%	90%	86%	83%
1997	8%	95%	86%	86%
1996	10%	95%	87%	86%
1995	13%	100%	90%	78%
1994	4%	100%	84%	65%
1993	12%	100%	94%	85%

Source: CQ's Politics in America (Washington, DC: Congressional Quarterly, Inc., 2010 and 2000); The American Conservative Union (http://www.conservative.org); Americans for Democratic Action (http://www.adaction.org); and Congressional Quarterly's vote studies (2009: http://innovation.cqpolitics.com/media/vote_study_2009; and 2010: http://innovation.cq.com/media/vote_study_2010).

his high ethical standards, but he did not win any popularity contests during his time in the Senate (in part because of his willingness to raise these ethics issues).

Feingold also had a reputation as a serious policy wonk. The Bipartisan Campaign Finance Reform of 2002 (BCRA), commonly known as the McCain/Feingold campaign finance reform law, was his signature piece of legislation. Feingold was also active in a broad range of policy areas including foreign policy (he was an early and strong opponent to the wars in Iraq and Afghanistan), the war on terror (especially his fight against torture of suspected terrorists), civil liberties, foreign trade (he is an opponent to many free-trade treaties because of their impact on domestic labor and environmental issues), and health care reform. Despite this range of policy interests, Feingold maintained strong links to constituents. The most prominent example was the promise he made in his initial campaign in 1992 to visit each of Wisconsin's 72 counties for a listening session every year. He maintained this commitment for 18 years. Surprisingly, his constituency service was not as strong as the other Wisconsin senator, Republican Herb Kohl. Perhaps the comparison is not fair, because Senator Kohl is widely regarded for having the most impressive constituency service operation in the Senate.[4]

All of these characteristics—his personal integrity, political independence, and policy interests—are simultaneously Feingold's virtues and vulnerabilities. While voters respect his integrity, his campaigns to change the Senate rankled some colleagues. Many voters valued his independence and commitment to various issues, but his strong positions sometimes alienated voters (and colleagues) on both sides of the aisle. In the end, his independence was not enough to inoculate him against the national surge of Republicans in 2010. One headline in the *New York Times* after the election read "Independents turn on one of their own."[5]

The Challenger: Ron Johnson as an Amateur Outsider

Given the competitive nature of electoral politics in Wisconsin, it was clear that Feingold would not be given a free pass for a fourth term. However, when a strong challenger still had not emerged early in 2010, most political observers thought Feingold was secure. One blogger expressed the typical sentiment, "Sen. Russ Feingold, the incumbent in Wisconsin's 2010 U.S. Senate race, seems poised to win reelection, with $3.6 million cash on hand in his campaign war chest (that's ten times more than any of his opponents), along with a record that reflects his status as a true maverick within the Democratic Party."[6] One big question mark clouded this picture: would Tommy Thompson, the popular former governor and Secretary of Health and Human Services under George W. Bush, challenge Feingold? When Thompson announced in mid-April that he would not run, it seemed that Feingold was secure. What the Republicans needed was their version of Herb Kohl (one of the wealthiest members of the institution that is sometimes referred to as a "millionaires' club") to run. With less than six months until the election, there was not time to raise the amount of money needed to fund a successful challenge to Feingold. Thus, it was almost a necessity that the Republican nominee would provide a substantial proportion of his or her campaign funds.

Shortly after Tommy Thompson announced that he would not run and less than a month before the Republican state convention, it appeared that Republicans got what they needed when Dick Leinenkugel, the beer magnate and commerce secretary under Governor Doyle, announced his candidacy. Dave Westlake and Terrence Wall also campaigned for some time, but neither gained much traction. A week before the Republican convention (on May 15), Ron Johnson, the owner of a small plastics company in Oshkosh and a political amateur, threw his hat into the ring. Then, Leinenkugel surprised everyone in a speech at the convention when he dropped out and threw his support behind Johnson. Johnson won the endorsement easily, taking more than 60 percent of the vote. As the *Wisconsin State Journal* put it, "Dick Leinenkugel had the name. Terrence Wall had the head start. But in the end, Ron Johnson had the votes ... His victory was shocking. To everyone. Including Johnson."[7] The primary was not until September, but when Wall dropped out (making bizarre allegations of voting buying at the convention by Johnson), the outcome was a foregone conclusion. Johnson ended up taking 85 percent of the primary vote (with 10 percent going to Westlake and the remaining 5 percent going to Stephen Finn).

Ron Johnson's nomination made sense from a practical standpoint: Republicans needed a candidate who was willing to spend millions of dollars and his strong business record and lack of political baggage would be pluses in a year in which anti-Washington sentiment was running high. Indeed, political amateurs were successful in races all around the country: the 39 candidates elected to the House in 2010 without any previous elective experience is the largest number since 1944, surpassing other "years of the outsider" such as 1952, 1974, and 1994. In the Senate, 11 of the 27 Republican challengers were amateurs and two others, in addition to Johnson, won their races (Rand Paul in Kentucky and Mike Lee in Utah).[8]

The success of political amateurs in the 2010 midterms creates a puzzle for the theory of ambition and strategic behavior. Current theory—the dominant version is the strategic politician hypothesis—predicts that in times of great political opportunity the most experienced politicians should run for office because current office holders time their attempts for higher office with the conditions that are most likely to lead to victory.[9] As noted in Chapter 1, this prediction is rooted in the strategic calculus employed by politicians that encompasses, among other things, the competitive position of the party, the relative success of others who have followed the same career path, and national tides (including the strength of the economy, the popularity of the president, and so on). Thus, in a year like 2010, one would expect a strong group of experienced candidates should have emerged to challenge Feingold, but none did.

Why then in the periods of greatest opportunity are proportionately *fewer* experienced politicians elected? As it turns out, in "high opportunity elections" (those in which the partisan division of newly elected seats is at least 2:1 and the winning party captures a minimum of 50 new seats in the House) candidates without previous political experience do better than in "normal" elections.[10] The 2010 midterms are consistent with that pattern. The relatively permeable nature of the political career structure, imbalance between the demand for and supply of viable candidates in high opportunity years, amateurs' risk-taking behavior relative to their more cautious and experienced counterparts, and amateurs' ability to exploit their outsider status and business backgrounds all contributed to their success in 2010.

The Campaign

Although the official GOP primary was not held until September, the party convention selected Johnson in May. So, the candidates for the general election were in place and the campaign began in earnest in early June. Feingold enjoyed a huge advantage in cash on hand and a small lead in the polls, but Johnson indicated that he was willing to spend what it would take to win. By mid-July,

Feingold's lead in the polls disappeared (and never came back) and the candidates locked into one of the most contentious campaigns in the nation. The next section will examine the dynamics of the campaign: the issues, the role of advertising, campaign finance, and outside groups.

Issues

The issues driving the campaign were the same as those in most Senate races: health care reform, the economy, the federal deficit and debt, and President Obama and the Democrats' response to the recession (specifically the stimulus bill and the role of the government in creating jobs). One additional issue was the contrast between how the candidates framed the incumbent: Feingold emphasized his independence and fighting for the interests of Wisconsin, while Johnson depicted Feingold as an out-of-touch liberal (and lawyer to boot) who had been in Washington for far too long. The latter was clearly Johnson's most effective argument—tapping into discontent with Washington and making the simple claim that 18 years was long enough resonated with voters—but Johnson also had to convince voters that he was a viable alternative who had enough knowledge and expertise to represent Wisconsin.

An early tactical decision Johnson faced was how closely to align himself with the Tea Party movement. Clearly, Tea Party activists would bring energy to the campaign, but too close of an association risked alienating a large bloc of moderate voters. At one meeting with a Tea Party group—the Rock River Patriots from Fort Atkinson—the perils of this balancing act became evident. In a 45-minute vetting session that was intended to demonstrate Johnson's bona fides on the Constitution, he did not provide strong enough answers on gun rights, property rights, and the Patriot Act (which is seen as an infringement on liberty by many Tea Party supporters).[11] Some Tea Party loyalists demanded stronger adherence to their views, but most recognized that Johnson was closer to them on the issues than Feingold. Johnson continued to meet with Tea Party groups throughout the campaign, but he never became completely identified with the movement.[12]

Initially, Johnson stumbled in his efforts to prove that he was a viable alternative to Feingold on policy grounds. Several early statements qualified as "gaffes" under Michael Kinsley's memorable definition of "when politicians say what they really think."[13] Two of the controversial comments were related to the BP oil spill in the Gulf of Mexico, the largest oil spill in U.S. history. First, Johnson seemed to say that he supported drilling for oil in the Great Lakes (he later said that he did not mean to say that, but rather was just expressing general support for more oil exploration and drilling).[14] Then, Johnson repeated his support of BP and big oil corporations more generally, which became even more controversial when it was revealed that he owned $100,000 of stock in BP. Another gaffe occurred when he stated that he supported free trade as "creative destruction," suggesting that it was necessary to outsource jobs overseas to create new jobs in the United States, which was a sensitive issue in Wisconsin given the number of jobs that had been lost in the manufacturing sector.[15]

Johnson was able to weather the storm created by these comments, but he made more trouble when he started talking about global warming. Previously, Johnson described believers in manmade causes of climate change as "crazy" and the theory as "lunacy" but then in an interview with the editorial board of the *Milwaukee Journal Sentinel* he said, "I absolutely do not believe in the science of man-caused climate change. It's not proven by any stretch of the imagination. It's far more likely that it's just sunspot activity or just something in the geologic eons of time." He added that excess carbon dioxide in the atmosphere "gets sucked down by trees and helps the trees grow."[16] The story was then picked up by national media outlets. It even made its way to late-night television where Jon Stewart said on *The Daily Show* that Russ Feingold is going to lose to some guy "who thinks that global warming is caused by sunspots and toaster ovens."[17]

Around this same time, Johnson also got in hot water with gun owners after saying that he was open to "licensing" guns like "we license cars and stuff."[18] Feingold ran a radio ad pointing this out, but Johnson quickly responded with a radio ad in which he said, "In my first days as a candidate, I used the wrong term in discussing my strong support for concealed carry rights for gun owners here in Wisconsin. I'm not a slick politician, and I made a mistake. It wasn't the first time, and it probably won't be the last."[19] His staff was worried about how much longer they would be able to play the "I'm the confused new guy card," but they continued the theme of not being a slick politician in ad that started running shortly after the global warming gaffe.[20]

"The Johnson Family" ad introduced voters to Johnson's kids who said nice things about their dad while reading awkwardly from cue cards. Johnson then cuts them off and says that he is not a career politician and his kids are not actors. The strategy worked: several new polls that came out after the gun rights and global warming controversies showed that the numbers had hardly budged— Johnson still had a narrow lead. Because of these experiences, the Johnson campaign cut back on the number of public appearances by the candidate (and they almost always were in front of small, friendly audiences) and limited the media's access to Johnson in order to keep the campaign "on message."

Johnson's television ads (discussed in more detail below) continued to hammer away on health care reform, the economy and creating jobs, and cutting budget deficits. In short, Johnson adopted the national GOP messaging strategy. This was especially true on the issue of health care where he talked about the need to "repeal and replace" the law that had been adopted. As critics pointed out, however, his issue positions did not go much beyond the 30-second sound bites. When pressed by a reporter to provide some details about *how* he would cut the budget, he responded, "I'm not going to get in the game here and, you know, start naming specific things to be attacked about, quite honestly."[21] His Web site offered no position papers, but short statements ranging in length from three to eight sentences on ten topics. The only one that was longer was the ten-paragraph entry on protecting Social Security and Medicare, an issue on which

Johnson was vulnerable because he had called Social Security a "Ponzi scheme" and indicated that he favored partial privatization of that popular program. The Web site made no mention of any foreign policy issues, which can be important in Senate races.[22]

The Johnson campaign had found an effective strategy of sticking to a general theme of "time for a change," creating jobs, and cutting the deficit, while limiting opportunities in which the candidate could "go rogue." There was one major hurdle that still remained: the three debates that both campaigns had agreed to (Feingold had argued for six debates). It hardly seemed like a fair fight: Feingold was a Rhodes Scholar, Harvard law school graduate, and policy expert with nearly 30 years of experience in public office; while Johnson was a plastics company owner who first got interested in politics less than a year before. Getting Johnson up to speed was going to be a major challenge for his campaign team. The campaign started more than a month before the first debate with "murder sessions," as Johnson called them.[23] The staff grilled him on a variety of issues they thought were likely to come up in the debate, tried to get him to memorize sound bites that he could use, and probed for any vulnerabilities. Johnson got frustrated with the sessions, sometimes throwing papers up in the air and leaving the room. Three days before the first debate, a staffer complained that the debate preparation was "off the rails."[24] Johnson knew that to be successful all he had to do was avoid a gaffe that would make the news or be used in a campaign ad. A relatively small audience watched the debate on live TV, so avoiding this collateral damage was key. Also, given the recognized mismatch in the debate and the expectations set for both candidates by the press, if Johnson could hold his own, it would be perceived as a win. As it turned out, Feingold won all three debates on the substance, but Johnson did not make any significant blunders and clearly exceeded expectations. Johnson had cleared the last hurdle; after the third debate, Johnson still led in the polls and it looked like it would be impossible for Feingold to close the gap.

Campaign Finance

The 2010 Senate race was the most expensive campaign in Wisconsin history, with the candidates spending more than $35 million between them with an additional $5 million coming from outside groups. Feingold spent $20.3 million and Johnson spent $15 million. In 2010, Feingold spent nearly twice what he did in his previous contest, and Johnson spent almost three times as much as Feingold's previous challenger (see Table 10.2). Johnson spent $8.7 million of his own money (57 percent of his total), while 92 percent of Feingold's money came from individual contributions, with the rest coming from political action committees. It is important to note that, because of the six-year term of Senators, Russ Feingold (and all senators) will raise and spend money out of a campaign account the entire time between his or her last election and the next campaign. For Feingold, this was between 2005 and 2010. Most of the money is spent in the year of the election, especially in a case like Feingold's where a challenger

Table 10.2 Campaign Finance Data for Wisconsin's Senate Campaigns, 2004 & 2010

Candidate and year	Disbursements	Receipts	Vote percentage
2010			
Russ Feingold (D)	$20,342,208	$20,803,357	47
Ron Johnson (R)	$15,043,252	$15,235,898	51.9
2004			
Russ Feingold (D)	$10,973,294	$10,973,294	55
Tim Michels (R)	$5,527,412	$5,533,163	44

Source: 2010 election results: *New York Times*, http://elections.nytimes.com/2010/results/wiscon-
sin; all other data: Center for Responsive Politics, http://www.opensecrets.org (accessed
February 15, 2011).

did not emerge until May of the election year. So while Feingold spent roughly
$5 million more than Johnson in total, he was actually outspent during the time
Johnson was in the race (see Table 10.3).

One of the ironies of the campaign was that Feingold was disproportionately
affected by the weakening of his signature campaign finance law. When the
Supreme Court ruled in the *Citizens United* case that corporations and labor
unions could directly spend without limit in federal elections, President Obama
warned in his 2010 State of the Union address that the decision opened "the
floodgates for special interests."[25] While the impact was smaller than anticipated,
Feingold bore the brunt of the outside spending in Wisconsin. "I've always been
a target in this stuff," Feingold said, "and this year, I'm getting the full dose: over
$2 million in these ads [criticizing him] that used to not be legal."[26] According
to the *Washington Post*'s analysis, 92 percent of the outside money in Wisconsin
favored Johnson.[27] The Center for Responsive Politics showed that about 80
percent of the $3.7 million that was either in support of or opposed to a can-
didate favored Johnson (and a large percentage of those ads were negative ads
against Feingold that emphasized the same themes as Johnson's ads). The other
$1.6 million of outside money was not tallied as supporting or opposing either
candidate, but all of that money was spent by conservative outside groups, such
as the Chamber of Commerce, the American Action Network, and the Faith &
Freedom Coalition.

Ad Wars

The millions of dollars in this race meant that both campaigns saturated the
airwaves with ads. According to data provided by the Wesleyan Media Project,
there were a staggering 58,423 discrete ad airings throughout the race (33,093
from the Johnson campaign, 20,937 by Feingold, and 4,393 from outside groups,
nearly all of which were either against Feingold or in support of Johnson). These
totals do not include another 2,241 ads that were aired before June 1. To begin
to put this in perspective, there are only five media markets in Wisconsin (plus

Table 10.3 Feingold and Johnson Campaign Receipts and Disbursements by Reporting Period, 2009–2010

Reporting Period	Russ Feingold			Ron Johnson		
	Receipts	Disbursements	Cash on Hand	Receipts	Disbursements	Cash on Hand
Beginning Cash as of September 30, 2009			$3,653,507.54			
2009 Year End						
(1 October–31 December)	$947,059.34	$421,469.42	$4,179,097.46			
2010 April Quarterly						
(1 January–31 March)	$1,344,408.23	$733,812.30	$4,789,693.39			$0.00
2010 July Quarterly						
(1 April–30 June)	$1,436,086.87	$1,396,782.35	$4,828,997.91	$2,032,627.87	$1,091,985.42	$940,642.45
2010 Pre-primary						
(1 July–25 August)	$937,733.16	$2,153,671.89	$3,613,059.18	$4,132,157.30	$3,458,176.08	$1,614,623.67
2010 October Quarterly						
(26 August–30 September)	$3,380,443.40	$2,939,548.99	$4,053,953.59	$4,479,511.05	$4,104,962.54	$1,989,172.18
2010 Pre-general						
(1 October–13 October)	$1,245,624.69	$2,315,320.74	$2,984,257.54	$2,232,753.00	$1,842,058.24	$2,379,866.94
2010 Post-general						
(14 October - 22 November)	$2,433,310.04	$3,903,445.95	$1,514,121.63	$2,338,230.56	$4,634,374.77	$83,722.73
Total	$11,724,665.73	$13,864,051.64		$15,215,279.78	$15,131,557.05	

Source: Compiled from candidate reports to the Federal Election Commission, Form 3, Lines 23, 24, 26, and 27, various dates.

Minneapolis/St. Paul and Duluth, Minnesota, which spill over into the western part Wisconsin and must be utilized if a candidate is going to reach voters in those areas by broadcast television). The ad campaign started in earnest on June 10. From that point to Election Day was 146 days, which means that an average of 80 ads ran every day in every media market for nearly five months! From September 1 through Election Day, Johnson ran more ads than any other Senate candidate in the nation and Feingold was second.[28] Overall, Wisconsin was second to Nevada in the total number of ads run, but more than a quarter of the ads in Nevada were by outside groups, whereas only 7 percent of the Wisconsin ads were not from the candidates' campaigns.

Perhaps the best indication of the level of advertising saturation in the last week of the campaign is that Johnson ran 35 ads in the Minneapolis media market for a total estimated cost of $72,210 (in contrast, Feingold only ran one ad in the Minneapolis media market at an estimated cost of $2,490, indicating perhaps than Johnson had more money to burn at the end of the campaign). While this is not quite like buying ads in the New York City media market to reach New Jersey voters, it is an expensive and inefficient way to reach voters in the western part of the state—about 95 percent of the people who saw those ads could not vote for Johnson because they live in Minnesota. (Both candidates also ran a greater number of ads in the Duluth media market, but the ratio of wasted advertising dollars was much lower there.) Johnson's tremendous volume of ads meant that he aired more ads than Feingold in 123 of the 146 days of the general election campaign.

In perhaps the only tactical error made by the Feingold campaign, they allowed Johnson to own the airwaves for more than a month at the start of the campaign: from June 10through July 12 Johnson ran 3,073 ads with no response from Feingold. Johnson ran three ads: "Real World," "Apple Pie," and "Tipping Point."[29] All three were positive, issue-based ads that introduced voters to Johnson, highlighting his background as a small businessman who knew how to create jobs. In "Tipping Point," he focused on the need to cut the federal budget deficit because failing to do anything about it is "inter-generational theft and it is immoral." Johnson controlled the airwaves at this important juncture and Feingold allowed his opponent to define himself in the eyes of the public. This violated the standard practice that candidates should define their opponent before their opponent can define themselves.

Feingold entered the fray with an attack ad asserting that Johnson favored drilling for oil in the Great Lakes. Johnson responded immediately with an ad accusing Feingold of mud-slinging, saying that he opposed drilling in the Great Lakes and that Feingold was the only Great Lakes senator to vote against the law that banned drilling in the Great Lakes. Politifact, a fact-checking Web site run by the *St. Petersburg Times* and several media other outlets, pointed out that the bill in question was an energy bill supported by President Bush and Vice President Cheney. Feingold voted against the bill because he thought it would continue the nation's dependence on oil rather than building sustainable energy (two other Great Lakes senators, Chuck Schumer and Hillary Clinton from New York, also voted against the law). Feingold was one of the earliest and strongest opponents of drilling in the Great Lakes, so the ad was misleading on several levels. Nonetheless, Johnson's response ad seemed to deflect attention away from the issue.

Feingold also countered with several ads criticizing Johnson's position on free trade. As noted above, the controversy was started by Johnson's comment that free trade was a necessary part of the process of "creative destruction." In another interview, Johnson seemed to praise China, saying it currently had a better business climate than the United States. Feingold's ads showed closed Wisconsin factories and businesses and stated that free-trade treaties "were directly responsible for these lost jobs, but Ron Johnson favors those deals."[30] Like the oil drilling ad, however, this issue did not seem to resonate with voters.

Johnson countered with ads that continued to hammer on the trifecta of health care reform, the economy and jobs, and deficits and the debt. Just over two-thirds of the ads that Johnson aired in the campaign were on these three issues (see Table 10.4). Other Johnson ads touted his background as a small businessman who created jobs, in contrast to Feingold, the career politician who believes that government creates jobs. In one of his most effective ads, "57," Johnson stood in front of a whiteboard and pointed out that there are 57 lawyers in the Senate (including Russ Feingold), but zero accountants and one manufacturer. "I am not a politician," he continued, "I am an accountant and a manufacturer. I know how to balance a budget and I *do* know how to create jobs."[31] This ad played on the common perception that there are too many lawyers in on Capitol Hill, and made the intuitive point that small businessmen are better at creating jobs than lawyers.

Feingold's ads were also a good mixture of attacks on Johnson and spots that built a positive case for himself. One ad that gained some national attention was "On Your Side," which may have been the only ad in the nation in which a Senate candidate actually defended the health care reform bill. The ad featured Wisconsin citizens who said how the health care bill was helping them and ended with the line, "Ron Johnson, hands off my health care."[32]

On the other hand, Feingold made a misstep with an ad called "No Vikings." The ad showed NFL players celebrating in the end zone after scoring a touchdown, including Randy Moss's infamous "mooning" of the fans in Green Bay. The ad stated that Johnson supporters were celebrating because they thought they were going to remove the toughest fighter against special interests from the U.S. Senate. The ad was pretty effective in trying to establish Feingold's underdog role, but there was one problem: the campaign had not gotten permission from the NFL to use the film footage. The campaign quickly made another version of the ad that removed Randy Moss and any other identifiable players, but the ad caused a few days of bad press. By the time election day came, Wisconsin voters were happy to be done with all the ads, especially given that more than 70 percent of Johnson's ads and nearly 64 percent of Feingold's ads were negative (see Table 10.4).

Table 10.4 Number of Ads Run by Russ Feingold, Ron Johnson, and their Supporters, 2010

Ad topics	Feingold		Johnson	
	Negative	*Positive*	*Negative*	*Positive*
Health care, Jobs, Debt			5,279	
Debt, Stimulus			3,321	2,919
Trade	2,708	2,172		
Veterans		3,381		
Candidate qualities		3,037	3,269	2,831
Candidate qualities, Jobs			1,708	1,296
Tax cuts, Health care	1,219			
Social Security	1,344		1,569	
Health care	449		1,651	
Economy (general)	1,403		1,336	
Economy, Jobs			2,679	2,338
Gun rights				245
Attack / Respond, Government loan	1,216		1,187	
Attack / Respond, Drilling Great Lakes	1,172		1,461	
Attack, Underdog role	1,583			
Attack, Opponent has no plan	2,176			
Totals (percent of the candidate total)	**15,083 (63.6%)**	**8,590 (36.4%)**	**23,460 (70.9%)**	**9,629 (29.1%)**

Election Day: Analyzing What Happened in Wisconsin

Returning to the question posed at the beginning of this chapter—why did Johnson win?—both micro-political and macro-political elements had an impact. Clearly, all of the factors specific to this race outlined above—the candidates themselves, the issues at the center of the debate, the money that was raised and spent, the ads that were aired, and the presence of outside groups—played some role. On the other hand, the national tides clearly dominated the Wisconsin Senate election. A fair assessment reveals that there really was not anything Russ Feingold could have done to win. Indeed, the Republican wave swept Wisconsin with a greater force than any other state in the nation. As evidence, consider that Wisconsin was the only state in which there was a party switch from Democrats to Republicans in a U.S. Senate seat, the governorship, majority control of the U.S. House delegation (which went from 5 to 3 Democratic to 5 to 3 Republican), and a flip in party control of both the state Assembly and state Senate. Feingold was caught up in this tide, losing by just over 105,000 votes out of 2.1 million cast (51.9 percent to 47 percent).

Exit polls offer a few more clues about the outcome of the election. One common explanation for Democratic losses in 2010 was not relevant for the Wisconsin Senate race: Feingold was not punished for his support of health care reform. The 21 percent of voters who said health care was the most important problem facing the nation narrowly voted for Feingold (52 percent to 48 percent). Also, a majority of voters (53 percent) reported a desire to expand health care reform (36 percent) or keep it as it is (17 percent), compared to only 45 percent who said they wanted to repeal it. Not surprisingly, 87 percent of those who wanted to expand health care voted for Feingold, and 89 percent of those who wanted to repeal it voted for Johnson (with 74 percent the "leave it as it is" folks going for Feingold). So health care was a complete wash.

A second common explanation for Republican success was that President Obama dragged down his fellow Democrats. In Wisconsin, voters' views on Obama helped Johnson, but the impact was not large. A small majority, 53 percent, of voters disapproved of the job Obama was doing as president and 87 percent of them voted for Johnson, but 89 percent of the 46 percent who approved of Obama voted for Feingold. When queried further about the impact of Obama on their vote, respondents were split: nearly all of the 27 percent who said that their Senate vote signaled support of Obama voted for Feingold, while the 34 percent who said their Senate vote was against Obama supported Johnson. Just over half of the voters who said their Senate vote was not a signal about Obama (37 percent of the total) supported Feingold.[33]

The "enthusiasm gap" and the inability to win the support of independents also help explain Feingold's defeat. Democrats had a six-point edge among people who voted in Wisconsin in 2008 (39 percent to 33 percent), but only a one-point margin in 2010 (37 percent to 36 percent). More critically, Feingold lost the independents by a 56 percent to 43 percent margin, while Obama carried them by 58 percent to 39 percent just two years earlier (a story that was repeated all over the country). Also, Feingold failed to mobilize young voters in the same way that Obama did: 18- to 29-year-olds made up 21 percent of the electorate in Wisconsin in 2008 (and 64.5 percent of them voted for Obama). Feingold carried the young voters (53 percent), but they comprised only 15 percent of the electorate in 2010. Turnout in Milwaukee, a Democratic stronghold, was also down substantially in 2010. Feingold did well in the urban areas (Milwaukee, Madison, and Racine/Kenosha) but it was not enough to overcome Johnson's edge in the suburbs and rural areas.

In his first interview after the election, Feingold was asked why a senator with such a strong reputation as an independent was not able to insulate himself from the partisan tides. He responded, "I think people got the mindset that they weren't going to make distinctions between different Democrats … People wanted to send a message. Sometimes elections are for that purpose. I respect that. I don't think it was a reflection on my record or what I was doing."[34] Feingold made it clear that money was not critical in deciding the outcome, while issues, at least in a general sense, were important. He said, "I certainly wasn't underfunded [in 2010]. I don't think another $100 million would have changed the outcome of my race. I don't think $100 million would have mattered because of the desire on the part of a lot of voters to send that message."[35] Earlier in the interview he elaborated that the message was targeted "particularly to anybody who was an incumbent, particularly to anybody who had supported the president's policies on some high-profile issues." He specifically referred to his support of the stimulus bill and health care reform as being the source of voters' desire to "send a message," but he also lamented that "a lot of the concern that was generated [on these issues] was not based on fact." Ultimately, Feingold concluded, the outcome of the race was "something that no amount of independence or facts could get around."[36]

While it might be tempting to dismiss this analysis as the rationalization of an incumbent who does not want to take responsibility for his defeat, Feingold's assessment of the election is accurate. It simply was a terrible year to be a Democratic incumbent with 18 years of Washington experience—even if much of that experience was built on bucking his party—in a competitive state; no amount of money and no tweaking of campaign tactics were going to change that reality. Mike Wittenwyler, a Madison election law attorney who had worked for Feingold in previous elections, observed "This is the kind of climate where you would vote your mother out of office. If you had a 'D' after your name, it was a liability."[37]

Conclusion

The sweep in the 2010 midterms left Republicans in Wisconsin overjoyed and Democrats demoralized. Still, Feingold tantalized his supporters in his concession speech on Election Night when he said, "It's on to the next fight, it's on to the next battle, it's on to 2012 and it is on to our next adventure. Forward."[38] Feingold later clarified that he is not planning on challenging President Obama in the 2012 primaries. Some have held out the possibility that he would run for the for the open Senate seat created by Herb Kohl's retirement.

Senator John McCain gave his long-time friend and colleague a heartfelt and remarkable tribute on the floor of the Senate a few weeks after the election. In an era of such polarized politics, it was refreshing to see such high praise for a senator on the other side of the aisle. McCain said,

> In his time in the Senate, Russ Feingold, every day and in every way, had the courage of his convictions. And though I am quite a few years older than Russ, and have served in this body longer than he has, I confess I have always felt he was my superior in that cardinal virtue.... I think he is one of the admirable people I have met in my life." And then at the end of the speech, McCain started to choke up when he said, "I have every expectation we will remain good friends long after we have both ended our Senate careers. But I will miss him every day. And I will try harder to become half

the public servant he is. Because his friendship is an honor and honors come with responsibilities.[39]

Ron Johnson has some big shoes to fill. He clearly brings a different vision than Feingold to the Senate about the proper role for Washington in the economy. He will be a strong advocate for limited government, a free market, and cutting government spending. He has six years to show the voters of Wisconsin that his argument during the campaign was valid—that he is a more effective voice for the state's interests than Russ Feingold would have been.

Notes

1. I should clarify what I mean by "upset"—the outcome of the race was not a surprise given that Johnson was comfortably ahead in all of the most recent polls. However, few people predicted this outcome at the beginning of the year.
2. David Hawkings and Brian Nutting, *CQ's Politics in America 2004: The 108th Congress* (Washington, D.C.: CQ Press, 2003), p. 1100.
3. Clay Barbour, "Feingold Ends Senate Service: Senator Often Stood Alone Against His Party," *Wisconsin State Journal*, December 28, 2010, http://host.madison.com/wsj/news/ local/govt-and-politics/article_0fb9e1b1-7dcb-53d6-b80b-f81f8840434b. html (accessed February 21, 2011).
4. Emily Badger, "Public Servant," *Milwaukee Magazine*, August 23, 2010, http://www.milwaukee magazine.com/currentIssue/full_feature_story.asp?NewMessageID =25789 (accessed February 21, 2011).
5. Katherine Q. Seelye, "In Feingold's Loss, Independents Turn on One of Their Own," *New York Times*, November 4, 2010, http://www.nytimes.com/2010/11/05/ us/politics/05 feingold.html?_ref=russelldfeingold (accessed February 21, 2011).
6. W. Zach, "A Quick & Dirty Rundown on Wisconsin's 2010 U.S. Senate Race," February 12, 2010, http://www.whowillwinthe2012election.com/a-quick-dirty-rundown-on-wisconsins-2010-u-s-senate-race/ (accessed February 21, 2011).
7. Clay Barbour. "Ron Johnson Surprises Many by Winning State GOP endorsement," *Wisconsin State Journal*, May 26, 2010, http://host.madison.com/wsj/news/local/govt_ and_politics/article_d4238718-6860-11df-8d93-001cc4c03286.html (accessed February 21, 2011).
8. See David T. Canon, "The Year of the Outsider: Political Amateurs in the U.S. Congress," *The Forum*, vol. 8 (2010), no. 4, http://www.bepress.com/forum/vol8/ iss4/art6/ (accessed February 23, 2011) for a more detailed discussion
9. Gary C. Jacobson and Samuel Kernell, *Strategy and Choice in Congressional Elections*, 2nd ed. (New Haven, CT: Yale University Press, 1983).
10. David T. Canon, *Actors, Athletes, and Astronauts: Political Amateurs in the U.S. Congress* (Chicago: University of Chicago Press, 1990).
11. Dave Umhoefer, "Ron Johnson Postpones Tea Party Sessions: Conservatives Unsatisfied by U.S. Senate Candidate's Responses," *Milwaukee Journal Sentinel*, June 16, 2010, http://www.jsonline.com/news/statepolitics/96528854.html (accessed February 23, 2011).
12. After taking office in January, 2011, Johnson declined to join the Tea Party Caucus in the Senate.
13. Michael Cooper, "Campaign Memo No. 1 Faux Pas in Washington? Candor, Perhaps," *New York Times*, June 25, 2008, http://www.nytimes.com/2008/06/25/us/ politics/25memo.html (accessed February 23, 2011).

14. The interview in which the statement was made, which was done by Wispolitics.com, can be heard at: http://www.wispolitics.com/1006/100610Johnson.mp3 (accessed February 21, 2011).

15. Christian Schneider, "The Making of a Candidate," *Wisconsin Interest*, vol. 19, no. 3 (November, 2010), p. 11.

16. Steve Schultze, "Sunspots Are Behind Climate Change, Johnson says," *Milwaukee Journal Sentinel*, August 16, 2010, http://www.jsonline.com/news/statepolitics/100814454.html (accessed February 23, 2011).

17. Schneider, "The Making of a Candidate," p. 14.

18. Quoted in Craig Gilbert, "Johnson Backpedals on Gun Licensing," *Milwaukee Journal Sentinel*, August 10, 2010, http://www.jsonline.com/news/wisconsin/100385719.html (accessed February 21, 2010).

19. http://www.youtube.com/ron4senate#p/a/u/0/Eb-tvzUXFAE (accessed February 21, 2011).

20. Schneider, "The Making of a Candidate," pp. 12–13.

21. Jack Carver, "Ron Johnson's Dubious Strategy: He Seeks Voters Support Without Telling them What He Stands For," *Isthmus*, October 29, 2010, p. 9.

22. See Ron Johnson's campaign Web site, http://ronjohnsonforsenate.com/home / issues/; and http://www.jsonline.com/blogs/news/102979384.html (accessed February 21, 2011).

23. Quoted in Christian Schneider, "A Candidate's Education: An Inside Look at How Neophyte Ron Johnson Learned the Ropes," *National Review Online*, November 17, 2010, http://www.nationalreview.com/articles/253421/candidate-s-education-christian-schneider (accessed February 21, 2011).

24. Schneider, "A Candidate's Education."

25. Text of the speech can be found at: http://www.whitehouse.gov/the-press-office/remarks-president-state-union-address (accessed February 22, 2011).

26. Robert Barnes, "In Wis., Feingold Feels Impact of Court Ruling," *Washington Post*, November 1, 2010, http://www.washingtonpost.com/wp-dyn/content/article/2010/10/31/AR2010103104314.html (accessed February 23, 2011).

27. *Washington Post*, "Wisconsin Senate Race," http://www.washingtonpost.com/wp-srv/politics/campaign/2010/spending/WI-S2.html (accessed February 21, 2011).

28. Erika Franklin Fowler and Travis N. Ridout, "Advertising Trends in 2010," *The Forum*, vol. 8 (2010), no. 4, http://www.bepress.com/forum/vol8/iss4/art4/ (accessed February 23, 2011); Craig Gilbert, "Johnson, Feingold led all Senate Candidates in Campaign Ads Last Fall," *Milwaukee Journal Sentinel*, January 12, 2011, http://www.jsonline.com/blogs/news/113351984.html (accessed February 23, 2011).

29. "Tipping Point": http://www.youtube.com/watch?v=XcRN8CQ90EE; "Apple Pie": http://www.youtube.com/watch?v=RMExLKHUyg0; "Real World": http://www.youtube.com/watch?v=GIZBNEGZelQ (accessed March 3, 2011).

30. http://www.youtube.com/watch?v=IiCP5wpUUdo (accessed March 7, 2011).

31. http://www.youtube.com/watch?v=06NXxd_qrtQ (accessed February 23, 2011).

32. http://www.youtube.com/watch?v=uS_RudqV1Gk (accessed February 23, 2011).

33. Exit polls are from http://www.cnn.com/ELECTION/2010/results/polls/#val=WIG00p1 (accessed March 7, 2011).

34. John Nichols, "Russ Feingold Speaks Out," *The Nation*, January 13, 2011, http://www.thenation.com/article/157719/russ-feingold-speaks-out (accessed February 21, 2011).

35. Quoted in John Nichols, "Russ Feingold Speaks Out."

36. John Nichols, "Russ Feingold Speaks Out."

37. Quoted in Seelye, "In Feingold's Loss, Independents Turn on One of Their Own."

38. Ibid.

39. John McCain "Tribute to Senator Russ Feingold," *Congressional Record*, November 20, 2010, S.8268, http://www.youtube.com/watch?v=QAVAk61JVDg (accessed February 23, 2011).

11 Chabot vs. Driehaus in Ohio's First Congressional District
The Rematch in the City of Seven Hills[1]

Randall E. Adkins and Gregory A. Petrow

In the 2006 elections Democrats swept both houses of Congress and, for the first time since 1994, they controlled both branches of the legislature. It was a Democratic wave. While many of his Republican colleagues lost in 2006, incumbent Steve Chabot survived with a narrow victory in Ohio's 1st Congressional District. In 2008, the political environment continued to favor the Democrats, but Chabot was unable to hold onto his seat. He lost to Steve Driehaus, the Minority Whip in the Ohio state legislature. Chabot, however, immediately set out to challenge Driehaus to a rematch in 2010. With the wind at his back, Steve Chabot rode the GOP wave created by the national tides and reclaimed the traditionally Republican 1st District.

Ohio's 1st Congressional District

Like ancient Rome, Cincinnati was originally built upon seven hills. These hills make up the heart of the 1st District, which includes most of Hamilton County and the southwest corner of Butler County. They border Indiana on the west and Kentucky to the south. More than three-fourths of the residents of the city of Cincinnati (primarily those who traditionally vote Democratic) live in the 1st District, which also includes the majority of the middle-class suburbs such as Forest Park, White Oak, and Norwood. The more affluent suburbs in the eastern part of the Cincinnati are part of the neighboring 2nd District.

In the past, Cincinnati has weathered economic storms well. The city's highly diversified economy has bolstered the metropolis against downturns in the economy. A majority of those employed in the 1st District, 60.5 percent, work in white collar jobs. Cincinnati is a national leader in consumer market research, consumer product development, and manufacturing. A number of different corporate entities are headquartered in the city, including Proctor and Gamble, the retail giant Federated Department Stores, and the Kroger supermarket chain. Manufacturing is also important to the district. Blue collar jobs make up 23.2 percent of employment, including General Electric's aircraft engine factory. The remaining 16.3 percent of the district work in the service industry.[2] In 2009, however, Cincinnati's unemployment rate grew. By March of 2010 it peaked at 11.0 percent and was still 9.3 percent on Election Day.[3]

After redistricting in the 1990s, the African-American population in the district almost doubled. By 2008, the 1st District had the second largest African-American population of any congressional district in Ohio and the largest African-American population of all congressional districts in the country that were held by a Republican incumbent.[4] Overall, the 1st District is 66.2 percent white, 28.6 percent black, about 1.9 percent Latino, and 1.2 percent Asian.[5] Racial tensions were strong even before the riots in 2001 that were spurred by the fatal shooting of an unarmed black male by a white police officer. In spite of the drop in crime since then, Cincinnati was still ranked by the Federal Bureau of Investigation in the City Crime Rankings as one of the 25 most dangerous cities.[6] Higher crime rates in the city have contributed to a boom in new suburban housing construction to the north of the city and to the south across the Ohio River in northern Kentucky.

In the decades preceding the 2010 election, the population of Cincinnati was declining. For more than a century the city was identified by the careful, conservative character of the German Catholic immigrants, who in recent years moved outside of Cincinnati to the suburbs. As Hamilton County's Republican base moved toward the beltway that encompasses Cincinnati and northern Kentucky, the city became noticeably more Democratic. In fact, by 2008 the city of Cincinnati itself was 45.8 percent black, and the more heavily black neighborhoods tend to vote very consistently for Democrats.[7] The portion of Butler County that sits in the 1st District was strongly Republican, and the heavily Republican suburbs in Hamilton County cast more votes than the city.

Because of the tension between the urban downtown and the suburbs, the 1st District has proved to be one of the most competitive electoral districts in the country at the presidential level. George W. Bush carried the district with 53 percent and 50 percent of the vote in 2000 and 2004, respectively. In 2004, Bush lost Hamilton County by a very narrow margin, but his larger margin in southwestern Butler County allowed him to carry the district by less than one percentage point. In 2008, the district surprisingly swung over to the Democratic column as Barack Obama won with 55 percent of the vote.[8]

On the other hand, the 1st District has a rather rich tradition at the congressional level of sending legislators that grew into Republican heavyweights to Congress. Former president William Henry Harrison was one of the first U.S. representatives from this district. He was elected in October of 1816 to succeed John McLean who was elected to the Ohio Supreme Court (McLean would later be appointed by President Andrew Jackson to the U.S. Supreme Court and served there for over 30 years). Harrison's time in the House was short; he served until the election of 1818 when he left Congress to run for a seat in the Ohio state senate.

Later in the 19th century the district was represented by Republican George Pendleton, the author of the famous Pendleton Act of 1883, establishing the United States Civil Service Commission. Written in response to the assassination of President James A. Garfield by Charles Guiteau (who was upset with the president for not offering him a political appointment), the Pendleton Act ended the patronage system of employment in the federal government as the Democratic and Republican presidents who alternated in office used the civil service system to protect those they appointed.

Probably the most notable representative from the Ohio 1st District was Nicholas Longworth IV, the husband of Alice Roosevelt, Theodore Roosevelt's oldest daughter. Longworth was elected to the House as a Republican in 1902. In the 1912 election, however, the Republican Party split into two factions, the Conservatives and the Progressives. Longworth's father-in-law, the former president, led the Progressives who bolted from the Republican convention in Chicago in June of 1912 and held their own convention a month later. Most of the former president's closest allies, including Longworth, continued to support President William Howard Taft. For those who expected to remain in politics, leaving the Republican Party was just too radical. Of course, this caused stress between Longworth and his wife. The Progressive Party ran a candidate in the 1st District, which allowed Democrat Stanley E. Bowdle to defeat Longworth by only 105 votes. Longworth returned to office, however, defeating Bowdle in both 1914 and 1916. He became the Speaker of the House of Representatives in 1925, where he remained until the Democrats took control of the House after the 1930 mid-term elections. Longworth is best known for strengthening the power of the Speaker while remaining very popular among members of both parties. Today, the Longworth House Office Building is named after him.

Until the 1970s, the district remained almost exclusively in the hands of the Republicans. Democrats temporarily wrestled control away from the Republican Party in the 63rd, 75th, 89th, and 93rd Congresses, but Thomas Luken was the only Democrat to hold this district for more than one term in the 20th century. After the district lines were redrawn following the 1980 census, Luken defeated incumbent William Gradison in the 1982 mid-term elections and held the seat until his retirement in 1990 when he was replaced in office by his son Charlie.

In the 1994 mid-term election, Republican Steve Chabot defeated freshman David Mann. Steve Chabot had previously run for the office, losing to Luken, in 1988. After 1994, Chabot won reelection, often by very narrow margins. Given the competitive and partisan nature of the district, Chabot's political fortunes appeared to be tied closely to the perception of the Republican Party nationally, winning less than 55 percent of the vote every year, except in 2002 and 2004 when Republicans did very well.

The Incumbent: Democrat Steve Driehaus

Steve Driehaus, another local product, defeated Chabot in 2008. Driehaus graduated from nearby Miami University in Oxford, Ohio, served in the Peace Corps in West Africa, and returned to the United States to earn a Masters in Public Administration from Indiana University. He eventually settled in Cincinnati, working in community development. While holding similar policy positions to Chabot on the budget and abortion, Driehaus was able to position himself as a more moderate alternative on issues where Chabot tended to take a less compromising policy stance, such as sustainable environmental policies and the expansion of government health benefits for children.[9] Overall, political analysts such as Stuart Rothenberg of the *Rothenberg Political Report* recognized Driehaus as a candidate to watch in 2008. Specifically, Rothenberg took note of Driehaus' proclamation that he was a "raging moderate." His positions suggested he rode the fence on many issues. For example, Driehaus is pro-life, but supports embryonic stem-cell research. He opposes a federal constitutional amendment to ban gay marriage, but he voted in support of Ohio's Defense of Marriage Act. Driehaus also believed that forces in Iraq should be withdrawn, but opposed setting timelines for withdrawal.[10]

In 2000, Driehaus got into electoral politics by winning an open seat in the Ohio House of Representatives. He represented the 31st state legislative district, which is incidentally completely contained within the boundaries of the 1st District. In campaigns that followed, Driehaus was never opposed in a primary and won reelection each time with at least 57 percent of the vote. He developed a reputation as a pro-life, fiscal conservative, and his strong work ethic in Columbus left him highly regarded. The *Cincinnati Enquirer* named Driehaus legislative "Rookie of the Year" and the Ohio Association of Election Officials named him Democratic Legislator of the Year in 2008.[11]

In 2006, Driehaus was recruited by the Democratic Congressional Campaign Committee (DCCC) to challenge Chabot, but sat on the sidelines. That year Chabot ended up winning narrowly, and the Republicans held onto two of the other three Republican seats in Ohio that Democrats tried desperately to capture. Given that he was elected as the Minority Whip in the Ohio House of Representatives in 2005, Driehaus chose instead to run for reelection. After Chabot's narrow victory margin in 2006, barred from running for reelection by term limits, Driehaus smelled blood in the water and decided to take the plunge and challenge the incumbent. After the 2006 election cycle was over, Driehaus started planning his campaign against Chabot.

Driehaus officially announced his intent to run on May 3, 2007. In response to the question of whether he could defeat Chabot, Driehaus argued that although John Cranley (the 2006 challenger to Chabot) had wider name recognition, he was actually better positioned to defeat Chabot. Like Chabot, Driehaus resided in Cincinnati's West Side neighborhood. This part of the city makes up almost one-third of the district. It is very middle class and heavily Catholic. Of the West Side Driehaus claimed, "I think that will be critical to us succeeding in the fall. We don't need to win in those areas, but we need to do well."[12]

Even though his voting record, once he arrived in Congress, did not offer confirmation of the fact, remember that Driehaus liked to call himself a "raging moderate." In fact, in his two short years in Congress, Driehaus never received a score lower than 80 from the liberal Americans for Democratic Action (ADA), and never received a score higher than 12 from the American Conservative Union (ACU) (see Table 11.1). While his voting record is not reflective of a moderate label, Driehaus was certainly less liberal than his predecessor, Steve Chabot, was conservative.

Table 11.1 Congressional Vote Scores for Steve Dreihaus and Steve Chabot, 1995–2010

Year	American Conservative Union	Americans for Democratic Action	Party Unity	Presidential Support
Steve Driehaus				
2010	8%	80%	89%	88%
2009	12%	85%	90%	85%
Steve Chabot				
2008	100%	15%	94%	64%
2007	100%	10%	94%	80%
2006	96%	10%	89%	95%
2005	96%	0%	95%	89%
2004	96%	10%	95%	79%
2003	96%	10%	95%	91%
2002	96%	0%	96%	85%
2001	96%	5%	94%	81%
2000	100%	5%	94%	21%
1999	96%	10%	89%	22%
1998	96%	0%	91%	27%
1997	96%	20%	87%	27%
1996	100%	15%	84%	34%
1995	100%	0%	94%	20%

Source: CQ's *Politics in America* (Washington, DC: Congressional Quarterly, Inc., 2010 and 2000); The American Conservative Union (http://www.conservative.org); Americans for Democratic Action (http://www.adaction.org); and Congressional Quarterly's vote studies (2009: http://innovation.cqpolitics.com/media/vote_study_2009; and 2010: http://innovation.cq.com/media/vote_study_2010).

Politically, Driehaus was for the most part in step with his party and the Obama administration. His party unity score was not less than 89 percent in either of his two years in Congress, nor was his presidential support score lower than 85 percent (see Table 11.1). By comparison, his predecessor Steve Chabot was about as likely to support President Bush, but he was much more likely to support his party on roll-call votes.

The Democratic leadership in the Congress and the Obama administration brought up a number of controversial issues during Driehaus' tenure in office. The three most important issues across the country tended to be the economic stimulus (the American Reinvestment and Recovery Act of 2009), an environmental bill that came to be known as "cap-and-trade" that was designed to deal with global warming (American Clean Energy and Security Act of 2009), and the health care reform legislation (the Patient Protection and Affordable Care Act of 2010). Driehaus supported both the stimulus bill and the cap-and-trade legislation.

With regard to the health care reform, Driehaus was part of the group of Democrats in the House, led by Representative Bart Stupak (D-MI), who threatened to block the health care legislation. They were concerned that as written it allowed federal funds to be used for abortion procedures. Eventually, Driehaus (and Stupak) agreed to vote for the health care reform bill after President Obama assured them he would issue an executive order that prohibited the use of federal funds for abortions.

The Challenger: Republican Steve Chabot

Born in Cincinnati, Chabot was educated at the College of William and Mary. After graduating in 1975, this cultural and fiscal conservative returned to Cincinnati and worked as a school teacher while he attended Northern Kentucky University law school at night. Early in his law career Chabot decided to get involved in politics, running for Cincinnati City Council in 1979 and again in 1983. He eventually won in 1985 and was reelected in 1987 and 1989.

Steve Chabot first ran for Congress in 1988, but lost. After serving a short time on the Hamilton County Commission, Chabot was poised to run for Congress again in 1994. This was the same year of the Republican "revolution" when the GOP picked up 54 seats in the House and wrestled control from the Democrats for the first time in 40 years. Chabot embraced the House Republican's "Contract with America" and defeated Democratic incumbent David Mann fairly handily with 56 percent of the vote. During his two years in the House, Democrats were angered by Mann's votes in support of President Bill Clinton's fiscal policies. In particular, organized labor was frustrated by his vote in support of the North American Free Trade Agreement (NAFTA). Mann was challenged in the Democratic primary in 1994, which left him vulnerable to Chabot in the general election. Chabot's campaign focused on attracting voters in Cincinnati's white, working-class neighborhoods and the western suburbs by emphasizing his humble, blue-collar beginnings. With Chabot cutting into his base of support, Mann ran television ads effectively running against President Clinton bragging that he voted against the president's "government takeover of health care." Chabot's campaign answered back with an ad morphing Mann's face into Clinton's while the announcer asserted that a vote for Mann was a vote for Clinton.[13] In the end, the national trends that favored the GOP allowed Chabot to emerge the victor, winning the support of suburban voters and many labor Democrats in the district.

In 1996, 1998, and 2000, Chabot defended his seat successfully, but never really won convincingly. By 2002 and 2004, however, his seat began to look safer as he won with 65 percent and 60 percent of the vote, respectively, against Democrat Greg Harris. Harris was a community activist and director of the Hamilton County Democratic Party. In the 2004 race, however, Harris received more than 116,000 votes, including 63 percent of the vote in Cincinnati. This number represented a higher raw vote total than any Democrat had ever received in this district.[14] Of course, numbers like this triggered Chabot's opponent from the 2000 election, Cincinnati City Council member John Cranley, to take another shot at picking off the seat. Even though it was a midterm election, voter turnout was only slightly lower than it was in 2000 and Cranley yielded almost as many votes in 2006 as he did in 2000. In this tough year for Republicans, Chabot held on to win narrowly with 52 percent of the vote.

The 1st District is a textbook example of a marginal district, but the close elections that Chabot faced did not seem to have a mitigating influence on his policy positions. As the data in Table 11.1 suggest, Chabot was far from a moderate during his time in Congress. According to both the ACU and ADA, he was among the most conservative members of Congress. Further, he was a strong supporter of the Republican Party in the House, and was among the strongest supporters of President Bush (until 2008 when he took positions opposing the president much more frequently). Throughout his tenure in office, Chabot consistently maintained a hard-line conservative voting record and acted as an advocate for conservative causes.

Chabot was a true fiscal conservative. His consistent voting record in opposition to tax increases led to very high ratings among anti-tax political advocacy groups. In addition, Chabot's criticism of government spending for both social welfare programs and "corporate welfare" were controversial even among the more moderate factions of the Republican Party. He regularly voted against programs like the State Children's Health Insurance Plan (S-CHIP), highway funding bills he claimed were full of wasteful "pork," and subsidies or tax breaks to support business.

Given his strong Catholicism, it is no surprise that Chabot was very conservative on social issues. During his 14 years in the House, he consistently voted against legislation that would expand abortion, receiving a 0 percent rating from NARAL Pro-Choice America[15] and an 85 percent rating from the National Right to Life Committee.[16] In fact, Chabot sponsored the Partial-Birth Abortion Ban Act of 2003, which was signed into law by President Bush. It is no surprise that Chabot's record is similarly conservative on other social issues like the teaching of intelligent design along with evolution in schools. He is also a staunch opponent of both gambling and gun control.

Finally, Chabot was a critic of both the Democratic and Republican leadership. In 1999 he stepped into the spotlight to serve as one of the floor managers of the Senate's impeachment trial of President Bill Clinton. Likewise, he was one of the first and loudest to call for Speaker Newt Gingrich to step aside after the disastrous 1998 midterm elections, when the Republicans actually lost five seats going against the historical trends (see Chapter 1).

After losing to Driehaus in the 2008 election cycle, Chabot wasted no time declaring his intent to win back his old seat. Chabot never polled well in the district, so it is somewhat surprising that a district with a Partisan Voting Index (PVI) of D+1 (as rated by the non-partisan *Cook Political Report*) sent to Capitol

Hill one of the most conservative members of Congress. Since his election to Congress in the Republican Revolution of 1994, he had always managed to win reelection by getting out the Republican vote in the suburbs. If Chabot could defeat Driehaus, it would be the second wave that he rode to Washington. By the end of the first quarter of 2009, Chabot had raised over $232,000—a substantial figure for a candidate not currently in office.[17] For Chabot this was serious business, and this time President Obama was not going to be running at the top of the ticket.

Chabot vs. Driehaus, Round One: The 2008 Campaign

Throughout the nation the electoral environment turned against the Republican Party following the 2004 election cycle. In 2006, the Democrats won control of both congressional chambers, and in 2008, they were looking to build larger majorities. Given Steve Chabot's narrow escape in 2006, his seat became one of the competitive congressional districts Democrats coveted as a possible pick-up. While Driehaus turned out to be a formidable challenger, he also benefitted from early attention from the Democratic leadership in the House and the DCCC.

Chabot faced a tough challenge that was relatively distinctive to his district. As noted above, the 1st District has the second largest black population (28.6 percent of voters) of any congressional district in Ohio and it had the highest black population of any congressional district in the country held by a Republican. A public opinion survey by SurveyUSA showed that African-American turnout in 2008 would likely decide the outcome of the race. In short, Driehaus needed the vote of African Americans to defeat Chabot. Overall, however, the district was still historically conservative and Driehaus hoped that the candidacy of Barack Obama might be the push that he needed to draw out higher than average black voter turnout. As a result, the Driehaus campaign developed a plan for courting black voters that included attending services at prominent black churches in Cincinnati, passing out campaign materials with photographs of Driehaus with then-Senator Obama,[18] and receiving visits from prominent members of the Congressional Black Caucus.[19]

Social issues had dominated the campaign discussion in the 1st District in recent election cycles before 2008. Democrats recognized that Republicans were better-positioned to win the battle over social issues, so they chose to nominate Driehaus, a pro-life Catholic, in response. With much of the country focusing on economic issues, Driehaus viewed his Catholicism and pro-life position as a form of "baseline" that was necessary for any candidate to have a chance of winning Cincinnati's West Side.[20] In support of this, Driehaus spokesman Joe Wessels argued that "It's not like [voters] are making a radical departure from the type of politician that they've elected from the West Side of Cincinnati before. They just see somebody [in Mr. Driehaus] who is maybe a little safer in these difficult times."[21]

Driehaus defeated Chabot with 52.5 percent of the vote, running behind Barack Obama who garnered 55 percent of the vote. Driehaus ran well in the precincts within the city of Cincinnati, which tend to be heavily Democratic, and he ran well enough in the more Republican suburbs outside of the city limits. Former Ohio Democratic Party Chairman, Jim Ruvulo, said, "That Chabot seat we dreamed about for years, but we never could get enough black voters and young voters to come out and care enough about it."[22] Steve Chabot said of his defeat, "The Democrats were saying about my district in particular that it would see a significant Obama factor. Apparently, they were right."[23]

Most of the seats that the Democrats focused on in 2008 were similar to the 1st District. They were Republican-leaning districts or states where Barack Obama's crossover appeal at the top of the ticket provided the additional votes needed for the Democratic challenger to win. Otherwise, Democrats needed to rely on voters to split their tickets without a good reason to do so.[24] An analysis of the 1st District race in 2008 indicates that this is clearly what happened.[25] While a number of factors ranging from the nationalization of the issues to voter registration patterns benefitted Driehaus, the most important factor benefitting him turned out to be the surge in voter turnout. The bigger the swing in voter turnout in each precinct over 2006, the higher the vote total for Driehaus in each precinct. The data show that the most likely reason for the surge in turnout was the Barack Obama's candidacy, and then Driehaus simply held onto most of the Obama voters. In 2008, Senator Obama was a highly charismatic candidate, and the electoral environment cut strongly against the GOP. Steve Chabot had weathered many difficult electoral challenges since capturing the seat in 1994, but Barack Obama was not running at the top of the ticket in any of those contests. Unfortunately for Driehaus, neither was Barack Obama running at the top of the ticket in 2010.

Driehaus vs. Chabot, Round Two: The 2010 Campaign

In January of 2010, SurveyUSA put a poll in the field the results of which showed that Driehaus was behind Chabot, 56 percent to 39 percent. This was certainly bad news for Driehaus. Anytime an incumbent falls below 50 percent he or she is in trouble. In this survey, Driehaus was not only below 50 percent, but he was behind by double-digits after only a year in office! Clearly, the incumbent had his work cut out for him.[26]

Drilling down into the poll, there was more news that was disconcerting to the Driehaus campaign. First, President Obama's approval/disapproval ratings were upside down in the 1st District. His disapproval rating was 55 percent and his approval rating was 42 percent. To put this in comparison nationally, the president was polling in Gallup organization surveys taken the same weekend at 50 percent approval and 43 percent disapproval. While Obama was rated equally poorly by men and women, and older and younger residents, a striking difference was how he was rated by whites and blacks. White disapproval ran 67 percent and his approval only 30 percent. Among African Americans, however, the president's approval rating ran 85 percent and only 14 percent disapproval. Second, the data in the poll showed that Driehaus' most loyal Democratic supporters, African Americans, were estimated to be 21 percent of the likely voters in November. For every percentage that African-American turnout rose, Driehaus could expect to gain one percent of the vote. Given that blacks make up 28.6 percent of the district, Driehaus could pick up a few percentage points by getting out the African-American vote. As one reporter framed it, his fate hung in the balance of the black vote.[27] Third, the survey results showed that if Driehaus voted in favor of the upcoming health care bill, 48 percent of respondents would view him less favorably, stating that their opinion of him would go down.[28]

Driehaus faced immediate criticism for the more important votes that he took on Capitol Hill. As mentioned earlier, after initially opposing the health care bill, Driehaus later chose to vote in favor of it after the president issued an executive order maintaining the restrictions on the federal funding of abortion. Chabot, of course, argued that if elected, he would fight the funding of the health care legislation.[29] The bigger issue for Driehaus came when he and a number of other Ohio Democrats were later attacked for their vote on the health care reform bill by independent groups who argued that their vote had opened the door to taxpayer-funded abortion. Driehaus found groups like Ohio Right to Life, Americans United for Life, and other pro-life advocacy groups, were actively trying to defeat him. The *Cincinnati Enquirer* published a letter to the editor written by the founder of the International Right to Life Federation, and the Susan B. Anthony List painted the words "Sold Out" on a bus parked by a rally at Fountain Square.[30]

Rather than run from his vote on health care reform, Driehaus, along with some Catholic groups and other anti-abortion supporters, used the president's agreement to sign an executive order banning the federal funding of abortion to claim victory. When the Susan B. Anthony List erected billboards claiming that Driehaus voted for taxpayer funded abortion, the congressman filed a complaint with the Ohio Elections Commission. Of the issue he said, "I've advocated strongly in the health-care bill that nothing goes to abortions and we were successful. It concerns me that people who legitimately care about the issue of abortion are willing to engage in misinformation for partisan gain." It did not help, however, National Right to Life, Ohio Right to Life, and Cincinnati Right to Life all endorsed his opponent, Steve Chabot. Even worse, a survey by the *Cincinnati Enquirer* showed that 77 percent of the support of voters that opposed abortion was going to Chabot.[31]

The health care issue remained a staple of the Chabot campaign. One television advertisement, entitled "Health Care Sham," flashed black and white shots of headlines from the *Cincinnati Enquirer* next to photos of Driehaus and Speaker Nancy Pelosi, while the narrator said:

> The *Enquirer* reports that Congressman Driehaus is set to vote no on health care. One day later, he voted for it. The *Enquirer* called the Pelosi-Driehaus

approach to health care reform "arrogant" and "a sham." Driehaus' vote hurts seniors, cutting $500 billion in Medicare and Driehaus' vote hurts small business, creating $500 billion in new taxes. Congressman Driehaus put his party leaders first, hurting us all.[32]

The references of arrogant and sham were made by the *Cincinnati Enquirer* editorial board, however, in reference to the administration's approach to health care, not Driehaus'.[33]

If this was not bad enough, Driehaus was accosted by angry Catholic voters at church festivals. Things got so bad, that the Driehaus campaign stopped publicizing where the congressman would be each day on their campaign Web site (although to be fair, Chabot was not very good at publicizing his schedule either). With the potential for enthusiastic opponents to take over a meeting, a tracker to catch a gaffe on video, or the real-time danger of generating a tweet on Twitter, candidates across the country found it better to guard their schedule closely, which left them open to the criticism of "ducking" the public.[34]

Certainly this race was going to tighten. Driehaus was a fiscal conservative, the former Minority Whip for the state House, and clearly a good campaigner given that he defeated a seven-term incumbent only two years earlier. A survey of registered voters fielded by We Ask America and published in early August, showed that the race had tightened to at least 12 points, 51 percent to 39 percent.[35] Further evidence that the race had tightened significantly came only two weeks later. American Action Forum, a conservative 527-style political organization headed by former Senator Norm Coleman (R-MN), published the results of a survey of likely voters showing that the race was much tighter than anyone thought. Chabot led by a mere two points, 47 percent to 45 percent.[36]

As Labor Day approached, the electorate in the 1st District was very clearly in sync with the national overall. Survey results showed that almost two-third of likely voters (59 percent) in the upcoming election felt that the country was "off on the wrong track" and less than one-third (31 percent) thought the country was "headed in the right direction." When asked what the most important issue was facing the United States, a resounding 53 percent volunteered the economy/unemployment/jobs. Government spending and health care were a distant second and third with less than ten percent each. When asked what issues were most likely to affect their vote in the fall election, respondents volunteered creating jobs (33 percent) and controlling government spending (22 percent). Given the national context, both issues favored the Republicans.[37]

Throughout the campaign, Driehaus' strategy was to remind voters in the 1st District that Chabot was really the longtime incumbent. In one ad that ran in late September entitled, "Words," the Driehaus' campaign compared Chabot's campaign rhetoric with his voting record over his seven terms in Congress. The advertisement uses an older and poor-quality video clip of Chabot plugging his credentials cutting federal spending, standing up to special interest groups, and privatizing Social Security. Over that the narrator contradicts Chabot's statements while the ad displays very specific textual references contrary to each of Chabot's statements.[38]

By the time early voting started on September 28, a poll sponsored by the *Cincinnati Enquirer* and conducted by SurveyUSA showed that Chabot pulled back out to a 12-point lead, 53 percent to 41 percent. One of the most interesting findings of the survey is that compared to previous elections, 67 percent of Republicans and 64 percent of Chabot's voters were more enthusiastic about the 2010 election. In contrast, only 43 percent of Democrats and 39 percent of Driehaus supporters were more enthusiastic. Part of the bad news for Driehaus was that SurveyUSA only projected the African-American vote to be 16 percent of the overall vote in the district, which was down five percentage points from their survey in January. [39] By this point in the campaign, the Driehaus campaign had failed to energize the black vote without President Obama running at the top of the ticket, which was a bad sign for his prospects on Election Day.

Campaign Finance in the 1st District

The candidates' finances are certainly one of the most important aspects of a congressional campaign, but that picture can portray very different things for incumbents and challengers. Obviously, the more money challengers raise, the more likely they are to win. The more parity between the incumbent and the challenger in terms of campaign fundraising and spending, the closer the election will in all likelihood be. Research by Gary Jacobson shows, however, that there reaches a point in a campaign where additional spending for an incumbent has a diminishing and sometimes even negative return. In simple terms, when incumbents are forced to raise and spend large sums of money, they are likely in big trouble because they are up against a quality challenger.[40]

In the campaign finance records for the 1st District over the past decade, these trends are crystal clear (see Table 11.2). In very good years for Republicans, 2002 and 2004, then-incumbent Steve Chabot won handily. He spent relatively little for a winning congressional candidate, just under $500,000, and still outspent his opponents 20:1 and 6:1, respectively. Chabot's next real challenge came in the 2006 election cycle when the Democrats were riding the anti-Bush wave. That year, Chabot outspent his opponent, Cincinnati City Councilman John Cranley, by a margin of 3:2, but Cranley raised more than $2 million and mounted a very strong campaign. As a result, the election results were much closer. Chabot won with only 53 percent of the vote and, subsequently, analysts shifted his district from the "safe" to the "marginal" column.[41] Chabot now looked vulnerable, so in 2008 the Democrats made a serious investment in the 1st District. In 2008, Driehaus raised less money than Cranley did in 2006, just under $1.5 million, but with money spent by the Democratic Party and other outside groups he found the resources he needed to take over Chabot's seat.

In the 2010 rematch, Chabot started raising funds almost immediately and by the end of 2009 had more than $500,000 cash on hand (see Table 11.3). By June 30, Chabot was one of only five Republican challengers in the country that led

Table 11.2 Campaign Finance Data for Ohio's 1st Congressional District Campaigns, 2002–2010

Election year	Disbursements		Receipts		Vote Percent	
	Chabot (R)	Opponent (D)	Chabot (R)	Opponent (D)	Chabot (R)	Opponent (D)
2010	$2,039,474	$1,971,653	$2,040,665	$1,930,201	51.5	46
2008	$2,410,292	$1,447,544	$2,349,745	$1,489,648	48	52
2006	$2,991,572	$2,021,495	$2,669,976	$2,024,604	53	47
2004	$479,225	$81,663	$610,087	$85,170	60	40
2002	$490,317	$23,388	$702,171	$25,975	65	35

Sources: 2010 election results: *New York Times* (http://elections.nytimes.com/2010/results/ohio); all other data: http://www.opensecrets.org (accessed February 15, 2011).

Table 11.3 Driehaus and Chabot Receipts and Disbursements by Reporting Period, 2009–2010

Reporting Period	Steve Driehaus			Steve Chabot		
	Receipts	Disbursements	Ending Cash	Receipts	Disbursements	Ending Cash
Beginning Cash as of September 30, 2009			$556,172.76			$504,670.14
2009 Year End (1 October–31 December)	$245,289.26	$41,831.66	$759,630.36	$134,039.00	$25,749.27	$612,959.87
2010 April Quarterly (1 January–31 March)	$301,446.21	$126,372.75	$934,703.82	$246,547.56	$57,596.98	$801,910.45
2010 Pre-primary (1 April–14 April)	$8,469.34	$48,400.83	$894,772.33	$7,595.00	$18,334.14	$791,171.31
2010 July Quarterly (15 April–30 June)	$230,672.12	$158,137.91	$967,306.54	$306,312.31	$90,333.19	$1,007,150.43
2010 October Quarterly (1 July–30 September)	$315,483.83	$860,217.76	$422,572.61	$423,992.69	$841,040.64	$590,102.48
2010 Pre-general (1 October–13 October)	$44,784.15	$245,997.10	$221,359.66	$70,897.13	$323,966.62	$337,032.99
2010 Post-general (14 October –22 November)	$160,309.44	$342,257.25	$39,411.85	$227,525.09	$556,422.30	$8,135.78
Total	$1,306,454.35	$1,823,215.26		$1,416,908.78	$1,913,443.14	

Source   Compiled from candidate reports to the Federal Election Commission, Form 3, Lines 23, 24, 26, and 27, various dates.

a Democratic incumbent in cash on hand and he continued to hold this advantage throughout the remainder of the election season.[42] All told, neither candidate really held a meaningful advantage in fundraising. Driehaus raised and spent just under $2 million, and Chabot raised and spent just over $2 million.

Chabot and Driehaus raised 34 percent and 46 percent of their funds from political action committees (PACs), respectively. Both candidates took in healthy sums from business and ideological PACs, but Driehaus also hauled in almost $300,000 from organized labor. There were a large number of PACs that donated the maximum ($5,000 in the primary phase and $5,000 in the general election phase), but there was one non-traditional PAC that really stood out from among the rest. ActBlue is a Democratic political organization that uses their Web site to bundle earmarked contributions made by individuals and pass them on to Democratic congressional candidates. In 2010, ActBlue funneled more than $200,000 to the Driehaus' campaign.[43] As of December 2010, ActBlue contributed more than $180 million to Democratic candidates for office.[44]

Outside money was not as influential in this race as it was in some others. This was either due to or the cause of Chabot's lead in the polls. Jacobson and Kernell's "strategic politician" theory argues that quality candidates make rational decisions and run for office when they have the best chance of winning, such as when the incumbent is retiring (see Chapter 1). Like candidates for office, campaign donors are rational too. As a result, if a candidate has pulled ahead into a double-digit lead, outside money will likely flow to a congressional race somewhere else so that it can make a bigger impact. This was the case in the 1st District. The race in the 1st District drew just under $600,000 in outside money that was spent independently of the candidate's campaigns, which is really very little. In comparison, the House race in Michigan's 7th District (see Chapter 13) drew the most outside money of any congressional race in 2010 (almost $9,000,000). The DCCC spent just over $86,000, of which 70 percent was spent in opposition to Steve Chabot. On the other side of the aisle, the National Republican Congressional Committee (NRCC) spent $85,000, all in support of Chabot. Two other conservative groups came into the district to spend on Chabot's behalf. The Campaign for Working Families spent almost $125,000 and Working America spent just under $103,000.[45]

It was likely that more outside money would have poured into the race in the final four weeks of the campaign. Given the Democrat's tenable position nationally, however, the DCCC made a decision on October 10, to pull more than $500,000 in advertising buys in support of Driehaus from the Cincinnati media market and shift them to congressional districts that they had a better chance of holding.[46] While Driehaus was the first Democratic incumbent to experience the feeling of abandonment, he certainly was not the last of the 2010 election cycle. Without the continued support of the DCCC, Driehaus was expected to go down to a resounding defeat. As will soon be seen, even though he lost, he clearly performed better than Democratic consultants and political analysts expected.

Analysis of the Vote

The election results were close in 2008, 52.5 percent to 47.5 percent, but they were even closer in 2010, 51.5 percent to 48.5 percent (see Table 11.4). This time, however, Chabot was victorious. Chabot won an outright majority of the vote in both Hamilton and Butler Counties, but he ran especially strong in the suburban precincts in Butler County. Those precincts, however, only make up a small fraction of the overall vote in the 1st District. The precincts within the city limits of Cincinnati represented Driehaus' electoral stronghold, where he won a resounding 73.1 percent of the vote. Thus, Driehaus won the urban vote within the city of Cincinnati, but Chabot took home the suburban vote in the remainder of the district. Unfortunately for Driehaus, there were more than twice as many voters outside of the city limits as there were inside of the city limits.

Between 2008 and 2010 there were other changes in voting patterns as well. Although Driehaus performed strongly within the city limits of Cincinnati in both election cycles, his share of the vote dropped 3.4 percent. On the other hand, Chabot won convincingly outside of the city limits of Cincinnati, and his vote share grew by 5.8 percent. In spite of the difference, the pattern is clear. Driehaus' level of support declined throughout the district and Chabot's level of support grew.

Examining the raw vote provides some additional insight into the election outcome. In 2008 when the presidential candidates were running at the top of the tickets, 296,138 people voted in the congressional election. It is a long-established fact that voters are less likely to turn out to vote in midterm elections than in presidential elections. Thus, it is no surprise that this number dropped in 2010 to 201,518. This is a loss of 94,620 voters, which represents a decline of 32 percent. A better comparison, however, is to the 2006 midterm congressional elections when 204,141 voters turned out. That number was just slightly higher than in 2010.

Within the city limits of Cincinnati, there were 39,814 fewer voters that turned out in 2010, and 54,806 fewer voters that turned out in the precincts outside of the city of Cincinnati. This represents 40 percent fewer voters turning out in the city of Cincinnati, but only 28 percent fewer voters turning out in the precincts outside of the city of Cincinnati.

In 2008, a surge in turnout fueled by the candidacy of Barack Obama led the Driehaus campaign to victory. In fact, Driehaus' share of the precinct-level vote was almost perfectly correlated with Senator Obama's (.99).[47] In the district overall, Obama ran about 2.5 percent ahead of Driehaus, but the fall-off from the presidential to the congressional vote was very small across the hundreds of precincts in the district. Driehaus hung onto virtually all of the Obama voters, in great part because he was considered to be a reasonable alternative to Chabot. In the end, Driehaus lost reelection by just 11,098 votes this time around. If he could have turned out his base of support in the precincts within the city of Cincinnati, then he was within reach of turning the rematch into an automatic recount.

Table 11.4 Comparison of Election Results for Ohio's 1st District, 2008 and 2010

	2008			2010			Change in Driehaus vote 2008 to 2010
	Total votes	Chabot (%)	Driehaus (%)	Total votes	Chabot (%)	Driehaus (%)	
1st District overall	296,138	140,683 (47.5)	155,455 (52.5)	201,518	103,770 (51.5)	92,672 (46.0)	–6.5
Butler County only	12,999	9,457 (72.8)	3,542 (27.2)	9,649	7,315 (75.8)	1,990 (20.6)	–6.6
Hamilton County only	283,139	131,226 (46.3)	151,913 (53.7)	191,869	96,455 (50.3)	90,682 (47.3)	–6.4
City of Cincinnati only	99,306	23,362 (23.5)	75,944 (76.5)	59,492	14,592 (24.5)	43,504 (73.1)	–3.4
1st District minus City of Cincinnati	196,832	117,321 (59.6)	79,511 (40.4)	142,026	89,178 (62.8)	49,168 (34.6)	–5.8
Hamilton County minus City of Cincinnati	183,833	107,864 (58.7)	75,969 (41.3)	132,377	81,863 (61.8)	47,178 (35.6)	–5.7

Source: Hamilton County: http://www.hamilton-co.org/boe/archiveresults.asp; Butler County (2010): http://www.butlercountyelections.org/results/files/nov2010SOVC. pdf, (2008) http://www.butlercountyelections.org/pdf%5Cnov08.pdf (accessed March 18, 2011).

Final Thoughts

The election in the 1st District drew national and even international attention in 2010. In many respects, the district is a microcosm of the country as
a whole. It includes urban, suburban, and rural voters, and a very significant
African-American population. One could say that the district is a bellwether
for the nation, especially in an election cycle where the issues are nationalized
like 2010.

Ohio, too, is known as a bellwether. Since 1944, the state of Ohio has voted
for every winning presidential candidate with the exception of choosing Nixon
over Kennedy in 1960. Clearly, the Republican Party returned to power in 2010.
Anyone who remembers the glory days of the Cincinnati Reds baseball team in
the 1970s remembers their nickname—the "Big Red Machine." Ohio in 2010
became the Big Red Machine of American politics. Republican John Kasich
wrestled the governor's office away from incumbent Democrat Ted Strickland.
Former U.S. House member and Bush administration official, Rob Portman,
won an open seat to replace retiring Senator George Voinivich. In addition, the
Republicans won five U.S. House seats from Democratic incumbents and now
hold 13 of the 18 House seats.

Not to be dismayed, even before he took office, Democrats put Steve Chabot
on public notice that they were going to come after him in 2012.[48] Given that
the Republicans will control redistricting following the 2010 Census, they may
feel the need to pack a few more Republicans into the district in order to parry
the Obama campaign and the Democratic contender that they are sure to nominate in 2012.

Notes

1. The authors wish to acknowledge the assistance of Elizabeth O'Connor.
2. Profile: Ohio's 1st District, http://www.cqpolitics.com/wmspage.cfm?docID=profile-
   000000027942 (accessed May 26, 2009).
3. "Cincinnati-Middletown, Ohio Unemployment," Department of Numbers, http://
   www.deptofnumbers.com/unemployment/ohio/cincinnati/ (accessed March 4,
   2011).
4. "Obama Success Boosts Other Democrats," *The Associated Press State & Local
   Wire*, October 16, 2008.
5. "Ohio 1st District Profile," *New York Times*, http://elections.nytimes.com/2010/
   house/ohio/1
6. "Study: 4 Ohio Cities Make Top 25 Most Dangerous List," *Dayton Daily News*,
   November 18, 2007, http://www.daytondailynews.com/n/content/oh/story/news/
   local/2007/11/18/ddn111907riskycityglance.html (accessed April 14, 2009).
7. "Cincinnati city, Ohio; ACS Demographic and Housing Estimates: 2005–
   2007," U.S. Census Bureau, http://factfinder.census.gov/servlet/ADPTable?
   _bm=y&-context=adp&-qr_name=ACS_2007_3YR_G00_DP3YR5&-
   ds_name=ACS_2007_3YR_G00_&-tree_id=3307&-redoLog=true&-_
   caller=geoselect&-geo_id=16000US3915000&-format=&-_lang=en   (accessed
   March 4, 2011).

8. http://www.cqpolitics.com/wmspage.cfm?docID=profile-000000027942 (accessed May 19, 2009).
9. "New to the House" *Washington Post*, November 6, 2008, p. A41.
10. Stuart Rothenberg, "A Crop of House Candidates Worth Taking a Look At," RealClearPolitics.com, March 31, 2008, http://www.realclearpolitics.com/articles/2008/03/a_crop_of_house_candidates_wor.html (accessed March 21, 2011).
11. "About Steve," driehaus.house.gov/about/index.shtml (accessed May 18, 2009).
12. Shira Toeplitz, "Driehaus Says He Can Beat Chabot," *Roll Call*, June 4, 2008, http://www.lexisnexis.com.leo.lib.unomaha.edu/hottopics/lnacademic/?verb=sr&csi=3624 (accessed June 12, 2011).
13. Brian Nutting and H. Amy Stern, *CQ's Politics in America 2002* (Washington, D.C.: CQ Press, 2001) p. 1017.
14. http://www.cincinnati-oh.gov/council/pages/-35528-/ (accessed April 16, 2009).
15. http://www.prochoiceamerica.org/choice-action-center/us-gov/congressional-record-on-choice/stevechabot.html (accessed May 20, 2009).
16. "Federal NRLC Scorecard - 110th Congress, Combined Sessions," National Right to Life, http://capwiz.com/nrlc/scorecard.xc?chamber=H&state=US&session=110&x=12&y=6 (accessed May 20, 2009). Typically, Chabot's NRLC rating was 100%.
17. Greg Giroux, "Ten Non-Incumbent House Candidates Topped $100K in First Quarter," CQ Today Online News – Politics, April 23, 2009, http://www.cqpolitics.com/wmspage.cfm?docID=news-000003102075 (accessed May 26, 2009).
18. Shira Toeplitz, "Black Turnout Likely to Decide Chabot's Fate," *Roll Call*, October 30, 2008, http://www.rollcall.com/issues/54_52/-29650-1.html (accessed March 21, 2011).
19. Ibid.
20. Julie Carr Smyth, "Cincinnati values vote at center of district fight," *Associated Press State & Local Wire*, September 1, 2008.
21. Sean Lengell, "Democratic Wave Seen Washing over the House," *Washington Times*, October 28, 2008, p. B01.
22. Mark Naymik and Stephen Koff, "He Was Strong in Democratic Areas, Cut into GOP Territort," *Cleveland Plain Dealer*, November 6, 2008, http://blog.cleveland.com/openers/2008/11/strategy_focus_pivotal_in_obam.html (accessed June 12, 2011).
23. Julie Carr Smyth, "Ohio Democrats Win House Seats," *The Associated Press State & Local Wire*, November 5, 2008.
24. Aaron Blake, "Democratic Challengers Do Not Yet Believe in Senator Obama," *The Hill*, March 26, 2008, p. 1.
25. Randall E. Adkins and Gregory A. Petrow, "Riding Obama's Coattails: The Democrats Finally Take the Ohio 1st," *American Review of Politics*, vol. 30 (Summer 2009), pp. 115–136.
26. "Results of SurveyUSA Election Poll #16208," http://www.surveyusa.com/client/PollReport.aspx?g=046a0e68-0886-4fdb-a800-56ec8556b852 (accessed March 15, 2010)
27. Quan Truong, "Driehaus' fate hangs on black vote," *Cincinnati Enquirer*, October 24, 2010.
28. "Results of SurveyUSA Election Poll #16208"; "Gallup Daily: Obama Job Approval," http://www.gallup.com/poll/113980/Gallup-Daily-Obama-Job-Approval.aspx (accessed March 15, 2010).
29. "Ohio's 1st congressional district," *The Economist*, September 2, 2010, http://www.economist.com/node/16943984/print (accessed March 4, 2011).
30. Sabrina Eaton, "Abortion foes attack like-minded Democrats" *Cleveland Plains Dealer*, September 21, 2010, p. A1.

31. Quon Truong, "Battle of the Steves: Driehaus-Chabot rematch a microcosm of the country," *Cincinnati Enquirer*, October 16, 2010, http://news.cincinnati.com/article/20101016/NEWS0108/10170336/Battle-Steves-Driehaus-Chabot-rematch-microcosm-country (accessed March 15, 2011).

32. http://www.youtube.com/watch?v=y8QzkwGxi0U (accessed March 15, 2011).

33. Quon Truong, "Adwatch: Health Care Sham," *Cincinnati Enquirer*, September 23, 2010, http://news.cincinnati.com/article/20100923/NEWS0108/9240340 (accessed January 19, 2011).

34. Jonathan Allen, "Vulnerable Dems Duck Public Events," *Politico*, September 11, 2010, http://www.politico.com/news/stories/0910/41849.html (accessed June 12, 2011).

35. "Triple Play in the Buckeye State," We Ask America poll release, http://weaskamerica.com/2010/08/13/triple-play-in-the-buckeye-state (accessed March 15, 2011).

36. "Survey of Likely Voters in Oh 01," http://americanactionforum.org/files/OH%2001%20Toplines.pdf (accessed March 15, 2011).

37. Ibid.

38. http://www.youtube.com/user/DriehausforCongress#p/u/2/j1QDINFw1yU (accessed March 15, 2011).

39. "Results of SurveyUSA Election Poll #17174," http://www.surveyusa.com/client/PollReport.aspx?g=80eccc67-aa69-41ad-be70-fca15d656922 (accessed March 15, 2011).

40. Gary C. Jacobson, *Money in Congressional Elections* (New Haven, CT: Yale University Press, 1980).

41. http://www.cookpolitical.com/charts/house/competitive_2010-11-01_12-12-36.php (accessed March 15, 2011).

42. Bob Benenson, "Can a Wall of Cash Hold Back the Tide?" *Roll Call*, August 6, 2010, http://www.rollcall.com/news/75792-1.html (accessed March 4, 2011).

43. "Top Contributors; 2010 Race: Ohio District 01," Center for Responsive Politics, http://www.opensecrets.org/races/contrib.php?cycle=2010&id=OH01(accessed March 15, 2011).

44. Act Blue, https://secure.actblue.com/ (accessed March 15, 2011).

45. "Top Contributors; 2010 Race: Ohio District 01," Center for Responsive Politics.

46. Chuck Todd, "Dems Pull Support from First House Incumbent This Cycle," MSNBC.com, http://firstread.msnbc.msn.com/_news/2010/10/11/5272642-dems-pull-support-from-first-house-incumbent-this-cycle (accessed March 15, 2011).

47. Adkins and Petrow, "Riding Obama's Coattails: The Democrats Finally Take the Ohio 1st."

48. Kyle Trygstad, "DCCC Targeting Marginal Districts in 2012," *Roll Call*, December 28, 2010, http://www.rollcall.com/news/-201962-1.html (accessed March 15, 2011).

12 Toomey vs. Sestak in Pennsylvania Senate Race

Moderation Doesn't Pay

Robin Kolodny

The drama of the 2010 Senate race in Pennsylvania actually began in the 2004 Republican primary for the same seat. The incumbent at the time, Republican Arlen Specter, eked out a victory over a younger, more conservative U.S. House member, Pat Toomey. This early warning was not lost on Arlen Specter, who spent the next several years wondering whether he could prevail in another Republican primary despite his 25 years in the U.S. Senate. At the time, Specter was one of the very few moderate Republicans left in Congress, and his anachronistic position led him to switch parties and become a Democrat in April 2009 in order to better position himself to hold on to his seat for a sixth term. Specter's 2004 experience and his 2009 party switch helped create the context for a battle over his Senate seat, but not the battle anyone originally envisioned.

Pennsylvania Politics

Known as the Keystone State, Pennsylvania, and especially its largest city Philadelphia, were very important in the nation's founding. Both the Declaration of Independence and the Constitution were signed in Philadelphia, and the state's political moderation and location in the geographic center of the country led to its nickname and pivotal status in the new nation.

Today, Pennsylvania retains its important place in American politics. Much of this comes from the electorally competitive nature of the state which is driven by features that lead to a political bifurcation. James Carville, a well-known Democratic political consultant for President Bill Clinton who worked extensively in Pennsylvania in 1991 and 1994, famously said that the state is Philadelphia and Pittsburgh, with Alabama in between.[1] The rural area of the state, found mostly in the northern tier and central section forming a "T" is known for being very conservative, Republican, politically active if sparsely populated. The areas around the cities of Pittsburgh and Philadelphia, where most of the state's 12.4 million residents live, are like most urban areas in the United States—heavily Democratic. The urban-rural split in the state is also reflected in that the areas that are part of the "T" are still economically dominated by agriculture, coal mining and steel production. The urban areas are more cosmopolitan and are home to Fortune 500 corporations like U.S. Steel, PPG Industries, and H.J.

Heinz. This combination makes Pennsylvania seem to be a microcosm of the United States.[2]

The Keystone State, like most states, is overwhelmingly white (82 percent); roughly 11 percent of residents are African American, while about 6 percent are Hispanic and 3 percent are Asian.[3] The fastest growing segment of the population is Hispanic Americans whose population increased by nearly 83 percent between 2000 and 2010.[4] Much of this growth was around the areas of Allentown, Lancaster, Reading, Hazleton, and Philadelphia. Pennsylvania is also home to a large senior citizen population (over 15 percent, which is higher than the national average of about 12.5 percent).[5] Nearly 30 percent of Pennsylvanians have a German heritage.[6]

Pennsylvania is a true "swing state." Voters have consistently switched between electing candidates of the two major parties, especially in statewide races. This trend is less so for presidential elections in recent years, however, as the state has voted to give its electoral votes to the Democratic presidential candidate in each of the last five elections. Even though Pennsylvania is a swing state, Democrats have a sizeable (1.18 million) voter registration advantage over Republicans. Many take this as a sign both of national trends in party identification (Democrats saw large gains across the nation in 2008), and the tenuousness of party as a predictor of vote choice or turnout.[7] As a result, it is not unusual to find one Pennsylvania senator from each party (as was the case after 2010), and to have the two parties alternate control of the governorship. While Republicans have held an advantage in controlling the state legislature, it has always been by the narrowest of margins. This is partly because of the "T" phenomenon described above. The two large urban centers normally produce Democratic winners at the U.S. House level, while the "T" selects Republicans. The electoral results in statewide races follow this pattern as well—Democrats do well in Pittsburgh and Philadelphia and Republicans get a lot of votes from the other parts of the state.

Typically, the partisans selected from the major parties are more moderate than in other regions of the nation that might be more skewed to one ideological perspective. Democrats in Pennsylvania are more likely to be pro-life (and especially Catholic) and more likely to be pro-gun than Democrats nationwide. Conversely, Republicans tend to be more pro-environment and more in favor of controlled development and social welfare programs than Republicans nationwide.

In 2010, Pennsylvania's gubernatorial seat was open, as the incumbent, Democrat Ed Rendell, was completing his second term and ineligible to run again. The state also held elections for the entire General Assembly (the state's lower house) and half the state Senate in addition to the U.S. Senate seat and the entire U.S. House delegation. Pennsylvania is also a closed primary and closed registration state. Voters may register or reregister with a new party affiliation up to 30 days before an election. Only registered party voters could vote in the primaries that were held on May 18, 2010.

The Context of the 2010 Senate Race

The U.S. Senate seat contest in 2010 turned into an open-seat race, but that was not originally expected. A critical part of the story of the 2010 election was focused on an individual who did not even end up running in the general election: Arlen Specter. First elected in 1980, he initially sought a sixth term, but not as a member of the party to which he had belonged since his first campaign in 1965. Because of his waning support within the Republican Party in Pennsylvania, demonstrated by his near-loss of his primary nomination in 2004, Specter decided to become a Democrat in early 2009. He believed that he would certainly lose the Republican nomination in 2010 to former Congressman Patrick Toomey (15th District, Allentown) who nearly defeated him in 2004. No one expected Specter to have a hard time winning the Democratic Party nomination as he was welcomed into the Democratic Party at the national level with open arms. This assumption proved to be incorrect.

Arlen Specter: Pennsylvania's Independent Senator

A Kansas native, Arlen Specter began his career as a lawyer after earning degrees from the University of Pennsylvania and Yale Law School. In 1964, he became assistant counsel to the Warren Commission, a committee responsible for investigating the assassination of President John F. Kennedy. Specter, although a registered Democrat, ran for Philadelphia District Attorney in 1965 as a Republican and won; he was reelected to that post in 1969. After a few years of electoral setbacks, Specter returned to practicing law until Senator Richard Schweiker announced his retirement, opening up the U.S. Senate seat for the 1980 election. Specter was elected to the Senate in 1980, when he defeated Peter F. Flaherty by less than 2 percentage points. He served in the Senate until 2011.[8]

Specter enjoyed 30 years in the Senate and holds the record for most years served in the Senate by anyone from the state of Pennsylvania. Throughout his career, he played an important role on the Senate Judiciary and Appropriations Committees. He is largely known for his more moderate stances compared to most other Republican elected officials. For instance, Specter took liberal positions in supporting abortion rights and affirmative action. He also took conservative positions in supporting gun rights and the death penalty. Specter's positions on these and other issues led to a very unusual voting record in the Senate. In an era of polarized partisans, Specter continually showed himself to be a moderate, often irritating his Republican colleagues. From his first year in the Senate, he received very low scores from the American Conservative Union (ACU) on the votes they tracked; that first year he only voted with the ACU's position 40 percent of the time (see Table 12.1). In fact, in his 30 years in office, he received scores of 50 percent or higher from the ACU only eight times. As one would expect with a low conservative voting record, Specter often voted with the Democrats. His vote ratings from the liberal group Americans for Democratic Action were typically above 40 percent, and his party unity scores

Table 12.1 Congressional Vote Scores for Arlen Specter, 1981–2010

Year	American Conservative Union	Americans for Democratic Action	Party Unity	Presidential Support
2010	0%	90%	97%	97%
2009	20%	75%	95%	96%
2008	42%	45%	62%	58%
2007	40%	60%	49%	63%
2006	43%	30%	61%	76%
2005	63%	45%	69%	85%
2004	75%	45%	70%	88%
2003	65%	25%	84%	89%
2002	50%	35%	60%	89%
2001	56%	40%	60%	87%
2000	62%	40%	67%	59%
1999	48%	40%	64%	53%
1998	33%	45%	41%	49%
1997	32%	70%	50%	71%
1996	50%	50%	63%	59%
1995	36%	55%	65%	49%
1994	46%	55%	55%	55%
1993	57%	45%	54%	42%
1992	30%	65%	41%	45%
1991	71%	40%	67%	68%
1990	48%	39%	53%	58%
1989	57%	40%	55%	66%
1988	33%	60%	48%	63%
1987	15%	80%	46%	40%
1986	33%	75%	27%	31%
1985	36%	55%	51%	61%
1984	36%	50%	67%	65%
1983	16%	80%	46%	59%
1982	26%	70%	50%	55%
1981	40%	50%	64%	77%

Source: CQ's *Politics in America* (Washington, DC: Congressional Quarterly, Inc., 2010 and 2000); The American Conservative Union (http://www.conservative.org); Americans for Democratic Action (http://www.adaction.org); and Congressional Quarterly's vote studies (2009: http://innovation.cqpolitics.com/media/vote_study_2009; and 2010: http://innovation.cq.com/media/vote_study_2010).

were very low compared to other GOP senators. Specter did show some loyalty to Republican presidents, but his highest presidential support scores came after Barack Obama was elected (and after he had switched parties). Specter's moderate reputation, however, brought him a good deal of influence in the institution. In years when the Senate was divided by only a few votes, both parties courted him to vote with them. Named one of *Time* magazine's ten best Senators in 2006, Specter was a formidable force in the upper chamber of Congress for many years.[9]

The 2004 Specter-Toomey Republican Primary

The 2004 Republican primary was the starting point for the 2010 race and it was anything but a sure bet for Specter. While he had held the seat for nearly a quarter century at the time of this election, his moderate record haunted him in this race. With a platform more socially conservative than his opponent, and with the support of many fiscally conservative organizations, then-Representative Patrick Toomey attacked Specter's moderate record, highlighting Specter's clashes with the conservative base. With the aid of organizations like the Club for Growth,[10] Toomey was able to cut Specter's early lead in the polls, which was up to 20 percentage points at times, down to just 6 percent right before the primary.[11]

Specter's support from important conservative figures such as President George W. Bush and fellow Pennsylvania Senator Rick Santorum, however, proved to make the difference. It was a close race with Specter garnering 51 percent of the vote and Toomey earning 49 percent.[12] Many ascribed the victory to endorsements from the aforementioned, which reminded Republicans of the importance of maintaining party control over the seat and of the upcoming presidential election that year. In addition, some commentators argued that this particular primary was indicative of the magnitude of the developing split within the Republican Party nationally.[13] Given Pennsylvania's historic preference for moderates, Specter was believed to be the best candidate to retain the seat for the GOP, especially when the Democrats were expected to (and did) select moderate Democratic Congressman Joseph M. Hoeffel (13th District – Northeast Philadelphia and Northern Philadelphia suburbs) as their Senate nominee.

Specter's Party Switch

As late as March of 2009, Arlen Specter declared that he would be running as a GOP candidate for reelection to a sixth term. Despite rumors that he would attempt to run as an Independent, Specter claimed, "I'm staying a Republican because I think I have a more important role to play there."[14] Just a month later, Specter announced that not only would he be leaving the Republican Party, but he would be running as a Democrat in 2010. A proponent of such policies as the $787 billion stimulus bill (the American Reinvestment and Recovery Act),

Specter was welcomed with open arms by the Democrats with President Obama stating to the senator, "You have my full support, and we're thrilled to have you."[15] The Republican leadership was not too fond of Specter's party shift, accusing him of jumping ship to avoid another difficult primary with Pat Toomey. Specter adamantly described his decision as evidence of an independently-minded politician, pointing to his moderate voting record. He also explained his move as the result of a larger ideological shift amongst his party: "Since my election in 1980, as part of the Reagan Big Tent, the Republican Party has moved far to the right… I now find my political philosophy more in line with Democrats than Republicans."[16]

Specter's switch immediately changed the dynamics of the 2010 Democratic primary. Joe Torsella, recent past president of the National Constitution Center in Philadelphia, planned to seek the Democratic nomination to oppose Specter in the general election, but withdrew when Specter switched (especially given his warm welcome into the Democratic Party). Representative Joe Sestak (7th District) hinted that he was considering challenging Specter in the primary, but did not officially decide to enter the race until August of 2009. At the time of Sestak's announcement, Specter's campaign war chest was almost twice that of Sestak and Specter was also ahead of him in the polls by a 2 to 1 margin.[17] Given Specter's long career, statewide name recognition, and high regard among the public and political elites alike, the general consensus was that Specter would have an easy time in the Democratic primary in 2010. Specter's approval rating was at 62 percent in November of 2008, and stayed above 50 percent through May 2009. His approval rating declined somewhat from May until December 2009, however, hovering around the 45 percent mark.[18] Meanwhile, the head-to-head matchup polls between Specter and Sestak consistently found Specter in the lead until April of 2010.[19] Therefore, during the remainder of 2009, most observers prepared to see a rematch between Arlen Specter and Pat Toomey in the 2010 general election.

Patrick Toomey: Specter Spoiler or Crest of a New Wave?

Patrick Toomey was born in Providence, Rhode Island. Upon his graduation from Harvard University in 1984, Toomey worked in the financial sector with Chemical Bank as an investment banker and at Morgan Grenfell, Co. (a London-based investment bank which was later bought by Deutsche Bank), where he eventually became director. In the early 1990s, Toomey moved to Allentown, Pennsylvania, where, along with his two brothers, he founded the restaurant business Toomey Enterprises, Inc., which launched Rookie's Restaurant and Sports Bar. The successful business eventually became a statewide chain.[20]

In 1997, Toomey decided to run for the U.S. House of Representatives after having been active with the Allentown Government Study Commission. In 1998 he won a clear, yet hard-fought victory over Democratic state Senator Roy Afflerbach for the 15th Congressional District seat. He held the seat through 2004, upholding his pledge to constituents to serve no more than three terms in

Table 12.2 Congressional Vote Scores for Pat Toomey, 1999–2004

Year	American Conservative Union	Americans for Democratic Action	Party Unity	Presidential Support
2004	100%	0%	98%	94%
2003	92%	20%	94%	93%
2002	100%	0%	96%	88%
2001	100%	0%	93%	93%
2000	95%	10%	92%	29%
1999	92%	5%	91%	28%

Source: CQ's *Politics in America* (Washington, DC: Congressional Quarterly, Inc., 2010 and 2000); The American Conservative Union (http://www.conservative.org); Americans for Democratic Action (http://www.adaction.org); and Congressional Quarterly's vote studies (2009: http://innovation.cqpolitics.com/media/vote_study_2009; and 2010: http://innovation.cq.com/media/vote_study_2010).

the House. While a member of the House, Toomey focused on fiscal issues, often challenging the Appropriations Committee and spending. He also served as a member of the Banking and Financial Services Committee and supported a flat tax as well as Social Security privatization. Toomey consistently demonstrated his fiscal restraint in the House, even opposing the Bush administration on the Medicare prescription drug benefit because of the cost. He also voted conservatively on a host of social issues. Toomey is a conservative through and through; he earned nearly perfect scores from the ACU and consistently low scores from the ADA while in the House (see Table 12.2). Toomey's challenge to Arlen Specter in the 2004 Republican Senate primary was portrayed as an epic battle between a true fiscal conservative and a "RINO" (Republican in Name Only). Toomey gained visible backing from the relatively new Club for Growth and became a hero to those who felt fiscal conservatism was being fully ignored.[21]

Out of a job after fulfilling his term-limit pledge, Pat Toomey took a position as the head of the Club for Growth in early 2005 after the group's founder, CATO Institute fiscal policy expert Stephen Moore, stepped down in 2004, creating an opening at the top of an interest group that was quickly gaining influence in American politics.[22] Toomey held this post until April of 2009 when he left to devote his energies to a full time run against Arlen Specter again. Two weeks after Toomey's resignation and activation of his campaign, Arlen Specter switched parties. In 2010, Toomey, without competition from Specter any longer, captured his party's nomination for the Senate seat.

Joseph Sestak: Reclaiming the Liberal Cause

Enter Joe Sestak. Born in Secane, Pennsylvania, Sestak is a graduate of the U.S. Naval Academy and holds a Ph.D. from Harvard in political economy and government. He served 31 years in the Navy, rising to the rank of 3-star admiral

Table 12.3 Congressional Vote Scores for Joe Sestak, 2007–2010

Year	American Conservative Union	Americans for Democratic Action	Party Unity	Presidential Support
2010	0%	90%	94%	95%
2009	0%	95%	96%	97%
2008	0%	90%	97%	18%
2007	0%	95%	95%	8%

Source: CQ's *Politics in America* (Washington, DC: Congressional Quarterly, Inc., 2010 and 2000); The American Conservative Union (http://www.conservative.org); Americans for Democratic Action (http://www.adaction.org); and Congressional Quarterly's vote studies (2009: http://innovation.cqpolitics.com/media/vote_study_2009; and 2010: http://innovation.cq.com/media/vote_study_2010).

before his retirement from military service. His first encounter with Washington, D.C. came during the Clinton administration where he served in the White House as Director for Defense Policy from 1994 to 1997. Sestak retired from the Navy in 2006 after commanding combat operations in both Afghanistan and Iraq.[23]

Upon his retirement, Sestak decided to run for the U.S. House of Representatives for Pennsylvania's 7th District (Western Philadelphia Suburbs to the Delaware border) where he grew up. He challenged 20-year Republican incumbent Curt Weldon, whom he trailed until three weeks before the election when the Federal Bureau of Investigation raided Weldon's daughter's apartment to procure evidence in an improper influence allegation involving the Weldons and Russian business owners.[24] Sestak won that election in 2006 and was reelected in 2008. While a member of the House, Sestak consistently earned grades of zero from the ACU and nearly perfect scores from the ADA (see Table 12.3). Hence, he was the mirror image of Toomey ideologically. Sestak also proved to be a loyal Democrat, as he voted with his party over 90 percent of the time in each of his four years in the House and repeatedly opposed President Bush and supported President Obama. Sestak supported Democratic legislation such as health care reform (the Patient Protection and Affordable Care Act of 2010) and the stimulus package (the American Reinvestment and Recovery Act). He served on the Committees for Armed Services, Small Business, and Education and Labor. Yet, in his two House terms, Sestak did not have an opportunity to become familiar to the remainder of the state, something he needed to prevail in a Senate race. He would spend most of 2010 trying to remedy that.

The 2010 Specter-Sestak Democratic Primary

What began as a race that many assumed would be uncompetitive—Specter was polling as a clear winner—the Democratic primary of 2010 in Pennsylvania ended up as a dead heat in the polls as early as a month before the actual election. As late as March of 2010, Sestak trailed Specter by 24 points in a

Quinnipiac University poll, and suffered from persistently low name recognition.[25] Despite Specter's endorsements from both the national and state Democratic establishments, however, Sestak began polling within a couple percentage points of the incumbent by mid-April, and most polls after that showed the race as a dead heat or Sestak leading.[26] Indeed, Specter was the only candidate to receive help from the Democratic Senatorial Campaign Committee (DSCC) in the 2010 primaries, demonstrating the considerable commitment to him from state and national Democratic officials.[27]

The primary campaign season mostly featured character attacks. A usually-confident Specter was on the defensive, reiterating his reasons for switching parties, as well as his electoral victory over Toomey in the previous primary season.[28] A storm of intrigue erupted over Sestak's claim on a cable TV show in February 2010 that the White House, using former President Bill Clinton as their emissary, had offered Sestak a job (rumored to be Secretary of the Navy) if Sestak would withdraw from the primary and return to his House seat.[29] While Specter supporters doubted Sestak's story, they said little, content to have the presence of White House heavyweights visit Pennsylvania on behalf of Specter speak for itself. After the primary, Toomey tried briefly to insist on an investigation of "job-gate," but given the White House's swift change of heart in embracing Sestak, the matter faded.

Sestak, similar to many GOP officials, questioned not only Specter's electability but his sincerity in becoming a Democrat, claiming that he was the true Democrat of the race. Two weeks before the primary, Sestak made a major ad buy in the state with an ad titled "The Switch." The ad included the following audio:

Sestak: I'm Joe Sestak, the Democrat. I authorized this message.

Specter: My change in party will enable me to be reelected.

Narrator: For 45 years, Arlen Specter has been a Republican politician.

George W. Bush: Arlen Specter is the right man for the United States Senate. I can count on this man. See, that's important. He's a firm ally.

Narrator: But now...

Specter: My change in party will enable me to be reelected.

Narrator: Arlen Specter changed parties to save one job: his, not yours.[30]

The video clip of Specter saying his goal was to be "reelected" became legendary, and was the talk of the media, pundits, and voters all over the state. The footage from the ad came from a press conference held by Specter in Philadelphia on May 1, 2009, defending his party switch on the grounds that his experience representing the state was so valuable to his supporters that they wanted to see him run however he could be elected. Specter also said he did not want to risk defeat at the hands of the Republican primary electorate.[31] The clip of George Bush calling Specter a "firm ally" came from one of Specter's own reelection ads in 2004. The ad titled "Three" showed Specter, Bush, and Rick Santorum sharing a stage with the announcer saying "Three for Pennsylvania" as they assemble for their event.[32] While Specter clearly thought through his party switch carefully and expected support from Independents and some Democrats (especially in the Jewish community), he had never before run in a statewide Democratic primary. Activist Democrats had backed opponents to Specter in the past. They were unhappy with his conservative fiscal votes, and his role in the confirmation hearings for Supreme Court Justice Clarence Thomas, particularly Specter's aggressive questioning of Anita Hill regarding her allegations of Thomas's sexual harassment. Knowing that many Democrats harbored no love for Specter, Sestak husbanded his resources to run the "Switch" ad intensely, launching it only 12 days before the primary election. The impact of this issue, and this ad specifically, is difficult to overstate. As the *Washington Post*'s Chris Cillizza noted, "Make no mistake: this ad is the make or break moment of the Pennsylvania primary. This is the ad that Sestak saw in his mind's eye when he decided to run against Specter despite the fact that the entire establishment— including President Barack Obama—had lined up behind his opponent."[33] On May 18, Specter only received 46 percent of the vote to Sestak's 53 percent. The general election race, between two ideologically polar opposite candidates, was now set.

Statewide Trends

While the macro-political forces outlined in Chapter 1 clearly helped Toomey win in 2010, they do not explain the disparate results in the U.S. Senate race and the Pennsylvania governor's race. While both Republican candidates won in the two statewide contests, Tom Corbett won his gubernatorial race by a higher margin (54.5 percent) than Toomey won the Senate race (51 percent).

The gubernatorial contest found Republican Tom Corbett running against Democrat Dan Onorato for the open seat vacated by Ed Rendell. Both candidates were from Allegheny County (which is part of metropolitan Pittsburgh). Tom Corbett was the sitting attorney general of Pennsylvania[34] and had a great deal of familiarity with the electorate due to his aggressive pursuit of corrupt lawmakers in Harrisburg during "bonusgate." This referred to the widespread practice of giving performance bonuses to state employees while they were engaged in campaign work for their bosses. Importantly, Corbett not only pursued ethical issues with Democratic lawmakers, he led an investigation against prominent Republicans, notably former House speaker John Perzel of Philadelphia; these efforts produced arrests and public trials.[35] Corbett also was a leader in the state-led lawsuits against the implementation of the Obama administration's new health care law; these lawsuits were very unpopular in the major cities.[36] Democratic candidate Dan Onorato was the executive of the state's second largest county, Allegheny.[37] Unlike Corbett, Onorato's exposure was only to the Western part of the state. Consequently, Onorato was quite unknown to voters in the eastern and northern parts of Pennsylvania.

The dynamics of the gubernatorial race affected the conduct of the senatorial race. Because both statewide races were approaching the same voters, party coordination seems natural. Indeed, the coordination on the Republican side, between Tom Corbett and Pat Toomey, was extraordinary. In the city of Philadelphia for example, neither campaign had an independent office. Instead, they formed a "Victory Committee" and deployed staff and resources jointly. The Democrats, on the other hand, had little formal coordination of their organizations. Coordination might very well have helped Onorato in the gubernatorial race, but Sestak certainly benefited by working separately from Onorato, coming within striking distance of Toomey on Election Day while the gubernatorial race was not nearly as close. Another likely factor in the diverging results is that many Pennsylvanians continued to split their tickets, a long-standing tradition in the state. Toomey defeated Sestak 51 percent to 49 percent, a vote margin of 80,229 votes. Corbett defeated Onorato 54.5 percent to 45.5 percent, a vote margin of 357,975 votes (see Table 12.4). Significantly, Tom Corbett won Democratic Allegheny County with a bare margin, but Sestak won it with more than 40,000 votes. The Toomey-Sestak race had a significantly closer margin despite the extreme ideological polarization of that race compared to the gubernatorial race.[38]

Issues and Money in Pennsylvania

The issues debated during the campaign were largely similar to those on the national agenda. The candidates differed substantially on who was better able to help the economy, which candidate understood how to create jobs, and who would preserve Social Security and Medicare. The contrast between the candidates on economic issues was even starker given the candidate's backgrounds:

Table 12.4 Pennsylvania Statewide Election Results, 2010

	Total votes	Percent	Statewide victory margin	Allegheny County victory margin
U.S. Senate				
Pat Toomey	2,028,945	51.0%	+80,229	
Joe Sestak	1,948,716	49.0%		+40,739
Governor				
Tom Corbett	2,172,763	54.5%	+357,975	+460
Dan Onorato	1,814,788	45.5%		

Source: Calculated by author from Pennsylvania's Department of State Election Returns, http://www.electionreturns.state.pa.us/ (accessed March 1, 2011).

Wall Street banker (Toomey) vs. military officer leading enlisted men in combat situations (Sestak).

Both candidates did what they could to focus on the company their opponent kept. Like many Republicans across the country, Toomey reminded voters of Sestak's support of President Obama (showing Sestak saying he would be "this president's closest ally") and Speaker Pelosi, by highlighting Sestak's 100 percent support of Pelosi's legislative agenda. Toomey also labeled Sestak as "liberal" and specifically highlighted Sestak's votes for the financial sector's bailouts (the Troubled Asset Relief Program, or TARP), the Obama stimulus package, cap and trade (the American Clean Energy and Security Act of 2009), and health care reform, while being careful to speak respectfully of Sestak's military service. One ad hit all these issues at once, as the narrator told voters, "It's sad what's happened to Joe Sestak. He served our country well. Then he went to Washington where he voted in lock-step with the extreme agenda of bailouts, debt, government health care, and job-killing energy taxes."[39] Another ad on health care enlists a physician from Newtown Square, which is in Sestak's district, who tells voters about how the new health care law "puts government between patients and their doctors," and how she "tried to discuss safe and effective reform with my congressman, Joe Sestak, but our local group of doctors couldn't even get an appointment."[40] Toomey's positive messages hit on familiar themes as well including his fiscal conservatism, which played well in a year like 2010.[41]

Since Toomey had not served in Congress in recent years, it was impossible to compare Sestak's recent votes to Toomey's. Instead, Sestak made much of Toomey's Wall Street background and his votes while in Congress from 1999 to 2004, and blamed him (along with George W. Bush) for the current "mess" and bad economic times.[42] Sestak also attacked some of Toomey's other positions on economic issues including eliminating corporate taxes,[43] and free trade practices with China.[44] These ads hit on the most important issues across the country—the economy and jobs—and were a fit in a state like Pennsylvania that had seen job losses due to free trade agreements. Given the state's relatively large senior population, it should be no surprise that Sestak attacked Toomey on his support for privatizing Social Security; an ad ran that featured several seniors noting Toomey's connection with Wall Street and their dependence on Social Security, and arguing that Toomey was "wrong for Pennsylvania" and does not "get it."[45]

Sestak used Toomey's own press clips (as he had against Specter) to link him to unpopular former Senator Rick Santorum. In one ad, Sestak's campaign calls Toomey "Pennsylvania's most right-wing congressman" and shows Toomey admitting that his" voting record is pretty hard to distinguish from Rick Santorum's"; the same ad also included Toomey calling Sarah Palin a "spectacular governor."[46]

Sestak also made a positive case for himself by pointing to his military service. He touted his "31 years protecting America," his role in "leading the fight against terrorism," and his responsibility while commanding "our sons and daughters in combat."[47] In order to counter the Toomey attack that he had voted

Table 12.5 Campaign Finance Data for Pennsylvania's Senate Campaigns, 2004–2010

Candidate and year	Disbursements	Receipts	Vote percentage
2010			
Pat Toomey (R)	$16,958,100	$17,045,467	51
Joe Sestak (D)	$12,112,579	$10,241,306	49
2006			
Rick Santorum (R)	$28,407,953	$28,641,536	41
Bob Casey (D)	$17,580,210	$17,929,395	59
2004			
Arlen Specter (R)	$21,891,958	$19,795,673	53
Joe Hoeffel (D)	$4,696,569	$4,689,980	42

Source: 2010 election results: *New York Times*, http://elections.nytimes.com/2010/results/pennsylvania; all other data: Center for Responsive Politics, http://www.opensecrets.org (accessed February 15, 2011).

in line with the Obama-Pelosi agenda, Sestak ran an ad that touted his independence, saying he "stood up to the establishment" in his own party during the primary contest against Specter, and claiming he would "always be an independent voice" who would "stand up to party bosses."[48]

The campaign was also remarkable for the relative equality in candidate spending. Most expected Toomey to out-spend Sestak, and while he did, it was by a small margin. Toomey looked very much in charge of the campaign early on as he began advertising heavily for himself immediately after the Democratic primary, mostly on cable television. Toomey's summer ads reminded voters of who he was, re-establishing his biography and experience with Pennsylvanians. Sestak made the most of what he had by advertising later in the campaign season than did Toomey and saturating the airwaves as heavily as he could. In fact, the candidate spending was much less substantial than by most of those in the 2006 or 2004 Pennsylvania Senate races (see Table 12.5) or compared to other high-profile competitive Senate contests in 2010. Despite the excitement of the national wave, the candidates did not see a splash of funds added to their personal campaign accounts. Instead, independent groups spent aside the campaigns.

Party and Interest Group Activity

Given the importance of this close race (it was on the list of seats Democrats probably needed to win if they were going to hold on to their majority in the Senate), the new environment created by the *Citizens United* decision, and the fact that it was now an open-seat race rather than an incumbent-challenger race, outside spending was inevitable. Outside groups did not disappoint as there was considerable spending in Pennsylvania. At least 16 outside groups ran television ads alongside the Toomey and Sestak campaigns (see Table 12.6). As expected,

Table 12.6 Campaign Activity by Outside Group in the Pennsylvania Senate Race, 2010

Group	Direct Mail	Radio Ad	TV Ad	Candidate Supported
Political Party Organizations				
Democratic National Committee	√		√	Sestak
PA Democratic Party (PA Victory 2010)	√			Sestak
Republican Federal Committee of PA	√			Toomey
Republican Party of Pennsylvania	√			Toomey
Democratic Senatorial Campaign Committee (DSCC)		√	√	Sestak
National Republican Senatorial Committee (NRSC)		√	√	Sestak
Unions				
PA State Educators Association (PASEA)	√			Sestak
AFL-CIO	√		√	Sestak
Service Employees International Union (SEIU)	√			Sestak
American Federation of Teachers (AFL-CIO)	√			Sestak
AFSCME	√	√		Sestak
National Education Association (NEA)	√	√		Sestak
"Traditional" Interest Groups				
PA Clean Water Action - Vote Environment	√			Sestak
National Shooting Sports Foundation	√			Toomey
National Rifle Association (NRA)	√		√	Toomey
NARAL Pro-Choice America	√		√	Sestak
Republican Jewish Coalition	√	√	√	Toomey
Sierra Club	√			Sestak
Realtors PAC	√			Sestak
National Federation of Independent Business (NFIB)	√	√		Toomey
U.S. Chamber of Commerce			√	Toomey
League of Conservation Voters			√	Sestak
"Citizens United" Interest Groups				
Faith and Freedom Coalition	√			Sestak
Campaign for America's Future	√	√		Sestak
Americans for Job Security		√		Toomey
Crossroads Grassroots Policy Strategies			√	Toomey

Group	Direct Mail	Radio Ad	TV Ad	Candidate Supported
Club for Growth			√	Toomey
Citizens for Strength and Security			√	Sestak
MoveOn.org			√	Sestak
People for the American Way			√	Sestak
VoteVets.Org	√		√	Sestak
Americans for Tax Reform	√		√	Toomey

Source: Compiled by author from mail collected in the greater Philadelphia metropolitan area and public files with political advertising invoices at Philadelphia area radio and television stations.

both the DSCC and the National Republican Senatorial Committee (NRSC) spent a considerable amount in independent expenditure ads.

The Pennsylvania Senate race ranked fourth among Senate races in the amount of outside money spent at $12.5 million.[49] Of that amount, $9.1 was spent on behalf of Toomey, and $3.4 was spent on behalf of Sestak.[50] Groups active in the race included those traditionally seen in U.S. elections including unions and pro-business groups, as well as groups focused on social issues such as abortion and the environment (although these latter groups did not spend a lot). For instance, the League of Conservation Voters tried to tie Toomey's past support of drilling to the BP oil spill and the National Abortion Rights Action League made an effort to criticize Toomey for his votes against abortion rights (the latter was also highlighted in an ad from the Sestak campaign). Also along traditional liberal-conservative economic lines, the AFL-CIO ran television ads on Sestak's behalf thanking him for supporting American union jobs and attacking the Chamber of Commerce on a host of issues including outsourcing. There were substantial late radio ad buys from American Federation of State, County and Municipal Employees (AFSCME) and the National Education Association (NEA) in support of Sestak which used actor Michael Douglas' voice as lead character Gordon Gekko in the movie *Wall Street* saying "Greed is Good." The U.S. Chamber of Commerce opposed Sestak's stands on "card-check," and the Republican Jewish Coalition ran ads on Toomey's behalf (which questioned Sestak's commitment to Israel). Both candidates saw a small amount of social issue spending in targeted areas. The National Rifle Association aired ads in support of Toomey, but only ran them outside the major metropolitan centers (i.e., in the "T" regions of Pennsylvania).

Perhaps more interesting is what new groups were active in the Pennsylvania Senate race and what groups were not. The Tea Party was largely invisible, although its supporters worked through the Club for Growth. *Citizens United-*style spending, however, especially by Crossroads GPS (the group formed with the help of former Bush adviser, Karl Rove), was significant. Pennsylvania would normally have supporters of the Tea Party movement actively campaigning, especially for a candidate like Pat Toomey whose previous House record was exactly in line with their views on government spending and taxation. On the other hand, Philadelphia's proximity to Delaware (illustrated by the fact that half of Delaware is in the Philadelphia media market) meant Pennsylvanians had too much exposure to the national taunting of Tea Party-supported Delaware U.S. Senate candidate Christine O'Donnell. While the "I am not a witch" ads gained much national exposure on mainstream and comedy news outlets, Philadelphians saw the ads in real time and were regaled with a steady stream of press coverage of O'Donnell, her Tea Party supporters, and the gaffes that seemed to follow them. Luckily for Pat Toomey, his past experience leading the Club for Growth allowed for the popular Tea Party messages to be delivered to the electorate without the stigma of a lampooned movement. Sestak had more *Citizens United*-style group expenditures spent against him, but much less spent on his behalf. The most significant effort was made by VoteVets.org. A widely broadcast ad featuring enlisted men expressing their disappointment in the way Toomey treated them at home (in contrast to Sestak).

In addition to all the spending by interest groups, the candidates each saw substantial investments from their Hill Committees—the DSCC and the NRSC. The DSCC poured in over $10.2 million, with about 80 percent of that going to attack Pat Toomey, while the NRSC spent $6.5 million, with nearly $5 million going to oppose Joe Sestak. The NRSC spent on ads that hammered themes similar to those from the Toomey campaign, including Sestak's votes on the stimulus and health care reform, and links to Pelosi and Obama.[51] The DSCC ads also hit on familiar themes from the Democratic side including Toomey's ties to Wall Street and votes on free-trade legislation.[52]

End Game

Going against the national trends, the race tightened up considerably in the last few weeks, and, for a moment, Democrats hoped that Sestak might pull ahead of Toomey. The race was indeed a cliffhanger with the media waiting until late in the night to declare a winner and both candidates keeping mum about the outcome. Some campaign operatives even thought there would be a recount and began traveling to governmental election offices late in the night. In the end, it seems clear that the national enthusiasm gap kept Sestak from winning.

After the votes were counted on Election Night, signs were present that the GOP wave was impacting nearly all of Pennsylvania. One indicator was that the U.S. House delegation switched from 12 Democrats and 7 Republicans to 7 Democrats and 12 Republicans. A clear victory by Pat Toomey was expected, then, given the way the state seemed to be voting. Toomey, however, won by only 2 percentage points. In fact, throughout the state, Joe Sestak consistently outperformed his Democratic colleagues further down on the ticket. For example, Delaware County, home of most of the 7th Congressional District which Sestak had represented, gave Democrat Bryan Lentz only 44.9 percent of the vote for the open House seat, but gave Sestak 56.1 percent in the Senate contest. This story was repeated in many other counties as well.

Despite the considerable presence of advertising in the race by the candidates, political parties and outside groups, voters were still trying to become familiar with the two Senate candidates and their personal stories. In all the Pennsylvania media markets, voters were inundated with ads for the open gubernatorial race, the Senate race, and an unusually high number of competitive U.S. House races. In many cases, voters endured advertising from neighboring states. This was especially true in Philadelphia where viewers not only saw ads from their home state but also viewed ads aired in the curious Delaware U.S. Senate race, and in the competitive U.S. House seat in New Jersey's 3rd Congressional District in the southeastern part of the state. By the time of the election, voters had a hard time sorting out federal from state issues, and which candidates supported which policies. Ultimately, these issues may not have mattered much as effective character framing and candidate familiarity played a big role in the Toomey-Sestak contest.

Perhaps the biggest issue for Democrats was not that their supporters voted Republican, but that they did not vote at all. Turnout levels in the heavily Democratic parts of the state were back to pre-2008 levels or lower. The youth and African-American vote energized by then-Senator Obama were not robust either. In terms of Pennsylvania's expected electoral geography, Sestak won only eight of Pennsylvania's 67 counties. These eight include Pennsylvania's four largest urban areas: Philadelphia (Philadelphia, Delaware, and Montgomery counties), Pittsburgh (Allegheny and Niagara counties), Erie (Erie County), and Scranton-Wilkes-Barre (Lackawanna and Luzerne counties). Compare this to 2006 when Democrat Bob Casey, Jr. defeated incumbent Republican Rick Santorum in 33 of the 67 counties. In this election at least, Pennsylvania's regions voted as predicted and those areas that tend to favor Democrats did not have robust turnout.

Exit polls confirm other forces that national and state observers expected. The election was driven by the economy. Nearly two-thirds of Pennsylvania voters said it was the most important issue facing the nation and over half said they were worried about economic conditions; these voters went overwhelmingly for Toomey. Interestingly, those voters who said they made up their mind about the candidates more than one month ago selected Toomey 52 percent to 48 percent. Those who made up their mind within the last month split nearly evenly between the two candidates, each getting 50 percent of these voters.[53]

The result that Arlen Specter feared—a Pat Toomey victory—came true. Joe Sestak's strong performance, however, makes it hard to prove that the choice of Democratic candidate was the decisive factor. Given Specter's party switch and the national conditions, Pat Toomey probably would have won even if he ran against the long-time moderate senator. Toomey appealed to rural and suburban residents who felt that the economy needed a new approach, and these voters turned out for him. Toomey will have to work hard to prove to the state's moderate, temperamental electorate that he can bring the economic recovery he promised.

Notes

1. Carrie Budoff Brown, "Rewriting Pennsylvania Political Geography," *Politico. com*, April 2, 2008, http://www.cbsnews.com/stories/2008/04/01/politics/politico/main3988061.shtml (accessed March 13, 2011).
2. Michael Barone, Richard E. Cohen, and Jackie Koszczuk. "Pennsylvania," *The Almanac of American Politics*, http://nationaljournal.com.libproxy.temple.edu/almanac/area/pa/ (accessed February 8, 2011).
3. Pennsylvania Data Center, "2010 Census Results," http://pasdc.hbg.psu.edu/Home/tabid/926/Data/Census2010/tabid/1489/Default.aspx (accessed March 13, 2011).
4. Ibid.
5. U.S. Census American Fact Finder, "2005–2009 American Community Survey 5-Year Estimates," U.S. Census, http://www.factfinder.census.gov/servlet/ACS-SAFFFacts?_event=Search&_name=&_state=04000US42&_county=&_cityTown=&_zip=&_sse=on&_lang=en&pctxt=fph&_submenuId=factsheet_1 (accessed March 12, 2011).
6. Ibid.
7. Tom Infield, "Pa. Voter Enrollment Off for Both Parties," *The Philadelphia Inquirer*, October 4, 2010, http://articles.philly.com/2010-10-04/news/24980721_1_voter-enrollment-new-voter-registrations-joseph-passarella (accessed February 26, 2011).
8. Jackie Koszczuk and Amy H. Stern, "Specter, Arlen, R-Pa," *CQ's Politics in America 2006: The 109th Congress* (Washington, D.C.: Congressional Quarterly, 2005), pp. 866–867.
9. Ibid.
10. At this point in its history, the Club for Growth was known as a bundling organization based on the EMILY's List model where the Club would inform its activist network throughout the country of its top tier candidates to help them raise significant funds.
11. Alex Kaplun, "Close Finish Expected in Specter-Toomey Primary," *Environment and Energy Daily*, April 27, 2004.
12. John Cochran, "GOP Primary in Pennsylvania Sends Mixed Message to Party Leaders," *CQ Weekly Online*, May 1, 2004, http://library.cqpress.com.libproxy.temple.edu/cqweekly/weeklyreport108-000001131890 (accessed February 26, 2011).
13. Kaplun, "Close Finish Expected in Specter-Toomey Primary"; Cochran, "GOP Primary in Pennsylvania Sends Mixed Message to Party Leaders"; and L. J. Jordan, "Specter, Toomey Primary for U.S. Senate Seat Comes Down to Fight of the Right," *Associated Press*, April 4, 2004.
14. Lauren Kornreich, "Specter Staying in the GOP—for Now," CNN.com, March 18, 2009, http://politicalticker.blogs.cnn.com/2009/03/18/specter-staying-in-the-gop-for-now/ (accessed February 26, 2011).
15. Ed Hornick and Deirdre Walsh, "Longtime GOP Sen. Arlen Specter Becomes Democrat," CNN.com, April 4, 2009, http://www.cnn.com/2009/POLITICS/04/28/specter.party.switch/index.html (accessed February 26, 2011).
16. Chris Cilliza, "Specter to Switch Parties," *Washington Post*, April 28, 2009. http://voices.washingtonpost.com/44/2009/04/28/specter_to_switch_parties.html?wprss=44 (accessed February 26, 2011).
17. Katharine Q. Seelye, "Democrat Taking On Specter," *New York Times*, August 5, 2009, p. A11.

18. "Pennsylvania Job Approval: Sen. Arlen Specter," Pollster.com, October 2010, http://www.huffingtonpost.com/2009/04/28/jobapproval-senspecter_n_726478. html (accessed March 1, 2011).

19. "2010 Pennsylvania Senate Democratic Primary: Joe Sestak vs. Sen. Arlen Specter," Pollster.com, May 2010, http://www.pollster.com/polls/pa/10-pa-sen-demprsvse.php?nr=1 (accessed March 1, 2011).

20. Michael Barone, Richard E. Cohen, and Jackie Koszczuk, "Senator Pat Toomey," *The Almanac of American Politics*, http://nationaljournal.com/almanac/person/pattoomey-pa/ (accessed February 8, 2011).

21. Philip Gourevitch, "Fight on the Right," *New Yorker*, vol. 80 (2004), no. 8, pp. 34–39.

22. The Club for Growth was founded in late 1999 not as a political action committee, but as a 501(c)4 bundling organization like Emily's List. Founded by CATO Institute fiscal policy expert Stephen Moore, the Club chooses to operate outside of the traditional Republican Party network, though vowing to support fiscally conservative Republicans exclusively. See Joseph A. D'Agostino, "The Club for Growth," *Human Events*, vol. 56 (2000), no. 11, p. 18.

23. Smartvoter.org, "Full Biography of Joe Sestak." http://www.smartvoter.org/2010/ 05/18/pa/state/vote/sestak_j/bio.html (accessed Mar. 1 2011)

24. "Pennsylvania 7," RealClearPolitics.com, 2006, http://www.realclearpolitics.com/ epolls/writeup/pennsylvania_7-11.html (accessed March 1, 2011).

25. Karen Tumulty, "Arlen in the Middle," *Time*, vol. 175 (2010), no. 11, pp. 26–29.

26. "2010 Pennsylvania Senate Democratic Primary: Joe Sestak vs. Sen. Arlen Specter."

27. Adam Nagourney, "Specter, After Shifting Parties, Faces Fire From Both Sides," *New York Times*, May 12, 2010, p. A1.

28. Thomas Fitzgerald and Tom Infield, "Specter – Sestak Senate contest tops primary slate," *The Philadelphia Inquirer*, May 18, 2010, http://www.philly.com/ philly/news/20100518_Specter-Sestak_Senate_contest_tops_primary_slate.html (accessed March 1, 2011).

29. Peter Baker, "The Politicking Behind an Offer To a Specter Foe." *New York Times*. May 29, 2010, section A, p. 1.

30. Chris Bowers, "Why Sestak's New Ad is So Devastating." Open Left, May 6, 2010. http://www.openleft.com/diary/18603/why-sestaks-new-ad-is-so-devastating (accessed March 1, 2011).

31. "News 8 Fact Checks 'Re-Elected' Ad" May 12, 2010, WGAL-TV, Lancaster-TV, http://www.youtube.com/watch?v=Fpw5KTvZKBI (accessed March 10, 2011).

32. http://www.youtube.com/watch?v=T2q7hei3T3E&playnext=1&list=PLAD5E84B EE7A785A4 (accessed March 10, 2011).

33. Chris Cillizza, "The Fix: Joe Sestak Launches Ad Linking Arlen Specter to George Bush," *Washington Post*, May 6, 2010, http://voices.washingtonpost.com/thefix/senate/joe-sestak-launches-ad-link-sp.html (accessed March 13, 2011).

34. He was elected to the position in 2004 and again in 2008. Between 1995 and 1997, Corbett was appointed attorney general by then-Governor Tom Ridge to fill the remaining term of the incumbent who was charged with mail fraud.

35. Angela Couloumbis, "Corbett campaign-fund appeal sent to Perzel," *The Philadelphia Inquirer*, October 6, 2010, p. B01.

36. Amy Worden, "Health-care Suit Infecting Politics; Pa. Attorney General Tom Corbett's Move to Fight Mandates Is Drawing Fevered Opposition," *The Philadelphia Inquirer*, March 28, 2010, p. B01.

37. "Dan Onorato," Vote Onorato.com," 2010, http://www.voteonorato.com/meet_ dan/biography (accessed March 1, 2011).

38. Onorato was being punished for instituting a "drink tax" in Allegheny County, a 10 percent tax on all alcoholic beverages sold at retail outlets (i.e., bars and restaurants). For instance, the Hospitality Political Action Committee of Western Pennsylvania (http://www.hospacwpa.com/the-allegheny-county-drink-tax-and-rental-car-tax/) made an explicit effort to keep Onorato out of Harrisburg, campaigning with the slogan "Dan Onorato [with a red slash through the name]: Remember the Drink Tax."

39. See, for example, http://www.youtube.com/watch?v=HBQurxkWQVM (accessed March 13, 2011).

40. http://www.youtube.com/watch?v=FAQ01PXd4wc (accessed March 13, 2011).

41. See, for example, http://www.youtube.com/watch?v=F4FYGnKl1SQ; and http://www.youtube.com/watch?v=By_K-5SxxX0 (accessed March 13, 2011).

42. http://www.youtube.com/watch?v=Q9SbDnoaYX8 (accessed March 13, 2011).

43. http://www.youtube.com/watch?v=7ujPSgdLrms (accessed March 13, 2011).

44. http://www.youtube.com/watch?v=OCtDW12e5oA (accessed March 13, 2011).

45. http://www.youtube.com/watch?v=_T39JPwb4tQ (accessed March 13, 2011).

46. http://www.youtube.com/watch?v=bd6ptMo8dgM (accessed March 13, 2011).

47. See http://www.youtube.com/watch?v=CfYP0DQCuF4; and http://www.youtube.com/watch?v=0W8wtetVPZA (accessed March 13, 2011).

48. http://www.youtube.com/watch?v=ZQ85l-7YXYs (accessed March 13, 2011).

49. It should be noted that this figure does not include that spent by the party committees. "Outside Spending," Center for Responsive Politics, http://www.opensecrets.org/outsidespending/index.php (accessed March 1, 2011).

50. Ibid.

51. See, for example, http://www.youtube.com/watch?v=IUio_j0eT5M (accessed March 13, 2011).

52. See, http://www.youtube.com/watch?v=rGLi2oINMHc; and http://www.youtube.com/watch?v=_kaiiJuz8a0 (accessed March 13, 2011).

53. Ibid.

13 Schauer vs. Walberg in Michigan's Seventh Congressional District

Money Helps Create the Wave

David A. Dulio and John S. Klemanski

Michigan's 7th Congressional District holds a unique place in U.S. House elections over the past ten years—there has not been a repeat winner in the five elections since 2002. In no other U.S. House district has such turnover occurred. The 2010 election produced results that were both similar and different than voters saw in the past. They were similar in that after the votes were counted, the incumbent officeholder was not returned to Washington, D.C. The election was different, however, in that the winning candidate was not a new face; one of the previous representatives forced a rematch to take back the seat he lost. The voters of the 7th District sent Tim Walberg back to Congress in 2010 when he defeated Mark Schauer, who had won the seat from Walberg only two years before.

The Schauer-Walberg contest was certainly influenced by the macro-political factors that helped build the GOP wave in 2010. Factors such as President Obama's low approval rating, an economic situation in Michigan that was more dire than that faced by just about any other state in the nation, a public that saw their nation and state headed in the wrong direction, and an increased excitement among Republicans to vote on Election Day. A number of factors specific to this district and the campaign, however, were also important to the outcome. The 7th District, for instance, was the epicenter for outside group spending in 2010, as more money was spent here by non-candidate entities than in any congressional district in the nation. This created a context of wall-to-wall television ads and political mail. In addition, the messages from the candidates provided the voters with a clear choice on Election Day, something that does not always happen in modern U.S. political campaigns.

In this chapter, we offer an account and explanation for why the Schauer-Walberg race turned out the way it did. We begin by describing the district, its people, and its politics. We then discuss the electoral context in which the race was fought. The bulk of the chapter is devoted to the four factors that had the largest impact on the outcome: the contrasting messages of the two candidates, outside spending by non-candidate groups, the Republican wave, and voter turnout.

Key Characteristics of Michigan's 7th District

Michigan's 7th District is comprised of five complete counties (Branch, Hills-dale, Lenawee, Jackson, and Eaton), most of Calhoun County, and a substantial part of Washtenaw County (including areas that are adjacent to, but do not include, the city of Ann Arbor). The district is made up, overall, of mostly rural areas and small towns. According to census data, about half (46.3 percent) of the population in the 7th District lives in rural areas, which is about double that of the U.S. average. Battle Creek is the district's largest city, with an estimated population of only about 53,000. Jackson, with roughly 36,000 residents, is the district's second largest city.

The district is largely white (89.6 percent), with small percentages of African Americans, Hispanics, and Asian Americans.[1] While not considered a wealthy district, the area's poverty rate (12.3 percent) is about that of the United States as a whole (13.5 percent) and a little lower than the state's (14.5 percent).[2] Unemployment in Michigan by November 2010 was at 12.4 percent, underscoring the importance of jobs as a campaign issue in this race. In Jackson (11.3 percent) and Battle Creek (9.9 percent), the November unemployment rates were also relatively high.[3]

While there is a strong farming tradition in the district, the economy in the past has relied heavily on the automobile industry for jobs. Only one major automobile assembly plant is located in the district—the relatively new General Motors Delta Township plant in Eaton County—but the district has been home to many automobile parts producers and some steel fabricators. The district also has a few health care facilities that provide some economic diversification, but farming and auto parts manufacturing have dominated the district's economy for a number of years. With a reliance on the auto industry, the industry's down-turn—including the bankruptcies of Chrysler and General Motors—has meant that the district had witnessed substantial increases in unemployment and pov-erty since 2000.

While the overall politics of the 7th District is conservative and leans Republican, the district has seen a number of close races since 2002. The *Cook Political Report*'s rating of R+2 illustrates this competitiveness and indicates that Republican presidential candidates performed only 2 points better in the district than they did nationally in the last two elections. Tim Walberg defeated an underfunded Democrat named Sharon Renier in the 2006 election (a Demo-cratic wave election), but only by a margin of 50 percent to 46 percent. Then, Mark Schauer defeated the incumbent Walberg by three percentage points in the "Obama wave" election of 2008. Part of this competitiveness is due to the nature of the district itself. While largely rural and socially conservative, the district has pockets of more moderate support that the Democrats have attracted in the past by focusing on economic issues. This has created a "bookend" effect in terms of the district's geographic politics. In the western end of the district, the Battle Creek area and Calhoun County typically vote Democratic. In the eastern end, Eaton County (outside of Lansing) and the Washtenaw County part of the district have leaned Democratic over the past 10 years. In the geographic middle are the socially and fiscally conservative counties of Hillsdale and Branch, along with Jackson County, which draws much of its social conservatism from a bloc of Catholic voters.

Schauer Gears Up for Reelection

The phrase "permanent campaign" is often bandied about in American politics. The concept refers to a continuous cycle of campaigning by elected officials to help ensure their reelection. Officeholders who know they will be running for reelection in as few as two years' time never stop polling their constituents, communicating regularly with voters, and raising campaign funds. After his election in 2008, Mark Schauer could be considered the poster boy for the permanent campaign in modern U.S. electoral politics.

Because his 2008 victory margin was slim, and his district was still considered to be Republican-leaning, some of Representative Schauer's actions illustrated clear signs of the permanent campaign, and he began to implement a reelection strategy immediately after taking office. This was an important decision because of the nature of the district and the likelihood of a strong challenge in 2010. According to Schauer Chief of Staff Ken Brock, "We viewed [the campaign and congressional office] as one continuous operation and organization."[4] This included an aggressive fundraising plan and a lot of communications to his constituents, but it also extended to decisions made regarding the congressional office.

In his classic work *Home Style*, Richard Fenno writes about the activities members of Congress engage in that help them achieve their goals.[5] Many of these activities surround the member's relationship to his or her constituency, or the style in which they will represent the district. Fenno argues that three components make up a member's "home style"—allocating resources between Washington and the district, explaining what they have done in Washington, and presenting themselves as a representative to the constituency.[6] In terms of allocating resources, Fenno notes: "Every member of Congress makes a basic decision with regard to his or her home style: How much and what kind of attention shall I pay to home? Or, to put it another way: Of all the resources available to me, which kinds and how much shall I allocate to activity at home?"[7] One of these decisions with respect to resources is focused on staff. House rules limit members to 18 full-time staffers. It is up to each member to decide how they will divide those staffers between the Washington office and the office(s) in the district. In most cases, a majority of staff is located in the D.C. office, with seven or eight staffers left for the district office.

In Schauer's case, however, he and his team decided that his office would be very district focused, believing this would help his reelection. For example, over half of the congressional office staff worked in the district office located in Jackson. In addition, the office's chief of staff was also based out of the Jackson office and spent more time there than he did in Washington. In short, Schauer's chief of staff described the strategy as being "very district heavy and D.C. light."[8] Schauer's home style was clearly going to include a major focus on voters in the district.

In addition, Schuaer's congressional office paid a lot of attention to communication with residents of the district.[9] The office sent a number of mailings to the district through the use of the franking privilege that allows members to send mail to their constituents with the bill paid for by the federal government. While this is reserved for "official business" only, it basically amounts to free advertising for members of Congress. Ken Brock describes Schauer's office's approach:

> We were also one of the top frankers in the country ... in terms of using paid communication from our congressional office. When you count the mass mail, the telephone town halls, and robo-calls from the congressional side we were among the top in the country. And again, this was from day one and this was part of our plan ...[10]

Of course, roll-call votes matter as well when it comes to an officeholder's bid for reelection. In Congress, Schauer voted with his party on the major legislation of 2009 and 2010. Recognizing that the national party and the Democratic brand both were in jeopardy in the run-up to the 2010 elections, however, Schauer did adjust his Hill behavior somewhat. This was true in terms of specific votes, but also in his decisions about co-sponsoring legislation, and in voting for amendments that struck out specific earmarks. In particular, Schauer voted against increasing the debt ceiling (which voters thought was too high), the second implementation of the Troubled Asset Relief Program (TARP, or what came to be known as the "Wall Street bailout"), and some of the most "wince-inducing" earmarks that had been attached to legislation.[11]

Moreover, Schauer took action on issues that were very important to his district. As Ken Brock noted:

> There were a number of ways in which he would take a look at opportunities to understand the populist discontent in the country and particularly in his district ... And we also looked for opportunities in his co-sponsorships ... Mark was very active with the trade caucus, if there were things that cut to the heart of the needs of the manufacturing sector, or that dealt with unemployment ... Mark was ... always quick to help out on the co-sponsorship ... And the bills, specifically, we worked on were pretty targeted to the needs of our community ... The biggest one ...was related to trade ... [and was] ... one we really trumpeted in the campaign and through the congressional communications ...

In this way, Schauer attempted to focus on local and district issues during the campaign by asserting some independence from the Democratic leadership in both the White House and in his own chamber. This strategy was designed to emphasize the policy differences between Mark Schauer and Tim Walberg, rather than making the election a referendum on national policies and the Democratic Party in general.

Ultimately, this strategy was not successful. While Schauer attempted to distance himself from the president and Speaker Pelosi as often as he could, many voters used a more narrow measure of his independence, and the areas in which Schauer tried to distance himself from his party paled in importance to the areas where he was more tied to his party leadership. Schauer voted for all of the major policies associated with the Democrats in 2009–2010.[12] President Obama's major legislative initiatives—health care reform (the Patient Protection and Affordable Care Act of 2010), the economic stimulus (the American Reinvestment and Recovery Act), and an environmental bill designed to deal with global warming (the American Clean Energy and Security Act of 2009), which came to be known as the cap-and-trade bill—took center stage in this campaign, as they did in many races around the country. In the end, votes on the "big three" were enough evidence for voters to conclude that he was in lock-step with the "liberal" agenda of Speaker Pelosi and President Obama. While Schauer tried to sell himself as a moderate and one who was representing the district, his votes on the most important bills of the 111th Congress made it difficult for him to support that claim. In fact, he had a 100 percent rating from the liberal advocacy group Americans for Democratic Action (ADA) for the calendar year 2009.[13] He also had party unity scores of 90 and 91 percent in his two years in the House as well as a presidential support score of 96 percent in 2009 (although it dropped to 88 percent in 2010).[14]

Schauer also was in continual campaign mode in terms of fundraising. In the words of Ken Brock, "We went right at it knowing we were going to have a tough reelection campaign."[15] The benefits of this were realized in the first fundraising quarter of 2009 when Schauer raised $388,000, which ranked near the top of all freshman members' fundraising totals.[16] This put Schauer on solid ground going forward and allowed the campaign to maintain a presence in the district.

The Pre-election Political Landscape

The context in which the candidates, political parties and outside groups would campaign for the 7th District's seat was not very different from other areas of the country. In short, the incumbent Democratic officeholder and President Obama were unpopular, as were their policies (with Schauer having voted for the "big three"). In addition, voters in the district viewed not only the nation but their state as off on the wrong track. These factors, coupled with the continued poor economy, made it a difficult year for a Democratic candidate in a district considered Republican-leaning. Clearly, Mark Schauer was going to have a difficult time retaining his seat, even though he had tried to create a home style that was very "district heavy" and position himself by paying attention to important concerns of his constituents.

Early polling in the race confirmed this reality and showed Schauer trailing by 10 points in January 2010 and similar margins not long after the August primary.[17] As the campaign between Schauer and Walberg heated up, the race tightened with some polls showing Schauer in the lead.[18] One poll conducted during the middle of October clearly illustrated the state of politics in the district. At this point in the campaign, President Obama's job approval rating was at 44 percent, which was 1 point below his national approval figure.[19] The residents of the 7th District also remained sour on the state of Michigan's economy as only slightly more than one-third of voters said they felt the economy was going to get better over the next six to twelve months. One bright spot for Mark Schauer was the fact that he was viewed more favorably than Tim Walberg, as 44 percent of voters had a favorable opinion of him compared to only 38 percent for Walberg.

Two other figures from the mid-October poll stand out as important pieces of the electoral landscape. Over 80 percent of all voters in the district reported that they were very motivated to vote in this election and 38 percent reported supporting the efforts of the Tea Party movement. These figures mirror the trends nationally. There was a wave of discontent and Walberg was able to ride it to Election Day.

Candidate Strategy and Message

The electoral landscape presented to the candidates created a very interesting set of circumstances each had to work within while trying to create a strategy for victory. Certainly part of this context were the factors noted above—low approval for President Obama, a poor economy in the district, and an electorate that seemed to be in the mood to fire officeholders they elected just two years before. But it also included those mentioned in Chapter 1, including a sour public mood and a frustration with Democrats in Congress and the legislation they had pushed through in the previous two years.

This created a political context that was eerily similar to the one present in 2006 and 2008 when Democrats made large gains—with one exception. In 2010, just as in the two previous cycles, one party was trying to make the election about national issues while the other was trying to make it about local issues. This year, however, it was the GOP trying to emphasize national issues while Democrats wanted to localize the elections. As Walberg noted: "It was clearly a national-issue race where it was the stimulus, cap-and-trade, the health care takeover, and the rampant and expansive move of government controlling more and more areas of our lives ... that is a national focus. Now, my opponent tried to bring [the race back to a] more local [focus]."[20] One potential problem with trying to nationalize an election, however, is that voters may feel that a candidate is not paying attention to issues that matter on the ground in the district. For the Walberg campaign, this was less of a concern in 2010. Part of their strategy was to take national issues and connect them to the local areas. On the issue of jobs, for instance, Walberg noted: "They were national issues that impacted local[ly]. In Michigan, of course, we think of jobs and the economy, I mean that's local."[21]

The importance of the health care issue was clear early in the race from a strategic perspective as well. As noted in Chapter 1, it was in August of 2009 during the district work period at town hall events that many Democratic officeholders began to first really hear and feel the disapproval that was present in their constituencies surrounding this bill. Rightly or not, Schauer was perceived as avoiding voters. According to one observer of the race, journalist Chris Gautz,

> ... a lot of people viewed [Mark] Schauer as [invisible] ... Throughout 2009 and 2010 during the health care debate, Schauer was nowhere to be found ... Schauer would not have town hall meetings about [health care]. He would not talk to [voters] beforehand, he would only have town hall meetings after he voted on it ... each time ... he had meetings to tell people what was in it and why he voted for it and how it was going to impact them, and people wanted the opposite; they wanted there to be discussion on the front end not afterwards.[22]

At the same time, Walberg held numerous town hall meetings, in an attempt to highlight the contrasting styles and substance between the two candidates. According to Walberg, his victory started with this strategic decision: "the foundation was laid, in what I think was great strategy ... to get me out, in total contrast to Mark Schauer, by being out doing town hall meetings, tele-town halls, [and] meet-and-greets all over this district, and [doing them] early on, even last August when Mark Schauer wouldn't."[23] His town hall meetings attracted large numbers of voters. Often these events did not include Walberg giving his opinion, but just listening to the people of the 7th District.[24]

Strategy in a campaign goes well beyond decisions about where to send a candidate and when to do so. Issues, and the candidate's positions on those issues, are critical. We noted at the beginning of the chapter that there were four main factors that impacted the outcome of this race. The first of these is the messages focused on by the candidates. A candidate's message is one of the most fundamental aspects of their campaign. Specifically, the message is a candidate's best reasons why a voter should choose that candidate over his or her opponent.

A common complaint about American elections is that candidates of the two major parties can sometimes appear to be very similar on important issues. Nothing could be further from the truth in the race for the 7th District. Mark Schauer and Tim Walberg could not have been more different on all of the major issues of the campaign. They provided voters with a clear choice when they entered the voting booth. This contrast was obvious in the messages the candidates developed to make their case to voters and in the communications they used to talk to voters. In short, the contrast between Mark Schauer and Tim Walberg was simple: Schauer supported the "big three" policies of health care, the stimulus, and cap-and-trade, while Walberg did not.

Walberg Follows the GOP Blueprint

The health care reform law was an important issue for the Walberg campaign. Walberg, like many GOP candidates, promised to vote to repeal the health care law once in Congress and then replace it with other policy alternatives such as expanding personal savings accounts, allowing individuals to purchase health insurance across state lines, tort reform, and giving individuals the same health care tax breaks as those provided to businesses.[25] Other issues were important, too. The Walberg campaign focused on framing these national issues as having an impact locally. It tried to connect the major issues to the difficult economic times people in the district were experiencing. Specifically, the cap-and-trade bill was often discussed as a job killer and the stimulus bill was often discussed in terms of wasteful Washington spending.

Walberg also took a page from the Republican Party "playbook"[26]—linking his opponent to President Obama and Democratic leadership (in this case Speaker Nancy Pelosi). Walberg's statements often referenced national Democrats and included references to the "Obama-Pelosi-Reid agenda."[27] In fact, Walberg's first television ad of the general election campaign began with the audio: "Mark Schauer's votes for Pelosi's trillion dollar stimulus … have devastated Michigan's economy …"[28] This approach is best summed up by another local journalist who wrote, "Republican Tim Walberg … paints Democratic incumbent Mark Schauer as a free-spending liberal in cahoots with House Speaker Nancy Pelosi and President Barack Obama …"[29]

Arguably, some of Walberg's attempts to use Pelosi and Obama to his advantage pushed the envelope, and some would argue he went too far at times. In mid-October, Walberg was meeting with voters at a coffee shop when he was asked a question about President Obama's citizenship. He responded by saying, "Well, I'm going to take him at his word that he's an American citizen."[30] He went on in his answer, however, to suggest that the Congress could consider impeaching the president should he fail to produce his birth certificate. This set off a firestorm of sorts in the media, including some attention on national cable news shows. The issue was raised in debates between the two candidates as well, and Walberg had to back off those remarks, saying in one debate that there was "no question at all" in his mind that Obama was a citizen.[31] In the end, this had surprisingly little impact on the outcome of the race, likely because it happened relatively late in the contest. If Schauer had more time to use it as an issue, it might have helped him more.[32]

Schauer Tries to Channel Tip O'Neill

Needless to say, the "big three" issues were not part of Mark Schauer's strategy to get reelected.[33] He could not very easily tout the fact that he had voted for each given the opposition to them among the public. The stimulus in particular was troublesome for Schauer. As scholars have shown for a long time, it is helpful for members of Congress at reelection time to be able to brag about back federal money they were able to secure for the district that would provide a benefit to the district.[34] In 2010, however, for a lot of people in the 7th District this was not helpful. Rather than benefits, people saw only more government spending.[35] Schauer's strategy for winning consisted of two main prongs: following the "all politics is local" adage of former House Speaker Tip O'Neill (D-MA), by focusing on issues that were important and close to the people in the 7th District, and trying to be the outsider candidate even as the incumbent officeholder. The public mood was not lost on the Schauer campaign; they knew being an incumbent in a GOP-leaning district was a tough position to be in during 2010. To combat this, they tried to make Schauer the candidate who was running against Washington at the start of the campaign. The campaign aired an advertisement early in the general election contest that featured Schauer sitting at the counter in a diner saying, "I must ask myself ten times a day, 'What is Washington thinking?' Bailouts for Wall Street, pay raises for Congress, spending your tax dollars on jobs in China. People are fed up and so am I."[36] Clearly, this was an effort to make Schauer look like the outsider who was going to go to Washington to bring about change the voters wanted. Of course, he was not the outsider and this proved to be a tough sell.

While there were a number of issues the Schauer campaign discussed during the course of the race, they focused on two for the most part—Social Security and trade. Every race in the country was dominated by the issues of jobs and the economy, but these two issues were also critical in the 7th. Pollster Bernie Porn of EPIC-MRA, one of the leading non-partisan firms in Michigan, noted: "In this race [the top issues were] clearly the economy and jobs as it was with every race. However, because of Walberg's own comments on Social Security and Medicare, and also outsourcing jobs, those are the things that Schauer was able to use ... to supplement his message about the economy."[37]

On both issues, the Schauer campaign was able to use Walberg's words against him. Nearly every ad the campaign put out included audio and/or video of statements made by Walberg. The Schauer campaign "put a tracker on Walberg starting in March ... [and] whenever he had a public event [they] had a person in the room with a video camera."[38] This can be a very effective tactic; when voters see an ad with the opponent making statements they are much more credible than a simple voice-over making statements about the opponent.

On Social Security, the Schauer campaign took advantage of statements Walberg had been making on the issue for several years. Most problematic for Walberg, and most advantageous for Schauer, was Walberg's statement that he would support privatizing Social Security; he also said he agreed with the statement that the system was a "Ponzi scheme."[39] The Schauer campaign made use of these statements in several advertisements including one that featured a number of senior citizens saying "... when you call Social Security 'worthless'... and a Ponzi scheme, and say you want to privatize our Social Security, Mr. Walberg, you're going to have to answer to us."[40] Throughout the campaign, Schauer hit on the theme of Walberg wanting to privatize Social Security—it came up in debates and the campaign used it to garner earned media attention. Walberg, when pressed on the issue, said he did not favor privatizing Social Security. But this did not stop Schauer from returning to it; in his final ad before Election Day, Schauer again hit Walberg on the privatization comments and promised he would always protect Social Security. Even Walberg admitted this line of attack was an effective strategy.[41]

The issue of trade, and in particular the North American Free Trade Agreement (NAFTA), was a powerful one in the district given the importance of the auto industry and the fact that the area had been hemorrhaging jobs for years, some of which went overseas or to Mexico. This issue was ripe for the Schauer campaign to use because of its importance to the public and because Shauer had used it effectively two years before in defeating Walberg. As we noted above, this was an issue that Schauer focused on in his legislative work while in Congress.

One of Schauer's early ads boasted about his vote "against spending your tax dollars on creating jobs in China."[42] Another ad at the end of the campaign continued the practice of using Walberg's statements against him and included the audio:

> … here's how out of touch Tim Walberg is: [video of Walberg speaking to voters] "It's not China and Mexico that we should really be worrying that much about. We're getting jobs back from China." Tim Walberg made it way too easy for companies to outsource out jobs to China. That's wrong. I'm fighting to end outsourcing. And I'm making sure we create jobs here and not China.[43]

Schauer returned to this theme in his closing ad to voters, but it was not enough to send him back to Washington.

Campaign Finance in the 7th District

Earlier, we noted Mark Schauer's fast start in terms of raising money after the 2008 election. Schauer continued this success and he raised $3,255,382 overall. Tim Walberg, using his experience and connections from having run and held office before raised $1,678,049. While both candidates raised a lot of money, these aggregate figures do not tell the whole story. In fact, Schauer had a large advantage. This was something new for Tim Walberg. In 2008 his fundraising was on par with Schauer's and in 2006 he dominated his novice political opponent, organic farmer Sharon Renier (see Table 13.1).

Schauer and Walberg faced two completely different funding challenges in 2010. Schauer raised a lot of money and held onto much of it because he had no primary opposition. Tim Walberg did not have that luxury. In short, Walberg had to spend money to even get to the general election. What made things more difficult was that his primary opponent in 2010 had considerable personal wealth. While Walberg won the primary easily (with 57 percent of the vote), he spent an unusually large amount of money for that race alone—about $800,000. What is more, he started the year at a significant funding disadvantage as Schauer had

Table 13.1 Campaign Finance Data for Michigan's 7th Congressional District Campaigns, 2006–2010

Election year	Disbursements		Receipts		Vote Percent	
	Walberg (R)	Opponent (D)	Walberg (R)	Opponent (D)	Walberg (R)	Opponent (D)
2010	$1,647,379	$3,261,651	$1,678,049	$3,255,382	50.1	45.4
2008	$2,128,559	$2,285,262	$2,112,214	$2,298,087	46.5	48.8
2006	$1,225,137	$55,794	$1,260,111	$55,682	49.9	45.9

Source: 2010 election results: New York Times, http://elections.nytimes.com/2010/results/michigan; all other data: Center for Responsive Politics, http://www.opensecrets.org (accessed February 15, 2011).

continued his aggressive fundraising through 2009 and ended the year with over $1 million in the bank while Walberg had only $280,000 in cash on hand (see Table 13.2). For the general election campaign, he ended up spending only about the same amount as the primary. In the end, Schauer outspent Walberg in the general election by about 4 to 1 (see the huge spending differences between the candidates in the last three reporting periods for 2010).

Candidate funding was not the story of this race, even though each raised a lot of money. The 7th District, rather, was the epicenter of outside spending during 2010. More outside money was spent by political parties and outside groups in the 7th than in any other district in the nation. According to the Center for Responsive Politics, in the 7th District alone, a total of $8,884,879 was spent by at least 35 separate organizations.[44] How much of this money was a result of the *Citizens United* decision noted in Chapter 1 we cannot say, but the decision certainly paved the way for this money to be spent and for some of the groups to be so active.

A variety of organizations spent substantial sums of money in this highly competitive race. Both parties' Hill Committees—the Democratic Congressional Campaign Committee (DCCC) and the National Republican Congressional Committee (NRCC)—were very active as each spent over $1.4 million. The Michigan Republican Party also spent a similar amount and helped ease the funding discrepancy between Schauer and Walberg.

The party committees picked up where the candidates left off in terms of message. The NRCC went after Schauer on his record the past two years in Congress by hammering him on "the big three" votes he cast and by tying him to the Democratic leadership. The NRCC ads continually mentioned the "failed stimulus" that Schauer voted for and his ties to Nancy Pelosi. One ad captured nearly all of the GOP talking points in 30 seconds:

> In Washington, one party has absolute power. Out of control spending, national energy tax, government takeover of health care, and Mark Schauer voted for it all. Schauer votes the Pelosi party line on spending, on our economy, on 94 percent of all the votes he cast....[45]

The DCCC also aired fairly predictable ads attacking Walberg on issues like Social Security and NAFTA. However, they unleashed a tactic that complemented what the Schauer campaign was trying to do in terms of making Schauer the outsider. In every television ad that we found aired by the DCCC in the 7th, Tim Walberg was referred to as "Congressman Walberg." One of their ads stated: "Congressman Walberg supported more unfair trade with South America as more than 300,000 jobs were lost. Walberg said outsourcing was good for the nation's economy, praised NAFTA ... Congressman Walberg just doesn't get it."[46] Clearly, this was an effort to tie Walberg to Washington at a time when Congress was experiencing unprecedented disapproval. As Walberg said after the election, "I was called 'congressman' more times than when I was in Congress during the course of the battle."[47] The DCCC also launched an attack

Table 13.2 Schauer and Walberg Receipts and Disbursements by Reporting Period, 2009–2010

Reporting Period	Mark Schauer			Tim Walberg		
	Receipts	Disbursements	Ending Cash	Receipts	Disbursements	Ending Cash
Beginning cash as of September 30, 2009			$903,537.61			$203,168.97
2009 Year End						
(1 October–31 December)	$327,880.65	$65,494.99	$1,165,923.27	$169,149.61	$92,071.48	$280,247.10
2010 April Quarterly						
(1 January–31 March)	$403,549.41	$129,313.62	$1,440,159.06	$167,824.49	$78,539.80	$369,531.79
2010 July Quarterly						
(1 April–30 June)	$406,488.21	$194,530.84	$1,652,116.43	$160,714.73	$165,848.21	$364,398.31
2010 Pre-primary						
(1 July–14 July)	$19,766.65	$19,274.04	$1,652,609.04	$26,456.12	$146,639.74	$244,214.69
2010 October Quarterly						
(15 July–30 September)	$546,405.06	$885,629.70	$1,313,384.40	$508,259.22	$301,388.82	$451,085.09
2010 Pre-general						
(1 October–13 October)	$157,897.42	$622,133.48	$849,148.34	$124,196.50	$175,866.33	$399,415.26
2010 Post-general						
(14 October–22 November)	$323,628.26	$1,157,691.18	$15,085.42	$255,507.50	$592,578.09	$62,344.67
Total	$2,185,615.66	$3,074,067.85		$1,412,108.17	$1,552,932.47	

Source: Compiled from candidate reports to the Federal Election Commission, Form 3, Lines 23, 24, 26, and 27, various dates.

on Walberg claiming that he "... wanted a new national sales tax on almost everything" and that "Walberg's tax would mean a 23 percent tax on groceries, clothes, even medicine, hitting the middle class hard." This issue was raised in several other districts across the U.S., but it was also a charge that the DCCC had rolled out against Walberg two years before.[48]

Millions more dollars were spent by non-party outside groups such as the Service Employees International Union (SEIU) ($437,567), and the American Federation of State, County and Municipal Employees (AFSCME) ($1,450,922) to help Mark Schauer, while Tim Walberg was helped by some new players in congressional elections including American Action Network ($370,000), American Future Fund ($506,761), and Americans for Prosperity ($322,763).[49] The ads by labor attacking Walberg aimed to tell voters that he had his chance in Congress and had been defeated before. For example, an AFSCME ad asks voters, "Now Walberg wants his job back? Haven't we been burned badly enough?"; an SEIU ad told voters, "We already gave Walberg the pink slip. This time let's make sure he gets the message"; and an ad from the Communications Workers of America stated, "Now Walberg wants his job back. But with a record like that, why would we ever rehire him?"[50]

One potential problem with outside groups coming into a district and communicating their own independent messages is that they can contradict the message of the campaign they are trying to help. The messages from these outside groups are fine examples of this phenomenon. The Schauer campaign, and the DCCC for that matter, clearly wanted to make Schauer the outsider and Walberg the insider, reminding voters that Walberg had been fired from his job in Congress once already contradicted this message. This kind of inconsistency in messaging can be difficult for a campaign to overcome.

The conservative groups that were active did not have this problem. They continued the same messages that the Walberg campaign and the NRCC were highlighting, including health care reform, the stimulus, the debt, and the cap-and-trade bill. They also featured heavy doses of Nancy Pelosi.

Some environmental groups spent money in the 7th as well. The Sierra Club spent about $90,000 on mailings attacking Walberg that were sent to about 160,000 homes.[51] The League of Conservation Voters (LCV) also spent about $380,000 on radio and television ads. It was an ad the LCV did with BlueGreen Alliance, however, that got the most attention in the race. The ad criticized Walberg for skipping a vote on a bill to help the auto companies and for voting against clean energy.[52] In the LCV/BlueGreen Alliance ad, the visuals arguably went one step further. The ad featured what was to be a movie poster that included a picture of Tim Walberg next to Iranian president Mahmoud Ahmadinejad and Saudi Arabian King Abdullah Bin Abdul-Aziz.[53]

Not surprisingly, much of the outside money (about 75 percent) was spent on advertising that opposed (rather than supported) one candidate or the other. In other words, much of the message to voters was negative. In addition, many of the claims made in the ads were subjected to "fact checks" of one kind or another by watchdog groups. They found many of the claims to be misleading—

such as the sales tax charge against Walberg—or downright false—such as the claim that Schauer had voted for the Wall Street bailout.

The impact of outside money in the 7th District cannot be overstated. In the end, about the same amount was spent in ways that helped Tim Walberg as was spent to help Mark Schauer—about $4.5 million on each side. This kind of spending saturated the airwaves and clogged mail boxes in the district. It was likely more of a help to Walberg, however, because of his campaign's lack of funding relative to Schauer's. Tim Walberg noted:

> When you look at our $1.6 million that we raised and spent, $800,000 of that during the primary and $800,000 during the general, we were outspent by Mark Schauer 4 to 1 … If there had not been the strong support from outside groups coming in to support us in the general, including the NRCC, including the state party, and including some of the business groups and others … it would have been very difficult to get the message out [with] all of the chatter that was out there from the millions that were expended by the other side.[54]

In the end, Schauer and his allies outspent Walberg and his allies by about $1 million on advertising.[55] Ken Brock, Schauer's Chief of Staff, noted that while it was a large part of the race, "We did not lose this race because of *Citizens United* or their ability to overwhelm us on the resource side."[56]

According to Walberg's campaign spokesman, Joe Wicks, the Walberg campaign was at a disadvantage immediately after the primary when a lot of money from left-leaning groups was spent in the district at a time when they had just spent a lot of their money for the primary and conservative groups had yet to get involved in the 7th. This, again according to the Walberg campaign, allowed Schauer to pull even in the race (see the polling figures referenced above). When conservative groups did get in the game, the Walberg lead reappeared.[57]

The Wave and Voter Turnout in Michigan's 7th District

One of the main reasons Tim Walberg was able to defeat Mark Schauer is linked to voter participation in the district. The 2008 presidential election saw a fairly substantial increase in turnout from four years before. Many voters that year were first-time voters who were inspired to vote by Barack Obama's candidacy, but Democrats generally also turned out at a higher rate than they had in 2004. Midterm elections always have lower turnout than presidential elections and 2010 was no different (see Chapter 14). It was the makeup of the voters who stayed home in 2010, however, that hurt Mark Schauer, and Democrats generally. A substantial number of voters who voted for Barack Obama and Democrats in 2008 simply did not vote this time. In short, voters who might have supported Mark Schauer did not vote at the same rate as they did in 2008.

Many of these voters were supplanted by Republicans who were caught up in the wave of 2010. So not only did Tim Walberg benefit from the decrease in

Democratic turnout, but an increased level of excitement among his own voters also helped him at the polls. Part of the enthusiasm in the Republican wave was a new interest, attention, and political activism that was associated with the Tea Party movement in 2010. There was a Tea Party presence in the Michigan 7th District race in 2010, but it is difficult to measure its scope or influence. Because it has been a grassroots movement and more or less leaderless, the Tea Party cannot be reliably tracked and understood in the same way that a formal political organization can. There are organizations in the Michigan 7th with Tea Party connections or sympathies, but the movement's real influence is more likely revealed by polling results that showed a fairly high percentage of voters in the district (38 percent) who agreed with the principles of the Tea Party movement (whether they were members or not).[58]

During the 2010 campaign, Tim Walberg recognized the presence of the Tea Party supporters as he met with voters. Walberg noted that "I think the Tea Party had a huge impact, regardless of vote counts. They forced Republicans—myself included—to respond to their demands. They forced us to not take them for granted.... We couldn't assume that they would vote for us...."[59] In part, because of the Tea Party movement, many people became more active during the campaign. These voters attended the town hall meetings, the candidate debates, and the "meet and greet" get-togethers sponsored by each campaign.

Tim Walberg defeated Mark Schauer by 10,783 votes, in a race that saw a total of 225,669 votes cast. Walberg's margin of victory (50.15 percent to 45.37 percent) was typically small for this competitive district. Each of the previous two elections was also close. In 2006, Tim Walberg survived the first Democratic wave election by narrowly defeating (50 percent to 46 percent) a relatively unknown opponent who raised and spent only about $55,000 on her campaign. In 2008, Mark Schauer rode the Obama wave to victory by about 7,500 votes, but it is worth noting he won his seat with less than 50 percent of the vote and by less than two percentage points (48.8 percent to 46.5 percent).

Key to his victory in 2008 was that Schauer was able to win his home county of Calhoun by almost 10,000 votes; he won as expected in Eaton and Washtenaw counties, and actually won in Jackson County, which is traditionally Republican and the second most populous county in the district. He also performed well in some conservative areas, almost winning Lenawee County (where he lost by only 934 votes out of 44,000 cast).

The 2010 voting results by county help illustrate how Mark Schauer lost his bid for reelection. First, the 225,669 votes cast in 2010 were less than the 245,026 that were cast in the previous midterm election of 2006; and lower turnout typically favors Republicans. About 4,000 fewer votes each were cast in Calhoun and Jackson counties in 2010 when compared to 2006, and about 3,000 fewer voters voted in Eaton County. These were winning counties for Mark Schauer in 2008, when 322,286 voters in the district cast a vote. This change in voter turnout was crucial for Mark Schauer's reelection and his campaign simply could not bring enough 2008 voters to the polls.[60]

Table 13.3 Mark Schauer Vote Percentages by County, 2008 & 2010

County	Schauer % of vote, 2008	Schauer % of vote, 2010	Difference
Branch	38.7	37.3	−1.4
Calhoun	55.9	50.0	−5.9
Eaton	49.6	48.8	−0.8
Hillsdale	34.9	32.6	−2.3
Jackson	48.2	43.9	−4.2
Lenawee	47.2	44.2	−3.0
Washtenaw	50.7	47.2	−3.5

Source: Calculated by authors from data available from the Michigan Secretary of State, http://www.mich.gov/sos (accessed January 20, 2011).

Obviously, the turnout numbers for a presidential election year cannot be compared to a midterm election year, but it appears that Mark Schauer suffered both from a Republican wave and a Democratic retreat in 2010. To make the two most recent election results more comparable, we calculated the percentage of each county's vote that Mark Schauer and Tim Walberg earned in 2008 and in 2010 (see Table 13.3)

The results are striking—Mark Schauer lost at least one percent of his share of each county's vote in 2010 compared to 2008, and in Jackson and Calhoun counties, he lost 4 percent and 6 percent, respectively. Put another way, Mark Schauer beat Tim Walberg in Calhoun County by almost 10,000 votes in 2008, but won his home county in 2010 by only 1,650 votes. He lost this election, in part, because of the political dynamics of 2010 but also because of the low voter turnout on the ground in the 7th District.

Conclusion

We have identified four important factors that contributed to Tim Walberg's victory over Mark Schauer in the 7th District congressional election. First, outside money can be considered a crucial factor to Tim Walberg's victory. The amount of outside spending in this race exceeded that of all other races in 2010. It was especially important to Tim Walberg's campaign because he spent about half of his total campaign funds to beat back a primary opponent. Thus, he was at a substantial funding disadvantage in the general election, until outside money on his campaign's behalf even the campaign spending field in this race.

The second factor is connected to outside spending, and that was campaign message differences of the two campaigns. Each candidate was well-credentialed; indeed, both had represented the district. Both had public records that dated back into their service in the Michigan state legislature, as well as their voting records as members of the U.S. House. A well-crafted campaign message that resonates with voters is only effective if a campaign can communicate that message effectively. The ability to reach voters with a message that fit well with the times and with the politics of the district in 2010 was crucial to Tim Walberg's victory. As Walberg's campaign spokesperson Joe Wicks put it, "I think the key to our victory was that once we had the funds in the general election to attach Mark Schauer to his record—that he voted for Obamacare, the stimulus, and cap-and-trade … our polling showed us that we would win."[61]

Third, the Republican wave brought excitement to Tim Walberg's campaign. The dissatisfaction by voters over the "big three" policies of the Obama White House and the Democratic majorities in Congress created a fervor among conservatives, especially the Tea Party. This wave led to the last factor important to the outcome in the 7th—an electorate that behaved much differently in 2010 than in 2008. Voters in more conservative areas within the district were more energized and active in 2010. Voters who supported Barack Obama and Mark Schauer in 2008 did not demonstrate the same enthusiasm and did not turn out in the midterm election. In the areas of the district where Mark Schauer had performed well in 2008, he was not able to match that performance in 2010.

For his part, incumbent Mark Schauer attempted to make the campaign a "Schauer versus Walberg" choice for voters. This strategy made sense, in large part because Schauer was at a distinct disadvantage if the election remained a referendum on the national policies that had angered and energized so many voters around the country. Moreover, Schauer tried to paint himself as a moderate, which was largely true on social issues. However, the major issues of the 2010 election were economic, not social. In the end, because he supported all of the bills criticized by Republicans and their supporters, Mark Schauer was unable to appear moderate or localize the election which was another piece of his strategy.

It might be easy to predict that the 2012 election will again be close, or that the incumbent will lose reelection, but we do not know yet what the district will look like after redistricting decisions are made. What we do know is that Republicans control all parts of the redistricting process in Michigan—majorities in the state legislature, the governor's office, and a majority on the state Supreme Court. This likely will bode well for Tim Walberg. Walberg is also aware that there is the potential for Democratic voters in the district to become re-energized. The 7th District has not proven to be incumbent-friendly over the past five elections; whether it will be in 2012 remains an open question.

Notes

1. American Community Survey, 2005–2009, "U.S. Census Bureau, Michigan 7th Congressional District," http://factfinder.census.gov/servlet/DTTable?_bm=y&-context=dt&-ds_name=ACS_2009_5YR_G00_&-mt_name=ACS_2009_5YR_G2000_B02001&-tree_id=5309&-redoLog=true&-_caller=geoselect&-geo_id=01000US&-geo_id=500$50000US2607&-search_results=01000US&-format=&-_lang=en (accessed January 10, 2011).
2. Ibid.

3. U.S. Bureau of Labor Statistics, http://www.bls.gov/eag/eag.mi.htm (accessed February 10, 2011).
4. Telephone interview with Ken Brock, December 1, 2010.
5. Richard Fenno, *Home Style: Members in their Districts* (New York: Little Brown, 1978). Fenno notes that members have three goals—reelection, good public policy, and power and prestige within the institution. The proximate goal—reelection—must be achieved before the other two can be.
6. Ibid, p. 50.
7. Ibid, p. 33.
8. Ken Brock interview.
9. This would qualify as explaining Washington behavior in Fenno's home style activities.
10. Ken Brock interview.
11. Ibid.
12. Ibid.
13. ADA scores taken from http://www.adaction.org/media/votingrecords/2009.pdf (accessed January 7, 2011).
14. Party unity and presidential support scores are from *Congressional Quarterly*; for 2009, see http://innovation.cqpolitics.com/media/vote_study_2009; and for 2010, see http://innovation.cq.com/media/vote_study_2010 (accessed February 6, 2011).
15. Ken Brock interview.
16. Gordon Trowbridge, "Mich. congressional freshmen get good fundraising start," *Detroit News*, April 16, 2009, http://www.detnews.com/article/20090416/POLITICS02/904160380/1024/POLITICS03/Mich.+congressional+freshmen+get+good+fundraising+start (accessed January 19, 2011).
17. These early polls were all done by Republican polling firms: National Research (Walberg 50 percent to Schauer 40 percent) between January 10 and 12, 2010; We Ask America (Walberg 44.9 percent to Schauer 37.4 percent) on August 4, 2010; and Ayres, McHenry & Associates (Walberg 50 percent to Schauer 40 percent) between August 16 and 18, 2010. See the *New York Times'* election section at http://elections.nytimes.com/2010/forecasts/house/michigan/7 (accessed January 18, 2011).
18. Ibid.
19. All other polling data in this section, unless otherwise noted, are taken from an EPIC-MRA poll, October 16–17, 2010. Poll data furnished by EPIC-MRA president, Bernie Porn.
20. Telephone interview with Representative Tim Walberg, December 9, 2010.
21. Ibid.
22. Telephone interview with Chris Gautz, November 29, 2010.
23. Tim Walberg interview.
24. Chris Gautz interview.
25. John Mulcahy, "Walberg addresses issues in coffee shop gathering," *The Daily Telegram* (Adrian), October 12, 2010, http://www.lenconnect.com/2010election/x123458475/Walberg-addresses-issues-in-coffee-shop-gathering (accessed February 2, 2010).
26. Naftali Bendavid, "Pelosi Key to GOP 2010 Playbook." *Wall Street Journal*, October 12, 2009, p. 4A, http://online.wsj.com/article/SB125530046902979049.html (accessed February 4, 2011).
27. Steve Carmody, "Michigan's 7th congressional district race," Michigan Radio, October 22, 2010, http://www.publicbroadcasting.net/michigan/news.newsmain/article/1/0/1715919/Michigan.News/Michigan/percent27s.7th.congressional.district.race (accessed February 2, 2010).
28. http://www.youtube.com/watch?v=9VZ0HNWUdXY

29. Andy Balaskovitz, "Mudslinging in the 7th," *City Pulse* (Lansing), October 27, 2010, http://www.lansingcitypulse.com/lansing/article-5016-mudslinging-in-the-7th.html (accessed February 2, 2010).

30. http://www.youtube.com/watch?v=bH96JOL7hNc. He had been asked a similar question in September while on a talk radio station and said he did not know because there was not enough information available, but that it was not an issue now because Obama was the sitting president.

31. Chris Gautz, "Mark Schauer and Tim Walberg repeat attacks, agree on little at third debate," *Jackson Citizen Patriot*, October 20, 2010, http://www.mlive.com/news/jackson/index.ssf/2010/10/schauer_and_walberg_repeat_att.html (accessed February 4, 2011).

32. Chris Gautz interview.

33. Schauer did defend his vote for health care reform during one debate when he was asked about it by saying, "I fundamentally believe that … every member of the public should have access to the same kind of health care I do." Quoted in Steve Carmody, "7th District debate ignites over Social Security, economy and health care reform," Michigan Radio, October 20, 2010, http://www.publicbroadcasting.net/michigan/news.newsmain/article/0/0/1715427/Michigan.All.Things.Considered/7th.district.debate.ignites.over.Social.Security..economy.and.health.care.reform (accessed February 5, 2011).

34. John A. Ferejohn, *Pork Barrel Politics: Rivers and Harbors Legislation: 1947–1968* (Stanford, CA: Stanford University Press, 1974); Steven D. Levitt and James M. Snyder, Jr. "The Impact of Federal Spending on House Election Outcomes," *Journal of Political Economy*, vol. 105 (1997), no. 1, pp. 30–53.

35. Chris Gautz interview.

36. http://www.youtube.com/user/SchauerforCongress#p/u/20/aIwLhkzI7D8

37. Telephone interview with Bernie Porn, President, EPIC-MRA, December 1, 2010.

38. Ken Brock interview.

39. *Daily Telegram* (Adrian). "Our View: Another round of electoral fact checks," October 20, 2010, http://www.lenconnect.com/opinions/editorials/x2048879369/Our-View-Another-round-of-electoral-fact-checks (accessed February 4, 2011).

40. http://www.youtube.com/watch?v=_A2SyZp0f-o

41. Tim Walberg interview.

42. http://www.youtube.com/watch?v=aIwLhkzI7D8

43. http://www.youtube.com/watch?v=kffDSY81g0w. We should also note that the quote from Walberg is not complete. In the full quote, Walberg says, "We're getting jobs back from China because of quality issues" (quoted in Chris Gautz, "U.S. Rep. Mark Schauer, Tim Walberg argue over ad about losing jobs to China," *Jackson Citizen Patriot*, September 24, 2010, http://blog.mlive.com/jackson-politics/2010/09/post_52.html (accessed February 10, 2011).

44. Center for Responsive Politics, "Outside Spending: Michigan 7th, 2010," http://www.opensecrets.org/races/indexp.php?cycle=2010&id=MI07 (accessed February 5, 2011).

45. http://www.youtube.com/watch?v=ipTOXN0S0Rg

46. http://www.youtube.com/watch?v=4tCrxpsPnG8

47. Tim Walberg interview.

48. Comparing the 2010 ad (http://www.youtube.com/watch?v=p2wbeuq9paI) with the 2008 ad (http://www.youtube.com/watch?v=aQkBotxvBxM) illustrates similar graphics and even some of the same actors (ads accessed February 10, 2011).

49. Michigan Campaign Finance Network, "Michigan 7th Congressional District 2010 Spending Summary," http://www.mcfn.org/pdfs/reports/7thMI_2010.pdf (accessed February 5, 2011).

50. Alex Isenstadt, "Outside groups' five favorite Dems," *Politico*, October 25, 2010, http://www.politico.com/news/stories/1010/44102.html (accessed February 5, 2011).
51. Ed Brayton, "Sierra Club targets Walberg," *Michigan Messenger*, October 20, 2010, http://michiganmessenger.com/42735/sierra-club-targets-walberg (accessed February 5, 2011).
52. Walberg did miss that vote on what anyone outside of Michigan calls the "auto bailout," but the ad fails to mention he was in the hospital recovering from prostate surgery.
53. http://www.youtube.com/watch?v=Ndkop6agAeQ
54. Tim Walberg interview.
55. Ken Brock interview.
56. Ken Brock interview.
57. Telephone interview with Walberg campaign spokesman Joe Wicks, December 9, 2010.
58. See the EPIC-MRA poll noted above.
59. Tim Walberg interview.
60. Vote totals for all elections were accessed through the Michigan Secretary of State's Web site, at www.michigan.gov/sos.
61. Joe Wicks interview.

The Wave Recedes, but Which Way Will the Tide Turn?

Randall E. Adkins and David A. Dulio

Since November of 2010 many Democrats have argued that the outcomes of the House and Senate elections were inevitable. From their perspective, the Republican landslide was a product of macro-political forces, culminating in a "wave" of public opinion they had to fight that was produced by a weak economy and an unpopular president. On the other hand, Republicans argue that the 2010 election was nothing more than a repudiation of the liberal policies pursued by the Obama Administration and the Democratic leaders in the Congress. To some degree both are right, but this particular election cycle presents issues that are actually much bigger than the partisan rhetoric suggests. As some contributors to this book recognized, after a wave crashes the shore, it recedes back into the ocean. Now that the 2010 Republican wave has receded, we can examine what was left behind and the aftermath of the 2010 election cycle.

The 2010 congressional elections were certainly historic and will be readily remembered for a number of reasons. First, 2010 was the third election in a row where the issues driving the election were nationalized. As a result, the Democrats picked up 31 House seats and five Senate seats in 2006, and padded their majority in the House with an additional 21 seats and in the Senate with an additional nine seats in 2008. In 2010, the Republicans turned the tables, picking up 63 seats in the House, and another six in the Senate. By comparison, the number of House or Senate seats picked up by either party from 1996 to 2004 were in the single digits in both chambers in each election cycle.

Second, as Jennifer Steen notes in this volume (see Chapter 5) the 2010 election offers a "course correction" for many U.S. House districts. In short, Republicans won in districts that Democrats gained in 2006 and 2008, but where Republicans had typically held an advantage. A total of 34 Democrats won seats in the previous two elections in congressional districts that traditionally favored Republicans. In 2010, Republicans won most of these districts back. Dave Schweikert (AZ 5th) and Tim Walberg (MI 7th) are good examples of these Republicans. Both candidates ran in districts that typically favor their party, albeit by a small margin. Both were able to win not just because of the tides of 2010, but because of the preferences of the voters in the areas in which they were running.

Third, the Republicans in the House clearly over-performed, surpassing nearly everyone's expectations by gaining 63 seats. The bigger question of the

2010 election was why the Republicans underperformed in the Senate. In the end, they remain four votes short of gaining control. Why were they unable to make greater inroads into the upper chamber? Clearly, in a wave election one would expect that the Republicans could pick off more than six seats.

There is a time-tested formula for winning campaigns: recruit a quality candidate, raise a lot of money and build a solid campaign organization, and make good use of polling to determine what issues to take advantage of and how to execute the campaign. We will look at each of these in turn to assess the 2010 House and Senate elections, and then discuss the consequences of the Republican takeover of the House.

Recruiting Quality Challengers

It is often said in politics that you can't beat a "somebody" with a "nobody" (see Chapter 2). In their "strategic politician" hypothesis, Gary Jacobson and Samuel Kernell argue that the best quality House challengers choose to run for office either when an incumbent retires or when the national tides are favorable to his or her political party and unfavorable to the incumbent's political party.[1] The 2010 election cycle was certainly a year when the national tides were favorable for Republicans. In some cases, long-term incumbents like House Appropriations Committee Chairman, Representative David Obey (D-WI) chose to retire. In other cases, long-term incumbents like House Budget Committee Chairman, John Spratt (D-SC) were defeated by quality challengers (in this case South Carolina State Senator Mick Mulvaney).

In the cases in this volume that deal with members of the House, both David Schweikert (AZ 5th) and Austin Scott (GA 8th) represent what Jacobson and Kernell call quality challengers. David Schweikert was a successful businessman and elected county-level official in the 5th District. Austin Scott was a long-time member of the Georgia House of Representatives. In addition, the Republicans recognized that some very successful incumbents were defeated in the Democratic wave elections of 2006 and 2008 by very close margins. In three cases presented in this volume, Republican candidates returned for a rematch and emerged victorious. Each of these candidates was well-known in the district and had a long record of public service. Charlie Bass (NH 2nd) was defeated in 2006, but after sitting the sidelines during the 2008 election he returned to recapture his old seat. In addition, both Steve Chabot (OH 1st) and Tim Walberg (MI 7th) lost by close margins in 2008, but once the tide turned they were able to ride it back to Congress in 2010.

The Senate, however, was clearly a different story in 2010. Given that Senate seats are often held by very entrenched and powerful incumbents, the selection process is much more visible, and the resources needed to run are much greater, the dynamics of recruiting quality Senate candidates will clearly be different. In most of the cases where the Republicans captured a seat from the Democrats, a quality candidate that held statewide or federal office won the race. In North Dakota, incumbent Governor John Hoeven won a resounding victory. In

Arkansas, U.S. Representative John Boozman defeated sitting Senator Blanche Lincoln. In two other cases, retired officeholders returned to run again. In Indiana, former Senator Dan Coats won the seat of retiring Senator Evan Bayh. In Pennsylvania (see Chapter 12), former Representative Pat Toomey emerged victorious.

Given the direction of the national tides, the Republicans were in a position to win additional seats. In many of these cases, however, they failed to nominate quality candidates with solid previous political experience. This was, in part, due to the success of the Tea Party movement within the Republican Party in 2010. Given the anti-establishment focus of the Tea Party, those who consider themselves part of the movement tended to support the less traditional, less experienced, and more ideological candidates. For example, in the Delaware Senate race, the Republican establishment recruited Congressman Mike Castle to run. Castle served as the at-large member of Congress from Delaware since 1993, having been elected or reelected nine times, and would likely have cruised to victory in the Senate election. Castle, however, was widely-recognized as one of the most moderate Republicans in Congress. As a result, Republican primary voters in Delaware decided to "jump the shark"[2] and nominate Christine O'Donnell, a candidate endorsed by the Tea Party movement. Given her on-camera gaffes (e.g., "I dabbled in witchcraft...."), how she responded to the gaffes (e.g., a television ad where she stated "I am not a witch."), and the parodies that both produced (e.g., *Saturday Night Live*), her campaign was unable to gain any serious traction.

There were also other states where Republicans "jumped the shark." In Connecticut, Republicans nominated *World Wresting Entertainment* CEO Linda McMahon. Some might argue the most important mistake that Republicans made was in not nominating a quality candidate in Nevada (see Chapter 2). Clearly, the Republicans had a chance to "Daschle" Senate Majority Leader Harry Reid (referring to their defeat of Senate Majority Leader Tom Daschle in 2006). The Republican Party establishment preferred the more mainstream Sue Lowden (or Danny Tarkanian), but Republican primary voters chose to nominate Tea Party activist Sharon Angle. As David Damore demonstrates in this volume, Reid ran a strong campaign in a bad year for a Democrat. Without Angle's assistance by running a poor campaign, the U.S. Senate might have needed to select a new majority leader.

Campaign Finance

General election candidates for U.S. House seats raised nearly $1 billion collectively in 2010, with Democrats and Republicans raising roughly equal amounts.[4] Republicans raised just over 52 percent of those funds. In some cases, Democratic incumbents raised twice as much as their Republican challenger and lost. For example, in Michigan's 7th District Mark Schauer's fundraising advantage in the general election was roughly 4 to 1, and in Georgia's 8th District Jim Marshall's fundraising advantage was approximately 1.4 to 1. There were clearly other races in the country where it was closer, like Ohio's 1st District where the Republican challenger Steve Chabot actually raised slightly more than the Democratic incumbent, and Texas' 17th District where Republican Bill Flores had to inject almost $1.5 million of his own money into his campaign to level the playing field with Chet Edwards.

Senate candidates raised almost $600 million collectively. Republicans raised just over 58 percent of those funds. In most cases, Democrats were successful at raising the funds needed to be competitive. In some states they were highly competitive; for instance, both Harry Reid and Barbara Boxer were able to successfully defend their seats in Nevada and California, respectively. In other states they were not; with Russ Feingold losing his bid for reelection a prime example. In Florida, however, Mark Rubio and Charlie Crist raised more than $35 million between them, and Democrat Kendrick Meek was forced to campaign in the fourth largest state in the country with less than $9 million. The Republicans were also good at securing serious candidates from the private sector that could self-finance a portion of their own Senate campaigns. In addition to Carly Fiorina (CA) and Ron Johnson (WI) mentioned in this volume (Chapters 4 and 10, respectively), John Raese, a business executive in West Virginia, spent almost $2.4 million of his own funds in a losing effort to take the seat formerly held by the late Senator Robert Byrd.

The Bipartisan Campaign Reform Act of 2002 was intended to simplify campaign finance and level the playing field between the two major party campaigns in each state or district. The campaign finance system today is anything but simple. In 2010, outside groups spent hundreds of millions of dollars to run advertisements, make telephone calls, distribute campaign-style literature, and engage in other activities to educate voters about candidates and issues. The parties' Hill Committees—the Democratic Congressional Campaign Committee, the National Republican Congressional Committee, the Democratic Senatorial Campaign Committee, and the National Republican Senatorial Committee—represent a large portion of that sum, spending money independently in states and districts, typically in opposition to rather than in support of a candidate. Other organizations that were not affiliated with the political parties accounted for more than 60 percent of this spending. These organizations come in many different shapes and sizes, including political action committees (PACs), super-PACs, 527s, and corporations and unions that want to spend money on behalf of a candidate for federal office.[5] In today's campaign finance climate, money could probably not flow more freely to where it is needed if it were completely unrestricted.

National Issues vs. Local Politics

Good polling is critical to winning congressional campaigns. Candidates must know how voters view the performance of the incumbent in office and what mix of local and national issues on the public agenda will resonate with voters. In some election cycles, national issues come to the forefront and in other election cycles local politics comes to the forefront. The 2010 election cycle was a year where local political concerns took a back seat to national issues in many campaigns. They were at the forefront of everyone's mind in congressional districts across the country and what we traditionally know as local politics took a back seat.

It is undeniable that the Democratic agenda of "change" that carried the day in 2008 impacted this election cycle. As we noted in Chapter 1, midterms are often referenda on the president who was elected two years before. Some voters clearly cast ballots in reaction to the policies that the Obama administration and Democrats in Congress had pursued during the 111th Congress. The American Reinvestment and Recovery Act—or the stimulus bill—and the American Clean Energy and Security Act of 2009—or the cap-and-trade bill—were the first two pieces of legislation that got the attention of many Americans. Arguably more important, however, was the Patient Protection and Affordable Care Act of 2010, or the health care reform law. This new law was unpopular among certain segments of the population, and these groups of voters turned out in greater numbers than those who supported the law. As we noted in Chapter 1, some analysts have shown that voting for these initiatives hurt Democrats, [6] which is consistent with other work that shows the public holds members of Congress accountable for votes that they take. [7]

Some of the Democratic incumbents chronicled in the preceding chapters were defeated on Election Day, at least in part, because of their votes for some or all of these legislative measures. Harry Mitchell in Arizona's 5th District was clearly one of these incumbents. His votes in favor of pieces of President Obama's legislative priorities, in combination with the Republican-leaning nature of their district, were problematic in his bid for reelection. The same can be said of Mark Schauer in Michigan's 7th District. Schauer voted for each of the "big three" bills (see Chapter 13) in the House. Again, those votes combined with a district that tilts toward the GOP made it difficult to survive in a year like 2010. Interestingly, Charlie Crist as governor of Florida did not vote in favor of any of these bills, yet he was tied to Obama for his rhetorical (and maybe literal) embrace of the policies early in Obama's term.

This does not explain all of the Democratic defeats, however. For instance, Jim Marshall in Georgia's 8th District and Chet Edwards in Texas' 17th District did not vote for health care reform or for cap-and-trade, yet they were both tied to Obama and Democratic leaders in Congress. Both tried to distance themselves from President Obama and Speaker Pelosi, but it was a difficult task in a strong Republican year with strong Republican challengers campaigning fiercely to link the incumbent to the president and Speaker Pelosi. Edwards ran ads telling voters how he stood up to Obama on the health care vote, and Marshall went so far as to say he would not vote for Pelosi as Speaker in the next Congress should he be reelected. In the end, this was not enough and even though these Democrats did not fully embrace the Obama agenda they voted for part of it which was enough for them to be tied to the Obama-Pelosi agenda and find themselves on the losing end of the vote on election night.

The results in Wisconsin were quite different. Russ Feingold's defeat showed that Democrats could lose even when they were not being punished for voting for President Obama's agenda. Voters in Wisconsin were not as angry about Feingold's votes for those bills and Obama was more popular there than many places around the country. Feingold, and some other Democrats across the nation, lost more because he was an incumbent Democrat than because he supported Obama.

An important factor in most races in 2010 was voter turnout. While the theory of "surge and decline" has been revised since Angus Campbell first wrote about it, the crux of the idea is still the same—the electorates of midterm elections and presidential elections are different. [8] In short, there is a surge of participation during a presidential contest (as well as an impact on voting behavior due to short-term political forces) and that surge then recedes during the next midterm election. The 2010 elections unequivocally were an illustration of the decline segment of the surge and decline theory.

A lot was made in 2008 about the large turnout when Barack Obama was elected. Indeed, all over the nation, many Americans who had never voted before went to the polls, and a large number of them voted for Obama and other Democrats. In 2010, however, many of those Americans did not vote and Democratic candidates suffered. In Michigan's 7th District this dynamic was clear in areas that incumbent Mark Schauer needed to do well in to be reelected; thousands fewer voters turned out to vote in his home county which helped Tim Walberg win back the seat. Similarly in Wisconsin, turnout in Milwaukee, a stronghold for Democrats, was down considerably from 2008. Moreover, the exit polls in that state showed that the surge in Democratic turnout from two years ago was not present in 2010, as the Democratic advantage in 2008 was 39 percent of the electorate to 33 percent Republican, but only 37 percent to 36 percent in 2010. The same effect can be seen in New Hampshire's 2nd District race. In 2008, "core Democrats" made up 48 percent of the electorate while "core Republicans" were just 21 percent of voters; in 2010, these figures were 39 percent to 36 percent, respectively (see Figure 7.4). In addition, in some places certain segments of the electorate turned out less than others in 2010. In both Georgia's 8th District and Ohio's 1st District, Jim Marshall and Steve Driehaus lost their bids for reelection, in part, due to a decrease in turnout from 2008, especially among African-American voters. A similar story was present in Pennsylvania, where African-American turnout was down from its robust levels in 2008. As Robin Kolodny noted, "Turnout levels in the heavily Democratic parts of the state were back to pre-2008 levels or lower." This is a pattern that repeated itself across the nation.

Obama's impact was felt another way in 2010. During his historic election two years prior, Obama won 52 percent of the independent vote. These same independent voters, however, left Obama and his party over the course of the next two years. As we noted in Chapter 1, independents' views of President Obama's job approval soured relatively quickly after he took office. Obama's approval rating among independents peaked at 66 percent in May 2009; it fell below 50 percent for the first time in July of that year and stayed under 50 percent after November 2009. With these approval ratings nationwide, it should not be a surprise that Democratic candidates (remember that in midterms that serve as a referendum voters express their displeasure with the president through their congressional votes) suffered. In Wisconsin, for instance, Russ Feingold—a senator who built a strong reputation as an independent thinker himself—lost the independent vote by a resounding 13 points, 56 percent to 43 percent. This was a trend across the nation. A full 56 percent of independents voted for Republican candidates in House races.[9] It was a similar story in Florida where in 2008, 52 percent independents voted for Obama but a majority (51 percent) voted for Republican Marco Rubio in 2010. As noted by Seth McKee and Steven Craig, however, independent voters tacked a bit to the right during 2010 which made it difficult for Charlie Crist to attract them to his campaign.

Some Republicans, however, did not get a great deal of support from independent voters. Carly Fiorina in California, for example, won a plurality of independent votes with 46 percent, but it was not enough for her to even come close to defeating Barbara Boxer. This speaks to another lesson that was reinforced in these election results—calling oneself a Democrat or a Republican means different things depending on where one is in the country. In short, Democrats in Wisconsin are different from Democrats in Georgia and Republicans in Texas are different from Republicans in California. Carly Fiorina ran against Barbara Boxer as a fairly typical establishment Republican. Voters in that state, however, do not respond well to Republicans of this mold. GOP candidates can win statewide in California, but they have a difficult time doing so as a stereotypical partisan.

The Aftermath of the Wave

The outcome of the 2010 congressional election changed politics in Washington for at least the last two years of President Obama's first term. Signs of this were everywhere early in the 112th Congress, especially in the House of Representatives where Republicans took control of the chamber. Here, policy alternatives that would never have been considered in a Democratic-controlled House are not only being discussed but passed by the new GOP majority including a measure to repeal the health care reform law (the Patient Protection and Affordable Care Act of 2010). While House Republicans can claim a victory as having delivered on a campaign promise, it is highly unlikely the repeal ever becomes law given that Democrats still control the Senate. Welcome to gridlock.

Clearly, this legislative result is linked to the election results. As we noted in Chapter 1, the 2010 cycle marked the first time that party control of the U.S. House had changed while a similar change was not seen in the Senate. Had Republicans taken control of the Senate they would be in a position to send legislation like a bill to repeal health care reform to President Obama. Of course, he would veto this particular measure, but might have been forced to sign other pieces of legislation.

Do Campaigns Matter?

There is a debate in political science about whether campaigns really matter and to what degree they matter.[10] We are firm believers that campaigns do in fact matter. Some of the cases presented in this volume, however, make the case that "there was nothing (s)he could have done differently to win." This would suggest that campaigns do not matter and that the outcome was predetermined by macro-level factors. This seems to have been the case with Harry Mitchell in Arizona's 5th District, Mark Schauer in Michigan's 7th, and Russ Feingold in Wisconsin. Either the authors of these chapters or observers of these campaigns made the case that the tide was so strong in 2010 that these Democratic incumbents could not have done anything to stem that tide. It may be that in some cases, congressional elections are so nationalized that in nothing a candidate from the disadvantaged party does can keep them from falling victim to macro-political factors influencing the environment. We would temper this slightly. Candidates of the advantaged party still need to execute their own campaign. The stage may be set by national conditions but they need to take advantage of those conditions and put together a strategy that will produce a victory on Election Day. A good example of a Republican *not* doing so was Sharon Angle in Nevada who was unable to unseat Harry Reid in the best of possible situations.

Another scenario is that the national tide is enough to make a race competitive but not enough to ensure a victory for the candidate of the advantaged party. Carly Fiorina in California is an example of this. Casey Dominguez noted that "Fiorina ran the perfect campaign against Boxer." This was not enough, however, to win. In part this was, in Dominguez's estimation, because Boxer ran a perfect race as well. It is also likely that the GOP wave moved the electoral landscape far enough in the GOP's direction in California to make the race competitive but not far enough that would allow a candidate like Fiorina to win.

Throughout 2010 many analysts questioned whether the wave had enough strength for Republicans to win control of the Senate. In the end, the GOP fell four seats short of a majority. While it is hard to make the case the GOP underperformed in House races during 2010, the case can certainly be made that they did in the Senate. In 2010, however, there were a total of 37 senate seats that were up for reelection (seats in Delaware, New York, and West Virginia were on the ballot to fill a vacant seat). Nineteen of these seats were held by Democrats, which meant that in order to take control of the Senate chamber Republicans needed to win 10. If the Republicans would have nominated a better candidate in races like Connecticut, Delaware, or Nevada, they might have won additional seats, but winning more than half of your opponent's seats while holding all of your own is a tall order to fill, even in a wave election.

One big problem with a wave election is that when there is a large number of incoming senators from one party in a class, that party must play defense six years later. As we have noted, Democrats had a great year in 2006. Now the time has come for them to defend those seats in the Senate. In 2012, more than 20 of the seats that are up for reelection are held either by Democrats or Independents that caucus with the Democrats. The good news for Republicans who did not take control of the Senate in 2010 is that they will have another opportunity to take control in 2012. The bad news, however, is that President Obama will be on the ballot again in 2012. How the presidential race impacts these congressional elections remains to be seen, but the formula for winning campaigns will remain the same: recruit quality candidates, raise a ton of money and build a solid campaign organization, and make good use of polling to determine what issues to take advantage of and how to execute the campaign.

Notes

1. Gary C. Jacobson and Samuel Kernell, *Strategy and Choice in Congressional Elections* (New Haven, CT: Yale University Press, 1983).
2. The term "jump the shark" is often used to describe a television show (or any other organization for that matter) that has abandoned its core premise, which in turn leads to deterioration in quality that is beyond salvage. More specifically, the term refers to an episode of the hit television show *Happy Days* where the lead character, Fonzie, absurdly jumped over a confined shark on water skis in order to prove his bravery. The television show continued after that for a number of seasons, but was significantly restructured.
3. "2010 Overview: Incumbent Advantage," Center for Responsive Politics, http://www.opensecrets.org/overview/incumbs.php (accessed March 21, 2011).
4. "2010 Overview: Stats at a Glance," Center for Responsive Politics, http://www.opensecrets.org/overview/index.php (accessed March 21, 2011).
5. "Outside Spending," Center for Responsive Politics, http://www.opensecrets.org/outsidespending/index.php (accessed March 21, 2011).
6. See, for example, the work of Eric McGhee (http://www.themonkeycage.org/2010/11/did_controversial_roll_call_vo.html), Seth Masket (http://www.huffingtonpost.com/seth-masket/the-price-of-reform_b_755785.html), and Brendan Nyhan (http://www.brendan-nyhan.com/blog/2010/11/a-first-take-on-election-2010.html) for examples.
7. Stephen Ansolabehere and Philip Edward Jones, "Constituents' Responses to Congressional Roll-Call Voting," *American Journal of Political Science*, vol.54, no. 3, pp. 583–597.
8. Angus Campbell, "Surge and decline: A study of electoral change," in *Elections and the Political Order*, eds. Angus Campbell, Philip E. Converse, Warren E. Miller, and Donald E. Stokes, pp. 40–62 (New York: Wiley, 1966). Angus Campbell's idea that there is a surge in turnout among independent voters during presidential elections and that partisans of the disadvantaged party will defect and vote for the candidate of the other party because of short-term political forces was challenged roughly 20 years later by another scholar named Campbell. James Campbell argued that the turnout surge in presidential elections was not among independents but among partisans and that vote choice effects from short-term political forces would be seen in independents rather than partisans. In both theories, the surge in turnout during presidential years comes back to more normal levels during the following midterm. For a description of the revised theory, see James E. Campbell, "The Revised Theory of Surge and Decline," *American Journal of Political Science*, vol. 31(1987), no. 4 pp. 965–979.
9. Exit poll data are from CNN.com, http://www.cnn.com/ELECTION/2010/results/polls/#CAS01p1 (accessed March 9, 2011).

10. Some scholars argue that campaigns have important effects on voters in terms of perceptions and behaviors and that these influence election outcomes. Others, however, argue that campaigns have little impact on election outcomes. For an introduction to this debate, see: See Thomas M. Holbrook, *Do Campaigns Matter?* (Thousand Oaks, CA: Sage, 1996); Daron Shaw, "The Effect of TV Ads and Candidate Appearances on Statewide Presidential Votes, 1988–1996," *American Political Science Review*, vol. 93 (June 1999), pp. 345–361; Daron Shaw, "A Study of Presidential Campaign Event Effects from 1952 to 1992," *Journal of Politics*, vol. 61 (May 1999), pp. 387–422; and Andrew Gelman and Gary King, "Why Are American Presidential Election Campaign Polls so Variable When Votes Are so Predictable?" *British Journal of Political Science*, vol. 23 (October 1993), pp. 409–451.

About the Contributors

Randall E. Adkins is the Ralph Wardle Diamond Professor of Arts and Sciences and chair of the Department of Political Science at the University of Nebraska at Omaha. He teaches courses on the presidency, Congress, political parties, and campaigns and elections. Adkins is the editor of *The Evolution of Political Parties, Campaigns, and Elections*, co-editor of *Cases in Congressional Campaigns: Incumbents Playing Defense* (with David A. Dulio), and is the author of numerous articles and chapters in edited volumes on the presidency and campaigns and elections. His research is published in *American Politics Quarterly, American Politics Research, American Review of Politics*, the *Journal of Political Marketing, Political Research Quarterly, Presidential Studies Quarterly*, and *Publius: The Journal of Federalism*. He is also a former American Political Science Association Congressional Fellow where he worked for the Hon. David E. Price (NC-4).

Charles S. Bullock, III, is the Richard B. Russell Professor of Political Science and Josiah Meigs Distinguished Teaching Professor at the University of Georgia. He has authored, co-authored, edited or co-edited 27 books and more than 150 articles. *Runoff Elections in the United States*, co-authored with Loch Johnson, won the V. O. Key Award as the best book published on Southern Politics in 1992. His most recent books are the 4th edition of *The New Politics of the Old South* (co-edited with Mark Rozell), *Georgia Politics in a State of Change* (co-authored with Keith Gaddie), *Redistricting: The Most Political Activity in America*, and *The Triumph of Voting Rights in the South* (co-authored with Keith Gaddie) winner of the V. O. Key Award as the best book published on Southern Politics in 2009.

David T. Canon is a professor of political science at the University of Wisconsin, Madison. He received his Ph.D. from the University of Minnesota in 1987 and previously taught at Duke University. His teaching and research interests are in American political institutions, especially Congress. His more specific research interests include racial representation, partisan realignments, political careers, and the historical study of Congress (especially congressional committees). He is author of *Race, Redistricting, and Representation* (winner of the 2000 Richard F. Fenno award for the best book on legislative politics), *The Dysfunctional*

Congress? The Individual Roots of an Institutional Dilemma (with Ken Mayer), *Actors, Athletes, and Astronauts: Political Amateurs in the U.S. Congress, American Politics Today* (with William Bianco), several edited books, and various articles and book chapters. He recently completed a term as the Congress editor of *Legislative Studies Quarterly.*

Stephen C. Craig is a professor of political science at the University of Florida. He is author of *The Malevolent Leaders: Popular Discontent in America,* editor of six books including *The Electoral Challenge: Theory Meets Practice* (2nd ed., with David B. Hill), and has published numerous book chapters and articles in professional journals. His research deals with attitude measurement, campaign effects, and various other aspects of contemporary public opinion and political behavior in the United States. Craig is founding director of the University of Florida's Graduate Program in Political Campaigning (established in 1985), and has worked extensively with both academic and political surveys in Florida and nationwide.

David F. Damore is an associate professor of political science at the University of Nevada, Las Vegas. He is presently working on projects examining interest mobilization in direct democracy elections and how state legislatures use the legislative referendum to pursue partisan agendas and preserve and enhance institutional autonomy. His research has been published in academic journals such as *The Journal of Politics, Political Research Quarterly,* and *Political Behavior.* Dr. Damore also regularly comments on Nevada political and policy issues for local, national, and international media outlets.

Casey B. K. Dominguez is an associate professor of political science at the University of San Diego. She received her Ph.D. in Political Science from the University of California, Berkeley, in 2005. Her research specialties are congressional elections, political parties, and the presidency. Dr. Dominguez has published articles on presidential elections, the presidential honeymoon, and party involvement in congressional primaries. Her ongoing research focuses on the development of presidential war powers and on the relationships between political parties and interest groups.

David A. Dulio is an associate professor and Chair of the Political Science Department at Oakland University where he teaches courses on campaigns and elections, Congress, political parties, interest groups, and other areas of American politics generally. Dulio has published seven other books, including *Cases in Congressional Campaigns: Incumbents Playing Defense* (with Randall E. Adkins), *Vital Signs: Perspectives on the Health of American Campaigning* (with Candice J. Nelson), and *For Better or Worse? How Professional Political Consultants are Changing Elections in the United States.* He has written dozens of articles and book chapters on subjects ranging from the role of professional consultants in U.S. elections to campaign finance. Dulio is also a former American Political Science Congressional Fellow on Capitol Hill where he worked in the U.S. House of Representatives Republican Conference for former U.S. Rep. J.C. Watts, Jr. (R-OK).

Victoria A. Farrar-Myers is Distinguished Teaching Professor of political science at the University of Texas at Arlington. Her research on the presidency, presidential-congressional relations, and campaign finance has been published in such journals as *Political Research Quarterly* and *Congress & the Presidency* as well as numerous edited volumes. She also authored, co-authored, or co-edited books including *Scripted for Change: The Institutionalization of the American Presidency*, *Legislative Labyrinth: Congress and Campaign Finance Reform*, and *Corruption and American Politics*. She has received such honors as the American Political Science Association Congressional Fellowship, a research grant from the Dirksen Congressional Center, and several teaching awards.

John S. Klemanski is a professor of political science at Oakland University, in Rochester, Michigan. His primary areas of research interest are campaigns and elections, and urban politics and policy. He is the co-author or co-editor of four books, on urban politics and policy, state legislative campaigns, and diversity in American politics. His research has appeared in *State Politics and Policy Quarterly*, *Judicature*, *Urban Affairs Quarterly*, *Journal of Urban Affairs*, *Economic Development Quarterly*, and *Policy Studies Journal*.

Robin Kolodny is an associate professor of political science at Temple University. During Academic Year 2008–2009, Kolodny was a Fulbright Distinguished Scholar to the United Kingdom, affiliated with the University of Sussex. She is the author of *Pursuing Majorities: Congressional Campaign Committees in American Politics* as well as articles on political parties in Congress, in elections, and in comparative perspective. Kolodny served as an American Political Science Association Congressional Fellow in 1995 and in 1999, she received the Emerging Scholar Award from the Political Organizations and Parties Section of the APSA.

Seth C. McKee is an associate professor of political science at the University of South Florida, St. Petersburg. He is a political behavior and institutions scholar of American Politics. McKee has published extensively on American politics, with an emphasis on examining the primary factors shaping partisan change in contemporary elections. He has published articles on topics such as political participation, redistricting, and voter preferences in presidential, gubernatorial, senatorial, and U.S. House elections. McKee received his doctorate from the University of Texas at Austin and he is the author of *Republican Ascendancy in Southern U.S. House Elections*.

Karen P. Owen is a doctoral candidate in political science at the University of Georgia. She holds a Masters of Public Administration degree from the School of Public and International Affairs at the University of Georgia. She has worked as a legislative assistant to U.S. Rep. Nathan Deal of Georgia, as a lobbyist at a Fortune 500 company, and as a public health legislative analyst at the Centers for Disease Control and Prevention.

Gregory A. Petrow is a political psychologist at the University of Nebraska at Omaha and a senior research advisor for Gallup. Petrow conducts research on the roles of identity and affect in politics, and also research on political discussion. He has published articles in *Political Science Quarterly*, *Political Psychology*, *Presidential Studies Quarterly*, and *Congress & the Presidency*. He is currently writing a book, *Leader Approval in Non-Democratic Regimes* (with Jonathan Benjamin-Alvarado), which features analysis of Gallup World Poll data.

Dante J. Scala is an associate professor of political science at the University of New Hampshire. He is a nationally recognized commentator on New Hampshire politics and presidential nomination contests. His work on campaigns and elections has recently appeared in *The Change Election* and *Pendulum Swing*.

Daniel Davis Sledge is an assistant professor of political science at the University of Texas at Arlington. He received his Ph.D. from Cornell University in 2010 and studies public policy and American Political Development.

Andrew E. Smith is associate professor of political science at the University of New Hampshire where his research has focused on elections, public opinion and the presidential nomination process. He has published in the *American Political Science Review*, and *Public Opinion Quarterly*. He is also been director of the University of New Hampshire Survey Center since 1999 and is nationally known for public opinion polling. He has conducted political polling for the *Boston Globe*, *USA Today*, and the *Philadelphia Inquirer* as well as Fox News, CNN, WMUR-TV Manchester, New Hampshire, WCVB-TV Boston, and KYW-TV Philadelphia.

Jennifer A. Steen is an assistant professor of political science at Arizona State University. Prior to receiving her Ph.D. from the University of California, Berkeley, she worked as a political consultant; her theoretical and empirical work on the American electoral process is complemented by her background in the rough-and-tumble world of political campaigns. Before pursuing her doctorate Steen worked for candidates in local, state, and federal elections and served as a county precinct captain, national convention delegate, and member of the Electoral College. She is the author of *Self-Financed Candidates in Congressional Election*.

Wayne Steger is professor of political science at DePaul University. His research focuses on political parties, presidential nominations, and presidential campaigns. Steger received his Ph.D. from the University of Iowa. He has published over 30 articles and chapters in academic journals and edited volumes. He co-edited *Campaigns and Political Marketing* and is a former editor of the *Journal of Political Marketing.*

About the Editors

Randall E. Adkins is the Ralph Wardle Diamond Professor of Arts and Sciences and chair of the Department of Political Science at the University of Nebraska at Omaha. He teaches courses on the presidency, Congress, political parties, and campaigns and elections. Adkins is the editor of *The Evolution of Political Parties, Campaigns, and Elections*, co-editor of *Cases in Congressional Campaigns: Incumbents Playing Defense* (with David A. Dulio), and is the author of numerous articles and chapters in edited volumes on the presidency and campaigns and elections. His research is published in *American Politics Quarterly*, *American Politics Research*, *American Review of Politics*, the *Journal of Political Marketing*, *Political Research Quarterly*, *Presidential Studies Quarterly*, and *Publius: The Journal of Federalism*. He is also a former American Political Science Association Congressional Fellow where he worked for the Hon. David E. Price (NC-4).

David A. Dulio is an associate professor and Chair of the Political Science Department at Oakland University where he teaches courses on campaigns and elections, Congress, political parties, interest groups, and other areas of American politics generally. Dulio has published seven other books, including *Cases in Congressional Campaigns: Incumbents Playing Defense* (with Randall E. Adkins), *Vital Signs: Perspectives on the Health of American Campaigning* (with Candice J. Nelson), and *For Better or Worse? How Professional Political Consultants are Changing Elections in the United States*. He has written dozens articles and book chapters on subjects ranging from the role of professional consultants in U.S. elections to campaign finance. Dulio is also a former American Political Science Congressional Fellow on Capitol Hill where he worked in the U.S. House of Representatives Republican Conference for former U.S. Rep. J.C. Watts, Jr. (R-OK).